Spring/Summer 1975

Spring/Summer 1976

Spring/Summer 1977

Spring/Summer 1977

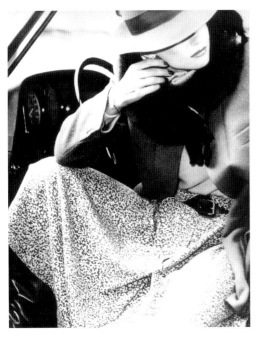

Fall/Winter 1977–78

Spring/Summer 1979

Fall/Winter 1978–79

Fall/Winter 1979–80

Fall/Winter 1979–80

Fall/Winter 1980–81

Spring/Summer 1981

Fall/Winter 1981–82

Fall/Winter 1982–83

Fall/Winter 1982–83

Spring/Summer 1984

Fall/Winter 1984–85

Spring/Summer 1985

Fall/Winter 1985–86

Fall/Winter 1985–86

Fall/Winter 1986–87

Spring/Summer 1987

Fall/Winter 1987–88

Fall/Winter 1984–85

Spring/Summer 1988

Spring/Summer 1988

Fall/Winter 1988–89

Fall/Winter 1988–89

Spring/Summer 1989

Fall/Winter 1989–90

Fall/Winter 1989–90

Spring/Summer 1990

Spring/Summer 1990

Fall/Winter 1990–91

Fall/Winter 1990–91

Fall/Winter 1990–91

Spring/Summer 1989

Spring/Summer 1990

Spring/Summer 1991

Spring/Summer 1991

Fall/Winter 1991–92

Fall/Winter 1991–92

Spring/Summer 1992

Fall/Winter 1992–93

Spring/Summer 1993

Spring/Summer 1993

Fall/Winter 1993–94

Fall/Winter 1992–93

Fall/Winter 1994–95

Spring/Summer 1994

Spring/Summer 1994

Fall/Winter 1994–95

Spring/Summer 1995

Spring/Summer 1995

Fall/Winter 1995–96

Fall/Winter 1995–96

Spring/Summer 1996

Spring/Summer 1996

Fall/Winter 1996–97

Fall/Winter 1997–98

Fall/Winter 1997–98

Fall/Winter 1997–98

Fall/Winter 1997–98

Spring/Summer 1997

Spring/Summer 1997

Spring/Summer 1998

Spring/Summer 1998

Fall/Winter 1998–99

Fall/Winter 1998–99

Spring/Summer 1999

Spring/Summer 1999

Fall/Winter 1999–2000

Spring/Summer 2000

Fall/Winter 2002–03

Fall/Winter 2002–03

Spring/Summer 2001

Spring/Summer 2001

Spring/Summer 2001

Fall/Winter 2001–02

Spring/Summer 2002

Spring/Summer 2002

Fall/Winter 2002–03

Fall/Winter 2002–03

Spring/Summer 2003

Spring/Summer 2003

Spring/Summer 2003

GIORGIO ARMANI

Royal Academy of Arts

Published on the occasion of the exhibition
G I O R G I O   A R M A N I
An exhibition organised by the Solomon R. Guggenheim Foundation
in cooperation with the Royal Academy of Arts.

Exhibition designed by Robert Wilson

Royal Academy of Arts
18 October 2003 – 15 February 2004

This exhibition is made possible by ⊛ Mercedes-Benz

ISBN 1-903973-41-4 (softcover, Royal Academy)
ISBN 0-89207-300-4 (hardcover, Royal Academy)

Guggenheim Museum Publications
1071 Fifth Avenue
New York, New York 10128

Catalogue design: Takaaki Matsumoto, Matsumoto Incorporated, New York
Cover photos by Tom Munro

Printed in Germany by Cantz

CONTENTS

This exhibition is made possible by  Mercedes-Benz

Richard Gere in Paul Schrader's *American Gigolo*, 1980

Giorgio Armani is widely regarded as one of the most important designers of the twentieth century. The Guggenheim's survey of his career explores the artistic, cultural, and social influence of nearly three decades of groundbreaking work.

The design characteristics of Giorgio Armani's creations—timeless elegance, effortless grace, simplicity, and a fresh modern sensibility—are all qualities that Mercedes-Benz has admired and embraced for more than one hundred years. We are proud to give our support to this landmark exhibition of such a legendary designer.

Our common passion for design and style was documented as early as 1980 when a Mercedes-Benz car and Giorgio Armani garments were paired in the classic film *American Gigolo*. The successful and charismatic main character of the movie, played by Richard Gere, both drove a black Mercedes-Benz SL (R107) and wore elegant clothing designed by Giorgio Armani.

We would like to thank the Solomon R. Guggenheim Foundation for curating an exhibition on the role of one of today's most inspiring designers. We are pleased to support its updated presentation at the Royal Academy's new space at Burlington Gardens. Mercedes-Benz is delighted to bring this remarkable presentation of Armani's work to audiences around the world.

Dr. Joachim Schmidt
DaimlerChrysler AG
Executive Vice President, Mercedes Car Group

Professor Phillip King CBE

Giorgio Armani: A Retrospective, organised by the Solomon R. Guggenheim Foundation in New York in co-operation with the Royal Academy, and presented with a spectacular and innovative design by Robert Wilson, celebrates the Italian designer's legendary career. The epitome of stylish, classic sophistication, Giorgio Armani is one of the world's most influential fashion designers and has been a style icon for over twenty-five years.

The Royal Academy is delighted that *Giorgio Armani* will be the inaugural exhibition in its new space, acquired in 2001. Burlington Gardens lies directly behind Burlington House, and its purchase represents the culmination of many years of planning and negotiation. Designed by the distinguished Victorian architect Sir James Pennethorne between 1867 and 1870, the building has always been a centre for intellectual life, for the arts and for education. From 1970 to 1997, it housed the ethnography collections of the British Museum and was known as the Museum of Mankind. The Royal Academy will use this landmark building for many diverse and original projects, and as a base for expanding on the activities of Burlington House.

Giorgio Armani marks another successful collaboration between the Royal Academy and the Guggenheim. Over the years, colleagues from our institutions, especially Thomas Krens, Director of the Guggenheim, and Norman Rosenthal, Exhibitions Secretary at the Royal Academy, have worked together on several highly significant and successful projects, most recently *1900: Art at the Crossroads*, which was held in London and New York, and *Paris: Capital of the Arts 1900–1968*, which was shown in London and Bilbao. *Giorgio Armani*, which originated at the Solomon R. Guggenheim Museum in New York in 2000 and was subsequently shown at the Guggenheim Museum Bilbao in 2001 and then at the Neue Nationalgalerie in Berlin earlier in 2003, visits London as part of a tour that will travel to Italy, the Far East and back to America.

An enterprise of this scope is always complex and cannot be realised without the goodwill and the practical assistance of many. We acknowledge a particular debt of gratitude to Giorgio Armani himself, for without his vision this exhibition would not have come about. We are extremely grateful to the many individuals at Giorgio Armani S.p.A. who have worked tirelessly on various aspects of the exhibition. We also express our sincerest gratitude to the internationally acclaimed artist and stage director Robert Wilson, whose specifically conceived design, using a dramatic combination of light, sound and architectural elements, has transformed our nineteenth-century building in Burlington Gardens into a spectacular contemporary environment in which to experience Armani's creations. In addition, we thank Elisabetta di Mambro of Change Performing Arts, together with all the members of Wilson's design team. We extend our warmest thanks to all our colleagues at the Guggenheim, especially Thomas Krens, Director; Lisa Dennison, Deputy Director and Chief Curator; Germano Celant, Senior Curator of Contemporary Art; Karole Vail, Assistant Curator; and Jessica Ludwig, Project Manager, who, working with Simonetta Fraquelli, Project Director for the Royal Academy, has skilfully helped us to bring this exhibition to fruition; and to Sascha Machiedo, the Academy's Project Manager for Fabrication, Construction and Installation. To all the members of the Royal Academy staff, whose names appear in the Project Team at the back of this catalogue, and who have been responsible for renovating Burlington Gardens and taking care of every aspect of this project, we extend our most heartfelt thanks.

We are especially grateful to DaimlerChrysler AG, the sponsor of the *Giorgio Armani* exhibition tour. Without their outstanding generosity and commitment, this project would not have been possible. We also extend our sincere thanks to American Express for their support.

PREFACE AND ACKNOWLEDGMENTS

Thomas Krens

When the Guggenheim Museum in New York presented the exhibition *Giorgio Armani* in fall 2000, it was a milestone for the institution. Although the Guggenheim had in the past included aspects of fashion design history in the context of larger art exhibitions, *Giorgio Armani* was the first time that the entire career of a single designer was presented in a way comparable to a retrospective of any other important visual artist: the entire Frank Lloyd Wright rotunda was given over to the display of Armani's fashion designs over a twenty-five-year period, and this exhaustive, scholarly catalogue was published to document and contextualize Armani's achievements. Moreover, the exhibition design, by Robert Wilson, was a major statement unto itself. Wilson engaged the Wright building with a drama and elegance that amplified many of the aesthetic and cultural themes implicit in Armani's design approach. The exhibition, a tremendous public and critical success, was followed in 2001 by a successful presentation at the Guggenheim Museum Bilbao; in this case, Wilson's design took on Frank Gehry's architectural masterpiece in a presentation that once again united three major artistic disciplines: fashion design, theater, and architecture.

In May 2003, *Giorgio Armani* entered another phase of its history, by beginning a five-city international tour that will maintain many of the fundamental features of the original Guggenheim presentations. The Royal Academy's new space at Burlington Gardens is the second stop on this expanded tour, which began at the Neue Nationalgalerie in Berlin. Updated to include important designs from the past three years, the exhibition now encompasses almost three decades of Armani's prodigious output. This catalogue, too, includes additional scholarship and images, to bring it fully up to date. And Robert Wilson will tailor his exhibition design to consider the unique architectural qualities of each new exhibition site.

Until Burlington Gardens, the architecture of each venue was decidedly modern—Wright's iconic Solomon R. Guggenheim Museum, Frank Gehry's groundbreaking Guggenheim Museum Bilbao, and Mies van der Rohe's glass-and-steel Neue Nationalgalerie. With Burlington Gardens, the exhibition

Installation view, Solomon R. Guggenheim Museum, New York.

Photo by Ellen Labenski.

Installation views, Solomon R.
Guggenheim Museum, New York.
Photos by Ellen Labenski.

moves into a very different context—a neoclassical building, complete with exquisite detailing, refined proportions, and strong historical presence. This strikingly fresh context offers new perspectives on Armani's quintessentially modern creations.

Armani's innovations in the realm of clothing design transformed the face of contemporary fashion and inspired an entire generation to rethink conventional, gender-specific modes of dress. The Armani look is synonymous with an androgynous elegance that is at once classic and casual. His reconfiguration of the traditional suit from a rigidly tailored garment to an unstructured, flowing form gave new emphasis to the male physique, which had long been suppressed in business attire. And his adaptation of the man's suit for women marked a liberating trend in womenswear.

Many contemporary designers have been influenced by the visual arts, while numerous contemporary artists have appropriated fashion as a means of self-expression. This exchange has been deeply significant for both fields and is a hallmark of culture at the outset of the twenty-first century. The Italian Futurists were among the earliest Modern artists to underscore the interrelationship between art and fashion. Giacomo Balla, for instance, advocated the idea of a totally designed environment, which included not only art and architecture, but also design and fashion in particular. Giorgio Armani has inherited the mantle of his Italian forbears. His vision encompasses a completely choreographed aesthetic experience, from his fashion designs to his home collections.

Giorgio Armani has been realized by the efforts and support of many individuals and institutions too numerous to cite here. Nevertheless, we would like to express our thanks to the incredible team of talented and devoted people who worked so diligently to bring this project about. We owe, of course, the greatest debt of gratitude to Giorgio Armani himself, whose incomparable work and vision we are celebrating. We are also grateful to the individuals at Giorgio Armani S.p.A. who have brought this exhibition to fruition. We recognize that this exhibition would not have been imaginable without the efforts and creative talents of its cocurators, Germano Celant, Senior Curator of

Installation views, Solomon R.
Guggenheim Museum, New York.
Photos by Ellen Labenski.

Contemporary Art, Guggenheim Museum; and guest curator Harold Koda, Curator in Charge, The
Costume Institute, The Metropolitan Museum of Art. Each has brought the expertise of his respective
field and his unique sensibilities to bear upon this show. Special thanks are also due to Susan Cross,
Associate Curator at the Guggenheim, who headed the curatorial team in New York.

In addition, we are pleased to have had the chance to work with distinguished visual artist
Robert Wilson, and to collaborate with Elisabetta di Mambro of Change Performing Arts and the rest
of Wilson's team. Wilson's unique exhibition design concept has transformed the museum, providing
a dramatic and incomparable setting for Armani's designs.

Robert Wilson would like to thank Alberto W. Vilar, Founding Patron of the Watermill Center, for
his generous support. The Byrd Hoffman Water Mill Foundation thanks the Aventis Foundation, the
Brown Foundation of Houston, Inc., the LLWW Foundation, Louis Vuitton Malletier, Montres Rolex S.A.,
Luciano and Giancarla Berti, Lisa and Richard D. Colburn, the Peter J. Sharp Foundation, the Scaler
Foundation, the Karan-Weiss Foundation, the Guttman Family, Gabriele Henkel, Katharine Rayner, as
well as the following World Sponsors and donors who support the work of Robert Wilson and the
Watermill Center: American Friends of the Paris Opera and Ballet, Giorgio Armani, Lily Auchincloss (in
memoriam), Bacardi USA, Inc., Monique Barbier-Mueller, Pierre Bergé, Deborah and Leon Black,
Melissa Cohn, The Cowles Charitable Trust, Ethel de Croisset (in memoriam), Dorothy Cullman, Zora
Danon, Heinz Duerr Stiftung, The Edelman Companies, Förderverein Watermill, Eric and Martine Franck,
Betty Freeman, Agnes Gund, Anne Randolph Hearst, Donald Kahn, Wendy Keys and Donald Pels, The
Earle E. Mack Foundation, Giovanna Mazzocchi, Katharina Otto Bernstein, The Overbrook Foundation,
Alfred Richterich, Mark Rudkin, Louisa Stude Sarofim, Lynn Schneider, Darthea Speyer, Robert Wilson
Stiftung, Robert W. Wilson, Neda Young, and anonymous donors.

We extend our sincerest thanks to the catalogue authors: Alberto Abruzzese, Professor of
Sociology, University La Sapienza, Rome; Donald Albrecht, Independent Curator and Adjunct Curator for

Installation views,

Guggenheim Museum Bilbao.

Photos by Erika Ede.

Special Projects, Cooper-Hewitt, National Design Museum, New York; Natalia Aspesi, journalist; Marshall Blonsky, Professor of Semiotics, New York University's Interactive Telecommunications Program; Andrea Branzi, architect and historian; Hamish Bowles, European editor-at-large, *Vogue*; Jay Cocks, screenwriter; Edmundo Desnoes, Professor of Semiotics, New York University's Interactive Telecommunications Program; Suzy Menkes, Fashion Editor, *International Herald Tribune*; Caroline Rennolds Milbank, fashion historian; Patrick McCarthy, Chairman and Editorial Director, Fairchild Publications; Catherine Perry, author and freelance journalist; Martin Scorsese, film director; Ingrid Sischy, Editor-in-Chief, *Interview* magazine; Franca Sozzani, Editor, *Vogue Italia*; and Valerie Steele, Curator, The Museum at the Fashion Institute of Technology, New York.

Takaaki Matsumoto is to be commended for his elegant catalogue design. Photographer Tom Munro is to be thanked for the new photography of the catalogue cover and back cover and so are Guggenheim photographers David Heald and Ellen Labenski for the beautiful mannequin photography.

Many individuals and institutions have provided essential support. We are grateful to Jay and Verna Cocks, who have been so generous and gracious in assisting on this exhibition and opening their closets to us. We greatly appreciate all those individuals who generously lent garments to this exhibition from their private collections: Kevin Costner, Robert De Niro, Dario Franchetti, Samuel L. Jackson, Ashley Judd, Diane Lane, Sophia Loren, Ricky Martin, Ornella Muti, Pat Riley, Julia Roberts, Diana Ross, Paul Schrader, and Tina Turner. We must thank the American Museum of the Moving Image, notably Dana Demeth, Curator of Popular Culture. We must also thank The Museum at the Fashion Institute of Technology, notably Director Dorothy Globus, Conservator Shirley Eng, and Curator of Costumes Ellen Shanley for their assistance and expertise. The assistance of The Costume Institute at The Metropolitan Museum of Art, New York, has been appreciated throughout the organization of this project. The Kent State University Museum was also extremely helpful; we thank Director Jean Gidruesedow, Collections Manager Anne Bissonnette, and Museum Registrar Lou Cinda Holt. Scott

Schuman also assisted us, lending essential materials from his personal library. A number of public figures kindly contributed quotations that reflect their relationship to and appreciation of Giorgio Armani and his designs. We are grateful to them all for sharing in this tribute.

An exhibition of this scope could not take place without the generous support of our sponsors. I would like to extend my sincere thanks to DaimlerChrysler AG, whose commitment to fine design is expressed by their enlightened and generous support of the *Giorgio Armani* exhibition tour. I am indebted to Hilmar Kopper, Chairman of the Supervisory Board—a longtime friend to the Guggenheim Foundation—and Prof. Jürgen Hubbert, Member of the Management Board, Mercedes Car Group. Without the leadership and vision of these two individuals, the expanded exhibition tour would simply not have been possible. For their creativity and dedication to this project, I would also like to thank Dr. Joachim Schmidt, Executive Vice President, Mercedes Car Group; Joachim-Justus Schneider, Director of Worldwide Marketing Communications, Mercedes-Benz and Maybach; and Burghard Graf Vitzthum, Head of Alternative Communications. We are also grateful to American Express for their support of this ambitious exhibition. In particular, I would like to thank David Herrick, President and Head of American Express Establishment Services, EMEA, for his enlightened support, as well as Philip Vergeylen, Vice President and Head of Marketing and Communications, American Express Establishment Services, EMEA, and Hugo Foulds, Director, American Express Public Affairs, Europe.

The Guggenheim staff for the London venue, whose names appear later on the Project Team list, deserve much credit for their hard work. Last but not least, we extend our thanks to the staff of the Royal Academy and in particular to Phillip King, President of the Royal Academy; Lawton Fitt, Secretary; Norman Rosenthal, Exhibitions Secretary; and Simonetta Fraquelli, Project Director.

Germano Celant

In 1980, when movie screens all over the world were showing Paul Schrader's *American Gigolo*, the shirts, ties, and suits of Giorgio Armani made their appearance as tools of seduction and enchantment, by means of which the gigolo, as played by Richard Gere, came to assume a magnetic, exciting, enigmatic and mysterious identity. The mass dandy was born. This behavioral model, conveyed by a system of mass communication, invited individuals—the spectators—to forge their own self-image, and therefore their own destinies, by means of clothing made up of the refined but mass-produced objects typical of prêt-à-porter fashion.

The American gigolo, unique in his good looks and identity, wants to attract and fascinate; however, living at once on his physical appearance and the availability of his body, which is put into circulation to satisfy the desires of others, he can be eccentric, but not too much so. His body, like his clothing—his second skin—must give off magic, so as to become an object of enjoyment, of furtive pleasure and momentary excitation. His whole being is therefore a bewitching universe capable of unleashing, with beauty as much as with purely visual conjuring, the magnetism binding seducer and seduced, actor and spectator. He is a cold and indifferent shadow that lights up by means of the mimetic virtuosity of his own attractiveness and that of his clothes; he is reflected in them and dissolves in them like an object of pleasure among other objects of pleasure. He is a lover, slave, prostitute, son, brother, father, boss—a being always spilling over into something else: a human entity capable of absorbing and incorporating others' desires in himself, like the very clothes he wears. He fills a void and his essence is a self-offering as a body-object passing over or through another body without changing its own physical or expressive state. He is not empty, but merely supple, like an article of clothing capable of absorbing any body, appropriating it and regenerating itself in it, transmitting a way of being while remaining the same—a neutral thing that negates and affirms itself at once, an open figure that implies all aspects and all types of body.

The gigolo is today's dandy. His style is not the excessive, unique one of his nineteenth-

Richard Gere in Paul Schrader's
American Gigolo, 1980

Oscar Wilde, 1875

century predecessor, which always straddled the boundary of incomprehensibility, for the gigolo remains frivolous and decadent, hiding behind a face that is a perfect, attractive mask. He is proud of pleasing others, ironic and refined, flawless in appearance and a snob. He turns his look, his outward aspect, into a mode of survival. Like an Oscar Wilde, a Barbey d'Aurevilly, a George Bryan Beau Brummel, Gere the gigolo crystallizes into an object among objects, a clothed body that makes style his manner of being-in-the-world. Nevertheless, compared to his predecessors, the Hollywood Ganymede does not parade an abundance or accumulation of fabrics and embroideries, of silks and dazzling, garish colors. Rather, he goes against the grain, opting for the minimal: subtle variations on one color, earth-tone monochromes, and the occasional, though rare, handcrafted fabric. He selects things as though wanting to avoid and deflect attention, entrusting himself to a secret, silent acceptability in which sweetness and softness are the true protagonists of his seduction, which interweaves the virile and the feminine. As he must indeed give of himself, he is forced to display an open character whose sexuality is fluid: he highlights the masculine, but does not suppress his feminine element, and thus cloaks himself in androgyny. He avails himself of a form of expression and a mask capable of mimicking—like his clothing and outer layer—the desire and pleasure of the other person. He thus avoids vulgarity and spectacle, dissolving the impetus and perfection of his limitlessly available body in the suppleness of the materials and colors that liberate its sensual form but grant him, in their uniformity and measure, a triumphant innocence.

Compared to his nineteenth-century referents, who refused to be part of the multitude and thought of the "fashionable" as something surprising and unusual and of refinement as the "high life," the gigolo is neither original, nor unique, nor rare, nor disturbing, nor different. Rather, he repeats gestures and behaviors he assumes will please others and lead to triumphs. At the same time, he is a multiple being; his existence depends on the assent of many people and on the plurality created by his expansion in space and time, brought about by the communicative vehicle that objectivizes him in the eyes of others: the cinema. The American gigolo is a figure multiplied in the eyes of millions; he is the product of an imaginary life onto which the fantasies and desires of the masses are projected. And so he becomes a mass dandy, a common being who makes the singular, unique function of the dandy plural, taking its sophisticated discourse and carrying it over into a popular dimension, that of a mass otherness capable of becoming an oneiric, planetary vision.

The Armani style that gave expression to the mass dandy was part of a renewal that occurred in fashion in 1975, when prêt-à-porter was born, transforming haute couture into mass fashion. The former's role as an absolute, elitist vision, with its useless forms representing a theatricality of prestige and power charged with old, mummified codes linked to social and economic subjection, came to an end, and a new realm opened up, one bound to an egalitarian mentality seeking to annul differences and disadvantages, to undermine roles and disparities in dress and self-presentation. Fashion left the inner sanctum of the chosen few, shed its cumbersome, off-putting theatricality, and became a transparent medium no longer bound to the aristocratic manner of certain identities, but now devoted to the narcissism of the many, if not everyone. It forgot its otherness and entered into everyday life, moving from a limited aesthetics to a generalized one that went so far as to include a reflection of all beings and all things, which thus became equivalent. This was a new dimension, no longer connected to a separate, autonomous universe, but to the spread of the literacy of mass taste.

At the same time, the search for fashion images and ideas became part of a decorative culture in which the reality of social status was transformed into images, into a simulation of individual identity. Clothing thus became an imaginary duplicate that served to legitimize and reflect one's social and economic desires, even when these were nonexistent. It became a stage set for the struggle between true and false, good and evil, original and copy, reality and travesty. It involved one's own display and styling, giving another meaning to subjectivity and to what lay beneath the clothing. It seemed to satisfy the demand for a less solemn, less gilded form of fashion, one suited to the new systems of mass communication. And in fact it became more public and reproducible. In particular, prêt-à-porter fashion, launched by Christian Dior and Yves Saint Laurent in 1975, found its strength in the notion of repetitiveness and the relationship between the original and the copy so perfect as to dissolve all difference and sense of primacy. This was a fashion of mimicry, based on the appearance of uniqueness, but produced by the thousands, with objects appearing and reappearing in infinite variants that continually created a sense of *ex novo* from one same thing.

In 1975, when, after a brief stint of medical study that taught him the relationship between design and anatomy, Armani began his adventure as a designer alongside Sergio Galeotti—an architect and thus someone who was able to recognize the roots of structural transformation in forms and volumes—he realized that the traditional concept of fashion was entirely inadequate for the profound social and intellectual changes that had taken place in the previous decade, which had led to an annulment of formal and behavioral differentiation between young and old, feminine and masculine, poor and rich, high and low. In a brief span of time, in fact, temporal and thematic differences were also annulled—between old and new, exotic and traditional. Everything became synchronic and replaceable, making every iconographic or material element mutable and permutable. Fashion was forced to adapt and become eclectic, no longer being able to keep to a single unitary, univocal principle that categorically reflected a social and sexual identity, which had frozen styles for decades. Now it exploded anew each season. It was no longer a vehicle of the dominant ideology—white, male, and European—but aimed instead at reflecting all cultures, adapting to the equivalency and reversibility of all choices, which could no longer be reduced to a definite unity. This indeterminacy undermined absoluteness and unidirectionality, which were replaced by a multiplicity based on the combination of elements. Sexual and social roles were blurred; the visible and the invisible, the naked and the clothed blended into one another.

Armani was one of the first to intuit this change of direction, which envisaged fashion as a

Actress Talitha Pol and husband Paul
Getty, Jr., Rome, 1971, dressed in
"couture" hippy style

Isabella Rossellini, Rome, 1970

Spring/Summer 1987

mass dream-vision in which clothing was an intermediary instrument of an egalitarian mentality as well as a crystallization of the desires and tastes of a broad swath of people wishing to forge their own identities. He understood that his role was to objectify an aspiration to be, which arose from a mass demand that reawakened to the forms of life after the generational rebellion of 1968. The explosion of individual creative freedom brought with it a liberation of clothing from the limits imposed on it by the social condition of fashion. The point was no longer obligation and rationality, but a personal and imaginative growth in which everyone could stake out his or her own unprecedented terrain of identity. Having been educated in a cultural epoch dominated by impersonal apparel—in particular the uniforms of the large manufacturers Facis and Lebole, which were sold at La Rinascente, the department-store chain where Armani began his adventure into the universe of fashion, and the uniforms of proletarians and the bourgeoisie, which canceled out the individuals wearing them in favor of a homogenized collectivity—Armani understood that clothing was instead part of the everyday management of one's appearance, a tool of personal symbology: "When I began to design, men all dressed in the same way. American industry called the shots, with its technicians scattered all over the world . . . all impeccably equal, equally impeccable. The Mao Syndrome. Everyone wore the same uniform, a bit wider here, a bit more tapered there, but the substance was always the same. You couldn't tell them apart. They had no defects. But I *liked* defect. I wanted to personalize the jacket, to make it more closely attuned to its wearer. How? By removing the structure. Making it into a sort of second skin."[1] An added epidermis, which the wearer would use to emphasize physical and psychological, emotional and ethical aspects; in other words, a form of self-possession and self-protection. Added to this was the awareness that clothing, aside from being a way to manage one's appearance and one's pleasures, was also a way to free oneself from social definitions based on age, economics, and gender, which high fashion had enforced to avoid a promiscuity of power, to the point that fashion had remained outside the workaday world and vice versa. Armani believed that the age of haute couture, which had operated in terms of pure creativity, isolating the beautiful from the useful and confining the pleasure of dressing to a luxury phenomenon, was past, and thought that prêt-à-porter clothes could lend dignity to fashion, which could actually come to influence and change the tastes of its consumers by opposing kitsch and vulgar notions of personal beauty. He did not conceive of fashion as an alternative capable of differentiating social classes, but rather looked to its possibilities as a cultural industry that would turn creative products into discoveries and aesthetic valorizations. Haute couture was utterly ill-suited to attempt to realize mass elegance, the possibility of which it denied and considered undesirable; it was not ready to meet the demand for differentiated but democratic signs. Indeed, if it had responded to these demands, it would have lost its identity: haute couture lives with the dandy and dies with the mass dandy.

All that remained was an item of mass production that continued to exalt the narcissistic image of the person, but was available to millions of consumers. "The true leader of fashion," Armani has said, "is industry. Prêt-à-porter, the manufactured garment, is the true force of fashion. Today fashion is that which is sold in great quantities, or at least in quantities that are visible when you walk down the street. High fashion for the wealthy and the very rich still exists, but the rule is that the articles shown on the runway, with a few corrections and a few modifications, must be capable of becoming clothes for everyone."[2] Fashion could not continue to affirm a social and economic split that at the time appeared quite visibly in its absolutizing differentiations, as witnessed in the films of that decade, from the garments by Roberto Capucci and Emilio Schuberth worn by the clerical and papal nobility in Federico Fellini's *La Dolce Vita* (1960), to the monochrome black of the upper bourgeoisie of Michelangelo Antonioni's *L'Avventura* (1960), to the motley and haphazard look of the proletarian class in Pier Paolo Pasolini's *Accattone!* (1961). Rather, fashion had to dissolve the distinctions, to reinvest clothing with a signic function that would become a surrogate identity. This was why Armani refused the oppositional approach, blurred the boundaries between power relationships and sexual differences, between feminine "being" and masculine "doing," and went in search of a new and different aesthetic and visual style that would produce "power" by itself— elegance as a mode of self-projection as person: "I believed in a new elegance, in a new fashion in step with the changes in women and the world: essence, simplicity, figure, rigour, sober beauty, restrained colours. This conviction suggested a way of being, and a way of operating in keeping with a new concept of the classic. I wanted to be more democratic, and to separate high fashion from the image of an applied art destined for only a few globetrotting jet-set millionaires. I thought about people. . . . I thought about a form of education of taste."[3]

He conceived of clothing as a mobile object, one not fixed to anthropological and social identities, but existing as movement and transition between the two. He established no absolute boundaries, but expressed instead a dynamic, nonstatic notion that went so far as to allow clothing to exist as an open-ended, formless condition covering the closed form of the body. This tearing down of walls of opposition clearly reflected a cultural climate in which hard ideological divisions were dissolved; Armani mirrored this in the production of objects of apparel that corresponded to the collapse of separateness and structure. On the level of separateness, his style sought a transition between the poles of masculine and feminine, and aspired to a fusion of differences. In this way, fashion no longer claimed to possess absolute values, but rather sought to move toward a neutral sexuality based on the design of clothing that might embrace both sexes. He created a single image that established a third way, by means of a new structural order and a new kind of fabric. His design aimed to let the product correspond not to a gender, but to a bodily pleasure, because what had mattered in earlier clothing was the sublimation of one's pleasure and sensibility. And since being "fashionable" meant sharing the aesthetic customs of a global mass of people—that is, recognizing oneself in others and sharing their general aspirations to elevate themselves—Armani began to interweave opposites: masculine and feminine, proletarian and bourgeois, local and international, classical and experimental, present and past, haute couture and prêt-à-porter, mass production and one-of-a-kind, structure and antistructure, the bodily and the bodiless.

In the language of fashion, this meant a deconstruction of the relationships between opposing signs, with the qualities of one form entering the other and vice versa. Armani began by destructuring the jacket, unhinging the system of rules and constants upholding its design; he changed proportions, exploited defects, and overturned rules in such a way that regularity and symmetry, essentiality and complexity, softness and rigidity, opacity and transparency, all became mutually integrated to create a sensual, natural style. A new way of dressing was born, based on a different manner of establishing the relationship between structure and movement, body and garment; the one does not command the other, but rather functions in terms of fullness and softness, and thus the body is no longer covered by the garment, but rather inhabits it, intertwines itself with it, forming a unity that establishes a total alliance between sensuality and thing. And since sensuality belongs as much to the masculine as to the feminine, Armani's 1975 destructured jacket threw the space of fashion open to nondifference, to garments that could be moved from one body to another. By this means, the designer realized that any schema could be abandoned, and that one could design things and garments whose functions do not derive from pre-established perspectives. He gave himself over to the outstanding givens of the object, from the composition to the details, from the materials to the cuttings, and from this made a model gratifying to all types: "All my work has developed around the jacket. It was the starting point for all the rest. My small but crucial discovery lies in having imagined a garment which falls over the body in a surprisingly natural manner. I experimented with new techniques, removing the lining, or the interlining. I have modified the arrangement of the buttons, and radically altered the proportions. What was previously considered a defect has become the basis for a new form: a new jacket. This creative procedure has generated a light jacket, as comfortable as a shirt, sensual even in its construction."[4]

This deconstruction called into question all the conventional and arbitrary definitions that have sustained the concept of difference. Difference survives when an element, of clothing or any other thing, refers only to a primary definition based on hierarchical oppositions—the most powerful and traditional of these being the institutional acceptance of the difference between masculine and feminine. Armani's destructured jacket identified a possible space for both, a third term that was not a term, a wrapping that was sexually blurred because it could be worn by either side. By working, in fact, with asymmetry, Armani challenged the binary, harmonious, stable symmetry of stereotyped forms indicated in the terms "masculine" and "feminine." His jacket was a tool of unstable identity that could adapt itself to any bodily context whatsoever, thus satisfying the emotional and psychological requirements of a femininity tending to the masculine as well as a masculinity that aspired to the feminine. The Armani style helped to bring about a crisis in all such clear-cut definitions; it situated itself in the area of androgyny. No more men and women, gentlemen and ladies, but timeless, bodiless people able to move about from here to there, from high to low, from aristocracy to the middle class, from young to old, from black to white, from the feminine to the masculine.

On the feminine level, this process of indistinction facilitated the decline of women's imitation of men. With Armani, the woman's body was removed from the competitive tension arising from the use of clothing as a sign of power and antagonism, because the garment was placed in the service of a naturalness and sensuality based not on travesty but on the personification of the feminine. The working woman was not forced to deny herself or redesign herself to be successful, or to assume the trappings of masculinity to be accepted and acknowledged; rather, she could cultivate her beauty and sensuality as vehicles of expression and existence. And the reverse could be done by men: "My fashion is not unisex, but it does insist upon more gentleness for men, and more strength for women. I know that in every human being there exist both masculine and feminine components, and that they

Fall/Winter 1994–95

Fall/Winter 1998–99

can be used to create a harmonious equilibrium, far from the extremist stereotypes of the macho man and the woman imprisoned in the squalid part of the doll-whore."[5]

For reasons of harmony, following in the footsteps of Gabrielle "Coco" Chanel and Paul Poiret—who were the first to present a woman's liberation through the elimination of decor and ornamental details and through the use of severity and simplicity—Armani designs linear, neutral garments that are architecturally soft. They live on the threshold of gender and function, so that day becomes confused with night, work with pleasure, artifice with naturalness: "I began to work in the field of women's fashion when women went around dressed . . . like flowers. I wanted a fashion that was for everybody. And I realized women did not have a way of dressing that was easy, modern, somewhat close to men's style. It was the time when women realized that they could stand up for their rights in a decisive manner, feminism, more or less, and also dressing in this new feminine spirit was very right."[6]

His language has generally been defined as minimal and classical. Minimal, because the designed garment satisfies simple and essential personal demands. It draws attention to the body by means of a cut and a style of workmanship, a material and color that become indistinguishable from the bodily shape wearing it. It keeps one's own identity alive but also underscores others that are linked to a higher quality of life, conveyed almost always through Armani's choice of fabrics and details that are elaborately constructed but simple in appearance. The style is also minimal because it does not accept the convolution of superficial, iconic mutations, but rather effects subtle variations and permutations of the same primary elements, which are repeatedly updated and renewed, keeping constant the method and concept—which is that of a body that absorbs the body, appropriating it in order to give it back regenerated and visually qualified. It is precisely here that the Armani style achieves its optimal result. In his clothes, the forms wrap and cover the body in a second skin that allows one to perceive the inside as much as the outside, by means of thin tissues and soft fabrics that assume the forms of the flesh like an inorganic epidermis. At the same time, this style is called classical because it prefers closed form to open form, the pleasure of the line, of muted colors, of unity to multiplicity, a sense of clear form to ambiguity—and because it prefers the process of removal and subtraction, using simple, incisive elements that always waver between the traditional and the advanced: "I am not so enthused when people say that I am a classicist, remote, distant from the present-day distress of being in style, and with this they feel that they have said the last word about my work. If, in my work, I begin with the rules of tradition, I do so because I am convinced that only by understanding these conventions can we go beyond them to truly change the form, the structure of the garment. To build a suit which is in conscious equilibrium between the tradition and the originality of my time."[7]

The Armani style is therefore surprising. It nullifies the conflict between dignity and sex, between dress and power. It also produces an aesthetic beauty on the level of the liberation of social minorities and sexualities; acquires public importance through diffusion and mass culture, while remaining open to the imaginary and the sensual; creates narcissistic commodities no longer determined only by functionality, but also by such models of symbolic identification as gender and status. It offers the freedom to move, through a change of style, from a local condition to an international one that coincides with globalization and the universalization of the bourgeois ideal that leads everyone worldwide to aspire to a comfortable, privileged, and elegant, but adventurous life. The Armani style is part of this modernization of middle-range tastes, for it provides a wrapping or garment that is not an elitist option, but rather a democratic one, on the level of aesthetic supply. And yet while it may remain economically at the high end of the spectrum, his product reflects the growing sophistication of the world's citizens, whose personalities are seemingly ever more oriented toward an enlightened search for self beyond all hedonism and spectacle.

Here, too, Armani tries to close the circle. When, in the 1980s, he opened fashion up to the exotic world of ethnic cultures, he drew his inspiration from the visual and spiritual treasures of Asia, in an attempt to interweave East and West: "My collections in the 1980s were full of references to the Orient. When I wanted to express the sensation of the greatest wealth of the decade, instinctively I turned to the images of a vague East, that of the Japanese samurai, of Imperial China, of the herdsmen of Mongolia, or of the maharajas of India, who have always fascinated me because of their dignity, composure, luxury, character. These images were useful to express an idea of opulence which was not hedonistic. In the 1990s the echo of a vague Islamic Orient has provided me with terms for the expression of an idea of simplicity and inner, spiritual wealth. This is an atmosphere which, with a few touches, alludes to a man who knows how to be gentle, and to a woman who knows her own mind. My interest in the Orient is not a stylistic whim, it is based on a certain spiritual affinity for the East and its cultures."[8]

But the inanimate materiality of the spirit in turn recalls the flesh, which is not its opposite but rather the place where the life force and instinctual and sensual power of the human being circulate. And since for Armani, fashion is life, living thought, the mutual attachment between garment and body takes place by means of the flesh, the very material nucleus that serves as the garment's support, in the absence of which there could be no discussion of fashion as existence or life. Another theme straddling the threshold of roles is that of the fabric's being able to pass gently from a condition as clothing to a condition as skin. Here the garment is no longer ornament, but pure sensuality; it is not something heavy and opaque adorning the body and rendering it solemn, but something immaterial and metaphysical underscoring the solid energy and beauty of the flesh.

Perhaps drawing inspiration from non-Western cultures, Armani, in 1990, interpreted the body as a transformer of energy, a kind of cauldron capable of receiving and transmitting nature's powers and giving them back in purified form. This passage from the carnal to the spiritual manifested itself in an exploration of design that put transparency at the center of its language. His fabrics began to acquire total freedom; not only did they destructure bodies, but they also destructured themselves in blending with the anatomical contours of their wearers. They represented hips and breasts, shoulders and torso, legs and back. An erotic relationship was thus established between nude body and clothing, the one not excluding the other. Dressing returned to ground zero, a point where such notions as full and empty collapse. It became the light, mischievous hieroglyphic of a sensual vortex from which masculine and feminine bodies emerged, regenerated. His garments clothed the body, but at the same time made its magnificence visible, and fashion became a union between the perdition of sensuality and the salvation of its covering. The Armani style reappropriated both and made them an integral part of one's everyday mode of existence.

This is why one speaks of Armani as formless, precisely because his forms are implicitly both seen and not seen. His garments move between the visible and the invisible, between the hidden and the desired. Fashion is thus transformed into a silent drama of sensuality, a magical action that transcends the limits of gender and sex. Armani's minimalism is a stripping down, in which the body—which is always nude—becomes a medium of communication. The garment defines its natural language, echoing its magnetism, which is communicated through contact between the two, in which the veil or transparency represents the search for an organic relationship between thing and person. In Armani's style, clothing is no longer the opposite of nakedness, but rather its inflection. Although it uses physical materials, its function is to resonate with the body's language. From this perspective, Armani goes against the fetishism of the garment; he rejects its value as effigy and the symbolism that moves it too close to an abstract concept. On the contrary, he fights for a living culture of fashion, which must not be simply a surface, but a focal point of emotional, spiritual, physical, and erotic energies. Hence the use of transparency, and the incorporeality of the fabrics and materials, which allow the flesh to re-emerge, no longer camouflaged or falsified, but exposed and sublimated in all its reality as a desired surface. The threshold of the socially forbidden has been crossed yet again: the coveted bodies cannot be touched, but the gaze may achieve a relationship of voluptuous immediacy with them. Transparency allows the eyes to possess from a distance, to infringe on reality and see the texture and colored nuances of a torso or breast. The diaphanousness of Armani's fabrics serves at once as a trap and a screen. It attracts desire and blocks it, seeks at once to draw in and repel, but above all it creates an active, living space, which is the infinite space of seductions. In Armani, the airy and the velvety, the satiny and the silky, reflection and color are nothing more than the other side of the destructured garment. They serve to bring to light what lies beneath the clothing; not to hide it, but to make it sexy: "It is true that I have always loved a certain discipline, a certain cleanness of line, but it's true that I also love to think that people dress to be sexy."[9]

And thus the body's substance is liberated, manifested with such force that it evaporates and ultimately dissolves into something resembling insubstantiality, something as evanescent as the fabric itself. At the same time, through the sort of dialectical interplay that underlies his style, Armani produces a contrary movement: he makes fluids coagulate; he solidifies and densifies colors and their lights. The intense chromaticism of his materials and the palpable thickening of the fabrics play an important role in his imagination. He aerates fluidity, but gives solidity and density to colors, which assert themselves with an uncertainty that prevents them from being fixed in one single state or another. They too, like the garments, are transitional; they point to "in-between" states likely to flow into one another. They are yet another attempt to avoid demarcation, which is why they are vague. But in the end they are Armani's colors—balanced greens and reds, blues and grays, beiges and creams that live on the borders of definition, propagating another vagueness. They participate in the integration of opposites, for they are assimilated with one another, juxtaposed or overlapped, in plays of soft and sandy variants that create the effect of blending and reverberation: "I am known as the stylist without colour, the inventor of *greige*, a cross between grey and beige. I love these neutral tones, they are calm, serene, they provide a background upon which anyone can express himself. It is a way to connect and combine the other colours. It is a base upon which to work, and it is never definitive, never dissonant, never a passing trend, it is always something that remains, a versatile basis over which, from time to time, to imagine other things."[10]

In Armani's noncolors, light often tends to slow down, to liquefy and thicken, as though having to pass through a murky transparency that imprisons it and turns it into physical mass. Armani's surfaces are dense with shadowy colors that condense and assume strong, solid shapes, as if wanting to become the atmosphere in which the flesh floats. Next to the strong sensual connotations of the flesh, colors can only be neutral, absent of precise definition, for they are a compact, deep background that highlights the lively, transitory fluidity of the body. They present no clear-cut margins, for they tend to constitute a uniform aggregate that remains indifferent and autonomous in regard to the masculine or feminine body of the model that inhabits it. Thus the Armani style appears bodiless and timeless, an open universe where past and future may intersect.

In conclusion, one could say that Armani has succeeded in combining various opposites that were separated and juxtaposed in fashion for decades. He has created contiguity and transition between already existing languages. Rather than keeping them distant from one another, he has integrated them, orchestrating more active relationships through interchanges of materials and genders, states of being and places. From color to color, from cut to cut, from destructuring to destructuring, change becomes a style based on the resonance of the immaterial in the material, the sensual in the spiritual. Armani works at interweaving East and West, local and global, covering and unveiling, fullness and emptiness, in order to re-absorb difference and equalize diversity. He pushes the different boundaries toward each other until they overlap—masculine and feminine, mass and dandy—in order to make a common notion arise between them and in them. He gleans sameness from contraries, and in this way his style marks a historic inversion in fashion. To continue to exist, fashion must not codify itself, but rather keep moving in order to remain itself. To Armani, a language that dissolves and is reborn to produce an elegance—that of the mass dandy, at once feminine and masculine—means "not being noticed, but being remembered."[11]

Notes

1.   "Armani Disarmed," *Emporio Armani* magazine (Milan) 14 (September–February 1995–96),

       p. 3.

2.   Ibid., p. 4.

3.   Ibid.

4.   Ibid., p. 3.

5.   Ibid., p. 6.

6.   Giorgio Armani in "Armani: The Artist as Entrepreneur," R.A.I. television special, 1998.

7.   "Armani Disarmed," p. 4.

8.   Ibid., p. 7.

9.   Giorgio Armani in "Armani: The Artist as Entrepreneur."

10.   "Armani Disarmed," p. 8.

11.   Paraphrased from ibid.: "Elegance doesn't mean being noticed, it means being remembered."

PRIVATE AND PUBLIC

Ingrid Sischy

Ingrid Sischy: Are you surprised by your life?

Giorgio Armani: Yes, absolutely. I never planned it out this way.

IS: When you were a kid, when you imagined the way your life would be, what did you see?

GA: Well, we children didn't have many chances to daydream. It was wartime. There were very real, everyday problems. I didn't have time to think about my dreams for the future. We were concerned with certain, very basic things: eating, getting cheap school books, and being able to go to the cinema on Sundays. We weren't allowed much!

IS: You grew up in Piacenza, which experienced a lot of bombing. How did that affect you?

GA: It was very difficult. The war affected everything. I didn't have a happy childhood. I experienced the death of two childhood friends from a war bomb. I was machine-gunned, with my three-year-old sister Rosanna; we were in the street and a plane flew over us, so we threw ourselves into a ditch. I was small and I covered my sister. It was traumatic. There were planes flying over us and we were under bombs all the time. Our parents used to wake us up at night to take us to the shelter. At three in the morning, with blankets, we'd all be there, all the children in the building. Once we had gotten over the shock of being woken up so brusquely, though, it was even fun.

IS: What were you like as a boy, from your perspective?

GA: I was an observer. I liked to listen rather than openly express myself. This trait is something that I've retained over the years.

IS: Can you describe a happy memory from your youth in Piacenza?

GA: I remember a family trip, possibly the only one, in a wonderful car with leather and metal spokes. It probably belonged to a friend of my father's and was an old 1930s model. We had parked this car by the side of a lake, and we were eating frittata. I have a wonderful memory of the beautiful sky, the light blue lake, the smell of the omelette and of the leather in the car.

Giorgio Armani on vacation, 1993

IS: After the war ended, you left Piacenza, right?

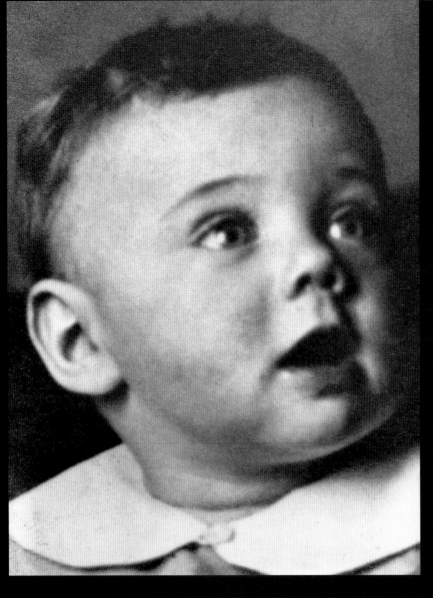

GA: Yes. We began a new life in Milan. It was a city of many ghettos—for the rich, for the middle class, for the poor. It was a very difficult time for our family. My parents were struggling to rebuild a decent life after the war. Milan seemed a big, tough city—very different from the quiet little provincial town of Piacenza.

IS: You were a teenager when you came to Milan. What would you do for fun?

GA: It was a totally different world from what it is today. On Sundays we'd go to the parks, a group of friends, and take photographs. Teenagers were much younger then than they are now. I was handed down my brother's clothes. We had no money to buy things.

IS: I imagine you were very aware, as a young man, of your family's struggles.

GA: Yes, I was very aware of the problems and could see the difficulties. But I was relaxed about them, too. I have to say I never suffered because I didn't grow up in a wealthy family. I was never envious of, say, some school friends who had more money. It never bothered me to see they were better off than us. I had a lot of serenity about this.

IS: Tell me about your parents. What did they do and what were they like?

GA: Well, my mother was a housewife. And my father at that time worked for a transport company. He was an accountant. He was extremely reserved, and he had problems after the war because he had been a member of a political group. He hadn't done anything, but things were black and white then. There was the right and the left, which meant he went through some difficult times. I think this affected him and demoralized him a great deal in his personal life, and in the life of the whole family. My mother was a very strong person who helped my father, and never let us feel underprivileged just because there wasn't much money. She always made us feel comfortable with ourselves. She was a wonderful mother, without being too overbearing. Possibly by keeping quiet she taught us much more than if she had said a lot. My mother was a very beautiful woman, and yet she dedicated herself wholeheartedly to the family, to us, the children, and this was a very important lesson for me. She never said very much, but what she did say was sufficient. She had a way of living with a great deal of dignity, even without money. This was something that had a real effect on me. I didn't want my mother to go without something because of me, or my father to make sacrifices and give up things for me. When the time came, I tried to be independent, to help the family in some way and not be a cause for concern.

IS: You have said that your mother's innate sense of style has been a constant inspiration. Tell me about this.

GA: Although my mother did not have a lot of money to spend on clothing, she nonetheless had her own style that was extremely personal. She took what she found interesting from fashion and ignored other trends that she disliked.

IS: Describe one of her looks, when you were still in Piacenza.

GA: Before the war, she would wear a lot of gray. Her clothes were simple styles, round-neck dresses in lightweight wool, possibly a brooch, a simple man's jacket, the checked jackets of the 1940s, but with a very understated look. She never gave way to exaggeration. My mother never wore hats, except once when she got married. She had a very striking face. She never needed much makeup; it didn't suit her. She had a very special beauty; not the beauty that I saw in some of my school friend's mothers, which was a bit artificial, with makeup and lipstick. My mother was less flashy, with a square face and very pronounced cheekbones. She was a woman who had succeeded in matching her style to her temperament, rejecting artificiality, ostentation, and caricatures. This rejection of so many things by my mother had a definite effect on me. But I never discussed fashion with my mother, and I didn't even think I would be particularly interested in fashion one day.

IS: What about your father's style? Did it make an impression?

GA: My father's sense of style was very similar to my mother's. Essential and even recherché at times.

IS: And what about your relationship to your older brother [Sergio, who died in 1995] and your younger sister [Rosanna]?

GA: We were very close, yet very independent. There were big age gaps between us, so we didn't have the same friends. Basically there was great mutual respect, total consideration, and an effort not to come into conflict with each other, not to invade each other's space. We had moments of great happiness all together. My brother always put on shows—he loved the cinema and theater and so he involved us in his creative efforts. Perhaps I received a sense of art, and a sensitivity to theatrical things, from my brother.

IS: Did your parents encourage it?

GA: Oh yes. The funny thing is, my parents met onstage, acting together. They often used to talk about it.

IS: Your grandfather also worked in the theater.

GA: Yes. He made wigs for the theater and he used to take me to the theater sometimes, to see what was going on.

IS: I read somewhere that you said when your grandfather took you backstage you were taken by the colorfulness of it all.

GA: I don't remember whether it was the colorfulness or the atmosphere. I remember, for example, when I went to the theater in Piacenza, which was an old municipal theater, like La Scala, but small. I must have been seven or eight, and I loved being in that place. I loved the smell of the stage.

IS: And when you started going to the movies, what did you see?

GA: I used to watch Italian films in Piacenza, but in Milan the American movies had arrived. The American musicals and westerns came to our screens, which I wasn't very fond of, I have to say.

IS: What did inspire you?

GA: A film that left me very emotional was *Ossessione* [1942] by Luchino Visconti. It had quite an impact on me. I knew nothing about the cinema, but I realized this film represented something very new. Until then, the cinema had been nothing but glamour, with all the women wearing suits and perfect hairstyles. Visconti's film was the opposite. It was humble, yet very sensual. The film probably awakened my consciousness of sensuality. I also remember seeing American films, with these American hunks in red-and-white gingham-check shirts. I looked for this type of shirt in Italy, but it didn't exist. Everyone told me what I was looking for were tablecloths from trattorias. (Laughs.) Some American films for Italian young people of that time were an education, a way of breaking out and seeing another world. I liked French films, too. Someone like Jean Gabin's films had a lot of emotions . . . passions. Then the new age of Italian cinema began, Neorealism, with directors like [Roberto] Rossellini, whose work I loved.

IS: When you moved to Milan after the war, what was your attitude about fashion and fashionable things?

GA: When I first came to Milan, I was only aware of the district where we lived. We did not live in the rich part of Milan, but in a part of Milan that was poor. It was a small area where you had your friends, the place where you played football, a second-rate cinema where you went because you didn't have the money to go to the center where the better, more expensive cinemas were. There were friends' houses where you took a bottle of Scotch and someone brought a record player. This is where we had our first romantic experiences—when the parents were out.

IS: When it was time for you to decide what to do with your life, why did you choose to study medicine? Why not become an actor, since you loved the movies so much?

GA: There was no open-mindedness at that time. If you were a man you had to be a notary, a lawyer, or a doctor. Being an actor was an impossible dream for me. Reading [A. J.] Cronin greatly influenced my ambitions. I wanted to dedicate my future to helping others—a very romantic vision. Of course, I discovered during my university studies that being a doctor is a job like others, not just a mission.

IS: When you had to leave medical school for military service, how did you feel?

GA: At the time, I was having doubts over which direction to take my studies, so having to leave for military service was the perfect excuse to clear my mind and take a well-needed break.

IS: You'd put in about three years on your medical studies, right?

GA: Yes. When I began my military service, I thought it would be like the military service I had seen in the movie *From Here to Eternity* [Fred Zinnemann, 1953]. That was the image I had. I even took my tennis racket with me. But it wasn't anything like the movie. Because I had done medical studies, I was assigned to the infirmary. It seemed that military life was about boredom and not the romance of friendship, or big men crying. I was mostly alone in the infirmary and spent most of my days painting. Then a flu epidemic broke out and I had sixty people in the infirmary. Anyway, some time later I had a short break from the service, and I asked if I could work in Milan. I was feeling frustrated in the service, and was thinking about what else I could do with my life. A woman friend of mine who worked at La Rinascente said there was a job in the advertising department. It has to be said that I forced Rosanna to do her first fashion photos, which I took to my interview there. The pictures were terrible, but the woman who was in charge of advertising at La Rinascente was very powerful and she liked me. She knew that I wasn't a photographer and that Rosanna wasn't a model, but she helped me get a job there. I believe in destiny. I managed to stay working at La Rinascente and finish my military service at the same time.

IS: When you gave up medicine for good, did your family understand?

GA: During that period, dreams were very relative. My family had economic problems; therefore, my main goal was to help them.

IS: How do you think your family would describe you as a young man?

GA: I think they would describe me as a very reserved person, without a very clear idea of what I wanted to do in the future, but with a great aesthetic sensitivity. I was almost never happy with the way my mother decorated the table, for instance. I always said no, I would do this or that instead. I had a very strong aesthetic sense.

IS: Was this true of your sister and brother, too?

GA: No. My sister, Rosanna, less so. My brother, Sergio, was very involved in other things. He was very attracted to girls, for example, and he was always out. He was very intelligent and very sensitive, though. That probably made life harder for him. My sister was very popular with women and with men, because she was very nice and very funny. Perhaps I was jealous of my sister at times, of her open-minded view of the world.

IS: The department store must have been a totally different experience after the army.

GA: It was. La Rinascente was the most important store in terms of understanding the fashion sensibility of the time. There were very smart people working there and they looked at the American department stores and at the ones in Switzerland, and they wanted to make La Rinascente a great center, not just a sales outlet.

IS: So what exactly did you do there?

GA: At first I assisted the people in charge of window dressing. Then I oversaw that work—checking to see that the windows were done properly. Soon I was moved to the fashion department, which assisted the buyers. My job was to help the buyers provide continuity and an appropriate atmosphere for the designers whose work they were ordering.

IS: Did you enjoy it?

GA: I was very much an observer.

IS: But you must have connected with it in some way. Did you find fashion exciting?

GA: I could see that at the time there were great French designers. Remember, I had had no education in fashion, no training in drawing or fashion design, absolutely none at all. I didn't work alongside the fashion greats, with a fashion staff, but with the craftsmen of fashion. I was very much afraid of failure. I knew I had to learn everything. After that experience at La Rinascente, word got around that I was good. I got a job working for [Nino] Cerruti. I did menswear for Hitman, Cerruti's new menswear line. It was a great experience.

IS: I'm curious: what was your relationship to fashion magazines then?

GA: When glancing at magazines, I knew there were big differences between what the public wanted and what the fashion magazines were proposing. This was the time that I was beginning to form strong ideas and opinions about fashion. It was also when the world of fashion was beginning to know my work. I had total independence and autonomy on the Hitman collection. It made a great deal of money and had a big turnover.

IS: You also created an advertising campaign for Hitman, which is now historic, because its point of view was revolutionary for the time.

GA: This was done with Oliviero Toscani, who took the famous photograph. It was a headshot of a man with long hair. You can see his hair moving, but not his face. The slogan said, "Hitman by Giorgio Armani." It was an honest photograph and a big success, but at first they said, "Armani, you shot a photo where you can't see the clothes. What did you do? No footwear, no fabric, we make fabrics, we make clothes!" I've still got the photograph. For the public it was something very new and it was brave of Toscani to do it. Now one sees a lot of fashion advertising like it. But this was the 1970s.

IS: Cerruti was one of the first Italian designers to show in Paris. Did that mean you were able to go there?

GA: I went to Paris only to observe the Cerruti shows. His Paris collections were not designed by me, and I was a little hurt by this. Sometimes some of the things that I did were taken and shown in Paris, though. Journalists would tell me it was obvious which pieces I had done. Working for Cerruti was a very important experience for me, because it taught me a lot and I was able to learn how to draw. For a young designer, to have a company behind you that is producing your work makes things much easier. Nino Cerruti taught me how to work and trusted me. By the time I worked with him, I had changed a great deal. I was no longer the boy I was at La Rinascente, a little insecure. I went to the office a little late every morning. I had bought a convertible Porsche. Secondhand, of course. I dressed well. It was the 1970s, so my hair was long. I took my dog with me everywhere, a boxer.

IS: Altogether how long did you work for Cerruti?

GA: Eight years.

IS: When Cerruti hired you, was it a big thing for you?

GA: Yes, but I think that going out on my own was actually the real "big thing." It wasn't easy giving up my job—it was safe, not difficult, and pretty well paid. I had no formal training in design or business. However, being young and naive allowed me to go for the new opportunity, ignoring the risks and my lack of experience. I was psychologically ready for a change. I realized that at Cerruti the chances for me to grow creatively were small. By then I had met Sergio Galeotti.

IS: I know how important this relationship was for you in life and work. I know, for example, that Galeotti was the one who pushed you to start designing on your own. Can you talk about this relationship and how it gave you both the confidence to flourish with the talents you had?

GA: I met Sergio through friends and realized right away that he had an unusual, youthful self-confidence and inner strength. He had this ability to make me examine what I was doing, what I could be doing and to reconsider my easy life at Cerruti. Sergio came from a small provincial town that was just too small for his liking. He was looking for a place where he could develop his personality and found Milan to be an energetic, active city. I helped him find a job in an architecture firm. When we embarked on our own company, he was often the one with the confidence. The most important part of our friendship was that we believed in each other and in each other's capabilities. When I was at Cerruti, Sergio would tell me that I was talented and could do other things. And there

was so much going on, in the culture as a whole and in fashion—especially between 1973 and 1975, with the extremes coming from Britain. There were also the changes being brought about by a new generation of feminism. Women needed a uniform for the mentality they were gradually acquiring.

IS: A uniform—or alternatives to what there was?

GA: Well, they definitely didn't need a floral skirt.

IS: And they weren't finding what they needed in the fashion magazines or in fashion.

GA: There seemed to be an aim to ridicule both men and women. What one saw was trends—clothes, for instance, that were obviously under the influence of Carnaby Street or the Beatles. It was media fashion.

IS: How did you personally dress?

GA: A bit like an office worker with a high salary. My clothes were made by a tailor. I would commission six outfits a year. I was working at Hitman and yet I didn't wear Hitman clothes! I realized it was time to look for a new reality. I started to think about how to leave behind traditional dress without becoming ridiculous. There had to be a way to design for the changes that were happening in the world without resorting to flowers.

IS: When you and Galeotti set up your first office in 1975, were you both scared that you might fail?

GA: Of course! When we hired our first employee, we told her to continue with her studies as we couldn't guarantee her future. Believe it or not, this person still works for me. She helps me remember what it was like in the beginning—the courage, the fears, the triumphs.

IS: Almost immediately when you started your own company, you revolutionized menswear with your now-famous unconstructed jacket. Tell me how it evolved. For instance, as a young man had you been dissatisfied with the clothes that you had found hanging in the stores?

GA: As a buyer, I found it difficult because I had to please a type of clientele who could spend money on clothing, yet the clothing had very little detail and made all the men look the same. I wanted clothing that could bring out a man's personality and compliment his body. Therefore, when I started on my own, I decided to get rid of all those "structures" in jackets. This was what was making everyone look identical. I experimented with letting the clothing fall over a man's body, bringing attention to this so-called "defect." The idea was to deconstruct the suit, providing more freedom and movement. I thought this was essential, allowing men a more personal and real look.

IS: When your revolutionary approach to menswear started to influence everything, did you sense that it would change fashion?

GA: I have made some personal contributions to fashion, but fashion moves and changes continuously. Nowadays, I make deconstructed jackets in many different ways, applying them to a modern lifestyle. Slimmer shoulders, a determined yet relaxed look. Most importantly, I want to remain true to my original concept: jackets without those confining internal structures that restrict the body.

IS: Then you did it again with women's fashion. You have said that both feminism and the style of your sister and her friends, who rejected stereotypical women's clothes, are what inspired you.

GA: I applied the same concepts to women's clothing, creating a new, sexy feeling of freedom. Of course, my family and friends were the first to experiment and test out my ideas.

IS: How would you describe the working dynamic between you and Galeotti?

GA: He was very clever. He gave me the freedom to design and he handled the contacts with the department stores. He didn't speak one word of English. And he had complete belief in what we were doing. I remember with one of the first collections, he refused to sell it to a big department store. We were nobody. And yet he said they had not made the minimum purchase. I could hear him explaining this in the background, and I was thinking: "What's he saying? What's he doing? Here we have the biggest department store and he's telling them no!"

IS: How long would you say it took you to find what we now think of as your voice as a designer?

GA: At least four seasons.

IS: Go back to what you did then. Did you work in the same way that you work today?

GA: I chose not to look at what was happening around me, from the fashion viewpoint. I started with a blank sheet of paper each season. Even today, it's a real drama—once I have found my way, it's OK, but to find the road, the solution, the path, is a big drama. I have a style to maintain, but I have to renew it and evolve it. Sometimes this renewal has led to collections that are too drastic.

IS: Such as?

GA: In the early 1980s I did a collection inspired by Japan that was too theatrical. The colors were not mine. After that I decided that for me there was only one way. And above all I learned not to listen to other people. That's dangerous.

IS: In the early days if you were going to listen to someone, was it Sergio?

GA: He was a good judge of my work. But he was very enthusiastic. Sometimes I felt that he was too readily pleased.

IS: In terms of the development of your vision, was there something that was going on somewhere, in another field perhaps, that inspired you, or that you felt connected to? Some parallel development somewhere that related? Something in art, maybe?

GA: Well, it was more indirect. At the beginning I was accepted above all by artists, actors, and architects, artistic types of people who understood how my jackets were constructed, who understood that the fault was not a fault but a quality. They understood that the suits I was designing were meant not to be restrictive. As these are the kind of individuals who wear old jackets, old pullovers, and like them when they are used and not when they are new, they felt a certain affinity to my fashion, and I felt one to them.

IS: Were there photographs that you saw that reinforced your vision, like the famous photographs of Picasso in his striped T-shirts?

13

GA: You mean from the end of the 1930s? They were the finest years in fashion. Very inventive. Very revolutionary. Not bourgeois. Yes, what one can see in photographs of, say, Dalí or Picasso from that time is the sort of atmosphere and class that I wanted to have in fashion. I tried to use that kind of idea and modernize it. There were also photographs of the young Gary Cooper that affected me. That was the style that I found very sexy—very strong, not stiff, not too constraining, relaxed. The suit does not cover the body, but instead puts it in evidence. But I have to say that an interest in these kinds of mixtures have also belonged to other designers. I'm thinking of [Yves] Saint Laurent first, [Gabrielle "Coco"] Chanel, and even [Jean Paul] Gaultier.

IS: Absolutely. What's interesting is how you all ended up with such different results. You've all come at it so differently.

GA: I've always tried to make clothes that are without references. That has sometimes been my problem with the fashion press. There haven't been easy references to explain what I've done.

IS: But there are a few people who you've said did, in fact, directly inspire you—like Matisse.

GA: How can you remain indifferent when you see a composition of colors in a painting by Matisse? You cannot remain unaffected by the way he paints a window, an interior in Nice, the street. There is such harmony, such invention and lightness in his work; this is what I like most, the philosophical simplicity. The simple flower becomes something unforgettable. I like Matisse's late works less. I find them more difficult to understand, and less poetic. But Matisse's work has given me a lot. It gave me the chance to use color in a very important way early on. Early Picasso has also been important to me: the purity of his drawings, their clarity, their spirit, and their modernity.

IS: How about Picasso as a figure?

GA: At times I find the myth a little embarrassing, a little heavy, overly self-important.

IS: While we are on the subject, are there any other artists whose work has been important to you?

GA: Giorgio Morandi.

IS: Of course.

GA: Morandi has a color palette very similar to mine. Three beiges, four grays. In his work, a slight variation makes all the difference.

IS: You've just touched on something that leads to the crux of what your work seems to be aiming for: Since establishing your vocabulary, you've always talked about a consistent vision. Doesn't your approach make it difficult for you in fashion, which seems to feed off changes and trends so much? You are going for the subtle Morandi approach, whereas fashion thrives on the idea of the new, even if it's old.

GA: In the world of fashion, if you don't follow the trends the press can ignore you. You are supposed to be yourself, yet at the same time follow the trends.

IS: How have you responded to this issue?

GA: By getting mad. (Laughs.) Fashion is made up of excesses, peaks, exaggeration, fanaticism. I'm against fanaticism. In the end I think the most difficult thing to do is the simplest thing. Fashion has to change. It has changed over the past fifty years, but it has to change more. I think people must not bow to dictates by those who deal with fashion in the broadest sense of the word. Specifying that skirts must be to the knee one season and shorter the next should end. I challenge that way of thinking. The fact that a woman looks good in one style doesn't necessarily mean she feels comfortable in another. People must not be the victims of input given by a group of people who decide what fashion is and what it isn't. It should be remembered that certain principles of elegance that were accepted thirty years ago are now obsolete. The mentality today is different.

IS: Tell me your philosophy about getting dressed up.

GA: Years ago, getting dressed up meant following certain rules that are very different today. It represented a special social coding, reflecting certain social classes. Today, there is more freedom from a visual point of view, and differences are masked. I pay more attention to the cut of an outfit and the quality of the material than to an overall head-to-toe look. A few years ago, elegance meant "super minimalism," but today I think elegance refers to something that is informal, relaxed, casual, and without excess. Dressing up is less about fur and pinstripes and more about the "Jackie O" black T-shirt and white chinos. Most importantly, it is a mentality that gives great value to simplicity.

IS: It seems like you've created the clothes for more movies than any other designer, which must be gratifying since you've had a love of movies since you were a child. How are your designs for movies connected to your other work?

GA: I am not a costume designer, so when I work on film projects, it is always directly related to my fashion. I have been lucky to have collaborated on so many films, such as *American Gigolo* [Paul Schrader, 1980], *The Untouchables* [Brian De Palma, 1987], *Stealing Beauty* [Bernardo Bertolucci, 1996], and the upcoming *Bounce* [Don Roos, 2000].

IS: What do you think when you watch something like the Oscars?

GA: It is a very interesting phenomenon when designers and stylists try to dress actors and actresses. Unfortunately, there are too many people—stylists, hairdressers, friends—who push the stars to choose retro outfits, rather than concentrating on what really suits them—often with disastrous results. I am lucky to have long-standing relationships with actors and actresses. If they attend the Oscars and decide to wear Armani, it is because they like Armani and feel good wearing it.

IS: Do you think there's a place for fantasy in fashion?

GA: Absolutely, a very big place! There is a strong need to innovate and personalize like never before. This sometimes means that you don't follow the trends for a season with the possibility of being ignored by certain fashion magazines. But it's necessary if you want to break away from clichés.

14

IS: It could be said that the contemporary fashion mentality would not be what it is if it hadn't been for what you have done in men's and women's fashion.

GA: To me, you shouldn't wear anything that defines you in a way that does not match your personality. It has to do with attitude, with the freedom to adapt what you are wearing to your needs. It's not about wearing something that looks like it doesn't belong to you, either psychologically or physically.

IS: Did your sister have a lot to do with how you came to understand what women wanted?

GA: I have great respect for women; I don't use women for personal amusement. In the 1960s Rosanna was something of a slave to fashion. Then I think she was embarrassed by this, as she had started to understand what her own style was. I love the way she dresses. She wears anonymous shirts and trousers, and she has an important face. The less fashion she wears, the more beautiful she is. She is very much like my mother. I dress like that, too. It is like a uniform. This is something I've always used for both men and women.

IS: But uniforms can feel authoritarian.

GA: No, I'm talking about something personal, not authoritarian—something that has no useless details, a nice cut, a nice shape, something that adheres to the body.

IS: The inevitable question to a designer is: How have other cultures influenced you in your work? It is always a tricky one because fashion's take in this regard can be very superficial, the same way it can get when it uses art for inspiration—it can be vampiric and touristy.

GA: You are right. It is easy to fall back on the theatrical and do costumes. But I must say that the East has had a definite influence on me, with its rational style of dress; a small jacket with a mandarin collar is the utmost in elegance and comfort. In all my collections there is definitely a touch of the East—always.

IS: I know you travel, but it also feels to me that when you touch on a theme, it can come as much from a photograph or from your imagination as from an actual journey.

GA: You have to use a theme to match it to your style and not vice versa. For example, I once did a Cuban collection, although I had never been to Cuba. I had seen a portrait of Diego Rivera, and this led to the collection. It was a collection that I dreamed up.

IS: Give me another example of how you work.

GA: One summer I had bought a necklace for my sister as a present, an archeological necklace that I had gotten from an antiques dealer. I was holding it in my hand. I could imagine a woman in the 1930s—the wife, say, of an archeologist who followed her husband in his work—and how she would dress. This led to an entire collection. It was based on this woman from the 1930s, brought up-to-date. Often my collections spring from an idea of this type, not from having researched a period of fashion. When I was young, I once created an eveningwear collection with a lot of embroidery. I wanted it to give the impression of a woman who, at the end of a long evening, returns home along the seashore and holds her skirt and her shoes up so that they don't get wet. That was the atmosphere of that collection; I wanted a relaxed look.

IS: Tell me about the recent collection that invoked the work of Vasily Kandinsky.

GA: I've always liked his graphic work. It wasn't a literal imitation of Kandinsky, but rather I wanted the clothes to have the same explosive energy that his work has.

IS: That energy is a good metaphor for what you've done with your business. But there was a moment, when your partner, Galeotti, died in 1985, when people assumed you were going to stop. Was there ever in your mind a question of stopping?

GA: It certainly was a moment of great despair and anguish. I had no other choice but to go ahead and bank on my confidence. I made decisions carefully, learning from my mistakes as I went along. It wasn't easy then, nor is it easier now. But I'm glad I was able to tackle it. The business was built up by me and by Sergio in a very emotional way. This is work that gives you no way out, no time to

breathe. It's a job that doesn't let you sleep, or really take a holiday, because your mind is always focused on it. It is a very difficult job, but enjoyable. We didn't do it out of a desire for wealth or fame. He'd always believed in my strengths, and I didn't want to disappoint him. Therefore there was a great desire to make it. I wanted to show that his confidence in my work was fully justified. I kept going for the same reason.

IS: You ended up not just continuing the company, but also taking on what he had been in charge of as well. Didn't you have obstacles when you also took charge of the business side?

GA: It was another challenge. Some said a designer cannot be a businessman too.

IS: Well, you've made mincemeat out of that cliché about creative types and business being oil and water.

GA: It was very difficult, though. I didn't really know my firm. I had left a lot of the responsibility to Sergio. He had many direct outside contacts and I had less. A lot of people said, "Ah, when Galeotti was here we did it this way." Therefore I had to get to know my firm, my people. I have to say that I've had some great coworkers, people who have helped me, although in the end the decisions are mine. My work is highly diversified, and I never work alone. I work with other people and I like the discussions of: Do you like this? Do you think this? Then I decide. I like to work this way. It keeps me alive, in constant tension.

IS: One of the most interesting collaborations between art and fashion that I have seen was the one you did with Robert Wilson in Florence in June 1996. [*GA Story*, performed in the Leopolda, a renovated nineteenth-century train station.] One of the tableaux in particular that the two of you came up with—the office tableau—always sticks in my mind. It was so riveting—the mix of style, lifestyle, and technology. It felt so prescient. Why do you think it is interesting for designers to work with other kinds of artists?

GA: I think that working only in your own field can make you lose some objectivity. A person who is outside your world can offer great insight. Bob Wilson's point of view on some of the clothing for that Florence show was essential to the outcome of the presentation.

IS: Over the years, you have also overseen your own advertising.

GA: Yes, with Rosanna handling it for a long time. Again the philosophy is to be at the service of the public. The public is represented by consumers, who mustn't be taken for a ride. It must be a sincere and direct relationship: "I'll make these clothes for you, I'll show them to you in the best possible way, in the atmosphere I consider appropriate, and, if you like them, go buy them." I think that often designers think they have to do certain things because they see general tendencies, but great equilibrium and great self-control are required.

IS: So, when you oversee an ad for a new women's perfume, say, what is in your mind in terms of creating a world for people to live in?

GA: The advertising has to show that I don't like women who, when they go into a lift, leave a tremendous waft of perfume in their wake.

IS: (Laughs.) You are known for being unswerving in your beliefs about what's right for Armani—even when everyone around you is pressuring you to do something else. Because you work in fashion, I'm sure there are people saying: "Giorgio, you have to be up to date, or Giorgio, this is the trend."

GA: In my opinion it's a question of great personal discipline: to have the strength to react to what comes at you from the outside. At times I wonder if I'm right to say no. Do I really have to say no to everyone? Sometimes you cannot express why it's a no. It has to do with something very personal in your mind, in your feelings and emotions. But sometimes you can say yes. In the end, you know what you wanted to do, in the months when you produced those drawings, those clothes, and you have to know this right up to the end.

Translated from the Italian by Roberta Armani.

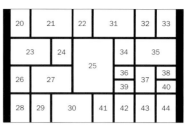
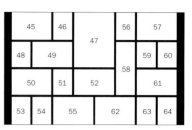

19

MILAN IN THE 1970S AND 1980S

Natalia Aspesi

For Giorgio Armani, one jacket was all it took to initiate his triumphant career and to change both the streetscape and the history of fashion. Certainly it was a special jacket, something new, which miraculously illustrated the needs and not merely the aesthetic of the moment. It was created to fit the restlessness and new authority of women, and to offer men the impetus to liberate themselves from the uncomfortable armor they had been using to protect their dignity and insecurities. These were the 1970s, dark years for Italy, above all for Milan, a city that was attempting to become the capital of high-style ready-to-wear, but was also, at that moment, the epicenter of the most tragic forms of social and political struggle.

Fragile commercial figures like fashion designers seemed anachronistic, out of place. This was a period when the country was being torn apart and the state structures were implicated, and precarious center-left governments, always led by the Christian Democrats, followed incessantly, one after another (eight governments from 1975 to 1980). Nothing was less current, less interesting, less important than fashion. Women who had discovered the advantages of ready-to-wear slipped quietly into the boutiques of Yves Saint Laurent, the favorite of the well-heeled bourgeoisie, which was still hesitant about Italian taste. But remembering the rotten eggs that protestors had hurled at their dazzling ensembles at the historic opening of La Scala in 1968, they camouflaged themselves on the street, disguised by unremarkable and irreproachable garments. Young women who dreamed of freedom through feminism and other political movements had rejected respectable pleated skirts and cardigans and were only buying stiff Afghan sheepskin jackets and mismatched, dyed garments from India. For the sake of the revolution, they even would have renounced being pretty, but not the very young Miuccia Prada, who distributed leaflets for the Communist Party dressed in French haute couture. Prada exhibited exemplary courage, since well-dressed young women were considered fascists and were accordingly isolated and sometimes subjected to insults and shoves.

Student demonstrations, Milan, 1968   Student demonstrations, Milan, 1968

It was with a certain hesitancy and anxiety that Armani embarked on a risky enterprise in 1975—the first collection bearing his name. He had rented two spaces in a building in the center of Milan, for one-and-one-half million lire a year. Behind closed doors, he worked with a marking pen and quantities of fabric, pursuing his still vague idea about clothing and thinking about the capital he would need to raise. He worked with two others: his dynamic and ambitious younger associate and companion, Sergio Galeotti, who had come from the architecture world and given him the courage to strive; and the mythical Irene, Armani's sole employee/factotum, to whom he had given permission to study during work hours because there was no certainty their small enterprise would have a future. Armani was developing his style, aloof and silent, outside the fashion of the moment. But he also remained detached from the enraged city, where the streets were thronged with marching protesters, facing off against police poised for war amid tear gas and shouted slogans, while students were occupying the universities and throwing out the professors and trade-union representatives. At that same time, the angriest broke away from the increasingly radicalized extremist groups, on both the right and left, and went underground, opting for terrorism. The streets of Milan were bloodied with the dead, victims of political ferocity. (In Rome, in 1978, the Red Brigades kidnapped and assassinated Aldo Moro, head of the Christian Democrats.)

This was the climate in which Armani brought his first women's collection to the runway, in a space at the Hotel Palace. According to Armani, "Maybe it was no big deal, but in the end Galeotti put on a record, at random, one that was very popular at that time by Inti-Illimani. The twelve models came out together on the runway and began moving to the lively beat of the music, and, incredulous, we heard applause." It was the applause of journalists, urged on by Count Franco Savorelli, who was lending a hand to his friend Armani. Having agreed to give up some of their precious time for the umpteenth new designer, the fashion press was dumbstruck by what it saw. Were these creations— simple, light garments, below-the-knee hemlines, soft trousers, jackets like shirts, without

Fall/Winter 1977–78   Spring/Summer 1979

ornamentation, impudence, or extravagance—beautiful or ugly? These clothes were simply different, outside the realm of Parisian high-fashion, which still dominated both women's dreams and the market, and also outside the Italian fashion industry designed by big French names, foremost among them Karl Lagerfeld, then Christiane Bailly and Emmanuelle Khan. Among the Italians there were designers like Kino Bert and Alberto Lattuada, or Qurino Conti and Walter Albini, who had established his label in 1973. It was a magical moment. Not only would Armani become a wealthy and established star, the king of made-in-Italy, within a few seasons and appear, seven years later, in April 1982, on the cover of *Time*, but without calculation, through pure instinct or perhaps a stroke of luck, he had understood his time while removing himself from its chaos and uncertainty. There was already a desire for change in the air, a longing for security and a future, and he was preparing that future's shapes and colors. Did this young man, reserved and still insecure, who had grown up in the provinces, in Piacenza, an ancient, agricultural city in Emilia, really have ideas that were so far-sighted? "It wasn't as if I had a burning passion, and I had never thought about getting involved with fashion. Other designers recall how they grew up amid the perfumed mysteries of their mother's closets, or how they began making clothes for their younger sisters' dolls. I have no memories of this sort. It is true the body fascinated me, and this was why I had decided to study medicine. I ended up in fashion by accident, but those were special times, occasions presented themselves unexpectedly, often, and people pursued paths without really understanding if they were on the right track." At most, Armani recalls, even as an adolescent, without realizing it, he felt dissatisfied with things that seemed aesthetically displeasing.

When Armani began working with the male clothing buyers at La Rinascente, the largest Italian department store at the time, the wholesalers were never able to provide what he thought should be obvious: black turtleneck sweaters, American-style shirts, jackets that didn't simply cover but rather adorned. And so Armani began to be involved with the body, no longer as a would-be doctor, but as a future engineer of elegance and behavior. Nino Cerruti, a businessman of great talent and foresight known for his men's fabrics and clothing (he didn't open a women's clothing boutique in Paris until 1976), discovered him there. Cerruti was surrounded by traditional clothing buyers, who hadn't realized that the world was changing, along with the way that men wanted to present themselves. Cerruti introduced the young Armani as his "stylist," a fairly new word in the fashion world, and Armani in turn began to fall in love with that world of fabrics and industrial production. While putting his faith in large-scale production and the demands of machinery, he rediscovered the value of the beautiful, well-made, elegant garment. He worked with Cerruti for eight years, and it was only during this period of discovery and development of his vocation that his personal talent began to flower. Even before leaving the company that had discovered him, Armani, as was the custom then, had also begun working anonymously for other ready-to-wear Italian labels, including those producing women's fashions, such as Sicons, Ginocchietti, and Gibò.

In this regard, he was following in the footsteps of other designers who would go on to achieve fame, from Gianfranco Ferrè to Gianni Versace. Beginning in 1967, after the usual and typically Italian quarrels, couture and ready-to-wear finally split definitively. Roberto Capucci, Valentino Schoen, and the other great Italian couturiers held their fashion shows in Rome. Krizia, Missoni, and many other new firms held their shows in Florence, in the famous White Room of the Pitti Palace. These were professional shows, without pageantry, with twenty houses presenting some twenty models each, all together, in an hour and a half. But in that crowd of models, the sharp eyes of the press and the American buyers had already noticed the originality of certain jackets, the surprising grace of certain men's fabrics used for women's clothing. Armani says, "I had my clothes tailor-made. It seemed indispensable to have them made to order, not out of snobbery, but because those mass-produced fashions made me feel old, shapeless, without glamour, and I wondered why they had to be so heavy, so awkward, like prisons that completely hid the body. At that time, fabric and lining were joined together with glue, which made the form rigid. I began to take everything away, padding, interfacing, linings, to look for fabrics that were classic in appearance but light, like those used in women's fashions. As far as possible, bearing in mind production costs, I wanted to apply the secrets of couture to ready-to-wear fashion. To emphasize the shoulders in jackets, but then let the rest undulate, adapt to the body, freed from all constraints. For the first time a creased, deconstructed garment became elegant." Men, used to the perpetual uniform of decorum and power, clearly were wary of this new image. It was enticing and comfortable, but seemed less protective of their mask of virility. Meanwhile, the powerless young in Italy, marching through the streets in protest, were dressed in the most disheveled way possible. They would never have dreamed of wearing a classic jacket, symbol of the despised bourgeoisie and their detested conservatism. But in 1980 a film, more beautiful than others at the time, appeared in Italian cinemas—Paul Schrader's *American Gigolo*. Those magnificent suits, perfectly cut to Richard Gere's young, rippling body, his costly, high-society gigolo wardrobe, full of gray suits, light-colored shirts, hundreds of ties, became the symbol of a new and unscrupulous urban elegance. Armani had designed them, and without doubt he helped turn Gere into a cult figure, someone with whom everyone, male and female, quickly fell in love, because of the melancholy seductiveness of his predatory character.

Armani's fashion immediately moved out of the Milan ghetto, away from Italian concerns, and spread beyond, to Europe and, above all, to the United States. To say that a cult began to form would only be a small exaggeration. This was prior to the 1980s, when not only Armani, but everything Italian was proclaimed triumphant on both sides of the Atlantic. The press, particularly the foreign press, crowned Armani king, blithely enthusing, "In Italy they have the Pope and Armani." Others went on, "Armani has done for fashion what Picasso did for painting. He has emancipated it, revolutionized it." When, with great reluctance and after sleepless nights, the Cerruti executive who had dreamed of neither fame nor wealth left his job, along with a salary he considered enormous, some $40,000 a

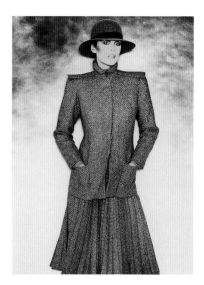

Spring/Summer 1976   Fall/Winter 1977–78   Fall/Winter 1978–79

year, he and Galeotti needed $10,000 in capital to get started. Just one year later, they were able to rent part of the Palazzo Caproni, one of the most beautiful baroque dwellings in the city, decorated with magnificent seventeenth-century frescoes. All timidity and fear had vanished, and he immediately furnished the gilded and voluted large rooms with ultramodern tables, sofas, and lamps of his own design. In 1976 the company's total sales already reached $90,000; in 1981 sales in the United States were $14 million, while total sales were $135 million, more than double the previous year.

To understand just how revolutionary Armani's fashion really was, how quickly it took over the world, first one needs to project oneself back to those revolutionary times in Italy. For example, it is important to remember that, during that crucial decade for Italian society, the intellectual bourgeoisie, looking down from on high and fueled by its cultural curiosity and financial advantages, was able to take an interest in the passage of fashion from couture to ready-to-wear and to adopt its variety, sense of fantasy, and freedom. But it was too deeply engaged in the political events of the country to look at this futile subject. The intellectual bourgeoisie sided with the young, signed petitions, participated in demonstrations, demanded the truth about mysterious deaths, victims of the police. In a word, they were aligned with the left, often outside the Communist Party, which had come to be considered too cautious and too caught up with the Christian Democrats, whose goal was anything but revolutionary. Within this passionate and enflamed climate, what room was there for fashion, despised for its frivolity and disengagement from reality? There was a unisex uniform for demonstrations: baggy pants and jackets, big shoes, camouflage colors, a scarf around the face, for concealment and for protection against tear gas, and at most an Indian shawl, jingling with mirrors, for her, or a Palestinian scarf, for him. These were spare, rebellious emblems, statements against waste and chic, against the sins of traditionalism and luxury, then considered tremendously right wing, reactionary, guilty. And yet during the 1970s Italian fashion was making an almost clandestine statement, detached from the disorder of the country and invisible in the streets. It could be seen behind the closed doors of important fashion houses, or on display during visits to Paris or New York or on holidays to places of indestructible worldliness, such as Capri or Saint Moritz. Other European countries were thrilled about it, even France, from a commercial point of view, though not in terms of information. (For years, no French journalist had come to Rome, Florence, or Milan to follow the fashion shows.) The reception was especially enthusiastic in the United States, which began to set aside sections for expensive Italian fashion in its most elegant large stores. There was the luxury of designers like Valentino, coming from the world of couture, the youthful grace of Krizia, the opulent practicality of Missoni, the early impudence of Versace, the urbane early statements of Ferrè. Italian ready-to-wear was well made, with beautiful fabrics, and still wavered between the rules of classical elegance and hippie romanticism.

We don't know whether Armani nurtured women's penchant for androgynous jackets without ornamentation, men's trousers, soft but severe-looking fabrics, and flat shoes because, after years of working in men's fashion, that was what he knew how to do best—or whether it was because he had truly understood that women were changing and wanted to find for themselves a different way of being feminine and seductive, a new image that would adapt, unambiguously, to their new needs and ever-stronger expectations, to the idea of achieving autonomy and social position, and that would also free them from their too-exhibited, overemphasized body, from the entire stage set of women's traditional clothing. In the United States, the period of marches and protests began to wane with the end of the Vietnam War in 1975. In Italy, the social and political disorder continued into the 1980s, but political passions, with the onset of terrorism, dissipated into fear, delusion, and clear popular rejection. It was an unexpected and rapid change, with a sudden, if watered-down, revival of *la dolce vita*, and the dreams and needs of the masses became something else, channeled toward consumption, wealth, light-heartedness, and a return to luxury without guilt. In Italy, Armani immediately brought an image of decorum and intelligence to this new social and individual passage. His work was not offensive or transgressive, nor was it ever opulent or vulgar. He offered a cosmopolitan elegance that ushered the country out of its recent dark ages and repositioned it in the world.

Translated from the Italian by Marguerite Shore.

Marshall Blonsky
with the collaboration of Edmundo Desnoes

Disemboweling the Jacket

Toward the beginning of *Made in Milan*, Martin Scorsese's 1990 filmic homage to Giorgio Armani, the designer is in his studio taking a scissors to the lining of a man's suit jacket opened before him. Cutting the bottom threads that bind inner to outer layer, Armani abruptly throws down the scissors and, grabbing the lining with his right hand, rips it up and away from the jacket—stopping at the shoulder to reach his hand deep into the sleeve. He yanks out the padding like so many entrails from a butchered beast. And there it is, disgorged—big, white, shapeless, ugly—to be thrown on the rug. The mildly startling moment, soundless save for the rip of the severed threads, condenses everything that can be said about Armani's attitude toward conventional structure, toward the rigid, the formal, the traditional.

Liberated from its unnecessary viscera, the beige skin is held aloft—Armani bringing it, *presenting* it to his Apollonian model (it could equally have been a Modigliani woman, so even-handed has Armani been in his gifts to the sexes), who deftly inserts his arms into it and, with a faint shiver of his tall torso, lets it fall from his shoulders. Armani rescues and transforms a traditional garment. Now it is an Armani.

"I created all my work around the jacket. It was my point of departure for everything," Armani explains to Scorsese.[1] "I had to defy convention to do this. But not by losing sight of all that's good in the past. I had to find a new way of inventing and thinking about clothing for a new era. It's a less formal time but it still requires its own style. I tried new techniques. Then I altered the way jackets were buttoned and radically modified the proportions. What used to be considered a defect became the basis for a new shape, a new jacket"—a wide shoulder, an elongated lapel, an unheard-of *dolcezza*, the sweetness of casualness, a plenitude of drapery.

Armani likes to say that modern clothes are a language, an expression of our individuality. And the whole world knows today that your individuality doesn't issue principally from your gender—

Spring/Summer 1989

boys to that showroom, girls to that. *Today* the world knows it, but it was Armani in the late 1970s who astonished women by making for them blazers and jackets that looked and felt and moved exactly as did those he made for men—softly armoring women's bodies in the identical way he was dressing men. This is why Armani says of the new individualism, which he helped form: "This is a shared victory for men and women. So much that now if a man won't go without a jacket, neither will a woman." A gift to efflorescent feminism from a man who in the 1960s had designed Nino Cerruti's menswear and who later designed uniforms for a male institution, the Italian Air Force.

I said earlier that Armani's model let the jacket *fall* from his tall shoulders, but *glide*, even *float* are perhaps better words for the effect. For the sports coat (that is what it is now!) appears so labile and light, silken and shimmering, it is as if it were a thing alive, delicate and exploring the space around the model.

"You see, it falls naturally on the body," Armani is telling me at almost the exact middle of his career, in June 1987. We are in his office in Milan, and he is sketching at his marble desk—atop it a delicate lamp illuminating his tanned face capped by pure white hair. (It's impossible to dye hair that color.) In a stroke of colored pencil on a piece of paper that I regret not taking home, he draws almost as a caress the sloping shoulder that would be his signature for fall/winter 1988–89 and into the 1990s. "*Le mot que je cherche, c'est . . . collant.*" He is speaking French, more to himself than to me. "The jacket should be running down the body without sticking to it, a second skin."

Do not underestimate this emphasis on something so seemingly humble as a jacket. Ripping the lining as well as the padding from that beige jacket only appears excessive (for Armani doesn't intend you, except on occasion, to wear jackets without lining). The ripping was a figural act, a metaphor: Armani was doing violence to, reconstructing tradition. For the modern jacket is not humble at all; it is the invention of the industrial-revolutionary patriarchy, part of a tradition that allowed the nineteenth-century bourgeois to enhance his upper body with a heavy, structured, tight suit jacket—before adding the last element, the tie, which forced him to button up at the neck to the point of strangulation. This completed the carapace. And the sign. The suit of many of our fathers through the middle of the last century, this carapace signified: "This breast, this brawn does not labor. It displays and commands. Look upward at my mind, which alone earns my salary and rules those who toil with their bodies."

The Eco in Armani

To understand that Armani makes signs out of clothes, it helps to remember a defining moment in the career of Umberto Eco. As Germano Celant recalls: "Eco was from the beginning in this core of intellectuals, Gruppo 63, whose semiologic approach completely changed the history of design and architecture. Whatever had been considered *arte minore,* minor arts, design, architecture, fashion, everything changed after Umberto. Naturally, after Roland Barthes, too. It is not by accident that Armani came along in the seventies. I knew the owner of Armani—he came up through a background of reading Umberto. Armani perfectly understands that clothing is semiotic. Attention to the meaning, to the language of fashion, this is the meaning of the boom called 'Made in Italy.'"[2]

A sign, the semiologists said, was a bit of an image instantly recognizable; a sign was what slapped you in the face by its difference from what came before it. And with Armani, every vestimentary "bit" is differentiated. No obvious browns but instead loamy mushrooms; shortened collars and cuffs; volumetrics where before was *près-du-corps* parsimony. One could go on. But let Armani explain difference through color: "I am known as the stylist without color, the inventor of 'greige,' a cross between gray and beige. I love these neutral tones. They are calm, serene. They provide a background upon which anyone can express him or herself."

Him or herself—not androgyny. "I've always had a rather carefree, easy-going woman in mind, but not one who's brazenly so," Armani says. "A woman who wants to dress, but not overstate who she is, or what part she plays in the world. A woman above all, and at all costs. A woman who knows how to live alongside a man with the sense of equality she deserves."[3]

Armani is a child of the semiotic, the deconstructive 1970s—and he has made millions of people worldwide understand clothes as a coded system of signs. "Clothes today are a language," Armani says. "We use them to communicate when we work and when we play." Sign consciousness informs his personality. His success is based in part on understanding the need to use instantly identifiable, differential images, something much more precise than simple branding.

You can test his use of difference by the way your own hand moves toward his clothes on a rack. If the lining is not sewn—or worse, fused—to the fabric at every possible point (remember the disemboweling?), you can hold a big piece away from the jacket without hurting it; you have revealed the suppleness of the garment. You can even crush folds of the fabric in your fist and, letting go, see the cloth spring back unrumpled; or if rumpled, all the better. Rumpling conduces, seduces, introduces you to the casually elegant slouch Armani prefers in women as in men. Try it on now: the Armani jacket cannot *plummet* from the shoulders; it makes it hard for you, man *or woman*, to play the rigid authoritarian patriarch. The jacket wafts, makes its moves with yours. It doubles your body with a textilian other. And everybody knows that a Father is one and the same, not two (I and the other), as Armani has now made possible. That is another of Armani's gifts to the genders: he was in the avant-garde of the attack on gender rigidity.

The Fabric of Our Lives

Because of his jackets' lissome nature, Armani can radically enlarge his repertoire of fabrics, adding the soft materials—like crepes and knits and leno weaves—previously rejected as too fragile. Armani's workshop revels in the versatility of fabrics.

The very word fabric comes from the Latin *fabrica*, workshop, and Armani insists on his

Fall/Winter 1988–89   Spring/Summer 2000

artisanal formation. "I've always put a lot of energy into choosing my fabrics. Maybe because fabric was my introduction to fashion. In fact, in the sixties I worked in a textile factory so I could really learn about fabrics. I remember enormous rooms full of looms that never stopped working, and noise, and people who seemed deaf. Though they were talking they didn't seem to hear each other. It was very hard work and I never thought I'd fall in love with it. Then little by little it became a passion."

From the minute you're in love with fabric, you're passionate about texture and its implications. "I want to eliminate the jacket's being a formal feature," he told the author in Milan, dressed in a blue T-shirt and black pants. "I want to render it very casual, very true, like a *pull*"—the French way to say pullover. A *pull* is a knitted thing: you can see the knit and the perl of its yarn, the very structure of the fabric. And suddenly we realize that from the very beginning Armani has made what the ancient rhetoric called the *impossibilia*: a deep surface, a profound surface for all his clothing. It has become a surface that can change, be seen through, both protect and reveal.

This Is Not a Tie

I have on my desk as I write a tie that I wore last night. It is a five-year-old, heavy, olive silk whose "striping" is not colored at all, but is rather ribbing, threads that have been made to surge from the surface, sometimes the thread becoming not a thread at all, but a fold. It is as if you were looking at a dried-up river, the ridges of its bed now visible. An ancient Green Sea. It *makes* you look *in*. Even the surface fabric of a tie has depth in Armani.

Imagine a woman at a cocktail party wearing Armani's metallic velvet beaded pants (fall/winter 2000–01)—but they are not beaded, they are composed of shiny black threads woven through the velvet, giving a wet look. The woman explains, leaning against a bookcase, that her garment has no weight: it is *in* the world of gravitas and *not,* at the same time. Over these trousers, she is wearing Armani's new one-button paillette jacket. "Such an incredible lightness of being," she murmurs. In every item with Armani's name on it, down to the lowliest tie, there is something to be found *inside—dedans*, *dentro*, as he might say.

The Depth of Surface

None of this is a matter of an Armani unconscious or subconscious. *Made in Milan* opens with a panorama of the cathedrals, the spires, the statues on spires, the putti, the palazzi, the colonnades of Milan as Armani, in voiceover, speaks of first coming to the metropolis "from a provincial city at a very vulnerable time in my youth to make my first real friends and meet my first responsibilities." He was alienated from the city: "Milan seemed very cold and big at first, then suddenly it was welcoming, rich in unexpected beauty to discover day by day. The old buildings here are not imposing and opulent like the ones in Rome. But they have a discreet elegance that almost whispers. Milan is not a city on the grand scale like Paris or London. But if you go beyond the narrow streets and past the house façades"—we are walking along with the camera of Nestor Almendros through an arch under a lantern into a courtyard—"you discover fantastic interiors. The small intricate gardens and intimate, refined settings are reminiscent of something exclusive and private, something from the past." You discover—and what you discover are marvelous interiors—not unlike when you watch models wearing Armani on a runway.

Encountering this exhibition—walking the Guggenheim's ramps like a model before a static audience of clothes—the viewer will perhaps viscerally grasp Armani's quarter-century-old intuition: that our fast-flowing times, where everything has to communicate instantly and move on, have banished depth. Depth is a category that pretends to penetrate surface and find gravity, passions, history, conflict, soul, origins, hidden motives, density, evil, sin, and abysmal precipices. Surface is about choice, speed, the visual, well-being, and fun; it is irreversible, aleatory, euphoric, flighty, cool, rootless, comfortable, detachable, changeable, and ahistorical.

First impressions are decisive. You're hired, you buy or throw away, you love or reject on the power of first impressions. Today we respect only the instantaneous and can therefore root in nothing. Entertainment is the name of the game, whether you are acting onstage or on the runway of the world's streets, or running for office. Or commuting, looking out the train window while listening to your Walkman or talking on your cell phone as you contemplate your laptop with your drink on the latest issue of *Vogue*. You could even be in a jet watching a film in which Richard Gere, Kevin Costner, or Robert De Niro is wearing Armani. Armani has broken down the separation between fantasy and reality, between celebrity and your everyday life. If you can't buy black label Armani, you can go to an A/X, or buy a rip-off, or even interpret his own dressing philosophy. Armani has become trickle-down fashion. He is everywhere.

"Armani effervesces in this country in 1982 with the April *Time* magazine cover story," Bruce Wolmer, editor-in-chief of *Art & Auction* magazine, recalled in a seminar this past spring. "For my generation, for the generation of '68, all of a sudden Armani comes along and marks a break. He marks a change of sensibility, challenges a kind of antifashion sensibility which had been prevalent throughout the seventies. All of a sudden Armani comes along and makes it possible for people interested in style in our generation to accept Armani in the way that you couldn't accept anyone else. I still have in the back of my closet my first blue-striped Armani suit. Wearing it was a radical departure from everything that was—even though the phrase didn't exist then—politically correct and sartorially correct. Armani marked the return of style and the return of luxury. For a lot of people of my generation Armani was the first designer we felt comfortable with." Armani inaugurated a new view of fashion, a new set of signs for both men and women. You *are* your appearance; reality is a matter of perception, not authority.

Surface appears individuated by apparel. The nude is not important, the clothes are. Before the 1970s, everybody wanted to undress reality, find the naked truth, the body behind the trimmings,

Giorgio Armani, collection show, Fall/Winter 1999–2000

what lay behind Salomé's seventh veil. Apparently very little. "The human body is not very attractive compared, for example, to a cheetah—that's why we have fashion," the late Alexander Liberman, Condé Nast editorial director, once said.[4] Our forefathers and mothers concentrated on undressing the other. We value dressing up.

When Lord Caversham in Oscar Wilde's *An Ideal Husband* (1895) accuses his son, Lord Goring, of being superficial and leading an idle life, Mabel Chiltern responds: "How can you say such a thing? Why, he rides in the Row at ten o'clock in the morning, goes to the Opera three times a week, changes his clothes at least five times a day, and dines out every night of the season. You don't call that leading an idle life, do you?" Wilde, the forerunner of the philosophy of surface, makes Lord Goring the very opposite, let us say, of the monk who never changes clothes, never eats out, and meditates in a cell. The power of surface—which Wilde understood—is not removed from what Armani supplies for dressing our age.

In the Beginning . . .

There is a poignant moment in *Made in Milan* when Armani is talking of his mother and father. (I suppose everything you say about your father and mother is poignant.) "I have many memories of my past, and my childhood. They have definitely influenced my work. I remember my mother's and father's elegance." On-screen is an album containing photos of his father at home, in tie and thinly rimmed eyeglasses, reading the paper; of his mother walking in the countryside in an ankle-length black dress, little Giorgio in white shorts right behind her. "A simple elegance. It was mostly an inner elegance since we didn't have a lot of money. I remember that my mother made my clothes. She made clothes for all her children. And we were the envy of all our classmates. We looked rich even though we were poor." And Armani on-screen slowly turns his head down, perhaps in shame, for even the remembrance of poverty brings shame.

But the very next words are: "I've always thought a lot about the images and aura of the past, my own past, my family's past, and the past of the cinema, which was the only entertainment we had when we were kids." The images he remembers from his childhood fuse with the images he saw on-screen. As a child, Armani discovered the power of the image, appearance, and the preeminence of perception. Images—electronically reproduced and easy to understand—pervade what we know and how we project ourselves upon the world. What we see is the basic source of our sense of reality. "All men [and women] by nature desire to know," wrote Aristotle, "and an indication of this is the delight we take in our senses; for even apart from their usefulness they are loved for themselves; and above all others the sense of sight." Sight sustains and perpetuates the image, which, like surface, has been traditionally considered superficial—a product of the intellectual and moral elites, who for centuries maintained power by controlling content and moral meaning. "Only a fool," as Wilde wrote, "wouldn't judge by appearances." The power of image is another of Armani's intuitions of the world we live in.

"I don't own what you might call a designer wardrobe." Maybe these are the most astonishing words Armani has ever uttered. He does not costume himself. "I have blue jackets, blue pullovers, and gray pants. In my mind it's like a uniform." He uniforms himself. "You have to know yourself and your own body and your personality to know how to dress. Maybe it's because I dress for work that I can't dress any other way." In short, he doesn't need to be the imaged, the fashionable man, he doesn't need to costume himself. But we do. To what end?

Armani's arrogant humbleness exists to highlight the rich mystery of his clothes. His simplicity reveals the many faces of his fashion signs. He is the unmovable mover, the demiurge of his creations. Armani is one and his manifestations are many.

Here he is orienting Laura and Susan, two models, as he prepares for a runway show. "Try walking, Laura, like a woman who moves down the street feeling the sensation of being in the center of the world." That, Marx wrote, is what it would be like *not* to be alienated. "Go . . . yeah, yeah, without rigidity . . . slowly Laura, even when you turn, do it gently. Now stop, as if you were window shopping, not as if you were on a runway. Okay, now with Susan. Watch Laura, do the same thing. *Molto gracilità*, relax Susan, don't be so rigid, put your hands in your pockets if you want, *si*." He shows the way of the modern flâneur. "Be a bit ironic. Smile. Smile at yourself, at your youth, at your clothes. *Vai*—go." And Susan ambles, all passion at rest.

This is what you need Armani's clothes for: to feel as though you were inhabiting, for a time, the calm center of things. What did Armani accomplish with his work in the last thirty years of the twentieth century? He made a soft army, a corps that, so far from being destructive, *creates* personality, protects you against failure, against maybe the biggest failure the late twentieth and early twenty-first centuries know—*disappearing into the background*. You can't disappear in his clothes, because they are subtle costume. Communication, as he says. Signs. Your moment in the light and in the shadow under the sheltering sky.

Notes

1.   This and all unidentified quotes that follow are from *Made in Milan*.

2.   Quoted in Marshall Blonsky, *American Mythologies* (New York: Oxford University Press, 1992), p. 389.

3.   Quoted in Anna Piaggi, "Armanology," in *Armani* (Milan: Franco Maria Ricci, 1982), p. 212.

4.   Quoted in Blonsky, p. 17.

ARMANI AND HOLLYWOOD

by Hamish Bowles

"Life is the movie, and my clothes are the costumes," says Giorgio Armani in *Made in Milan*. But if Armani's great contribution to fashion history has been to liberate classic clothing components, to relax and soften and to bring a sense of real-life sportswear comfort to a couture approach, still the roots of his aesthetic seem to lie in the flickering magic of the silver screen. Even Armani's runway presentations are evocative of a visit to an old-fashioned cinema palace. The audience assembles in the subterranean theater of the designer's Milanese palazzo, ranked on tiers of black seats. The arrival of the big screen luminaries—of Sophia Loren, or Claudia Cardinale, or Gwyneth Paltrow— signals that the screening is about to begin. Abruptly, the house lights go down, plunging the audience into darkness for a moment. And then, misty screens begin to light up. Only here, the screens are a trail of translucent light boxes that form the runway's path.

Armani's use of color in his fashion shows is equally cinematic. Against his favored neutral palette, his sparing bursts of vivid color hit with the impact of Dorothy's descent from Kansas (where everything is reassuringly black-and-white) into the Technicolor playground of Oz. Or of MGM designer Adrian's fashion-show sequence in George Cukor's 1939 film *The Women*, another firework display igniting the monochrome antics of its larger-than-life stars.

And the clothes, too, hint at the glory years of the Hollywood studios. Armani's signature androgynous suits, with their insouciant built-in slouch, evoke the mannish off-screen wardrobes of sirens like Marlene Dietrich and Greta Garbo. Even when he indulges his most elaborate evening fantasies, there is a subtlety of coloration and decoration that suggests a George Hurrell portrait or a glamour goddess lighting up the darkness of the movie house. All is shimmering suggestion, like the opalescent lighting that Josef von Sternberg contrived to deify Dietrich's screen appearances.

Armani's intimate involvement with present-day Hollywood seems therefore an inevitable one. This relationship had its genesis in the wardrobe he created for Richard Gere in Paul Schrader's 1980 film *American Gigolo*. Here, the character's clothing—an essential tool of his trade, and a token of his success—had a screen presence almost as potent as the actor in his breakthrough role. His costuming for the movie established Armani as the industry's menswear designer of choice. In the decade to follow, many of Hollywood's preeminent actresses made their own playful sartorial decisions when establishing what to wear to high-profile industry events like the Academy Awards ceremonies. They were rewarded with eviscerating criticism from the fashion and entertainment press. Armani stepped in to woo them with his uncontroversial elegance and low-key glamour that hinted at the poised style of those luminous stars who had once been dressed and groomed by their studios for such public appearances. By 1992, columnist Liz Smith was asking, "Could the Oscars exist without Giorgio Armani?"[1] and *Women's Wear Daily* could write of "the Armanization of the Academy Awards," suggesting that, "no one can criticize you if you're wearing an understatedly elegant Giorgio Armani . . . making all that glitter and bunting seem extraneous."[2]

Armani has developed symbiotic relationships with today's stars. "My rapport with Hollywood is not a one-night-a-year proposition," he told the *Los Angeles Times* in 1995.[3] Indeed, it suggests rather his lifelong fascination with the movies, and has been an essential element in Hollywood's current romancing of the fashion world.

Notes

1. Quoted in "Designers: Endangered or Extinct?," *Women's Wear Daily*, April 7, 1992, p. 1.

2. Merle Ginsberg, "The Scoop on the Oscars," *Women's Wear Daily*, March 17, 1992, p. 4.

3. Judith Michaelson, "And the Designer Is . . .," *Los Angeles Times*, March 26, 1995, p. 28.

Winona Ryder

The Armani tuxedo has long been the epitome of taste, class, and success. After winning an Oscar while wearing mine, I can now say Armani also signifies luck and good fortune. I am totally devoted.

Matt Damon, *Actor*

In my opinion fashion is deeper than the way it appears in the fashion défilés [runway shows]. I think fashion is the summary of a few basic elements, which, following the natural laws of good taste, never change. The fashion world, in recent years, has looked like a mad carousel of shocking images that mainly propose how to strip rather than dress the human body.

Entering into Armani's world is like landing into the peaceful eye of a typhoon, into the perfect calm, into a style that cannot be shaken by the winds of sensationalism.

His line has a soul that can't be defined: you say "how beautiful," and that's all. An Armani dress doesn't give you doubt or uncertainty. It's an Armani and that's all you need.

Sophia Loren, *Actress*

When you wear an Armani gown, you can be sure of two things: all-out glamour and comfort. When you think of being in Armani, you always know you will not be pinched, corseted, or bound. One only feels beautiful and comfortable, as if in a pair of favorite jeans.

I remember buying my first Armani suit, establishing a long relationship with Mr. Armani. Such beautiful tailoring, such fine fabrics. But Mr. Armani's gowns have always held a soft spot in my heart. I have been lucky enough to wear quite a few, including a blue beaded one I wore to the Academy Awards. I hardly felt "dressed up" because I was so at ease in the gown, but it gave me an undeniable feeling of glamour. The fabric and beading reminded me of a star-filled night under the skies of one of our California deserts, a magical-looking piece. I could still wear it today and feel very modern. That is the essence of Armani.

Rita Wilson, *Actress*

I suppose I wear Armani because it suits who I am, someone who cares for comfort, fit, and subtle fabrics. I don't need to be the flashiest person in the room, just the most confident.

Jodie Foster, *Actress, Director, Producer*

42

My style is Armani. No one (nowhere at all in the world) ever asks me, "What are you wearing?" It is always and only Armani. I like the simplicity, the refinement, I recognize myself totally in his modern essential and minimal line, I like the lightness of his fabrics, which follow the body's line without ever encumbering it. My movements are free, and in harmony with my life as an active, free, and contemporary woman.

Claudia Cardinale, *Actress*

Top row: Julia Roberts, Liam Neeson, Jessica Tandy, Lucrezia Lante della Rovere, Robin Williams; second row; Winona Ryder, Margherita Buy, Freddie Prinze, Jr., Jenna Elfman, Clint Eastwood; third row: David E. Kelly, Martin Scorsese, Arnold Schwarzenegger and Maria Schriver, Mel Gibson, Debbie Mazar; fourth row: Warren Beatty, Faye Dunaway, Eleonora Giorgi, Luca Barbareschi, Phil Collins; bottom row: Lilly Gruber, Tim Robbins, Claire Forlani, Tina Turner, Gary Sinise.

When I first met Giorgio Armani in 1979, he made me the best-dressed American there was. Today, he's made everybody around the world the best-dressed person they can be, and we all love him for it. Thank you, Giorgio.

John Travolta, *Actor*

Giorgio Armani personifies respect. He clearly respects all aspects of his work—the design, the fabric, the color, the craftsmanship, and the person. I am always very comfortable in Armani and that translates into confidence and ease. Even his high heels are comfortable. I suppose that makes him not only a wonderful designer, but a magician as well.

Julia Roberts, *Actress*

What makes Armani the premiere designer of our time is his extraordinary ability to combine style, texture, cut, and color. His classic grace defines elegance and, like all great artists, he makes simplicity look easy.

Annette Bening, *Actress*

Top row: Billy Crystal, Isabella Rossellini, Angelina Jolie, Lawrence Fishburne, Lena Olin; second row: Penny Marshall, Mark Wahlberg, Mira Sorvino, Fanny Ardant, Thora Birch; third row: Jewel, Djimon Hounsou, Charlize Theron, Christie Brinkley and Peter Cook, Jeff Goldblum; fourth row: Katie Holmes, Diego Abatantuomo, Roberto Benigni, Monica Bellucci, Lisa Kudrow; bottom row: Diane Keaton, James van der Beck, Lisa Rinna, Gabriel Byrne, Gioia Marchi.

I was very happy that Giorgio Armani was able to provide the wardrobe for my world tour. His clothes feel elegant and sleek—they are perfect. I have so much respect for him—here is a man who, after twenty-five years in business, is still fueled with creative energy, and he continues to be at the top of his field!

Ricky Martin, *Singer*

Above and beyond what he has contributed to the world of fashion, I view Giorgio as a designer in the broader sense of the word, as an architect for the human form. As such I consider him a genius, purely and simply one of the great artists of the twentieth century.

Eric Clapton, *Singer*

My relationship with Mr. Armani started nearly twenty years ago when he lent me a stunning ensemble, which I wore to the Kennedy Center Honors: a black, long-sleeved, beaded, fabulous-shouldered tunic over black satin pajamas. I felt then, for the first time, something that I still feel today when I put on Armani: it is possible to be dressed up and remain yourself. When wearing Armani at any of the fancy events that I've had to attend in the past years, I have never felt like a mannequin—stiff, self-conscious, and alien to myself.

Glenn Close, *Actress*

Giorgio Armani changed the face of women's fashion beginning in the '70s. Thousands of confused women placed their confidence in him and were overnight transformed to "best dressed."

Anjelica Huston, *Actress*

I looked up the word "class" in the dictionary: "held to be in the highest rank of excellence and having lasting significance." For a brief second I thought I saw the name "Armani" there, but maybe that was just in my mind.

George Clooney, *Actor*

Top row: Kevin Costner, Keri Russell, Tom Hanks, Ashley Judd, Kevin Spacey; second row: Lauryn Hill, Ben Affleck, Emmanuelle Béart, Sean Connery, Gwyneth Paltrow; third row: Alicia Silverstone, Jean-Michel Basquiat, Sharon Stone, Caroline Kennedy Schlossberg and John F. Kennedy, Jr., Russell Crowe; fourth row: Natalie Portman, Denzel Washington, Diane Lane, Leonardo DiCaprio, Julia Louis Dreyfus; bottom row: Salma Hayek, Ed Harris, Candice Bergen, Emma Thompson, Pete Sampras.

To tell you the truth, and Giorgio knows this, I really don't know anything about fashion, and I knew even less before we made American Gigolo. But it was daring, forward-thinking design that influenced a generation of other designers, wearers, and wannabe movie dreamers. The best fabrics in the world. And he is a gentleman.

Richard Gere, *Actor*

Why do I wear Armani? Because there are things of his that are fifteen years old that I still wear. Because he takes seven colors to make just one. Because he has classic, good sense, and classic cuts, like Savile Row, that you can always wear.

I first discovered Armani while filming American Gigolo *and I have been wearing his clothes ever since. He has also become a personal friend. I did a runway show for Giorgio too, one of his earliest.*

Armani makes things easy. There's always something from Armani I'll look good in on or off the set. His clothes are sexy, good-looking, classic, and comfortable.

Lauren Hutton, *Actress, Model*

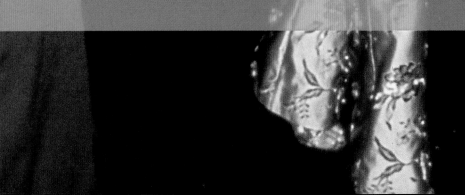

His designs come to life as soon as I put them on. I think Giorgio's philosophy is that a woman should be complemented by her clothing, not overpowered by it. That really works for me.

Michelle Pfeiffer, *Actress*

Wearing Armani as John Shaft gave me a remarkable feeling of confidence and cool. The clothing, especially the leather jackets, helped me as an actor to embody a new kind of heroism, sexiness, and suave in playing a '70s film icon and moving him into the new millennium. Armani is a true innovator and genius of design because he allows a man so much self-expression and individuality in dressing—yet always at a level of world-class taste.

Samuel L. Jackson, *Actor*

1

1. Woman's evening dress, spring/summer 1997. **2. Woman's evening pants ensemble,** fall/winter 1995–96. **3. Woman's evening pants ensemble,** fall/winter 1995–96. **4. Woman's evening pants ensemble,** fall/winter 1995–96.   Armani has often endowed apparel with a metaphor for celebrity in the form of a peekaboo game of personal revelation and concealment. The undeniable self-exhibition and exposure of many of his designs are

2   4

3

invariably linked with a skillful obfuscation of the most private and personal. As with his own public persona, there is no apparent guardedness, but the carefully placed beading and reflective zones of sequining in the eveningwear illustrated here assure that any nudity or disclosure is securely orchestrated.

5

6

7

5. Woman's evening shorts ensemble, spring/summer 1995. **6. Woman's evening bustier and skirt ensemble,** spring/summer 1988. **7. Woman's evening bodice and skirt ensemble,** spring/summer 1988. **8. Woman's evening jacket and skirt,** spring/summer 1988. History is not entirely shed by Armani, but appears in his work only in conjunction with contemporary materials and forms. Here, romanticism is marked with a Milanese edge as

8

he inverts elements of historical dress. His subjection of the crinoline and the corset to inside-out reversals results in a modernist infrastructural expression. Like the moulted skin of a python, the stiffened casings of nineteenth-century dress form vestigial enclosures to more supple and silken gowns beneath.

64

9

10

9. Woman's evening gown, spring/summer 1997. **10. Woman's evening pants ensemble,** spring/summer 1997. **11. Woman's strapless evening gown,** spring/summer 1999. **12. Woman's strapless evening gown,** spring/summer 1999. **13. Woman's strapless evening gown,** spring/summer 1999. The Armani aesthetic is invariably discreet, with elaborate beaded embroideries often muted in their expression if not their application. Rich combinations of seed and bugle beads, varied sequins, faceted stones, and pearls are frequently so densely applied as to form a high relief. But in

11

12

13

a kind of perverse reversal, this baroque abandon is either softened by a tone-on-tone palette that obscures the legibility of the richly encrusted forms, or veiled by complementary-colored silk mesh. Armani's glitter is like the nacreous surfaces of a grotto, or old mirrors in a candlelit hall, in which flash and dazzle are reduced to an adumbral glow.

GENDER

LIBERTY, EQUALITY, SOBRIETY

Suzy Menkes

The Duke of Windsor, that icon of masculine elegance, had a habit of casting off—literally and metaphorically—the "buttoned-up" rigidity of royal life. "It was my impulse, whenever I found myself alone, to remove my coat, rip off my tie, loosen my collar and roll up my sleeves," he wrote in *A Family Album*, his 1960 memoir. "The Duchess likes to describe this process as my 'striptease' act."[1]

Cut to Martin Scorsese's 1990 documentary *Made in Milan*, where Giorgio Armani is conducting his own fashion "striptease"—ripping out from a jacket the lining, the interlining, the padding, the facings, and anything that makes male tailoring formal and constricting.

The Duke might have made fashion history by being the first man to insist on hand-tailored sports jackets as soft and supple as a shirt. But Armani democratized the unstructured jacket, produced it industrially, and suited it to everyman—and everywoman.

By bringing comfort and freedom of movement to tailored uniformity, Armani marked twentieth-century fashion and underscored its linear, masculine quality. This androgynous style reached its apogee in the 1980s as the aerodynamic, modern, unisex pantsuit.

"I think I succeeded," Armani has said, "In the difficult task of transferring the concept of sobriety from the men's wardrobe to women's way of dressing."[2] The result is so natural, easy, and low-key that it is hard to credit Armani with a fashion revolution. The image is set in the stone-beige colors he favors. Running-water colors. Or, as he describes them, "colors of dawn and dusk."[3] The silhouette is fluid, shadowing the body—an easy jacket, square-shouldered in the power-dressing era but now rounded and softened. The slouchy pants flow, rather than grip, and take movement in a long stride.

Armani entered fashion via menswear, working for eight years from 1964 for Nino Cerruti, launching into womenswear with his own label only in 1976. That menswear thread has never been broken. Jackets and pants remain the linchpin of his look, even if dresses have long since been absorbed into his fashion vocabulary and active sportswear is a forceful part of the Armani empire.

The Duke of Windsor, 1949

Woman in Edwardian jacket and skirt, ca. 1898

"To me, the jacket is the perfect piece of clothing, as important an invention as jeans and the T-shirt," he told the London *Times* in 1991.[4] That was more than a decade after Richard Gere in Paul Schrader's 1980 film *American Gigolo* brought Armani to public attention and uttered the immortal words: "Who's acting in this scene, me or the jacket?"

An Armani outfit is designed to walk off the runway into the street. "When I started, my idea was always to make men and women seem contemporary but never ridiculous or obsessed by fashion," Armani told this writer in 1999.[5]

His principles are akin to the minimalist ideas of the Bauhaus: design free from meaningless ornament "so that the eye may delight in perfection of proportion and of surface," as British *Vogue* described the new style in 1927.[6] It is summed up in the mantras of the architect Mies van der Rohe, "God is in the details" and "less is more."

To understand Armani's achievement, you have to see him as a link in a chain that goes back to the introduction of "tailor-made" outfits in the Belle Epoque and continues through Gabrielle "Coco" Chanel in the 1920s–30s and Yves Saint Laurent in the 1960s–70s.

The concept of tailoring—a male preserve since Neoclassical times—edged its way into women's fashion via Edwardian jackets and skirts and riding outfits. But it was the conjunction of the streamlining of industrial design, Bauhaus modernism, the linear geometry of abstract art, and the emancipation of women in the 1920s that moved female fashion away from the decorative and status-conscious toward the functional.

Chanel was the progenitor, the designer who appropriated elements of male clothing to give women a realistic, self-possessed wardrobe that offered ease, comfort, functionality, and freedom. Other designers like Jean Patou contributed to the new energetic sportiness that emerged in the fluid pants, sweaters, and cardigan jackets of the 1930s, but Chanel is identified with the truly radical departure in women's dress.

Chanel, "Ford Dress," 1926   Christian Dior, New Look, 1947

Significantly, Armani himself is drawn to the period when newly cropped hair and flat figures announced the "garçon" or boyish look for women. "The thirties and early forties have always influenced me," he has said. "There was an elegant simplicity—a clean white blouse, a simple shirt, a duster, a slim lamé evening dress. By the fifties, fashion was getting too extreme."[7]

It is no wonder that Armani rejected the immediate postwar look. The recidivist fashion era ushered in by Christian Dior's 1947 New Look wrenched women away from the new classicism and burgeoning equality with men and propelled them backwards to a feminine, romantic, nostalgic past.

It was left to the young Saint Laurent to take up the feminist cause. The wardrobe he created in the 1960s allowed a well-dressed woman, as he himself put it, to need nothing more than a blazer, a raincoat, a roll-neck sweater, and a pair of flannel pants. The tuxedo that he reinvented for women was the ultimate expression of twentieth-century fashion: pants for equality and jackets for women standing shoulder pad to broad shoulders in a man's world.

But if Saint Laurent was the architect of a new mode of dressing for an entire generation of women, his style remained traditional in two areas. Although he was in the vanguard of the Parisian ready-to-wear movement, the designer was, and is, quintessentially a couturier, his artistic heart beating for custom-made clothes at the elevated level of haute couture. His fashion revolution also stopped short of challenging the male-female status quo. For all the tailored masculinity of Saint Laurent's daywear and tuxedos, at night women were offered the sinuous romance of draped and embellished dresses.

As the feminist movement gathered momentum and questions of gender bubbled up, it was not only women, but men too who were changing. Although the initial thrust of androgyny was for women to take on men's clothing, its ultimate effect was the softening of the male carapace of tailoring that had its distant origins in the medieval suit of armor. But if the coalescence of male and female attire was the essence of twentieth-century style, fashion also witnessed the struggle to free

Fall/Winter 1989–90

the body from constricting clothes. Women discarded the corsets that had molded the female silhouette for four hundred years. Flexibility and freedom applied also to men's clothes. The logic of the pre-Armani era was that the suit maketh the man. A bespoke tailor would rebuild a pigeon chest, stiffen the spine, whittle the waist, and generally improve on the imperfect. "There was a stereotype male with rigid silhouette and stiff shoulders," said Armani. "Since then men have accepted a lot. It is not a question of being formal or casual. But of a different mentality. An elegant man or woman of today is not the same as twenty or thirty years ago. When you think now of a man dressed like an old-style English country gentleman, it looks like play acting."[8]

You could argue that the old-fashioned tyranny of tightly laced underwear and hefty, sculpted suits has simply been replaced by the modern tyranny of the gym. But bodily physique is now the undisputed foundation of style—and has been since sports clothes became general leisure wear from the early 1980s. When Armani injected the ease of sportswear into tailored suits, it was not just a reflection of how a new generation felt about clothes, but also a reaction to their gym-honed bodies.

That is why the visualization of male pride in the 1980s became a body rippling through its light covering, as seen on Don Johnson wearing an Armani jacket over a taut T-shirt in *Miami Vice*, the cast of Brian De Palma's 1987 film *The Untouchables* in sleek Armani suits, or the designer himself in his signature T-shirt and jeans.

The triumph of the soft pantsuit for women coincided with the supermodel era, when the body beautiful became at least as important as the clothes. Although Armani himself eschewed the cult of celebrity models, his clothes were designed to cover a female silhouette sculpted by working out. The design innovation for both sexes was to produce on an industrial scale a soft covering for the hard body.

Perhaps only in Milan, the heartland of modern industrial design, could a tailor have envisaged making factory-line slipcovers for the human frame—reminiscent of the beige calico

Spring/Summer 1993   Spring/Summer 1999

shrouds that are placed over basic chairs at every Armani event. The secret of the new suits lay in the fabric research that Italian manufacturers had undertaken in the postwar period. With Como silk undercut by production in Asia, Italian mills focused on synthetic fabrics and their blends with natural fibers to answer the high-performance, low-maintenance needs of modern society.

Armani was in the vanguard of this fabric innovation and to this day he says that as much time is spent on developing intriguing textures and surface finishes as on the design prototypes that he personally fits, often sitting on the floor like a traditional tailor. The jackets thus retain the elegance of the uncomplicated, while slithery "wet" or rougher "dry" finishes give depth to their noncolors.

Armani remains a rational designer, a creator of clothes for the workplace and the street. His forays into more exotic designs for evening are mostly vacational inspirations—sarongs from tropical islands, colors drawn from lagoons and coral reefs, sequined sheaths like mermaid scales—all symbols of escape from everyday reality.

Is the tasteful mimimalism for which Armani has become so well known still enough for the new millennium? Just as postmodern artists have challenged abstraction and the total elimination of the superfluous and the decorative, so postfeminist women are beginning to hanker after a wardrobe that is based less on menswear and that allows for some essentially female or "girly" attributes. Young men also crave the bravura sexiness of the peacock male, exemplified by biker hardness or rocker flamboyance.

Armani has responded with color (for both sexes) and with pattern (mostly geometric and abstract, although sometimes orientalist). He has also recut male and female silhouettes closer to their natural forms. And he has lightened up fabrics so that his famous women's pants or cardigan jackets might be reduced to just a gauzy wisp.

But it is hard to believe that Armani is ever going to break the visceral link between rational design and the ascetic luxury of fine fabrics cut with quiet elegance. To do so would be to negate his essential rigor and purity. Powerful designers, like other artists, draw from an interior wellspring of creativity. However fashion flows, they follow their own currents. And Armani's instinct is for liberty, equality, sobriety.

Notes

1. Duke of Windsor, *A Family Album* (London: Cassell, 1960), p. 105.

2. Quoted in Olivia Lowe, "Giorgio Armani," *Yes Please*, December 7, 1990, p. 7.

3. Conversation with the author, Milan, June 30, 1999.

4. Lisa Armstrong, "Why Armani Can't Keep a Straight Face," *The Times* (London), July 4, 1991, p. 15.

5. Quoted in Suzy Menkes, "Giorgio Armani: Celebrating 25 Years in 2000," *International Herald Tribune*, July 2, 1999, p. 14.

6. See *The Twenties in Vogue* (London: Octopus Books, 1983), p. 98.

7. Quoted in "Giorgio's New Glamour," *W*, February 18, 1991, p. 116.

8. Quoted in Menkes, p. 14.

Franca Sozzani

In 1976 I had yet to be led astray by the world of fashion. I had very clear ideas: I liked pants, blouses, and jackets. Yves Saint Laurent and Walter Albini were my points of reference. But now there was a new name on the scene: Giorgio Armani. Although he had already made numerous appearances in *L'Uomo Vogue* (not my choice of reading matter at the time), he was virtually unknown to the female public. Almost twenty-five years have passed since then, and who can claim that they have never heard of Armani now? How can he still be so successful after so long? What has happened over the years? How has he managed to capture the desires of women of all ages from countries that are so different in terms of culture and custom?

As I say to editors and photographers when I need to explain something: "Find a concept and half the work is done. Be true to your concept and you will create a style." But it's not that easy to achieve! Armani has always based what he does on a very precise idea. And there is more: he has arrived where he is today by always believing in a specific concept. All the awards he has received over the past few years have effectively been given to him for the consistency of his work. That has always been his aim, but it is also just the way he is. He is direct, happy to please, but not to indulge. He has never compromised, either in terms of style or image or in his dealings with journalists. That has been the key to his success. "It is my opinion and I share it," wrote M. B. Monnier in 1840, almost a century before Armani was born.

Armani started just one revolution, twenty-five years ago, by placing a man's jacket on a woman and combining it not just with a shirt and waistcoat, but with corsets or pieces of precious fabric covering bare breasts—a bit like what is seen in fashion shows at the start of this new century. At that time, the kindest chose to believe that he had done so as a last-minute replacement for a jacket that had turned out wrong! Nowadays, anything goes under the banner of creativity, and daring in order to astonish is the starting point for anyone wanting to be a designer. Yet since this initial upheaval, Armani's long story revolves around just a handful of common denominators that

Jacket and shorts ensemble from the
Spring/Summer 1986 collection,
sketched by Giorgio Armani, 2000

Evening gown from the Fall/Winter
1986–87 collection, sketched by
Giorgio Armani, 2000

have stood the test of time, changing incrementally as tastes have evolved. Armani's decision *not* to astonish is a courageous choice, for journalists love to be astonished.

For Armani, the development of fashion is linked to the search for new materials and details, which he applies to what have become his calling cards: jackets and overcoats adapted from menswear, embroidered cardigans, see-through skirts over pants, tops, shawls, evening dresses that borrow the form of a man's vest, lacy black and white petticoats and corsets. An entire essay could be devoted to the thousand ways he has interpreted the basic features of the tuxedo. Colors and noncolors—it would be possible to discuss his muted palette until the end of time. Armani is precise even here. There is no question that he comes very close to the opinion voiced by the highly elegant Elsie de Wolf: "It's beige, my color."

Speaking about someone's work is almost as sensitive as discussing the private life of a famous person. The work is not just what you see, it is what lies behind it as well: the dreams, the choices, the creativity, the difficulties in turning an idea into reality. Taking all of this and producing a garment—and then multiplying this process by two hundred, twice a year for twenty-five years, for both women's and men's collections—is a slightly crazy endeavor. Continuity is a great deal harder than the fleeting, bright spark; it is also exhausting, unless the concept and passion are stronger.

What are the fundamental aspects of Armani's work? What garments and colors will be instantly recognized as Armani, no matter where they are seen? In my opinion, his work can be divided into four basic categories that encapsulate the designer's vision: androgynous, minimal, ethnic, and eveningwear derived from the form of the tuxedo.

Androgynous

"Masculine" is the most frequently used adjective in describing Armani's pantsuits for women, and reference has often mistakenly been made to women dressed like men when talking about Armani's style. I do not think there is any interpretation that could be further from his original idea. The man's garment is only the starting point, not the undisputed protagonist, of Armani's female wardrobe. The idea of a man's suit on a woman—a jacket with tie and waistcoat, pants with pleats—comes from Saint Laurent, who combined these elements of male dress with a female touch in the form of high heels (*very* high heels, even platforms). Armani does the exact opposite. With him, the man's garment is taken to pieces and refashioned on a woman: the lapels are widened, the shoulders are rounded, and the bosom is emphasized—or sometimes even exposed when the front of the jacket plunges low enough. Low sandals and embroidered slippers accompany these outfits, almost as if to emphasize that all this male inspiration must be transformed into something more soft and gentle. No heels, men's shoes, or other ambiguous "fetishes": the Armani woman is feminine, gentle in her movements, the exact opposite of lesbo-chic or business style.

Each season the jacket is reexamined and renewed by Armani: it does up at the side, ties at the bosom, crosses at the back, fastens at the neck, or the lapels rise to form the neckline of an Indian guru's jacket. Sometimes it does not do up at all and has only a scarf underneath. It might get shorter, reaching only the waist, or increase to three-quarter length like a ladies' riding habit from the beginning of the nineteenth century. It is redesigned, reproportioned, and given a thousand variations: drooping collars, even with flounces; soft martingales at the hips; tapered sleeves brushing the arms. It might be tight-fitted to emphasize the shape of a woman's body and buttoned with the classic four buttons, or tied in blouse cuffs and soft ruches to lend—even to the starkest of garments—a feminine touch.

Armani has also stolen the cardigan from the men's wardrobe. Originally it was small, tight-fitting, and tapered, hugging the hips, with small, low pockets that allowed women nonchalantly to place their hands in their pockets. A woman should be free, knowing, and relaxed, Armani seemed to be saying, as if clothes are just a game for her, a way of being able to move as naturally

Evening gown from the Fall/Winter
1986–87 collection, sketched by
Giorgio Armani, 2000

as possible. In the 1980s the cardigan became wider, falling over a body that would have been naked except for the long, light, embroidered skirts barely covering the legs. Floral and geometric patterns were introduced to the staid English gentleman's cardigan.

Another item beloved by Armani is the waistcoat. In its transposition to womenswear, it is never given a masculine shape; the origin is clear, but never appears literally. It becomes a micro top that changes continuously, as if by magic: made smaller or larger, depending on whether it is worn beneath a jacket or alone with a skirt or pants; pleated, folded, decorated, or layered. It crosses over at the front or buttons at the bottom, or even right up to the neck, almost like a clergyman's garb. And above all, it comes in all lengths, even extending toward the floor in the form of a long dress.

Armani is not the romantic, affected man of the twin set. He is a man of contradictions, feminizing what is masculine. The bomber jacket, which became a status symbol for men of all ages in the 1950s and later a standard feature of Armani's men's collections, has been transformed by the designer into a small "jewel" to be worn in the evening, made of various precious fabrics, often embroidered or beaded, including velvet, satin, silk crepe, and Scottish taffetas.

Minimal

"Minimal," a term adopted from the art world, has become synonymous with "pure," "clean-cut," and "linear." In fashion, it is a deliberate challenge to the arrogance of luxury, gold, and embellishment. Minimalism was brought to life in the 1980s by the Japanese designers Rei Kawakubo and Yohji Yamamoto, who went against the trends of the time in doing so. It reappeared in the early 1990s, when there was a general rebellion against the excesses of the previous decade, and now it is once again in decline. And yet it is the only way to dress for anyone seeking true *style* in fashion and not merely the latest trend.

Armani is minimal, naturally. Little has changed for him, from 1975 to today. He believes that cuts must be simple, clean, and as straight as possible—which is why he has always chosen masculine shapes, because they do not lend themselves to an overemphasis of decoration. Favoring linearity does not necessarily mean sacrificing decoration altogether, or avoiding embroidery and jewelry. Rather, it is about not indulging in artificial, uncomfortable, or impossible shapes, seeking self-gratification in stylistic virtuosity that, more often than not, leads one to ask, "Who on earth is going to wear that and, even if someone did, where would they go dressed that way?"

Years ago, the much-feared fashion and style critic John Fairchild commented of Gloria Guiness (that icon of elegance par excellence), "Miss Guiness was the chicest of all in a black cardigan and black skirt." Guiness herself said, "I don't believe in fashion. I believe in consistency." Seemingly simple garments created using luxurious materials and with meticulous attention to details that are almost invisible to the untrained eye have always been synonymous with luxury and elegance, a maxim confirmed by the words of Diana Vreeland, the legendary editor of American *Vogue*: "I like to be very luxuriously dressed. I like to have on the most luxurious black cashmere sweater, the most luxurious black satin pants."

Various criticisms have been made of the minimal style. It has been accused more than once of being boring, uncreative, unstimulating, too rational, and passionless. Armani has also frequently been accused of coldness, due not only to the linearity of his style, but also to his choice of models: thin, lanky women without the conventional markers of female sensuality, with their hair up in waves, a chignon, or simply fastened back with grips or small caps. Truman Capote referred to this type of aristocratic and distant beautiful woman as a "swan," the description commonly applied to four of the most celebrated icons of style: Guiness, C. Z. Guest, Slim Keith, and Babe Paley, all of whom dressed—or dress—simply to be elegant and never to try to stand out. "Whoever looks only for fame is not bound for glory," claimed the French statesman Félix Faure. It is always a choice: should you

Evening jacket, overskirt and
pants ensemble from the Fall/Winter
1988–89 collection, sketched by Giorgio
Armani, 2000

Evening gown from the Spring/Summer
1990 collection, sketched by Giorgio
Armani, 2000

work toward the moment or toward a long-term place in history? Go for the ridiculous thing that makes
the news, or a style that will become legendary?

Ethnic

Any history of fashion cannot fail to mention how designers have always drawn on the customs of
far-off lands or simply those of their own countries of origin. This is certainly the case with Cristóbal
Balenciaga, who loved his native Spain, and with Saint Laurent, who has looked to Arabic traditions,
particularly those of his adopted country, Morocco. For Armani, the ethnic is more an idea,
a fragrance, a memory, an infatuation. It is like a thread running subtly from one country to another,
uniting all the most important influences from these places of dreams, experiences, and journeys.
It may be a flower or a color, a shape, a hairstyle, a piece of embroidery, a piece of jewelry, a bag,
or just a way of moving. The countries or regions whose cultures he has alluded to range from India to
Japan, China, Indonesia, Polynesia, and Northern Africa. The allusions are vague and undefined,
personal reinterpretations of the original source. Indian gurus' jackets are transformed into
embroidered golden vests worn over flowing pants, or become overcoats cut like frock coats, opening
over wide, ruched skirts. The "guru" collar then moves to China, and the body of the jacket becomes
wider. On to Japan, and the sleeves deepen to form a kimono, with old pottery patterns serving
as decorative motifs printed on silk or taffeta. The sleeves fall off and small collar lapels appear,
taking us to Indonesia, where tiny waistcoats are combined with long mesh wraps specked with
colored stones and glass beads that offer glimpses of tight, ankle-length pants beneath. The wrap
rises and ties above the bosom to become a strapless evening dress in lace or printed velvet,
or shortens to caress the hips and cover a longer, patterned wrap in a play of multiple
transparencies. Now the bosom is wrapped tightly in small strips, evocative of an Indian or Polynesian
bandeau. The shawl found in wardrobes around the world, from Spain to Africa, Russia, and Turkey,

Woman's tuxedo from the Fall/Winter
1992–93 collection, sketched by
Giorgio Armani, 2000

Evening mini dress and shorts
ensemble from the Spring/Summer
1991 collection, sketched by
Giorgio Armani, 2000

even Italy itself, enlivens even the most linear of outfits. It may be square, rectangular, or triangular, large or small, used as a belt, sash, skirt, or an entire outfit, or to perform its usual function of covering the shoulders, head, or body. It may be made of lace, wool, velvet, silk tulle, or damasked fabrics, fringed, decorated, patterned, colored or black, or perhaps even covered with big black-and-white flowers. Throughout Armani's oeuvre, enormous or minute flowers are dyed onto all types of fabric to evoke kimonos or saris, djellabahs or caftans.

For Armani, ethnic style is not so much a way of discovering the folklore of a people, a way of reproducing their costumes and traditions; rather, it is a means to capture the innate elegance that most, if not all, cultures retain when they remain in touch with their own history. He is fascinated by this intrinsic elegance, and it is this that he attempts to appropriate, while leaving behind the obvious. Avoiding folkloristic clichés is as difficult as transforming these visions and interpretations into new forms of clothing.

Eveningwear

Black tie for a gala evening, the tuxedo marks the man's entry into society. It is a symbol of luxury, precision, and class. Very few elements can be used to create it: a double-breasted or single-breasted jacket with a shawl collar; matching pants; a waistcoat; a white shirt with pleated or smooth front, pearl buttons or hidden fastenings, and double cuffs with cufflinks; a black or white bow tie in velvet or any other colored fabric; a sash pleated and fastened at the back; plus an overcoat or three-quarter-length coat, with a white or geometrically patterned silk scarf. Each element has been adapted and reinterpreted by Armani in his eveningwear designs for women, with additional touches of irony.

A black bow tie appears to hang, untied, over a jacket, as at the end of an evening, its edge embroidered in contrast to create the trompe l'oeil effect. Elsewhere, a jacket retains the conventional shawl collar in black satin, but is fabricated in lace and held in by a high sash or embroidered like something out of the Cotton Club. Or it might be entirely traditional in all aspects but its fabric: a gray daytime wool. It might be fastened with a pearl button or a short string at bosom height, but whatever the case, it is so fitted and feminine that a tie can be used without making it look masculine.

The tuxedo's other elements are equally transformed. The bib front is interpreted in honeycombed piqué, cotton, embroidered organza, velvet, vertical-pleated satin, lace, very light chiffon, or jacquard silk. Narrow, pleated cuffs fastened by cufflinks gradually widen into a white top for a black velvet evening dress, the two buttons fastening the giant cuff at the bosom. The waistcoat might be more reminiscent of a bib front made of a tie fabric, buttonless and barely covering the bosom. The pants, whether white, polka dot, striped, or simply black, frequently have trim along the sides and are fastened with a different-colored sash. The shirt is often replaced by a scarf, which might also be knotted as a long, out-of-proportion tie. Black or white gloves with satin wrists—worn in sharp contrast with bare arms—take the place of jewelry. All so simple.

This apparent simplicity encompasses all of Armani's work. The women who choose to wear his clothing are austere, but never harsh. Sophisticated and reserved, they have little patience for continual changes in fashion. They are, in other words, the embodiment of the concept that has guided Armani through the years: you do not change with the times, you change when the time is right. Staying true to himself and ignoring seasonal fads or the enthusiastic comments of journalists when they want to launch a new trend at all costs, Armani might well ask, in the words of James Thurber, "Why should I be a nonconformist like everybody else?"

THE MENSWEAR REVOLUTION

Patrick McCarthy

The fashion world is divided into two kinds of designers: those with influence and those without. One list is considerably shorter than the other, and it almost inevitably begins with the holy trinity of Christian Dior, Gabrielle "Coco" Chanel, and Cristóbal Balenciaga. In the 1960s and 1970s Yves Saint Laurent was—by universal agreement—added to the list, but after him there was a long period in which new candidates would emerge, raise hopes, cause debate, and then inevitably fall away.

Until, of course, Giorgio Armani arrived. It all sounds terribly subjective but, in fact, the test for admission to these exalted ranks is both objective and simple: a designer must actually influence the way people look. Not a few people, not a tiny group of fashion insiders—though it usually begins there—but a broad, wide-reaching cross section of the real world. The litmus test is unforgiving. Few pass, but when they do the breakthrough is as clear and understandable as most truths are. And not all that difficult to predict.

From almost the very first sighting of Armani—in 1975—there was an audible gasp of recognition within the fashion world. Here was a contender. The unconstructed blazer that Armani unlined and unleashed was the fashion shot heard around the world: headline writers fell over themselves proclaiming not only a sartorial revolution but the birth of a star. Actually, Armani was one of those overnight successes that took a dozen or so years to gestate, but that is always a much duller story. Nowadays we are used to the superstar designer—Tom Ford, Calvin Klein, Miuccia Prada—but in the mid-1970s they were still a rarity. The exceptions were French—Saint Laurent, Hubert de Givenchy, Pierre Cardin—but it had taken each of them at least a decade to build a worldwide following, and by 1975 Paris had a musty air about it. There was a hunger for something new, something spectacular, and Armani provided just that.

Armani emerged in a world still reeling from the flower-power gurus of the 1960s. The bell-bottomed, garish colors of Carnaby Street held an enormous sway over the way many fashionable young men dressed, at least in their private moments. Brooks Brothers, and its European and Asian

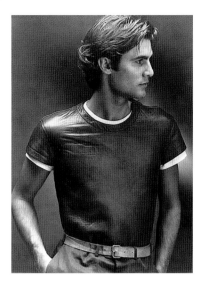

Spring/Summer 1977

Spring/Summer 1984

equivalents, controlled the rest of their time. In the early 1970s Cardin launched a kind of counteroffensive with his stiff peacock suits—tight pants, high armholes, a silhouette that screamed "Continental." The Cardin suit was the antithesis of what any self-respecting, laid-back hippie (or uptight preppie) would wear. It was into this schizophrenic stylistic morass that Armani jumped headfirst.

"My work has always demanded that I be very secure, that I have no doubts," Armani once observed,[1] and the unconstructed blazer that he launched certainly had that air of authority. Armani, quite literally, ripped the guts out of what most men had been wearing for generations. Gone were the linings and the padding and the shoulders. In their place was a light-as-a-feather jacket of remarkable simplicity and elegance with sloped shoulders, narrow lapels, and a new, long length.

There was a deliberately rumpled quality to Armani's new jacket, but there was also an exhilarating sense of casual luxury. The Armani cut was refined but virtually undetectable, while his textures were both liberating and stunning. Only a designer of Armani's genius could have actually transformed nubby fabrics—until that time universally dismissed as frumpy and old-fashioned (or worse)—into the essence of cool.

Indeed, cloth is as important to Armani as anything else in his fashion arsenal. "Fabric is the reason for my success," he says. "Draping fabric on a body is the most sensual thing that can happen. It must drape in your hand and have a union with the body. There is fabric that jumps out of my hand, that repels. I can't have it near me."[2] Nor can he have it near any of his customers. From the very beginning, there was a suppleness to Armani's material that not even the best Savile Row tailors could match. The research that Armani and his colleagues undertook with the fabric mills of Lake Como led to all kinds of breakthroughs in texture and weight and actually signaled a second Italian fashion revolution. The hardened cloth that had traditionally been the mainstay of menswear disappeared overnight. In its place were soft, sensual, downright sexy fabrics that caressed the body as clothes never had before.

Indeed, sex was what sold Armani. Long before muscled pecs and bare skin became a staple in men's fashion advertising, Armani realized that there was a growing, completely untapped market of men who wanted to flaunt their bodies. Armani was one of the first designers to realize that gyms actually existed, that they had moved beyond their eccentric bodybuilder origins, and that the search for a better physical form would have enormous implications. The male form was rapidly changing, especially among young professional men, and that change would require a whole new wardrobe—both literally and figuratively.

Armani's foresight did not occur in a vacuum, as he is the first to admit. "In the 1970s there was this great push to create a new kind of jacket," he recalls. "I remember when I was working for [Nino] Cerruti coming up with all kinds of new shapes, but, of course, nothing ever caught on in a big way. It was then that I realized, well, you have to take . . . the traditional jacket, which has been with us one way or another for hundreds of years, and work within it. And then there was the idea back then of wearing a blue blazer and tie over jeans. That was supposedly the ultimate, and though it looks dated now, it opened up this notion of a jacket as sportswear. The problem wasn't the jeans, it was the jacket. A traditional jacket is actually very limiting."[3]

Armani's solution was both noisy and subtle. He understood intrinsically the yearning for something new, but he also realized that this yearning was tempered by convention. "Men's fashion doesn't exist in the way women's fashion does," he notes. "A woman sets out to be intentionally different from everyone else. A man—most men—want to be individual, but in a context that has its own language."[4] And the jacket is the crucial component of that language. "You have to realize," Armani says, "that just moving a button an inch or two changes the feel dramatically. Move it down, and it's very relaxed and casual. Move it up, it's more dandified. The same with the lapels: narrow, high lapels recall the turn of the century, wide ones the 1940s and all that implies."[5]

The irony is that Armani's New Look—and it was as important as Dior's New Look—sprang from a career in traditional Italian menswear. Armani, the son of a transport-company accountant in Piacenza, forty miles south of Milan, grew up during World War II and can still recall waking up screaming during air raids. His grandfather, Lodovicio, had a shop in Piacenza that made wigs for the local theater company, and he often took his grandson backstage with him, an experience that Giorgio found both frightening and exciting. Armani's parents pressured him to go to medical school, and he endured it for three years or so before military service intervened. In 1957, while finishing his service, Armani took a job with La Rinascente, Italy's largest department-store chain. He started in window display but quickly moved over to a department ominously called the Office of Fashion and Style. "I began to understand about fabrics and the importance of rapport with the public," he says. "It's one thing to design clothes, but it's something else again to hang around the sales floor watching the public react to them."[6]

In the early 1960s Armani went to work for Cerruti, who was shaking up his family's textile business with a new men's fashion line. "You look respectable," Armani remembers Cerruti telling him during their first interview. "You will do."[7] The new Cerruti collection was a big success in Europe, and soon Armani had offers from other Italian fashion houses to design collections for them. At first the ever-cautious Armani resisted, but after a few years he decided to leave Cerruti and set himself up as a design consultant for such companies as Sicons, Ungaro, and Zegna. The "design consultant," in fact, was an Italian invention that came into being as the country's largest manufacturing companies tried to carve out a place for themselves in the burgeoning world of high fashion. Walter Albini, Karl Lagerfeld, and Gianni Versace were all design consultants at the time, and it became a cynical guessing game among the press each season to speculate on who had designed which collection. At first, a company usually pretended that its owner had actually created the collection and denied any knowledge of outside consultants. But as the consultants themselves became more famous, companies realized that their names had a commercial value, and inevitably the word would "leak" that Armani had worked on this or Lagerfeld had worked on that. The whole system came full circle in the mid-1980s, when the consultants started to demand that, despite their high fees, their names could not be connected publicly to these companies in any way.

Like his competitors, Armani used the income to establish his own business, and in 1975 Armani and his partner, Sergio Galeotti, launched Giorgio Armani S.p.A. Their only employee was a receptionist—a student, in fact. "We paid her so little we had to let her study on the job," Galeotti once recalled.[8] Success, however, came quickly, even by the fashion world's standards. In 1976, the company's first full year of operation, sales totaled about $90,000. Five years later the figure was $14 million. Ten years later it was above $100 million. Armani often credits Galeotti both with pushing him to open his own house and with providing the management structure that allowed the company to grow so phenomenally. And anyone who knew the strong, fierce, and charming Galeotti does not doubt his pivotal role in the history of Giorgio Armani. But above all else, the house of Armani rested on the design talents of Armani himself, something both friends and competitors acknowledge. "Discovering a man like Armani is impossible, because he discovered himself," Cerruti once observed when he was asked if he took credit for inventing Armani. "He had a natural talent, and he is self-taught. He would have stood out from the crowd in any case. Men like Armani are so rare that when one emerges even the blind are aware of it."[9]

It certainly did not take very long for the world to discover the new fashion house on the Via Durini. Both the press and the stores responded to Armani instantaneously. And so did Hollywood. In fact, the movie community adopted the designer more fervently than any other group. Both Armani and Galeotti recognized the importance of that in marketing his name and growing his business. When the chance to participate in a major motion picture—American Gigolo—presented itself, neither Armani nor Galeotti hesitated. At first the star was to be John Travolta, but that later changed to Richard Gere, which was a major stroke of luck for Armani. Gere, with his toned body and handsome face, was the perfect Armani model—sexy, young, and slightly dangerous. And he clearly loved clothes, at least in the film. American Gigolo was a visual homage to Armani's sleek silhouette and startlingly subtle colors. If anyone had any doubts about the commercial viability of his menswear—or its equally important "coolness factor"—American Gigolo wiped them away.

Indeed, from the very beginning Armani has been aware of the strategic importance of appearing "cool." Dressing actors was one way of reinforcing that strategy, but so was dressing the studio executives and producers who are the real powers in Hollywood. Armani and his colleagues understood the growing fascination with those executives long before anyone else in fashion did. The Armani company went out of its way to encourage agents at Creative Artists Agency, for example, or vice presidents at Twentieth Century Fox to visit its stores in Los Angeles and New York. It was the first fashion company to employ full-time staff members in both New York and Los Angeles to identify celebrities—actors, musicians, sports figures—it should seek to dress. It was also the first—the very first—fashion house to understand the importance of Oscar night as a major marketing opportunity, for both men and women. Now that the lead-up to the Academy Awards has become a hysterical blitzkrieg, with competing fashion labels offering money and clothes to even the most minor players, it's hard to remember that there was a time when most of the nominated actresses wore dresses created by studio costume designers and most of the actors didn't have a clue who made their tuxedos. Armani changed all that.

He also transformed the advertising of men's fashion. Armani emphasized the sexuality of his clothes in a way that had never been done before. He and his principal photographer, Aldo Fallai, exulted in the sensuality of his materials and the casualness of his cut. Shirts could be worn with a tie or wide open to reveal a hypertoned chest. Trousers were loose but revealing. Suits were tailored to flatter and flaunt. Fabrics had a sheerness that was barely acceptable even in women's fashion. The styling of Armani's advertising was unexpected and provocative: shirts without collars, jackets

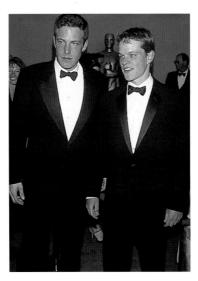

Michael Ovitz, former head of Creative
Artists Agency, wearing Armani

Ben Affleck and Matt Damon at the
71st Annual Academy Awards, 1999,
wearing Armani

with massive pockets, polo knits with suits, naked torsos everywhere. "I find nothing more prissy and ridiculous than a grown man stepping out in a pristinely clean 'outfit,'" declared Armani. "There really is nothing more démodé than that."[10]

The unconstructed blazer was inevitably copied by other designers in both Europe and America, and by the late 1970s it had become an industry standard. It was then, and only then, that Armani reversed himself and decided to experiment with the classic Savile Row suit. Inspired by movie heroes from the 1930s and '40s, Armani put back all of the elements he had previously pulled out. His new "power suit," as it was immediately dubbed, had wider lapels, stronger shoulders, and both padding and linings. Armani also lowered the "gorge"—the broadest point between lapels—to construct what would become the most tailored garment he has ever created. Later still, as this look was copied and risked becoming a caricature of itself, Armani changed course again—and took the entire world with him. In the late 1980s his reinvention of the sack suit, that creaky old American institution, was not only a testament to his influence, but also to his mastery of technique. Who else could make oversized jackets and wide pants look not only fashionable, but sultry? Who else could have an army of downtrodden male models—shoulders stooped, hands in pockets, eyes averted—march down a runway and have millions of men wanting to look just like them—at $2,000 a suit?

Ah, the prices. Armani does not come cheap. Nor does he have to. The success of his career is not explained simply by design genius. There is a commercial powerhouse at work here as well. Since 1986, after the death of Galeotti, Armani has not only been his company's chief designer but also its chief business strategist. Occasionally, he will bemoan his backbreaking work schedule, but only occasionally. Behind the Technicolor blue eyes and under the perfect white hair lies the brain of a brilliant businessman who has enjoyed his pivotal role in shaping how the fashion industry works today.

Fall/Winter 1979–80   Spring/Summer 1994

In recent years much has been made of Armani's aloof lifestyle. He is suspicious of outsiders, the refrain goes, which is why he lives just buildings away from his office and surrounds himself with a small clique of friends, most of whom work for him. He almost never leaves Milan, observers note, and when he does it is to go to a small desert isle near Sicily called Pantelleria. He refuses to delegate power, they say, and when he does surrender some it is almost inevitably snatched back soon after. Armani, they claim, revels in his image as a fashion monk, like Balenciaga before him.

In some ways the naysayers are absolutely right. Armani does love his reputation as someone apart from the herd. "Let the others do it their way," he once pronounced royally. "We will do it ours."[11] Still, the entire thrust of his design career—in menswear as well as womenswear—has been inclusive. Armani loves seeing people wearing his clothes and—loath as he is to admit it—loves to know that there is a whole army of designers who have copied his style. His mission, a rather democratic mission at that, has been to return elegance to clothing without abandoning the ease and comfort that crept in during the 1960s. His ideal model may be tall, good-looking, and muscled, but the joy actually comes when someone short, bald, and fleshy looks magnificent in his clothes. Fashion, as we all know, is about many things. But it is mostly about beauty—and the bringing of beauty to places it has never been before.

Notes

1.   Quoted in Marian McEvoy, "Armani's Clean Sweep," *W*, October 26, 1979, p. 28.

2.   Quoted in Andre Leon Talley, "The Blazer's Edge," *Women's Wear Daily*, May 16, 1978, p. 20.

3.   Quoted in Mark Ganem, "Armani: King of the Jacket," *Daily News Record*, April 3, 1989, p. 11.

4.   Ibid.

5.   Ibid.

6.   Quoted in Jay Cocks, "Suiting Up for Easy Street," *Time*, April 5, 1982, p. 65.

7.   Ibid.

8.   Ibid.

9.   Ibid.

10.   Quoted in Ganem, p. 11.

11.   Quoted in "Armani's Season," *Women's Wear Daily*, February 24, 1987, p. 1.

ANDROGYNY: UNDOING GENDER

by Susan Cross

Growing out of the anti-Establishment protests of the 1960s and the burgeoning feminist movement, new attitudes toward once-rigid definitions of gender developed in the 1970s. This outlook soon manifested itself in new styles of dress that broke with traditional patterns of gendered fashion. While much of the focus was on the constrictions of women's dress, Armani began his career by freeing men from their own limiting uniforms, allowing them to express a more sensual side traditionally associated with the feminine. Ripping out the stiff lining of men's suiting and substituting conventional fabrics with luxurious cashmere and silk, Armani made clothes that accentuated the previously hidden male form. Creating clothes that draped softly over hips and chest, the designer introduced a more casual and sexier look for once buttoned-up men.

Not long after his deconstructed jacket revolutionized menswear, Armani began designing them for women. As he eroticized male dress, he provided women with a similar look of comfort and ease while maintaining both a sexy elegance and a look of intelligence and confidence. In addition to his fuller cuts, Armani cleverly used materials in unexpected ways, adopting womenswear fabrics such as wool crepe for men's suits and designing T-shirts for professional women in other woolens traditionally seen on men. He also eschewed the dark hues of traditional menswear and the pastel colors conventionally assigned to womenswear, and chose instead a neutral palette of taupe and beige for both.

Twenty-five years after Armani designed his first collection, he continues to acknowledge the mutability of gender by making clothing for men and women that is nearly indistinguishable. He has looked to other cultures' vestimentary customs to find softer, more acceptable feminine modes of dress for men, adopting the loose tunics of Northern Africa and India, harem pants, and the sarong of the South Pacific and Asia for both his men's and women's collections. In his subversion of customary sartorial rules of gender, Armani has also inverted conventions, allowing men to play a more feminine role and women to adopt a more masculine mien. The result is a kind of cross-dressing that for much of the twentieth century has been limited to women. As witnessed in advertisements from the spring/summer 1995 and 1998 campaigns, for example, Armani switched the accessories associated with one gender for those of the other, dressing a woman in a sleek pinstriped suit and tie, and a man in a relaxed, zippered shirt with a silk paisley fringed scarf.

Armani plays with such traditional signifiers of gender, both undermining and capitalizing on their cultural meaning. In an image from the fall/winter 1996–97 campaign, a woman sits on a motorcycle in a pose reminiscent of Marlon Brando. She wears a collared shirt and tie, like those usually seen on men, on top of which is layered a floral shirt and necklace more typical of a woman's wardrobe. In an image from spring/summer 1997 a man is shown wearing a similar floral shirt, but in place of the tie is a more fluid scarf draped casually around his neck. His hair and face hardly differ from that of the woman in the earlier photograph. His delicate looks and the sinuous textiles he wears hark back to the 1930s and the male film stars of the time, such as Tyrone Power, who was framed in both a feminized and eroticized light.

A fall/winter 1993–94 image exemplifies Armani's obfuscation of traditional gender. A man and a woman both wear versions of a three-piece suit. The sloping shoulders of the man's suit appear less armorlike than that of his counterpart, whose suit is more formal and rigid, with a high, stiff collar and thick, padded shoulders. While she maintains a slightly more assertive stance, the man has traded a matching waistcoat for a softer vest, which lends him an air of leisure. Combining, transposing, and confusing conventional male and female attributes in this way, Armani has created an androgynous aesthetic that liberates clothing from its traditionally gendered strictures.

92

left: Fall/Winter 1996–97, right: Spring/Summer 1997

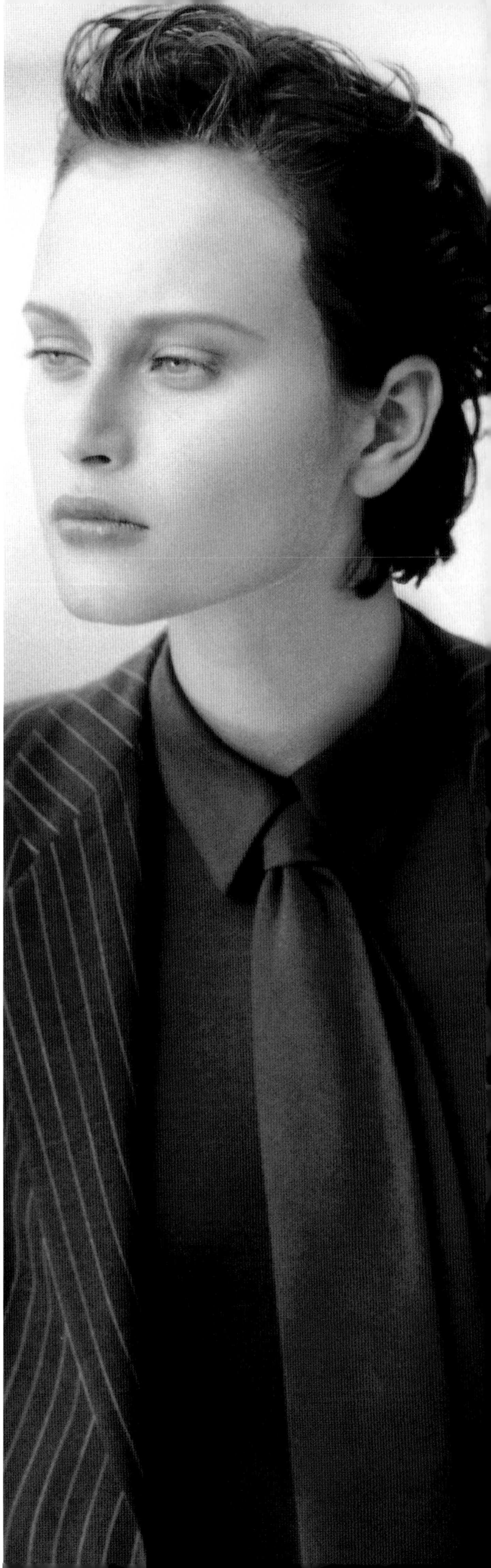

left: Spring/Summer 1998, right: Spring/Summer 1995

following two pages: Spring/Summer 1997, Fall/Winter 1995–96

Fall/Winter 1993–94

THE ARMANI LOOK

by Catherine Perry

All the elements of style—not just clothes, but hair, makeup, even models—are an integral part of defining a designer's signature image or "look." In a world based on invention, adaptation, and often fickleness, the challenge for fashion designers to produce the look of the moment can directly conflict with the ultimate task of maintaining a particular identity. Consistently, for more than twenty years, Armani's distinctive style has been clean, uncontrived, and elegant, distinguished by an uncomplicated and refined ease.

Typical of this look is the interpretation of urban business style represented by examples from Armani's fall/winter 1984–85 and spring/summer 1998 campaigns, which invoke the seriousness of a powerful "player" softened by an easy, latent informality characteristic of the designer's clothes. The Armani woman often assesses her world through generously shadowed, smoky-lidded eyes that smolder under penciled brows. Her skin and lips are pale and matte. Rather than relying solely on the standard stable of instantly recognizable faces, Armani uses less-famous models whose features project intelligence, power, and self-confidence.

Nothing Armani does is rigid or stiff, and even his more coiffed heads are swept back and soft. Hair for men and women is generally the same length, the slightly longish male locks implying a looseness and freedom. Even when hair is dressed and controlled, as pictured here in the fall/winter 1991–92 and fall/winter 1985–86 campaigns, it is run through with the same subdued sexiness and mussed elegance. An exception is the slicked-back, shoe-polish hair influenced by theater and film of the 1930s seen in the designer's campaigns from fall/winter 1990–91 and fall/winter 1992–93, which recall the famously androgynous look of Marlene Dietrich and the arch, Deco style of Adolphe Menjou. The parallel treatment of men and women in this campaign mimics the ungendered feel of many of Armani's clothes. This urbane, cosmopolitan sensibility appropriates a bygone glamour while projecting the designer's invariably modern, sophisticated feel.

More recently, in his campaigns for fall/winter 1998–99 and fall/winter 1997–98, for example, Armani has responded to the street with a slightly edgy and tousled, hand-through-the-hair feel. Even with this more youthful image, Armani maintains a familiar sophisticated, smart identity. Rather than subverting the traditional elegance of Armani, this look of "mad, bad, and dangerous to know" only informs it with a new, sharper bite. Ultimately, the Armani style resides in the unimpeachable authority of the clothes, and in the confidence and attitude they inspire.

103

Fall/Winter 1997–98

104

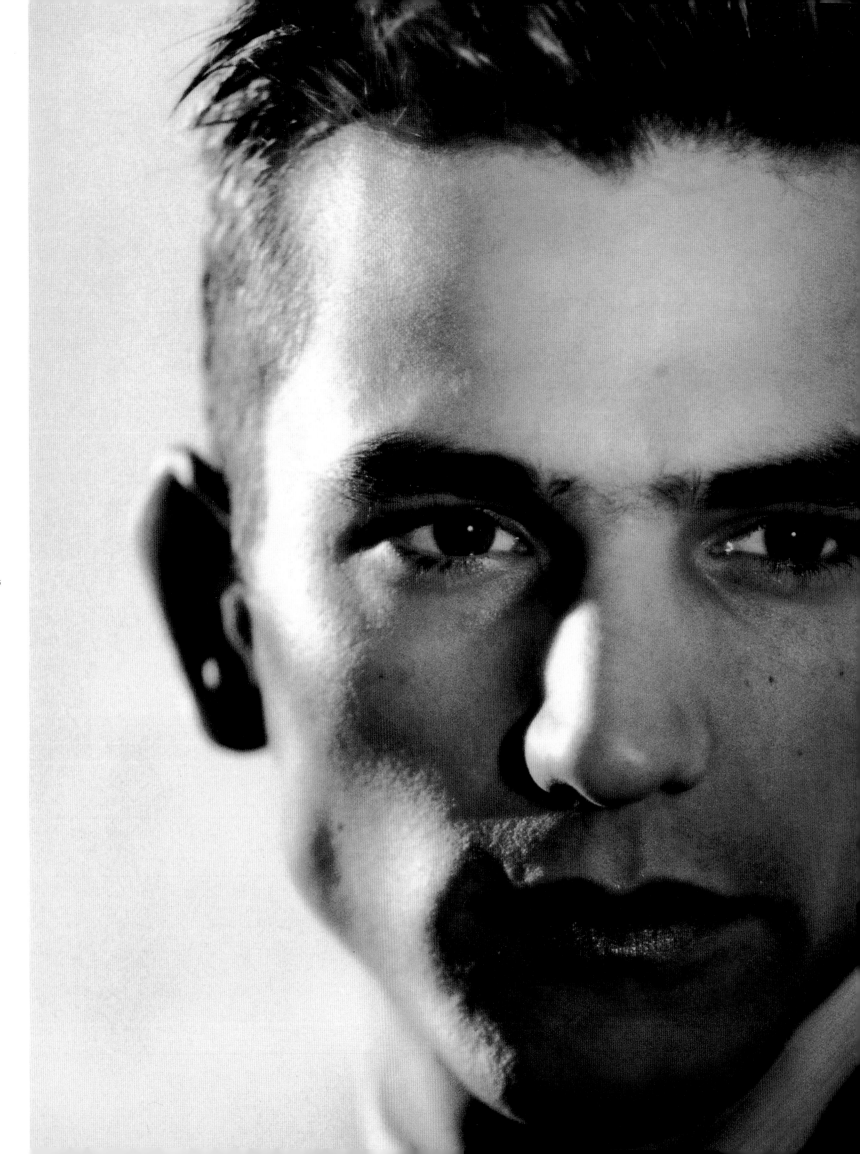

Spring/Summer 1998

108

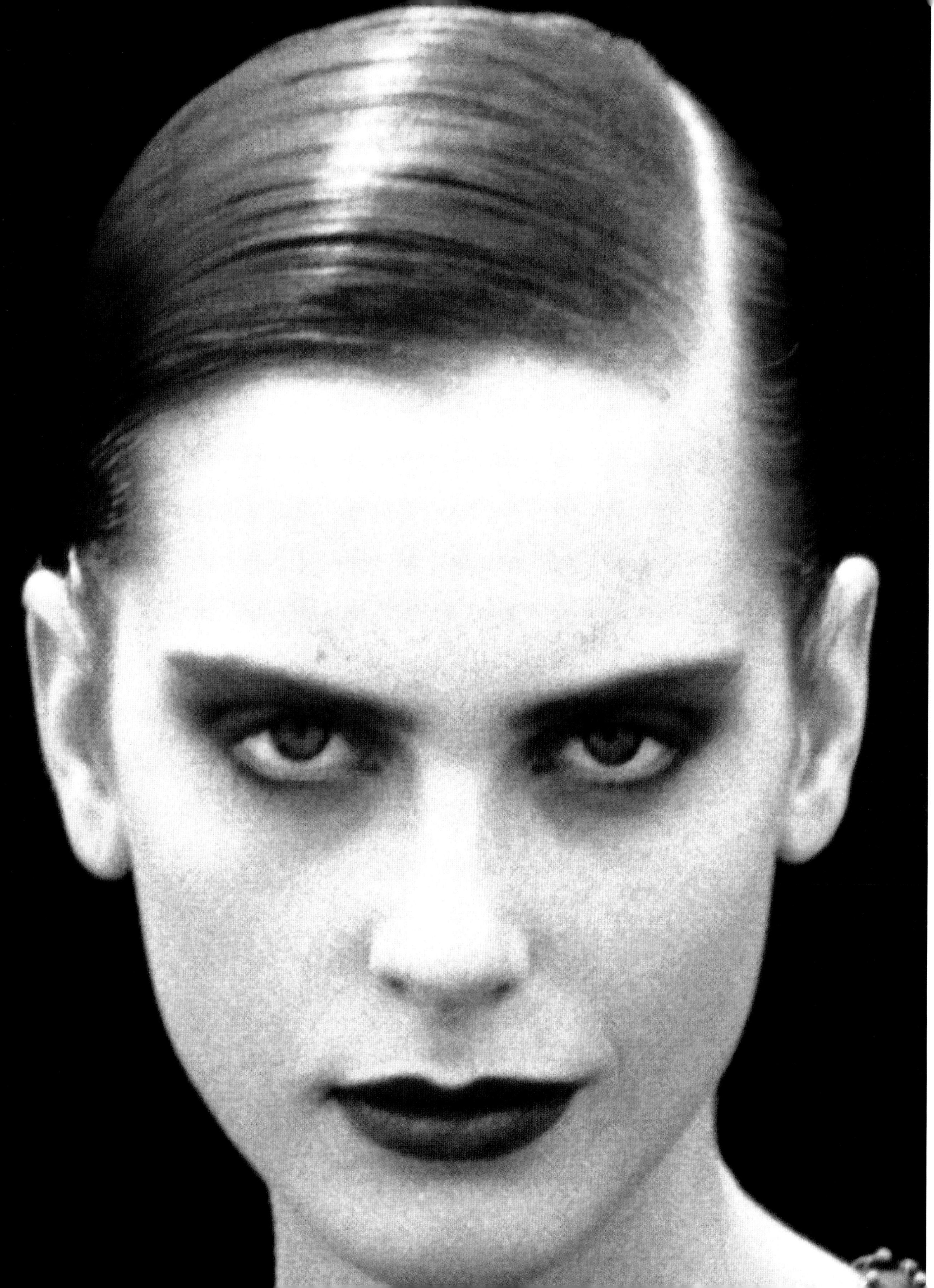

110

Fall/Winter 1992–93

Fall/Winter 1991–92

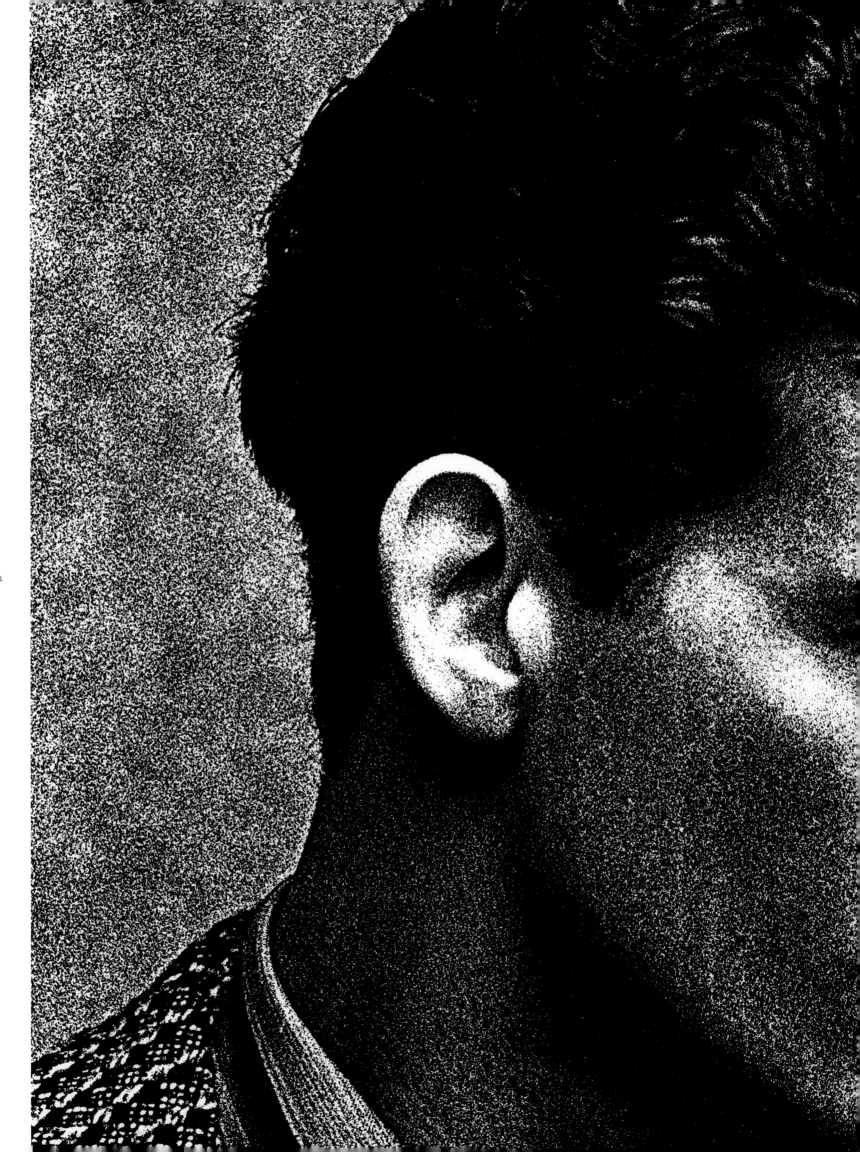

115

Fall/Winter 1985–86

116

TRADITIONALISM: REDOING GENDER

by Susan Cross

While Armani subverts traditional gender dress codes with his more androgynous designs, he also creates garments that reinforce stereotypes of difference. Following the iconic, genderless suits down the Armani runway might be embroidered Scarlett O'Hara gowns for women or Stanley Kowalski "muscle tees" for men. These more traditional uniforms of feminine and masculine identity seem to radiate a certain playfulness, an air of dressing up from an attic trunk filled with clothing from another time. Indeed, Armani has likened his clothes to costumes, and it appears that one can inhabit a myriad of personae by wearing them. Dressing for both men and women is treated as a masquerade: the powerful executive can become a sultry femme fatale or coy princess, and the sensitive dandy can transform himself into a heroic adventurer or confident jock. The unstable nature of gender constructions becomes clear in the range of roles Armani offers us.

The same designer credited with contributing to the liberation of women's fashions in the footsteps of Gabrielle "Coco" Chanel has also mastered a sartorial tradition that projects pure femininity. For his fall/winter 1978–79 womenswear collection, Armani paired flamboyant boas with heavy, coarse wool jackets and suits. Combining in one ensemble this fetish of hyperfemininity with a fashion convention associated with the masculine mimics the same freedom of choice that Armani offers in one's closet: hanging right next to the serious black Armani suit Michelle Pfeiffer wore to the Academy Awards in 1989 might be the sultry, transparent, beaded skirt and tank she wore to the Emmy Awards in 1998.

An advertisement for the spring/summer 2000 women's collection features a triad of Lolita-like beauties in barely-there bikinis, sheer hot pants, and cropped tanks, striking poses reminiscent of pinup or calendar girls. This representation of woman (or girl) as object of desire is one of a number of guises traditionally offered to women that we can now choose to appropriate and re-create. Armani offers other such guises, too: a sequined red ball gown with ballooning skirt from fall/winter 1993–94 elicits memories of a 1950s film star, while a reserved plum gown from fall/winter 1989–90 recalls a patrician grande dame from the 1910s. A Belle Epoque–inspired black dress with veil and gloves from spring/summer 1989 conjures an image of the enchanting young widow, a role that straddles the boundary between fantasy subject and object: with the experience and worldliness her position implies, the widow can be seen as an independent character in control, a seductress, or as the innocent prey of others' desire without the shelter of her husband/protector.

For men, too, Armani expands the cast of characters. The fantastic identities that men have classically adopted through clothing are those that tend to be formed in boyhood: the soldier, the cowboy, the athlete, and the adventurer. Accessible in the form of fatigues, trench coats, and aviator jackets, these personae offer the nerd inside or the boy next door a chance to be a hero—though in fact the macho ideal that this clothing represents may exist only in the apparel. Early in his career, Armani appropriated the trench coat, a remnant of World War I that later became a symbol of the romantic explorer or maverick detective. In an image from Armani's fall/winter 1975–76 menswear campaign, a group of men in trench coats and Eisenhower jackets stare out at the camera with the nonchalant assurance of seasoned militarymen. This bravura is translated into a sleeveless tank and drawstring pants in the spring/summer 1997 collection. Emphasizing a muscular physique, the sleeveless tank or T-shirt can signify both the strength and discipline of an athlete or the brutish sensuality of a laborer. A corduroy hunting jacket worn over a vest and scarf dating from fall/winter 1993–94 gives men the chance to re-create the role of the country gentleman or master of the hunt, though the casual, slightly mussed styling alludes to a more earthy incarnation: the gamekeeper from D. H. Lawrence's *Lady Chatterley's Lover*, who plays the part of Lord of the manor.

left: Spring/Summer 2000

following two pages: Special collection, uniforms designed for the Italian military commissioned by *L'Uomo Vogue*, 1977

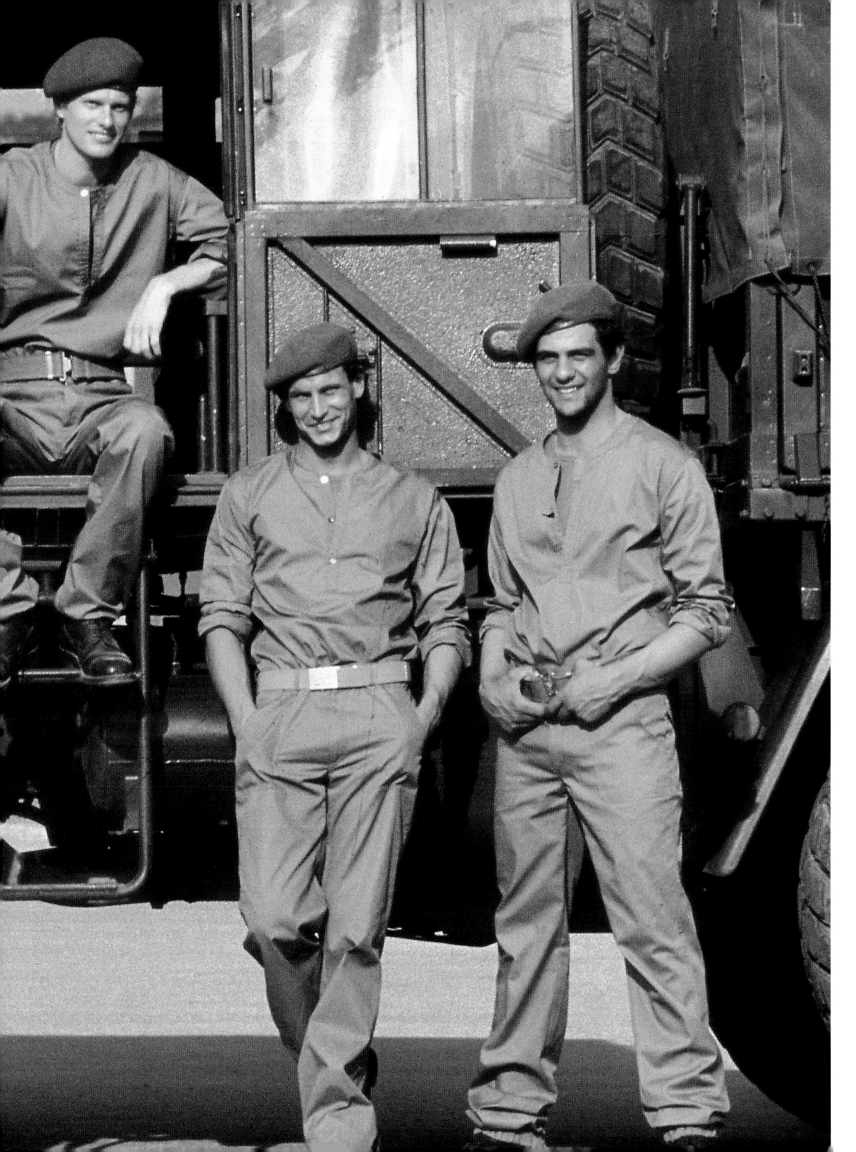

120

left to right: Fall/Winter 1993–94; Fall/Winter 1989–90; Spring/Summer 1992; Spring/Summer 1989

122

left to right: Spring/Summer 1997; Fall/Winter 1993–94; Spring/Summer 1982; Fall/Winter 1986–87; following two pages: Fall/Winter 1975–76

124

125

CHANGING ROLES

by Susan Cross

As women asserted themselves in the workplace in the 1970s, "dressing for success" entered the fashion lexicon. Armani had begun designing chicly masculinized jackets and suits for women as early as 1976, and by the mid-1980s the Armani label had become synonymous with the power suit. Female executives dressed in the elegant but serious Armani-designed ensembles, which were at once symbols of success and a way to obtain it. His loosely draped suits drew attention away from the feminized body, and their broad, padded shoulders lent a sense of authority and protection like a suit of armor.

For some, the suit symbolized the equality many feminists were fighting for. For others, it represented another patriarchal convention that equated success in the workplace with a male role model. Many women did not want to lose the choice to be feminine and believed that equality should not be predicated on being like—even dressing like—a man. Armani's suits are often lauded for having offered the first credible option, with their soft, sensuous fabrics, fluid lines, and nonconstricting cuts. But at the same time, the designer also provided women a more conventional expression of femininity, in the form of slinky dresses and flowery frocks. In other words, Armani allowed women to escape the burden of being either/or.

Suggesting the multivalent nature of identity, advertisements for both the Armani suit and his more conventional gowns have asserted the image of the successful woman at work and at play, by day and by night. The scenarios they describe seem to offer women more than an image of equality, but also one of control. A campaign from spring/summer 1992, for example, features a woman in formal eveningwear, presumably ready for a night out, seated next to a man dressed—or more accurately, underdressed—in pajamas and loungewear. Reclining, chest bared and in a state of repose within the Moroccan interior, her companion is reminiscent of an Odalisque—conventionally a libidinal representation of the feminine and the exotic.

This inversion of customary roles is similarly evident in ads for the spring/summer 1989 and 1991 collections and in another from the spring/summer 1992 campaign, in which women dressed in tailored suits are accompanied by partners who sport a more casual look. In the earliest image, an implied economic hierarchy is coupled with one of experience: the woman appears considerably more worldly than her boyish counterpart, whose shorts suit (reminiscent of the uniforms of young English schoolboys) infantilizes him to a degree. At the same time, this could be considered a form of liberation, an opportunity for men to relinquish the cultural expectation for them to be in charge; instead, women can take that role. In an image from the fall/winter 1999–2000 collection, two women unabashedly dance together, no longer needing a man to take the lead.

127

left: Spring/Summer 1992, right: Spring/Summer 1992; following two pages: Spring/Summer 1992, Spring/Summer 1989

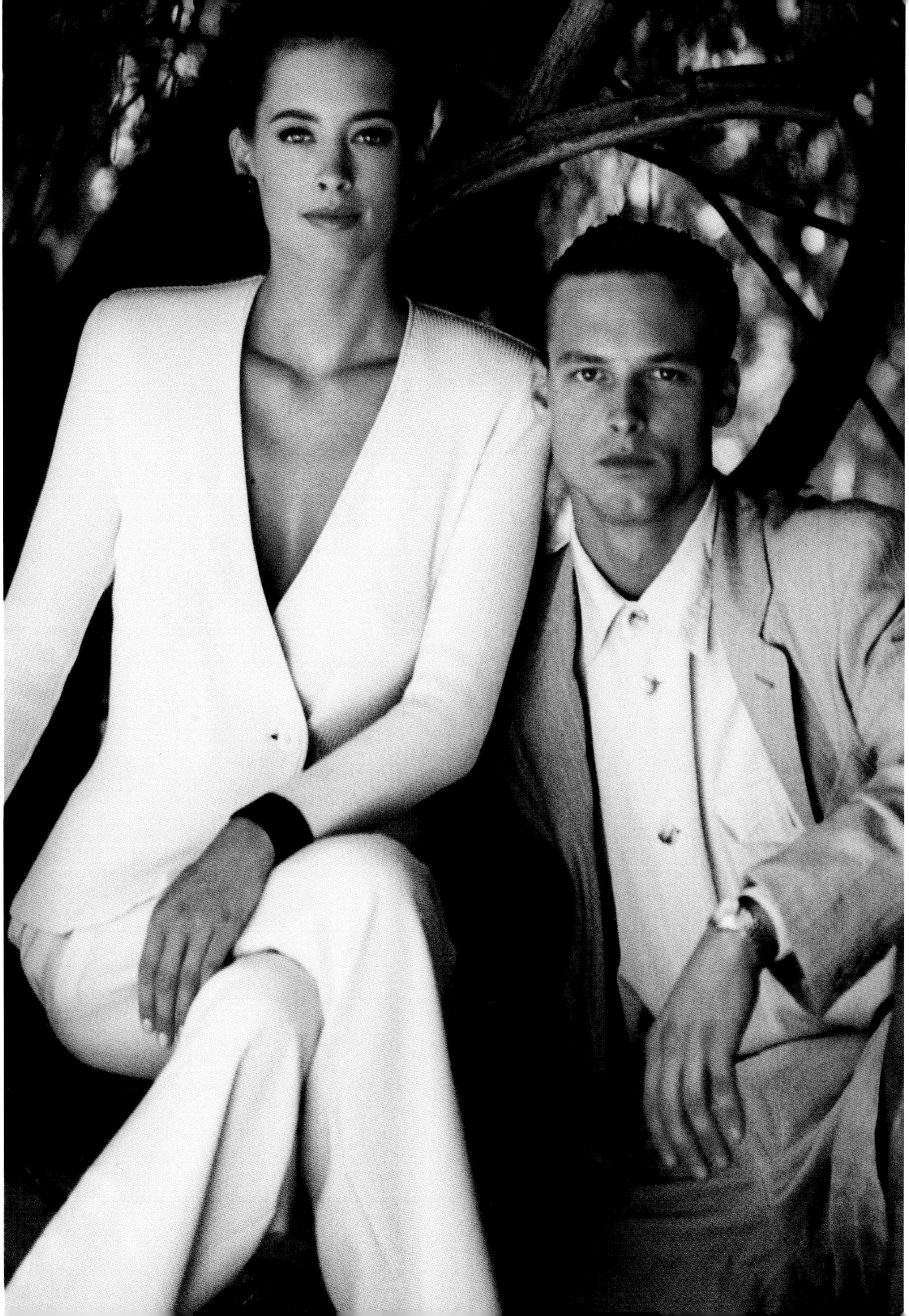

131

133

14

15

16

14. Man's blouson jacket ensemble; jacket: ca. fall/winter 1978–79; pants: ca. fall/winter 1982–83. **15. Man's shirtjacket ensemble;** shirtjacket: ca. fall/winter 1982–83; pants: ca. 1980–85. **16. Man's sports jacket and sweater vest ensemble,** fall/winter 1994–95. **17. Woman's jacket and skirt ensemble,** spring/summer 1987. **18. Man's vest ensemble,** fall/winter 1994–95. **19. Man's jacket and sweater vest ensemble,** fall/winter 1993–94.   Historically womenswear, with its accommodation and encouragement of decorative expression, has been the primary vehicle for dress with explicit stylistic quotations. In Armani's oeuvre, however, it is in menswear that references to regional, historical, and occupational precedents

17

18

19

appear most clearly: an academic sweater vest and tweeds, and an ensemble worthy of a stroll through the Tyrol, are gently edged to refinement by the designer's nuanced accretions of texture and pattern, while retaining the essential characteristics of their sources. In Armani's ensembles for women, even those with details directly appropriated from menswear, such references are often so mutated that the original inspiration has been all but obliterated. In the woman's ensemble above, only the textiles can be associated with the commonplace menswear coordination of plaid jackets and solid trousers.

20

21

22

20. Man's sports jacket ensemble, fall/winter 1992–93. **21. Woman's suit,** fall/winter 1979–80. **22. Man's three-piece suit,** fall/winter 1990–91. **23. Woman's pantsuit,** fall/winter 1998–99. **24. Man's suit,** fall/winter 1990–91. Armani's collections for both men and women suggest a variety of strategies in tailoring. While his designs are evidently anchored in the traditional metier of the tailor's art, which uses the shaped pattern piece to establish fit, Armani has extended the possibilities of the cut, subtly in his menswear and more aggressively in his womenswear. The gray wool

23

24

woman's suit above left is given a draped cinch at the waist that is antithetical to the tailor's craft and more characteristic of a dressmaker's approach. On the other hand, the plastron-like lapel treatment of the woman's pantsuit to the right alludes to the handiwork of that ultimate practitioner of traditional tailoring skills, the maker of bespoke military uniforms.

140

25

26

27

28

25. Woman's jacket and pants, fall/winter 1994–95. **26. Woman's pantsuit,** fall/winter 1995–96. **27. Woman's three-piece pantsuit,** fall/winter 1993–94. **28. Woman's jacket and pants,** fall/winter 1993–94. **29. Woman's pantsuit,** ca. fall/winter 1985–86. **30. Woman's suit,** fall/winter 1994–95.   More than any other article of dress, the jacket was the precipitant of the Armani revolution. Fitted or loose, paired with narrow pants or trousers eased to the fullness of a skirt, the Armani jacket—despite the restricted number of its components—has been subject to a seemingly

29

30

endless stream of discrete permutations. Armani's innovations, beyond the evisceration of excess padding, can be as dramatic as the reformation or eradication of a lapel, or the articulation or camouflaging of the waist. More often, however, they are as subtle as the slightly shifted stance of buttons: generally a raised placement for women, a lowered one for men.

142

31

32

31. Man's suit, fall/winter 1982–83. **32. Man's suit,** fall/winter 1978–79. **33. Woman's pants ensemble with overskirt,** fall/winter 1996–97. **34. Man's suit,** ca. fall/winter 1995–96.   The first evolutionary step of the Armani power suit for men was in the direction of the reduction and elimination of any superfluous infrastructure. As Cristóbal Balenciaga had done in his haute-couture collections for women in the 1950s and 1960s, Armani strives to achieve his shaping almost exclusively through the hang of fabric and ingenious seaming. Unlike the Spanish master, however,

33

34

Armani's impulse to greater drape and sensuality has resulted in an almost fluid expression of the body. Yet despite this easing of propriety away from stiffness into comfort, Armani's business dress has retained its aura of authority. In the woman's ensemble pictured above, the neatly knotted tie introduces the probity of male business attire to an outfit otherwise characterized by a breezy informality, thus reversing the modus operandi that generally characterizes his menswear approach.

35

36

35. Woman's jacket and pants, spring/summer 1998. **36. Woman's jacket and pants,** fall/winter 1995–96. **37. Woman's "Bermuda" suit,** spring/summer 1992. **38. Woman's suit,** fall/winter 1980–81.   Even Armani's women's ensembles that invoke the characteristically linear cut of traditional menswear retain an essential sensuality. The two ensembles with black jackets and striped trousers suggest the British "city suit,"

37

38

though they have shed the conventional waistcoat and shirt. Other boardroom ensembles are leavened by the exposure of leg: Bermuda shorts are revealing while maintaining a business-like modesty, and an elongated double-breasted jacket allows, but controls, the splaying of a wrap skirt.

146

39

40

39. Woman's "muscle tee" top and skirt, fall/winter 1998–99. **40. Woman's cowl top and pants,** fall/winter 1998–99. **41. Woman's jacket and pants,** fall/winter 1998–99. **42. Woman's evening gown and coat,** fall/winter 1998–99. **43. Woman's evening gown and jacket,** fall/winter 1998–99.   While gender transpositions from menswear to womenswear occurred prior to the twentieth century, especially in riding habits, it is only

41

42

43

in the last hundred years that they have gained such wide currency in other forms of womenswear. From "muscle tees" and hooded sweatshirts interpreted for dressed-up sportswear, to Bond Street suitings applied to women's jackets and coats over evening gowns, Armani has extended the parameters of the feminine encroachment into the masculine wardrobe.

148

44

45

44. Woman's evening jacket and pants, fall/winter 1991–92. **45. Woman's evening suit,** fall/winter 1991–92. **46. Woman's evening ensemble,** fall/winter 1985–86. Often, Armani embellishes textiles representative of the traditional male wardrobe—herringbone, glen plaid, rep-striped silk twill—with a variety of sequined and beaded embroideries. By using sequins to glaze over a printed rendering of a glen plaid, or by disposing bugle

46

beads directionally to create a dimensional relief to herringbone, Armani applies associations of menswear and daywear to womenswear and eveningwear.

150

47

48

49

47. Woman's evening gown, fall/winter 1986–87. **48. Woman's evening ensemble,** fall/winter 1992–93. **49. Woman's evening gown,** fall/winter 1992–93. **50. Woman's evening gown,** fall/winter 1992–93. **51. Woman's halter-top evening gown,** fall/winter 1997–98. **52. Man's tuxedo,** spring/summer 2000.   The Armani tuxedo emerged in the 1980s as the ubiquitous formal garb of choice among men who sought eveningwear that

50

51

52

retained all the elegant sobriety of the style with a new, flatteringly comfortable cut. In a series of playfully elegant transpositions for women, Armani has taken the venerable tuxedo into the surreal and elegant world of Cecil Beaton and Elsa Schiaparelli.

152

53

53. Woman's pants ensemble, fall/winter 1998–99.   Armani's work often resists the assignment of specific sources, historical or conceptual. Here, a heathered wool bouclé suggests the pointillist speckling of gray flannel, but the sturdy construction of that hardy fabric is dissolved into an airy weave that exposes the body. The design creates an ensemble that in its mixed semiotic signals alludes to one thing while presenting its opposite.

WORLD CULTURE

THE SANDS OF TIME: HISTORICISM AND ORIENTALISM IN ARMANI'S DESIGNS FOR WOMEN

Caroline Rennolds Milbank

Few clothes speak more eloquently of modern life than those of Giorgio Armani, who has defined professional dress for both sexes for a quarter of the twentieth century and beyond. His influence is immeasurable. An Armani suit, with its almost palpable allure, has something of the power of a talisman. Yet behind the contemporary simplicity and ease of his clothes (even at their most minimal), there often lies a hint of *autre temps*, *autre moeurs*. Sometimes the reference is ambiguous: a curved line might suggest anything from a suffragette's suit to a Polynesian pareo. Occasionally the translation is direct, providing a new screen through which to view another time or a seemingly distant culture.

Well before the first fashion designer existed (and most agree that Charles Frederick Worth created the profession when he opened his couture house in 1858), fashion often invigorated itself by looking to the past. Such borrowing was the essence of fancy dress, a rage that spanned centuries and continents (and that is the ancestor of Halloween and pre-Lenten celebrations today). Donning a costume has never stopped having the appeal of stepping outside one's own skin temporarily. And there is romance in wearing an article of contemporary fashion that features revived details from some time ago. In fashion, a dress made in one period in homage to another offers a look at both times, emphasizing the similarities, differences, or just plain tension between the two.

Historical references in Armani's clothes provide a bridge between a lost world—whose elegance can be viewed in retrospect as oppressive—and a contemporary reality, in which sterility can be the price paid for greater freedoms. Combating some of the harsher elements of the brave new world are Armani's winsome details from the past. Frogs that might have marched in formation down the front of a hussar's uniform lie sinuously across the front of one of his crepe de chine blouses. Bias-cut cuffs flutter languidly like eighteenth-century *engageants*. Evening skirts, in tulle and chiffon, have the fragile heft of those worn by Edgar Degas's bronze ballet dancers. Jackets evoke the medieval doublets or pages' tunics of Florentine painting, not just in their shape and line, but also in

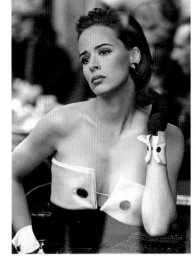

Fall/Winter 1994–95   Fall/Winter 1992–93

their mien: Armani's clothes share a stillness and precision with figures in a painting by Giotto.

It is almost impossible for a fashion designer not to be indelibly marked by the era of his youth. For Armani, the 1930s were formative in defining his spare, elegant, fluid aesthetic. Any one of his bare, almost liquid evening dresses summons the time vividly. But it is the use of men's clothes from the golden age of male elegance—the period between the two world wars—to inspire women's dress that is the dominant theme of Armani's work. At his most playful, he reinterprets articles of male attire entirely. A man's tie, untied, becomes a barer-than-bare evening blouse, the old school stripes rendered in sequins and beads. French cuffs comprise the entire strapless bodice of an evening gown. A man's bow tie forms the bodice of another evening gown, or hangs like a watch fob from a woman's pocket.

Menswear is the source of such favored materials as chalk- and pinstripes and plaids (a gray plaid with a black-and-white grid is to Armani as black-and-white houndstooth was to Christian Dior). These might visually resemble their tweed and woolen forebears, but, updated in blends of wool, silk, and rayon and other synthetics, they suit an increasingly atmosphere-controlled, seasonless life. Shirtings are often interpreted for women in soft silks. Joining the traditionally male silhouette and materials in Armani's designs for women are an almost relentlessly neutral palette and details of men's tailoring, including besom pockets, band collars, and plays on classic lapel treatments.

Besides the transposition of elements from male uniforms to women's clothing, a juxtaposition that has zigzagged alluringly across the twentieth-century fashion timeline, there can also be found in Armani's oeuvre the influence of boy's clothes from a bygone era. A Depression-era schoolboy might be the source for elegant ensembles of knee-length shorts, short cardigan-style jackets, cut-in sleeveless T-shirts, and visored caps. Rounded, soft collars, a frequent leitmotif, date back to turn-of-the-century productions of J. M. Barrie's play about the boy who never wanted to grow up: Peter Pan.

Starting perhaps with the nineteenth-century English firm of Redfern, known for exquisitely tailored riding habits, many couturiers and designers adapted aspects of men's clothes for women. Usually this took the form of imposing male elements upon the female silhouette. How Armani transformed the way women dress has to do not so much with the specific elements he has appropriated, but with his particular way with fit. Jackets draped seemingly casually—like those sported by big-band leaders in the 1930s and later—have just as much insouciant swagger on women as on men today, serving to remind us of the contrast in dress of the sexes just seventy years ago, a period when only the most daring toyed with androgyny and women borrowing men's clothes borrowed their formality as well.

By dressing both men and women in pants, jackets with broad shoulders, and flat shoes, Armani accomplished seemingly effortlessly what was a quest for many twentieth-century designers: the desire to devise a unisex uniform. Earlier experiments by designers from Pierre Cardin to Rudi Gernreich can be viewed in hindsight as quaintly futuristic: riffs on bodysuits, jumpsuits, body jewelry, and shaved heads in helmets. What made Armani's new uniform succeed was its relaxed, unstructured shape. By softening the tailoring of the jacket, the keystone of the male work uniform for at least 150 years, Armani came to clothe the end of an era in the most comfortable armor ever made.

Armani didn't stop with revolutionizing classic business attire. Acknowledging the changes being wrought by the third industrial revolution, he went on to expand the vocabulary of what constitutes a suit. In 1989 the designer told *The New York Times* that he wanted to "change the form of things." His aim, he said, was to make designs that looked "as if a woman took a piece of fabric and threw it over her body in a natural gesture."[1] He accomplished this by turning away from traditional Western tailoring methods and toward the East. Place traditional garments of European and Eastern origin side by side on a table and the most obvious difference between them becomes instantly clear: one is constructed of variously shaped pieces of fabric sewn together to encase a figure, while the other is likely to be made of a flat piece of material with minimal cutting and stitching. The sari, for example, is worn the way it comes off the loom, and the *burnous* (a hooded cloak worn in parts of the Middle East) is rectangular and can be laid flat. When a flat garment is put on a rounded figure, the result is that the fabric hangs in soft folds. Armani successfully melded this sense of *flou* into a vernacular based on Western tailoring.

In his logical progression from the soft jacket, Armani has experimented with various elements and proportions that point East. Alternatives to the classic pantsuit of blazer and trousers include ensembles made with vests over tunic shirts reminiscent of standard male dress from, among other places, India. Other tunic shirts acquire the presence of a jacket with the addition of bib fronts, like those of Northern African djellabahs or Moroccan caftans. Knee-length or longer tunics or coats worn over pants could have stepped out of a Persian miniature painting. Wrapped jackets recall short informal men's kimonos from Japan. Single-breasted jackets buttoning down the front and stand-up collars are Armani Nehru, and many of the soft suits take the Mao uniform into the realm of luxury.

Eastern effects provide not just softer lines, but also specific shapes and patterns: harem skirts appear on evening clothes as well as on such tailored day pieces as a camel-hair coat; batik birds, cloud scrolls, and chrysanthemum petals decorate jackets, pants, and skirts; the use of transparency recalls piña cloth; Zouave braid, simplified (as are most of these references), adorns clothing and accessories. While historically orientalism has painted Western design in brilliant palettes and patterns, Armani is drawn most often to the simplest of Eastern wear, the subtleties of rough, plain, coarse, worn peasant clothing having more appeal (and more workable modernity) than court clothes.

Eastern clothing having a modernizing effect on Western women's dress goes back to the nineteenth century. To escape the binds of corsets and voluminous crinoline skirts, a handful of daring women—activists and/or actresses—began to adopt the daringly shocking wearing of pants.

Spring/Summer 1994

Spring/Summer 1988

Fall/Winter 1989–90

(In an age when legs were known as limbs, clothing that defined them was almost unspeakable.) The first commonly worn ensemble based on pants for women was modeled after Turkish trousers (full and modestly gathered at the ankles); these came to be known as bloomers after their most renowned wearer, the American reformer Amelia Bloomer. As a revolutionary statement the look didn't last long, although bloomers continued to be worn for active sports, which were becoming increasingly popular. Curiously, it was not until high fashion turned its attention to Eastern effects, including harem trousers, with no more intent than to transform women into exotic birds of plumage, that the real seeds of modern fashion were sown.

The fertile moment was 1910. Suffragists were giving solemn speeches wearing masculine bifurcated costumes when the theatrical costume and set designer Léon Bakst turned the world of fashion on its ear with his zeitgeist designs for the Ballets Russes production, in Paris, of *Scheherazade*. Couturiers, master jewelers, and artisans of all sorts were profoundly affected by the exhilarating palette and radically diaphanous near-nudity of the dancers' harem costumes. Bold socialites, having already dipped a toe in the water by wearing Persian fancy dress, bought versions of the new look from Bakst, Paul Poiret, and others.

In 1990 Armani paid homage to this turning point with a group of Bakst-inspired designs, including a version of one of the most riveting designs of the twentieth century: the Persian tunic designed for Gertrude Vanderbilt Whitney by the Russian costumer. Heiress, wife, and mother, as well as artist, patron, and museum founder, Whitney became in effect a work of art herself in 1913 by posing wearing her Bakst-commissioned ensemble four times: she was photographed by Baron Adolf de Meyer, sculpted in silver by Emanuele de Rosales, painted life-size by Howard Cushing in a mural he installed in her Long Island studio, and drawn by John Singer Sargent. Like such contemporaries as Rita de Acosta Lydig, Natasha Rambova, Mata Hari, and the Italian beauty the Marchesa Casati, Whitney was presenting an avant-garde artistic self to the world when she dressed this way.

Gertrude Vanderbilt Whitney,

photographed by Baron Adolf de Meyer

in 1913.

Armani seems to appreciate that while the past holds allure for the present, this attraction is often tempered by mixed feelings. Sending out his pared-down ensembles on his light-box runway, he often gives the models the finishing touch of gloves, the one accessory (with the possible exception of the fan) associated most strongly with Victorian etiquette. As the punctuation to clothes that can go from a business meeting in one time zone to a soccer meet or benefit in another, these serve as touching reminders of just how far women have come. For the very elegant ground-breaking Whitney, wearing trousers would remain a part of her downtown, artistic, woman-of-accomplishment identity; her uptown heiress-wife-mother-hostess self wore proper ladylike skirts. In reviving her most artistic look and translating it into the easiest of evening ready-to-wear more than seventy-five years later, Armani reminds us of how, thanks in no small part to him, these selves today can be and are one and the same.

Note

1.   Bernadine Morris, "Huzzahs for Armani's Soft and Slithery Collection," *The New York Times*, October 13, 1989, p. B20.

A PLACE IN THE SUN

by Susan Cross

Like an adventure tale whose amalgam of fiction and memory evokes far-away destinations that exist only in the imagination, Armani's clothes and his advertising similarly transport us through space and time to exotic locales. As in a dream, we are never sure exactly where, or even when, the scene takes place, but there is a sense of familiarity and comfort, as with a face we can't quite place.

Armani's nostalgic and romantic visions mirror the revival of eclectic historical styles and cultural traditions characteristic of postmodern society, which has been defined at least in part by the advent of multiculturalism and the recognition of Western civilization as one among many cultures, all of which are equally valued. Simultaneously, technological advances have created a profusion of images and information that have helped to establish the new world culture, in which Japanese tatami mats furnish American homes and denim jeans are found throughout the world.

This convergence of cultures takes visible form, in Armani's designs, in ensembles that might combine a hint of a Japanese obi with a suggestion of a Northern African djellabah or a Mao jacket. (Like that unrecognizable face, however, the original garments are never quite identifiable.) This pastiche of sartorial customs results in something of a universal vision of dress, which parallels Armani's creation of clothing that crosses the division of sexes: his clothes erase lines equally between genders, social strata, and cultures.

Armani's clothes seem to bring us back to a simpler time and place—one that has never existed outside of longing. This sentimental fantasy reappears in Armani's advertising, which is often set in sunny, desertlike landscapes or white-washed villages, or in their cool, tiled interiors. Reminiscent of Morocco, Algiers, Polynesia, or perhaps Bali, these seductive but unknown locales represent the fulfillment of a simultaneous desire for the past and the future, for refuge and for adventure. Dotted with palm trees, these sites invoke the oasis that Armani offers us from restricting dress and customs.

In an image from the spring/summer 1978 menswear campaign, a muscular model leans against a burlap sack; he appears as if he might be taking a rest from lifting the mysterious goods contained within: coffee from South America or spices from India? In another image, the same model again creates this moment of leisure despite his more formal attire, as, dressed in a suit, he reclines against a palm tree with a book in his hand. This notion of freedom is the thread connecting Armani's clothes and the manner in which they are represented. Though the loose-fitting garments associated with hot climates are those that often inspire Armani—the sarong, the caftan, the harem pant—his more tailored clothes still retain that same fluid, languid elegance. Even in the tropical setting of the spring/summer 1990 womenswear campaign, a formal gown and an oversized suit look at home because of their relaxed styling.

Along with the juxtaposition of cultural references, the coupling of high and low is typical of Armani. A beaded ensemble from the spring/summer 1994 women's collection is based on the everyday tunics worn by Northern African men. Combining a brightly striped, collarless work-type shirt with a man's dress suit or cropped Indian-influenced pajama pants with a tailored woman's jacket in his spring/summer 1992 campaign, Armani creates the casual air for which he so well known. Like the clothing, the Moroccan interior against which these ensembles appear conjures the slow, languorous rhythms of hot, sultry climates.

Just as Armani refers to cultures around the world, he also invokes the Western colonialist past in his spring/summer 1994 campaign. Set against the backdrop of an archeological dig, the images remind us of the romantic past that Armani is mining—an idealized, impossible place that exists in the marriage of opposites that Armani brings to his clothing.

Spring/Summer 1992

Spring/Summer 1978

Spring/Summer 1990

Spring/Summer 1992

Spring/Summer 1989

173

Spring/Summer 1994

54

54. Woman's overshirt and pants, spring/summer 1994. **55. Woman's shirt and skirt,** spring/summer 1994. **56. Woman's evening pantsuit,** spring/summer 1994. **57. Woman's pants ensemble**, fall/winter 1994–95.   From the sun-bleached, earth-toned palette and simple shirt and pant forms of everyday menswear seen in parts of the Islamic world, Armani has created luxurious though understated apparel for women. His allusions to regional costume typologies are often of the most mundane examples: the bib-front tunic shirt, the loosely fitted vest, the cotton caftan. In the

55

56

57

four ensembles illustrated here, Armani has replaced the quotidian muslins and durable plain weaves of Northern African and Middle Eastern apparel with the luxury of Italian textiles. Silk gauze and organza substitute for rough crinkled cottons, and glass bugle beads are used to render the effect of woven stripes that are the common adornment of light Berber wools.

58   59   60

58. Man's sports jacket ensemble, spring/summer 1991. **59. Man's suit,** spring/summer 1990. **60. Woman's jacket and pants,** spring/summer 1993. **61. Woman's jacket and sarong pants,** spring/summer 1994.   Armani's imagination does not appear to be circumscribed by the specific realities of his travels. Near and Far Eastern traditions are assimilated and digested, but so transformed in his designs as to be only the faintest of

adumbrations. The signs he uses to suggest an orientalist "other" are generally more allusion than they are quotation. A sand-toned palette, a shirttail-like overskirt, or a knotted closure at the waist of pants are typical of the small evocative details on which Armani's fictive geographies rely.

62

63

64

62. Woman's pants ensemble, fall/winter 1994–95. **63. Woman's jacket and dress,** spring/summer 1994. **64. Woman's jacket and pants,** fall/winter 1994–95. **65. Woman's evening gown,** fall/winter 1994–95. **66. Woman's floor-length dress,** fall/winter 1994–95. Here, layering, tonal mixes of richly textured fabrics, and an ostensible simplicity of cut suggest the clothing of Northern Africa and the Near East. But, as in much of

65

66

Armani's work, the apparent rusticity of the textiles and seemingly rudimentary pattern pieces are only a subterfuge. Textiles with sophisticated crepe and gauze weaves or complex knitted and crochet-effect patterns have been engineered into carefully manipulated geometries that belie the subtle mastery of their construction.

182

67

67. Woman's evening vest and pants, spring/summer 1994. **68. Woman's evening dress,** spring/summer 1995. **69. Woman's evening dress,** spring/summer 1995. **70. Woman's evening vest, overskirt, and pants,** spring/summer 1993.   The fields of elaborate floss embroideries and passementeries that enrich caftans and djellabahs are interpreted here in elaborate beadwork on silk organza. Yet while the floral and small

68

69

70

geometric motifs were inspired by Islamic patterns, the sheerness and zonal exposure of these dresses and ensembles are in radical opposition to the clothing paradigms that are their source. Even as extrapolations of specific regional styles, they unabashedly express the sensibilities and mores of the high-fashion system of the West.

71

72

73

71. Woman's evening tunic coat and pants, fall/winter 1990–91. **72. Woman's evening pants ensemble,** spring/summer 1990. **73. Woman's evening dress and pants,** fall/winter 1994–95. **74. Woman's evening jacket and skirt,** spring/summer 1995. **75. Woman's evening jacket and divided skirt,** spring/summer 1995. **76. Woman's evening "polonaise" ensemble,** spring/summer 1988. While most of Armani's work that alludes to the Islamic world finds its sources in peasant and nomadic dress with their spare ornament, strong textural appeal, and simple forms, the

74

75

76

designer is inspired as well by Persian and Mughal miniatures, and the fictive world represented by the nineteenth-century orientalist painters. In addition, patterns and colors from tiles, carpets, and antique textiles percolate through his eveningwear. But no single element is transposed without interpretation, while his sources become obscured in a febrile cultural fusion.

77

78

79

77. Woman's evening vest, overskirt, and pants, spring/summer 1994. **78. Woman's evening jacket and pants,** spring/summer 1994.
79. Woman's evening pantsuit, fall/winter 1990–91. **80. Woman's evening jacket and pants,** fall/winter 1995–96. **81. Woman's evening jacket
and pants,** fall/winter 1990–91.   Chinese artifacts and costumes—from Shang bronzes and mandarin badges to Ming ceramics and Manchu robes—

80

81

emerge here as contemporary eveningwear. In Armani's designs, however, patterns of identifiable provenance are often mixed with elements of deliberately obscure origins. In his synthesis of the recognizable with the unfamiliar, Armani has taken undeniable poetic license. The result is a chinoiserie with elements at once studiously esoteric and wildly inchoate—both historically charged and convincingly modern.

82

82. Woman's evening gown, fall/winter 1995–96. **83. Woman's evening dress with overshirt,** spring/summer 1998. **84. Woman's evening ensemble with wrap skirt,** spring/summer 1998.   Armani looks to the Far East in the eveningwear pictured here, but though his rendering is faithful in parts, it is also inarguably subjective, like Roland Barthes's "reading" of Japan in *Empire of Signs* (1982). Motifs derived from Chinese dragon robes and

83

84

Japanese decorative arts are described in elaborate seed and bugle beading, a technique alien to both Asian cultures. Additionally, dragonfly and mugho-pine patterns and a rainbow border are situated, juxtaposed, and repeated in a fashion not seen in their original sources. Most notably, Armani reduces to body-cleaving sheaths the voluminous layering of Manchu court dress and the padded waist of the obi-wrapped kimono.

85

86

85. Woman's evening jacket and culottes, fall/winter 1982–83. **86. Woman's evening jacket and pants,** fall/winter 1990–91. **87. Woman's jacket and culottes,** fall/winter 1980–81.   The fall/winter 1980–81 season, which was characterized by severely planar, origami-like geometries, surprised a public who had preconceptions about Armani's vocabulary of relaxed and supple forms. To this day, however, it is one of the designer's favorite collections. Inspired by Akira Kurosawa's 1980 film *Kagemusha*, the collection ranged from space-age evening ensembles based on the armor of

87

feudal Japan to sportswear that sourced the short jackets and *monpei* trousers still worn by farmers in rice fields. Over the years, the designer has reprised elements from that collection, but has further invested them with a graphic sensibility more akin to the costumes of the Russian Constructivists than to traditional Japanese dress.

192

88

89

90

88. Woman's evening shirt and floor-length skirt, spring/summer 1997. **89. Woman's evening shirt and pants,** fall/winter 1997–98. **90. Woman's evening jacket and pants,** spring/summer 1997. **91. Woman's evening tunic coat and pants,** fall/winter 1990–91. **92. Woman's evening jacket and pants,** fall/winter 1990–91.   Here, clothing elements from the Malay peninsula and the Indonesian archipelago are the basis for sportswear-like

91

92

evening ensembles. Small, tight shirts are paired with siren-fitted beaded skirts or transparent trousers; the long sashes that secure jackets and overshirts in the originals have been eliminated or displaced. Further, the mixing of Chinese and Nepalese influences with the batik patterns more typical of Indonesia results in a convincing synthesis of place and culture that in fact exists only in the designer's imagination.

93   95

94

93. Woman's strapless evening ensemble, spring/summer 1993. **94. Woman's evening vest, overskirt, and pants,** spring/summer 1993.
95. Woman's one-shouldered evening ensemble, spring/summer 1993. **96. Woman's evening blouse, pareo, and skirt,** spring/summer 1990. **97.**
Woman's strapless evening ensemble, spring/summer 1990.   In these evening ensembles, wraps and overskirts allude to the sarongs and pareos

96

97

that function as the basic modules of Pacific Basin dress. Prints of dense vegetation and idyllic tropical pastorals recall the paintings of Henri Rousseau and Paul Gauguin, invoking the natural splendors of Southeast Asia and the South Pacific as transmitted through the nineteenth-century European imagination.

98

99

101

100

98. Woman's evening tank top and skirt, spring/summer 1993. **99. Woman's evening jacket, overskirt, and pants,** spring/summer 1993.
100. Woman's evening dress and pants, spring/summer 1993. **101. Woman's evening jacket, overskirt, and pants,** spring/summer 1993. **102.**
Woman's strapless evening gown, spring/summer 1993. **103. Woman's strapless evening gown,** spring/summer 1993. **104. Woman's strapless**
evening gown, spring/summer 1993.   The Southeast Asian men's fashion of suit jacket over sarong or dhoti-style bottoms is transposed here to

102

103

104

women, embellished with pattern, and reconfigured through the multiple layering of sheer parts. Eveningwear is treated as sportswear, with interchangeable elements of such lightness and transparency that they billow in movement or collapse in body-revealing folds, rather than encumbering the silhouette. In a typical Armanian mixing of cultural forms, the three Polynesian-style gowns on the right are as indebted to Southeast Asian ceremonial skirtcloths as they are to Tahitian pareos.

ARCHITECTURE AND DESIGN

THE ELEGANCE OF THE EVERYDAY:
THE INTERIORS OF GIORGIO ARMANI

Donald Albrecht

Clothing, it's been said, is the first level of architecture. Both art forms protect the body from nature and reflect a person's taste. Throughout his thirty-year career, Giorgio Armani has adapted his fashion sensibility to architecture and interior design in the spaces in which he lives and works. Collaborating with many architects and interior designers, including Michael Gabellini, Gabriella Giuntoli, Keith Hobbs, Peter Marino, and Giancarlo Ortelli, Armani visually unites his diverse settings—from residences in Italy and the south of France to offices in Milan—with neutral colors, sumptuous materials, and simple forms. A worldview that prizes comfortable and casual elegance defines the Armani style.

Armani's interiors wear their clothes on the inside. Tented dining rooms and canopied beds are softly draped pavilions within harder-edged buildings. As in his clothes, Armani's interior-design aesthetic is based on opposition: translucence and opacity, pattern and solid, modern and traditional, East and West, black and white. Reflecting the same language of juxtaposition, the buildings Armani lives and works in are powerful historical shells in which he fashions modern, upholstered fantasies. In architecture, as in fashion, good bones matter.

Fabric, texture, and pattern—the building blocks of fashion—understandably play essential roles in Armani's interiors. Armani defines space with gently draped fabric in the same way he clothes the body in silk, linen, and wool crepe. The rippling horizontal ribs of a translucent tunic in Armani's fall/winter 1990–91 women's collection reverberate in the dining room of his former home on Milan's Via Santa Cecilia, where Japanese-inspired bamboo screens thinly veiled the backlit ceiling and lush landscaped garden beyond. The rough stucco and stone exterior of his house on the Mediterranean island of Pantelleria contrasts with its soft, smooth interior, and its roof undulates like white sails in suspended animation. Fusing primitive and sophisticated, the house is a distant cousin of the late-1930s villa built by Curzio Malaparte on the island of Capri, immortalized during Armani's formative years by Jean-Luc Godard in the director's 1963 film *Le Mépris* (*Contempt*).

Giorgio Armani's former office at Via Borgonuovo 21, Milan

The canopied pavilions at Armani's homes in Saint-Tropez and Pantelleria are large, tented outdoor rooms with the scale and domestic finish of indoor spaces. Just as Armani often inverts clothing conventions in his fashions—decorating a bustier with jeweled appliqué and making it the top of a dress rather than hiding it underneath—he creates similar indoor-outdoor inversions in his homes.

Armani also juxtaposes old and new. In the main reception area of his former headquarters in Milan's seventeenth-century Palazzo Durini, which he occupied from 1977 to 1982, simply shaped low sofas and ottomans, overstuffed and loosely shrouded in white cloth, were set within a vaulted gallery of epic proportions, rococo decoration, and huge mirrors. The effect was surreal and ghostly, evocative of the underworld in Jean Cocteau's classic 1946 film *La Belle et la Bête* (*Beauty and the Beast*). A lone black telephone, which seemed to float above a white marble table, suggested the presence of unseen visitors.

This forbidding reception area upturned expectations and revealed how Armani can surprise. In the midst of sophisticated elegance, he is not above a touch of gentle provocation. Just as his beaded dresses recall lingerie, his office's low, soft couches suggested languorous eroticism. And in the ultrarefined, urban setting of his Milan apartment, Armani has unleashed a hint of the jungle in the form of a sculpture of a black panther ready to pounce.

This love of opposition can also be seen in the work of filmmaker Luchino Visconti, an artist Armani greatly admires as an avatar of European culture and refinement. Both filmmaker and fashion designer share an obsessive attention to detail and a love of luxury. In Visconti's 1963 masterpiece *Il Gattopardo* (*The Leopard*), characters in opulent costumes dance in glamorous interiors like models on a fashion runway. In his *Gruppo di famiglia in uno Interno* (*Conversation Piece*)— released in 1975, the year Armani launched his label—the main characters inhabit two different apartments in the same historic building, one of which is overdressed baroque, the other sleek

Fall/Winter 1990–91

Dining room in Armani's former apartment
at Via Santa Cecilia 5, Milan

mid-1970s modernism. The contrast between them propels the plot.

Armani's interiors extend traditions of twentieth-century modern interior design. Aware of Italy's unparalleled architectural legacy, the nation's postwar architects and designers showed a remarkable capacity to respect tradition while embracing avant-garde forms, materials, and technologies. Italian architects such as Franco Albini deftly renovated historic masonry structures by installing minimal, lightweight furnishings in metal and glass, as in the Museo del Palazzo Bianco in Genoa (1951). Postwar Italian design gained greater respect internationally, with Milan, Armani's home base, positioning itself as the center of design activity. At the same time, the high-style decor in the films of postwar Italian directors from Michelangelo Antonioni to Bernardo Bertolucci burnished the country's aesthetic reputation. *Italy: The New Domestic Landscape*, the landmark exhibition organized by Emilio Ambasz and presented at the Museum of Modern Art, New York, in 1972, solidified Italian design's authority, setting the stage for the rise of Italian fashion designers such as Armani.

Even more significant in Armani's evolving aesthetic were 1930s interiors by French designer Jean-Michel Frank, who "unfurnished" a room in order to decorate it, just as Armani "undresses" a woman in order to clothe her. Frank moved in the stimulating world of prewar Paris fashion, designing interiors for such tastemakers as Lucien Lelong, Elsa Schiaparelli, and Guerlain. Like Armani, he achieved a harmonious classicism that straddled tradition and the avant-garde. Like Armani, he prized proportion, balance, and refinement and replaced excess with austere forms and well-crafted details. "One doesn't work in centimeters," Frank said, "but in millimeters."[1]

In his interiors, Armani adopts Frank's style of carefully orchestrated ensembles of simple, generously scaled furnishings, rich materials, a limited palette, and vernacular traditions. Armani's apartment on Milan's Via Borgonuovo, set within a late-sixteenth-century building, re-creates the spirit of Frank's own 1930 Parisian home and his masterpiece, the 1936 Paris apartment for Charles and

Spring/Summer 1991

Chimney corner in Charles and Marie-
Laure de Noailles's Paris apartment
designed by Jean-Michel Frank, 1936

Marie-Laure de Noailles. Armani's living room features a Frank-designed sofa and screen, walls of light-hued oak, and club chairs upholstered in raw silk. The carefully edited selection of boldly scaled lamps and objects mimics the Frank originals and recalls the way Armani accessorizes his couture collections with single pieces of overscaled jewelry.

Armani's former office in the same building, too, was pure Frank. Credenzas were tableaux of casually arranged books and mementos. Frank-style club chairs provided seating for guests. The centerpiece was a trestle table—a traditional workhorse of the farmhouse or factory—made elegant with ample proportions and high polish. Its utilitarian sources were echoed in metal industrial drafting lamps.

In this approach, which elevates the vernacular to the formal, Armani found a stylistic counterpart to his fashions. Staples of Armani's collections year after year are T-shirts, cardigans, and pullovers recontextualized through masterful tailoring and the use of exquisite fabrics.

Armani, in fashion as in architecture, discovers inspiration in the everyday and the elegant. He is the visual arbiter of a global empire, not only capturing the public's imagination with his distinctive style of comfortable, casual refinement, but also transforming his personal vision into a defining philosophy of modern life.

Note

1.   Quoted in Léopold Diego Sanchez, *Jean-Michel Frank* (Paris: Editions du Regard), p. 18.

Andrea Branzi

In Catholic cultures, elegance of clothing has always been seen as a useless pretense, a worldly vice unsuitable to a moral public that finds in modesty the motifs of conservation and thrift. This culture—even today—often sees fashion as a minor, mercantile, almost vulgar phenomenon. Thus fashion emerged in Italy without any true roots, with few and isolated prophets and a market that had never been consolidated. Certainly, the system did not seem destined to produce a great number of talents within a short period of time.

But this was not the first time that Italy had defied expectations, that a negative environment had produced its exact opposite in terms of aesthetic production. Renaissance culture, for example, emerged within the fractured, uncertain, and conflict-ridden political context of fifteenth-century Italy. One might almost say that Italians appear to have the capacity to invert or at least interrupt the usual cause-effect relationship, so that aesthetic production moves in the opposite direction from the context within which it is created. This has happened not only in art, but also in design and fashion.

The rupture that was the early Modern movement in Italy formed a new link in a vast chain of previous ruptures, which in their totality paradoxically constitute a specific and recognizable cultural continuity. Ruptures and faults produced by the weakness of cultural systems are continually subjected to recurrent crises, and precisely because of this cultural producers have found unexpected openings to the new and unforeseen that make up for the lack of established power, which often produces rigidity and a rejection of innovation.

At the beginning of the twentieth century, the Italian avant-garde looked pessimistically upon myths of progress, which was seen by the Futurists as the producer of change without end and without purpose, and by the Metaphysical artists as a suspended existential condition that offered no answers because there were no questions. This pessimism had its roots in the unexpected cultural and industrial upheavals in society at the end of the nineteenth century—upheavals that were animated by a polemical energy, a radical opposition that found release in aesthetic research

Spring/Summer 1995   Spring/Summer 1980

and its underlying theories. Amid a lack of real political transformation, and in the absence of broader effectual conditions, Italian policies and strategies often seemed to assume the form of art, design, or clothing, affirming the powerful role of aesthetics and its capacity to achieve extreme and clever syntheses.

More attention needs to be paid to the period when the phenomenon of Italian fashion began to assert itself in the world, and to the general meaning that Italian fashion had at that time. The late 1970s saw a rise in theories advocating complexity, understood as the dismantling of markets and large political units, within a society that was experiencing the advent of the postindustrial condition in terms of conflict (including terrorism). Within this context of uncertainty and fragmentation, within this socially provincial environment where grand politico-ideological alignments were in decline, Italian fashion under Armani brought about an authoritative change, defining its general role in terms of postmodernity and in opposition to classical modernity.

According to their traditional roles, one would have expected technology to produce certainties and stability, a solidity of ideas and design, while fashion—seasonal, ephemeral, capricious, produced by unpredictable creative types for a market of opinion leaders—would be relegated to a role of perennial hedonistic uncertainty. Instead, beginning with Armani, and then with other great Italian designers, fashion has offered, on an international level, an unfaltering and elegant continuity. For a society increasingly uncertain of its statutes and its role, and often still terrified of the future, fashion has provided a true aesthetic identity. Europe and the West (and Japan as well) saw themselves reflected in Armani's extraordinary statement, which offered both aesthetic certainty and clothing that stimulated the senses. With Italian fashion, the first real superstructure industry emerged, one capable of operating with very little investment and reaping very high profits based on great funds of charisma and intransigence.

In the world of electronic markets, where everything changes like the wind, where progress

Spring/Summer 1977

is the producer of continual obsolescence, Italian fashion was the first to break this cycle. Through the young Armani, it invented the evergreen of an elastic and moderately evolutionary neoclassicism, which contained the complexity of a turbulent, restless market and a decadent and corrupt society.[1] But, like true neoclassicism, which stands neither within nor outside the mediocrity of history, it neither participated in nor judged this world. If it has not yet succeeded in "saving the world with beauty" (as Fyodor Dostoevsky said), at least it has attempted to save beauty from attack by the world.

Armani's public debut in the latter half of the 1970s was announced in two deliberate products: the unstructured man's jacket (without shoulder pads) and the structured woman's jacket (with shoulder pads). From the point of view of design culture, one might say that Armani focused his attention on the joint—on a nodal aspect of the garment's sartorial structure, ignoring other questions secondary to its design. Thus he produced a slight shift in the parameters of classical beauty, directing it toward different references—such as Indian fashion. It was not a question, however, of ethnic style or Eastern quotations. For men, classical beauty has always entailed the structural and geometric continuity of the shoulder with the volumes of the torso and the body, while for women, clothing had to express fragility and brevity, in order to emphasize the curves of the hips and breasts. In contrast, Indian parameters of beauty are less unitary (or perhaps more polytheistic), in the sense that the human body is viewed not as a single, compact volume, but rather as a totality of autonomous figures, which describe a composite divine beauty made up of almost separate and dynamic parts. Shiva, who dances within a circle of flames, fittingly describes the sublime elasticity of Indian beauty.

With Armani, it almost seems that the male and female shoulders changed roles. The unstructured shoulders of the man's jacket define a more flexible, thoughtful male, and could be worn by a young gentleman, more likely the owner of a silk factory than of an ironworks. And the female shoulder belongs to an expansive woman, articulated in separate and harmonious volumes. Thus these garments of absolute simplicity fit within the best tradition of Italian modernity, which has always avoided the rigidity of Reason. They are the fruit of an Enlightenment of old that has never experienced revolution (there is no moralism or minimalism), and which extends from the times of Giuseppe Parini up to Franco Albini and Piero Manzoni.

During the years in which Armani came to the fore, Milan consolidated its role as a major exporter of beauty products. As is typical of the history of Italian aesthetics, this was accomplished in opposition to the general reality of the country and fueled by an energy that thrives on contention with its context. Fashion, design, and corporate communications became a sort of mobile system of identity for an ugly, violent city, threadbare in its public spaces, but beautiful, elegant, and refined in its private spaces—its houses and courtyards, the secret interiors of a bourgeoisie that was sensitive but had never assumed a public role. Thus Milan became synonymous with elegance, quality, and intelligent design.

Throughout the 1980s and 1990s, Milan—more than Paris or London—held the reputation as a center for innovation. It did not specialize in one particular commodity, as Carpi was known for its knitwear, Sassuolo for its tiles, or Prato for its textiles. Rather, the city and its surrounding district became known for its general approach to design, a creative vocation for research and innovation in both technical and aesthetic terms that may be applied equally to design, fashion, communications, or applied technology. It might almost be said that this city, which has the greatest concentration of designers and stylists in the world, exports innovation in many and various industries to many and various regions internationally. It is a place where technologies are tried out at their highest level of performance—that is, the aesthetic.

In part, Armani's success is aligned with Italy's substantial textile system, with its perfect spinning machines that guarantee the high quality of the country's fashion-production industry. One of Armani's accomplishments has been his ability to provide fashion with a broader definition, one that goes beyond the elaboration of signs, colors, and accessories. Armani was the first great designer to see his clothing as an integral part of a broader spatial universe, one that extended from the fashion runways to his stores, his houses, even his reserved lifestyle. But he has also provided a loftier definition of textiles, viewing them as participants on the public stage, as cladding for people, as a mass component of the urban landscape. Armani's collaboration with Marco Rivetti's GFT group was an occasion to experiment with a new unity between fashion's aesthetic and technical components. This unity helped to establish higher standards throughout the clothing industry, in Italy and abroad.

In doing so, Armani was an indirect participant in the evolution of society. Just as jazz has served to modify the entire sound of popular music, and as high art in the twentieth century has contributed to the development of visual mass communications, the contribution of fashion is not limited to the presentation of new models, but rather can intervene to modify the quality of a society's entire textile system. This is no small thing. Textiles are perhaps one of the material elements that best represent the level of a society's well-being. The quality of the threads, the endurance of the fabrics, the density of the knitwear, the definition and stability of the colors are all part of the perceptual basis of the economic and cultural wealth of a social group.

Along with the hegemony of England's woolen goods, the United States' close-woven cottons, and India's silks, Italy's textiles are a visual element, a mobile icon of its industrial culture, understood not only as a commercial reality, but more broadly as a decorative and thus social surface. In this way, fashion enters the sphere of energies that profoundly transform the material world. It can be placed among those evolutionary forces that raise up vast oceans of mass identity. In addition to the direct and immediate contribution of new forms of draping, then, the contribution of great designers like Armani must be evaluated in terms of the subtle weaves, the warps and the wefts, of the grand surfaces of mass society.

Note

1. When I speak of Armani's classicism, I am not referring to historical revivals, or to a proposal of systems of improbable certainties; rather, I am speaking of an open system of signs, a recognizable but incomplete code, and thus one that can be updated, one that is more concerned with quality than with style.

ARMANI AND ARCHITECTURE

by Lisa Panzera

Armani's collaborations with important architects are well known. Peter Marino designed Armani's flagship Madison Avenue store in New York, and Claudio Silvestrin his store on Place Vendôme in Paris. Michael Gabellini is currently at work on a three-story building on Via Manzoni, Milan, which will house several of Armani's boutiques, while Tadao Ando is renovating the Nestlé warehouse building, also in Milan, which will house Armani's new runway. All of these ambitious design projects express the beauty and simplicity of Armani's aesthetic.

Armani's home on Via Borgonuovo, Milan, indicates how clearly his life and work overlap: not only is it just buildings away from his headquarters down the street, but it is also—for now—the location of the runway where he presents his collections each season. Aesthetically, too, his home speaks to this convergence of life and work. The low beige sofas and pristine surfaces of its interior are indicative of the spare minimalism that dominates his clothing designs, a sleek modernity that is belied by the exterior of the building, a heavy stone structure located in an arcaded *cortile*. Using this typical Milanese facade as a foil for his elegant interior, Armani knowingly and intelligently exploited the contrast.

Parallels between Armani's clothing and the architecture that surrounds him abound. Perhaps most evident among these is the fact that his garments assume the colors of Milan itself: beige, gray, and "greige" (a color of the designer's invention). The architecture that Armani inhabits also reflects his penchant and talent for taking a well-known, long-established design—such as the suit—and, while keeping it recognizable, making it comfortable to live with and in. Just as he transformed the interior of his Milanese palazzo, Armani has stripped his vacation homes—in Pantelleria and Broni, Italy, and Saint-Tropez, France—of uptight formality in order to create simple and comfortable spaces to share with friends and family.

Pantelleria, a tiny, rocky, remote island off Sicily, has been described by the designer as a wild, magical, and sensual place. It is clearly a locus of deep inspiration. The rugged stone structure, pebbled white archways, and tented and canopied beds of his home on the island recall the novel plaids, beaded fabrics, and overlapping layers of transparent materials that have appeared in many of his designs.

Prominent in all of Armani's spaces is the play of surface qualities, and this is mirrored in his clothing, particularly in the feel, weave, and drape of the materials he uses. The influence of foreign cultures is also evident, as it is in his clothing designs: Moroccan tea sets and Japanese bamboo shades echo the long beige tunics and transparent, ribboned fabrics that have played central roles in his collections. But the presence of these elements points to a broader characteristic found throughout Armani's clothing: the Italian palazzo with modern furnishings and Japanese screens in Milan and the rustic refuge with sheer canopies and Northern African elements in Pantelleria equally underscore Armani's ability to mix elements from widely divergent sources.

Courtyard of Palazzo Durini, Milan,

Giorgio Armani's former offices

212

Armani's former offices in the Palazzo Durini, Milan, following two pages: Armani's vacation home in Pantelleria

217

Armani's vacation home in Pantelleria

Armani's apartment at Via Borgonuovo 21, Milan

Armani's apartment at Via Borgonuovo 21, Milan

following two pages: Runway at Via Borgonuovo 21

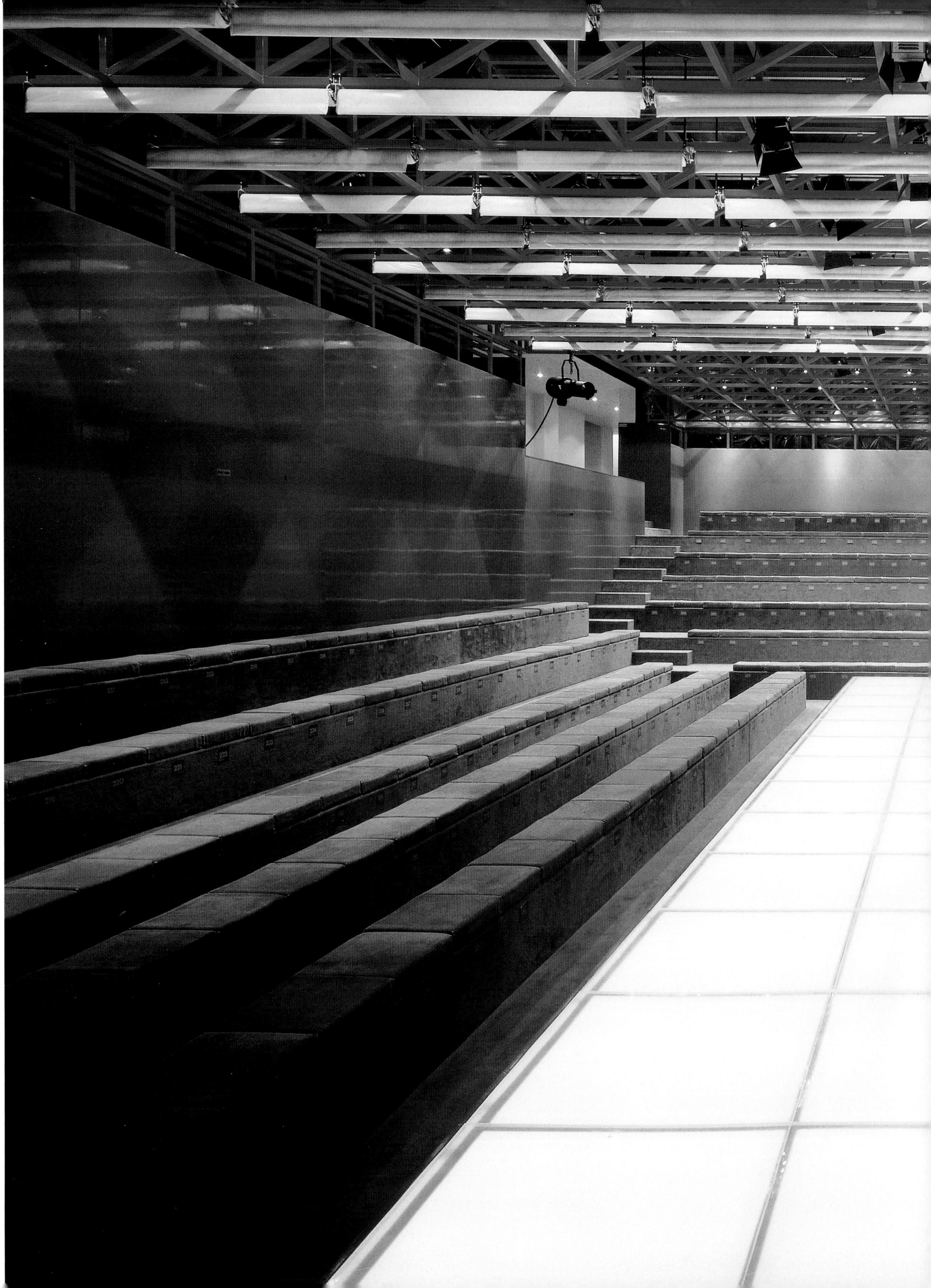

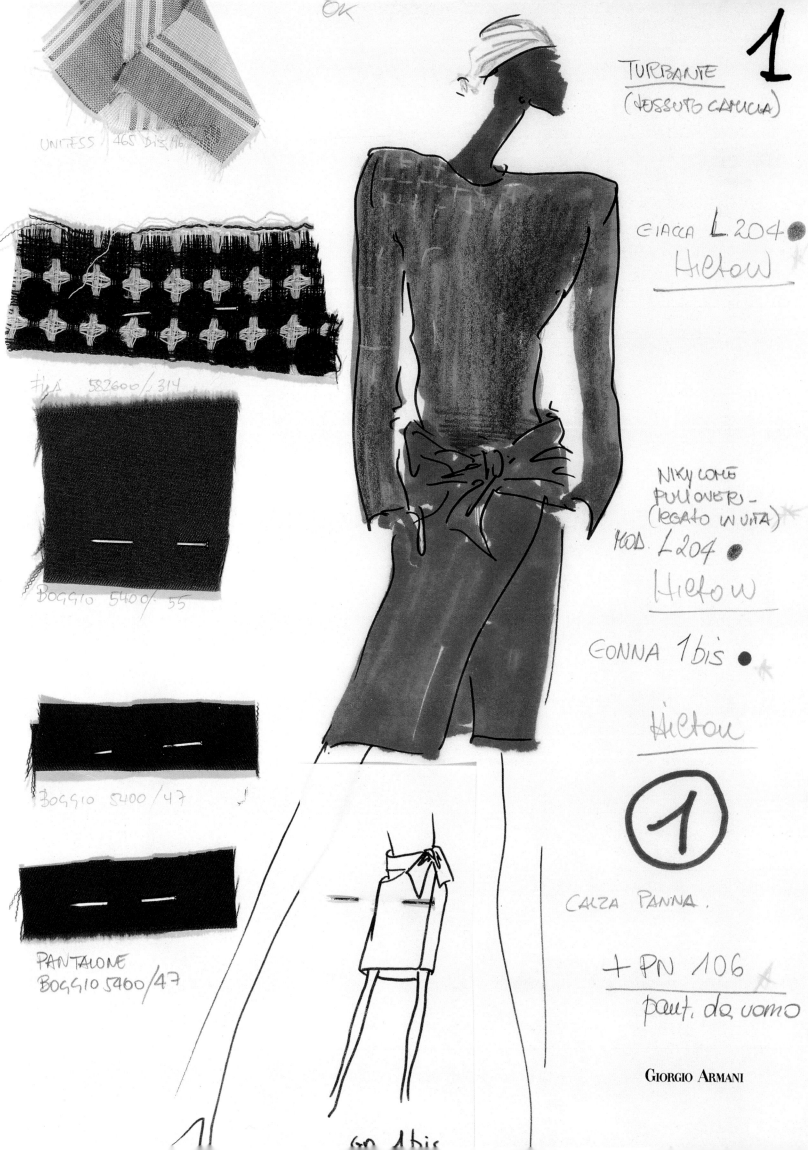

OK

TURBANTE **1**
(tessuto camicia)

UNITESS / 465 bis/46

GIACCA L.204 ●
Hilton

fire 582600/314

NIKY COME
PULLOVER -
(legato in vita)
MOD. L 204 ●
Hilton

BOGGIO 5400/55

GONNA 1 bis ●

Hilton

①

BOGGIO 5400/47

CALZA PANNA.

PANTALONE
BOGGIO 5400/47

+ PN 106
pant. da uomo

GIORGIO ARMANI

224

ARMANI AND TEXTILES

by Catherine Perry

Armani's use of textiles reveals a precise understanding of line and surface paired with an irreverent playfulness. Armani was the first designer to use two or even three different tweeds per garment, and his groundbreaking combination of traditional patterns—glen plaid with Prince of Wales checks or pinstripes, for example—gave birth to new and creative interpretations of classic looks. Traditional weaves were reborn and assumptions about these textiles, and of how to employ them, changed forever.

Layering—as in his conjunction of tweeds—is a central motif in Armani's work. Layers, both literal and implied, are achieved by his manipulation of texture and pattern as well as by the convergence of opposites: rough and refined, structured and loose, elegant and sporty, masculine and feminine. In adopting traditionally masculine fabrics, not just in menswear, but in women's suits and elegant dresses, Armani infuses these fabrics with unexpected glamour. Twill, a typically utilitarian weave, takes on a surprisingly light and feminine look when applied to skirts and suits. Wool crepe artfully maintains the authority of a suit while adding surface dimension with a nuanced delicacy, the crepe offering a fluidity and drape not possible with more traditional, heavier weaves.

Armani's talent for reinventing traditional concepts is evident in his incorporation of new technologies: his summer-weight fabrics such as silk, linen, and hand-finished wool, often appear to be organic even when they incorporate antiwrinkle surface treatments or lightweight technofibers. But this talent is equally evident in his novelty variations of classic patterns, such as houndstooth and herringbone, and in his technique of printing, not weaving, them on silk, wool blends, and even leather. Armani uses the pile or nap of the fabric to manipulate his patterns: naps of different lengths or directions, for example, create variations in color and design. In other instances, he uses the dimension of the fabric surface to help define the pattern, incorporating small peekaboo checks on a man's faux velvet shirt or silk-screening houndstooth on suede or wool blends. In fact, surface and texture often subvert structure as the defining element of Armani's clothing.

Along with the nap or pile of a fabric, Armani introduces surface dimension through the use of such innovative materials as corded silk, or by adopting techniques such as embossing on leather or fabric; beading over prints, checks, or lace; and quilting and basket weaves. The structure of his textiles ranges from heavy and coarse, the texture of burlap, to web-thin, the transparent delicacy of gauze.

Armani's love of art and its influence on his designs is evidenced by his use of patterns. His early prints and florals are complex: tiny flowers in relief on fabric printed with larger ones, or small abstract patterns whose negative space makes up a larger pattern. These latter are especially intricate, creating an organic unity that results in a muted elegance rather than chaos. Patterns may also be deceptive, appearing to have been printed on the fabric, while in fact being either woven into its structure or shaved into its pile surface. Embroidery and beading add another element to pattern and texture; often, they are used to create stripes or geometric patterns, or are sewn over printed or woven patterns or atop lace layered over florals. Appliqués, tassels, satin rosettes, and details like braided satin add dramatic and eccentric accents to Armani's idiosyncratic elegance.

225

facing page:

Sketch for Fall/Winter 1982–83

following three pages:

Sketches for Fall/Winter 1982–83

page 229:

Sketch for Fall/Winter 1997–98

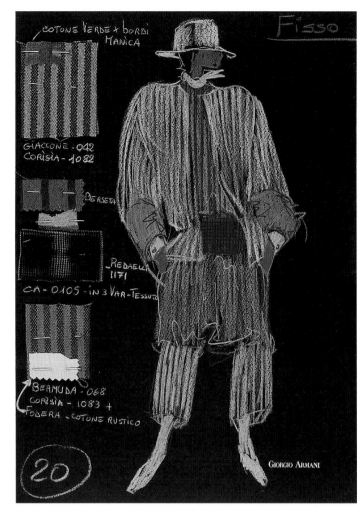

226

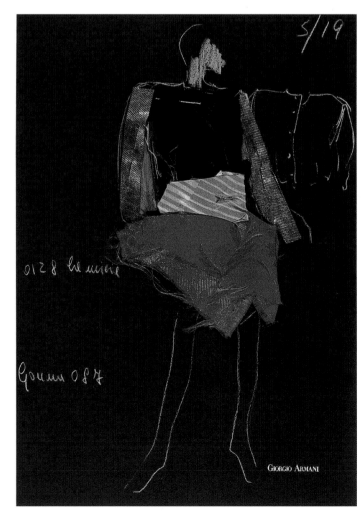

FISSO

SOPRA GIACCA
CORISIA - 1086

GI. 09
CORISIA - 1087

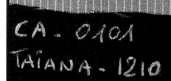

CA. 0101
TAIANA - 1210

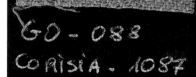

GO - 088
CORISIA - 1087

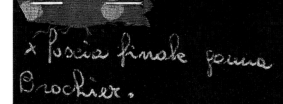

x fascia finale forma
Brochier.

⑰

GIORGIO ARMANI

227

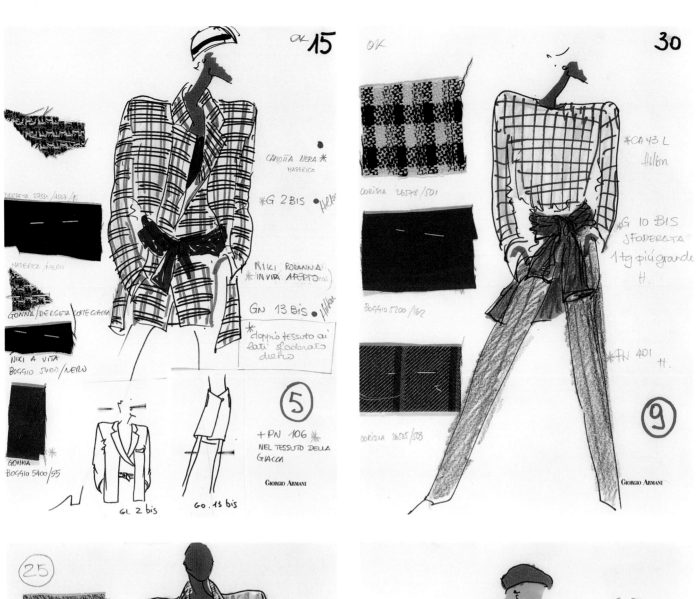

CANOTTA NERA ✳
MASERICA

✳ G 2 BIS ●

NIKI ROSANNA!
✳ IN VITA APERTO 6

GN 13 BIS ●

✳ doppio tessuto ai
lati sfoderato
dietro

⑤

+ PN 106 ✳
NEL TESSUTO DELLA
GIACCA

DERSETO 27331/4567/15

MASERICA NERO

GONNA/DERSETA SOTTE GIACCA

NIKI A VITA
BOGGIO 5400/NERO

GONNA
BOGGIO 5400/55

GI. 2 bis   Go. 13 bis

GIORGIO ARMANI

✳ CA 43 L
H6/6n

G 10 BIS
SFODERATA
1 tg più grande
H.

● PN 401
H.

⑨

CORISIA 26578/501

BOGGIO 5200/162

CORISIA 26585/508

GIORGIO ARMANI

228

㉕

GIORGIO ARMANI

G. 27

PN 7

GIORGIO ARMANI
B 11

V2 BIS

- GONNA IN VELLUTO
NERO SOIE DE TR.
FRANCE.
ART. 1005

229

- CORPINO
RICAMO: SHAMEEZA GA1
AL CAMPIONE

GIORGIO ARMANI

105

105. Woman's pants ensemble, fall/winter 1993–94. **106. Woman's pantsuit,** spring/summer 1995. **107. Woman's pantsuit,** fall/winter 1993–94.

Armani's affinity for a Bauhaus reductivism does not manifest itself as a blind functionalism. Rather, collarpieces, the skirt of a jacket, or the finish

106

107

of a lapel can become an ornamental flourish derived from a vestigial structural component. Form-giving details of tailoring and industrial techniques, sometimes refined and often mundane, are enlisted in a dual purpose: to shape and dress a garment.

234

108

109

110

108. Woman's suit, fall/winter 1995–96. **109. Woman's evening pants ensemble,** spring/summer 1999. **110. Woman's evening pants ensemble,** spring/summer 1998. **111. Man's leather coat ensemble,** fall/winter 1999–2000.   Here, Armani expresses a contemporary modernism by embracing the sensuality of materials and forms while applying a rigorous paring of extraneous ornament. Elements that are arguably less structural than decorative function as reinforcing signs of the designer's narrative intentions: the net skirt over trousers, for example, situates the ensemble

111

as eveningwear with gender transposition. On the other hand, connotative aspects of some designs are the serendipitous consequence of structural innovation. For example, a faintly Chinese-style jacket is actually the result of a reconsideration of the function of the lapel, and the tough, knife-edge street style of a leather coat is predicated on the lightness of a hem finish.

113

112

112. Man's suit, fall/winter 1991–92. **113. Man's raincoat and suit,** ca. fall/winter 1984–85. **114. Woman's evening dress and pants,** spring/summer 1993. **115. Man's coat and suit,** fall/winter 1999–2000. **116. Man's suit,** fall/winter 1999–2000. In menswear, Armani is known for his reduction and displacement of the padding and interfacings that constitute the construction of the traditional suit. Yet despite this transformation—and his introduction of textiles of unconventional weaves and weight that lent an unprecedented suppleness and comfort—his

114

115

116

237

earliest designs retained elements of the prevailing silhouette. Quickly, however, his collections offered a relaxation of these conventional style lines. As in a woman's coat or suit jacket by Cristóbal Balenciaga, Armani's tailoring obtains its fit as much from fabrics gliding away from the body as it does from contouring over the body's forms. In a conceptual reversal, the designer imposes a stiffly segmented geometry to a woman's evening ensemble. Even as he softens tailoring, Armani confounds expectations and introduces a crisp linearity to his dressmaking.

117

118

117. Woman's evening jacket and shorts, spring/summer 1992. **118. Woman's evening mini dress and shorts ensemble,** spring/summer 1991.
119. Woman's evening gown, fall/winter 1994–95. **120. Woman's one-shouldered evening gown,** spring/summer 1994.   Surface ornament, in Armani's hands, is implemented less for its decorative potential than for its capacity to alter a textile's physical properties. He uses beading as

119

120

texture and for its effect on the "hang" of a textile, producing, for example, a mail-like jacket or a heavily draped wrap dress. This interest in the mutable characteristic of materials is seen in the gown above (second from right), where the cloth's liquid folds freeze into tight pleats and stretch to a thin film like the transformation from water to ice and steam.

121

122

121. Woman's evening gown, spring/summer 1992. **122. Woman's one-shouldered evening gown,** spring/summer 1997. **123. Woman's evening gown,** spring/summer 1997. **124. Woman's evening gown,** spring/summer 1997. **125. Woman's one-shouldered evening dress,** spring/summer 1998. For all his attraction to the infinite variations of cloth and the three-dimensional potential of dress, Armani is essentially a modernist. Shorn

123

124

125

of excess, his gowns are often reduced to addressing a fundamental question of clothing construction: how to support the fabric's fall over the body. Like the biomorphic engineering of a Santiago Calatrava bridge, the expressive functionalism, reinforced edges, and curvilinear audacity of the shoulders and necklines bring aesthetic consideration to the most basic structuring of dress.

126

126. Woman's evening gown, spring/summer 1989.   The stark piping pattern of this gown delineates a projection of regularity onto the emphatically irregular contours of the body. Like the bias tapes that mark style lines on a dressmaker's dummy, the lines establish a series of pattern pieces. This simple geometric configuration of strictly orthogonal zones requires a sophisticated manipulation of the grain of the fabric. Paradoxically, unlike most of Armani's modernist seaming, the structural complexity of the gown's cut is not reflected in its ornament.

CINEMA

ARMANI, FILM, AND FASHION

Valerie Steele

Giorgio Armani has been influenced by films both in his clothing designs and his advertising. He has also been involved in many film projects, providing the on-screen wardrobes for actors and actresses and, in some cases, designing film costumes that then influenced his own collections. In all three areas—fashion design, advertising imagery, and film costume—he has exerted a powerful influence on the way people dress in the real world. There are many facets of his relationship with cinema— from the significance of Marlene Dietrich's androgynous style on Armani's designs for women, to the dissemination of the Armani style via films such as Paul Schrader's *American Gigolo* (1980).

The relationship between fashion and cinema has, of course, been the subject of considerable discussion ever since the 1920s and 1930s, when Hollywood movies focused attention on the styles of the stars. Fashion was clearly an important component of box-office appeal. Fashion publicity for upcoming films was widely disseminated, and consumers could acquire versions of studio styles through retail outlets such as Hollywood Fashions and Cinema Shops. Indeed, fan magazines, such as *Photoplay*, insisted that "Your Clothes Come from Hollywood."[1] Screen styles functioned simultaneously as dramatic spectacle, as a consumer guide to fashion trends, and as a way to emulate the stars.

The academic discourse on cinema costume has grown out of feminist film theory. Central to this critical endeavor is the argument that the image of woman is a "construction." By deconstructing this image, feminist film theory unveiled the fabrication of femininity. The paradigm of voyeuristic looking (the "male gaze"), which dominated early feminist film theory, was subsequently complicated by other theoretical paradigms that allowed for the possibility of alternate readings of filmic imagery. Significantly, the images of Dietrich were central to this analysis.[2] With the rise of queer theory, the fashioning of masculinities also became the subject of critical attention, and a more nuanced picture of cinematic style began to emerge. Identification with a film star might present viewers with models for self-determination, but the significance of that identification was no longer self-evidently hegemonic.

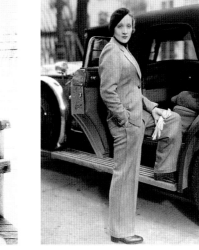

Fall/Winter 1990–91   Marlene Dietrich, 1930s

There is no doubt that glamorous stars influenced popular perceptions of how men and women should look, dress, and behave. In particular, Dietrich's fondness for trousers, both on- and off-screen, had a powerful impact on fashion in the 1930s and later. Dietrich's legs were notoriously exposed for her role in Josef von Sternberg's *Der blaue Engel* (*The Blue Angel*, 1930). Later the same year, she appeared in von Sternberg's *Morocco*, wearing a top hat, white tie, and tails, in a performance notable both for its gender ambiguity and for its erotic appeal to both men and women. Whether photographed onstage, on-screen, or on the street, Dietrich provided a range of iconic images that entered the collective visual lexicon.

"First, I uncovered my legs, and people were excited over that. Now I cover my legs, and that excites them, too," she told *Motion Picture* magazine in 1933. In "Marlene Dietrich Tells Why She Wears Men's Clothes!" Dietrich explained that "Women's clothes take too much time—it is exhausting, shopping for them. . . . Then the styles change—and it must all be done over again, every few months. It is very extravagant to dress as most women do. Men's clothes do not change; I can wear them as long as I like." Practicality was not the only issue, however. She continued, "I am sincere in my preference for men's clothes—I do not wear them to be sensational. . . . I think I am much more alluring in these clothes."[3]

Dietrich was frequently photographed off-screen wearing trousers and mannish tailored suits. Her transgressive self-presentation was imitated by other women, especially in Hollywood, resulting in "wild protests from the men." One newspaper article from 1933 referred to Hollywood as "Trouser-Land," and declared that the authorities "View with Alarm the Strange Spectacle of Women in Trousers." It was said that Dietrich "pioneered the fashion," and a "professor of abnormal psychology" gave his opinion that the trousered mode was the result of women's "blind striving for accomplishment in a man's field." Another newspaper article reported that "radicals declare that within another year working women will be wearing tailored suits to the office and store."[4]

Alfred Hitchcock, *Notorious*, 1946

In the 1930s, women's social and sexual modernity was more a question of image than reality, but it became more real by virtue of the growing acceptance of the pose. In fact, it was not until the 1970s that many women wore pantsuits to their place of work. Although it took a long time, women's appropriation of man-tailored pantsuits marked a pivotal moment in the history of women's rights. Many designers have been associated with this radical transformation of the female wardrobe, including Gabrielle "Coco" Chanel, André Courrèges, and Yves Saint Laurent, but there is no question that Armani was among the most influential. Fashion writers agree that Armani "evolv[ed] a new way of dressing for women that was not just a simple appropriation of items from the male wardrobe but the use of them as a source upon which to build. He developed a style for the working woman that had an understated, almost androgynous chic."[5]

In numerous interviews, Armani has stated that Dietrich's style was a powerful influence on his own work. In April 1995, the Berlin Martin-Gropius-Bau even mounted an exhibition entitled *Armani vis-à-vis Dietrich*. Certainly a comparison of period photographs of Dietrich with Armani's advertising imagery reveals a long-term infatuation with her style. The pantsuit in which Dietrich scandalized Hollywood in 1933, for example, provided the direct inspiration for several ensembles in Armani's collection of fall/winter 1990–91. Not only is there a recognizable resemblance in color and cut, but at least one advertising photograph, shot in nostalgic sepia tones, is styled with the same type of beret and gloves that Dietrich used to accessorize her notorious outfit.

Another series of advertising images used model Amber Valletta as a stand-in for Dietrich. In one picture, she wears trousers with the same pose of arrogant authority that Dietrich assumed. In another, she smolders in a sequined gown that recalls the one Dietrich was sewn into for her stage performances later in her career. (When drag queens impersonate Dietrich, they usually adopt this type of sparkling skin-tight gown.) Of Dietrich's films, Armani has mentioned in particular "the always-inspiring" Billy Wilder film *Witness for the Prosecution* (1957), in which she wears a dandyish dark

Steven Spielberg, *Raiders of the Lost Ark*, 1981

Spring/Summer 1982

suit and plays a woman who is not what she seems.

There are many more examples of direct influences from Armani's favorite films to his clothing designs, some more significant than others. Ambiguity and deception also characterize Alfred Hitchcock's *Notorious* (1946), a spy thriller starring Cary Grant and Ingrid Bergman. Grant, of course, epitomized the suavely elegant "Man about Town," as Richard Martin and Harold Koda observed in their influential 1989 book and exhibition *Jocks and Nerds: Men's Style in the Twentieth Century*.[6] In *Notorious*, Grant and Bergman play complex and mysterious characters—and they do so in remarkably similar checked suits, which seem the visual embodiment of their checkered lives. For his collection of fall/winter 1984–85, Armani created men's and women's clothing characterized by the same nuanced textures and patterns. Here, surfaces achieve primacy, and structure recedes into the background.

Martin Scorsese's *Taxi Driver* (1976) may have inspired Armani's spring/summer 1995 collection, with hot pants like those worn by Jodie Foster's teenaged prostitute, as well as a graphic black-and-white ensemble derived from the clothing worn by Harvey Keitel's pimp. Although attractive enough, these designs were not particularly directional. In contrast, Akira Kurosawa's masterpiece *Kagemusha* (1980) inspired Armani's magnificent samurai collection of fall/winter 1981–82, for which he designed leather body armor that still looks avant-garde today. Elegant, but more conventional, were the white evening dresses of spring/summer 1992, apparently inspired by the bias-cut gown worn by Dominique Sanda in Bernardo Bertolucci's study of Italian fascism, *Il Conformista* (*The Conformist*, 1970). Armani's fall/winter 1982–83 collection was inspired by Steven Spielberg's *Raiders of the Lost Ark* (1981), another film set in the 1930s.

Armani's advertisements also frequently utilize the poses and lighting techniques made famous by the glamour and publicity pictures of the stars of classical Hollywood cinema. Indeed, it appears that Armani has been influenced at least as much by the still photographs produced by the film studios as by the moving pictures themselves. This is perhaps not surprising, since it is the mythical aura of the star that is most relevant to the creation of a fashion image. Today the cult of personality is no longer restricted to Hollywood stars, and viewers of an Armani advertisement are implicitly invited to insert themselves into the stylistic performance represented before their eyes. This dynamic is made more complex still by the undeniable fact that Armani himself has attained star status and may be able to confer it on those who wear his clothes, which are immediately recognizable as such.

Of course, Armani designs have also appeared in films. Armani's first project was *American Gigolo*, for which he provided Richard Gere's wardrobe. According to publicity releases, no fewer than thirty Armani suits and jackets were featured in the film, along with numerous beautiful shirts. The clothes were chosen directly from Armani's menswear collection. These were not "costumes" especially designed for *American Gigolo*. Yet the identity of the Armani label was crucial to the definition of Gere's character as "an elite male prostitute in Beverly Hills," who is paid in sartorial gifts as well as cash. Indeed, according to journalist Judith Thurman, "His shopping trips provided the film's true sexual excitement."[7] In addition to seeing his clients buying him Armani clothes, we also watch the gigolo going through his closet and lovingly laying a selection of clothing on the bed. This scene is pointless in terms of the plot, since after packing a suitcase, the character never actually goes anywhere. In other words, the primary function of scenes like these is to establish that he is an Armani man.

According to Italian fashion writer Giovanna Grignaffini, people already had an image of Armani, so within the context of the movie, the clothes functioned as a sign "of verisimilitude." Not only were Armani's clothes immediately recognizable to a movie audience as items of "designer clothing," the clothes were "also perceived as being in the realm of values."[8] In other words, the public already knew that Armani clothing signified casual, expensive, sexy elegance. However, as Martin and Koda argue, different national audiences may have responded differently to the meaning of Gere's costuming; in their view, it was the film that "taught an American audience to understand the Armani menswear style."[9]

Certainly, *American Gigolo* reinforced an emerging image. As Armani told *Gentleman's Quarterly* in 1979, his style was "a study in making men look sexier."[10] Armani's clothes drew attention to the body at a time when men were increasingly willing to be perceived as sex objects. (This was also the period when Bruce Weber created Calvin Klein's men's underwear advertisements.) Significantly, however, an Armani wardrobe was also a status symbol, albeit one for a new age that valued both personal liberation and financial success. What made Armani clothing perfect for *American Gigolo* was the way it functioned as the tangible sign of money *and* sexual charisma. By 1982, Armani's reputation was so high that such movie stars as Jack Nicholson, Dustin Hoffman, and John Travolta, as well as Gere, were eager to tell a journalist from *Time* about their own Armani clothes.[11]

"Armani disarmed men and their clothes erotically without unmanning them," suggests Thurman. "He freed them to be looked at and desired by women (and other men)."[12] He accomplished this, I would argue, by creating a style based on the famous "unconstructed" jacket made of soft luxury fabrics. It was this jacket that was featured most conspicuously in *American Gigolo*, although Gere was also often shown in his shirt, and he undressed to exercise or make love. Since a desirable phallic hardness was visually represented by the hard body, clothing no longer needed to function as a defensive carapace but could instead be dedicated to the satisfaction of what Freud called "the libido for touching."[13] As Martin and Koda observe, the softer unconstructed jacket implies a "sportswear-like informality" that contrasts with the "unyielding structure" of the traditional business suit. They also note that "the shirt is often a focal point of the Armani ensemble," and they compare it with "the cascading luxury of Gatsby's shirts."[14]

Both film and fashion are an interpretation of the spirit of the time. This is true even of period costume dramas, like Brian De Palma's *The Untouchables* (1987), set in 1920s Chicago, when the gangster Al Capone battled Treasury officer Eliot Ness, and for which Armani created some five hundred garments. These costumes were not intended to be accurate historical reproductions. Instead, Armani made it clear that he wanted to interpret period style according to his own vision. For this film he created pinstriped suits with a high gorge and four to six buttons. Many of the actors also wore vests, period-style hats, and broad-shouldered topcoats. Perhaps inevitably, his cinematic designs ended up influencing the collection he was preparing for fall/winter 1987–88. Even without accessory weaponry, the collection emphasized physical power via the strength of the shoulder line.

Throughout the 1980s and 1990s, Armani worked on so many film projects—at least one hundred—that in most cases only the stars were likely to qualify for "costumes by Armani" or even "selected costumes by Armani." For example, Tom Cruise and Renée Zellweger wore sharp, stylish "costumes by Giorgio Armani" in Cameron Crowe's *Jerry Maguire* (1996), whereas actors in lower-budget films might have access, at most, to a "wardrobe by Giorgio Armani and Emporio Armani." Although individual actors are probably exquisitely aware of such distinctions, they are mostly irrelevant to audiences. Many viewers do see the screen credits, however, and are quite aware of product placement in films. Gregory Hoblit's 1996 film *Primal Fear* was not a fashion film the way *American Gigolo* was—in other words, Armani's clothes did not function as a virtual protagonist in this film—nevertheless, the suits and ties that Richard Gere wore in *Primal Fear* did effectively enhance his role as a smart and sympathetic lawyer. Likewise, for the new version of *Shaft* (2000), directed by John Singleton, Armani designed a streamlined, contemporary wardrobe. He reinforced the the ultra-cool, tough detective character of John Shaft, played by Samuel L. Jackson, using raw-edged sleek tailored leather jackets, sexy knits, and skull caps made from luxury fabrics. No doubt Armani, through his work for the film industry, will continue to create fashion trends and win new fans.

251

Notes

1.   Sarah Berry, *Screen Style: Fashion and Femininity in 1930s Hollywood* (Minneapolis and London: University of Minnesota Press, 2000), p. 16.

2.   Jane Gaines and Charlotte Herzog, eds., *Fabrications: Costume and the Female Body* (London and New York: Routledge, 1990), pp. 1–27. See also Gaylyn Studlar, *In the Realm of Pleasure: Von Sternberg, Dietrich, and the Masochistic Aesthetic* (Urbana: University of Illinois Press, 1988).

3.   Quoted in Berry, *Screen Style*, pp. 145–47.

4.   Quoted in Berry, pp. 154–55.

5.   Richard Martin, ed., *Contemporary Fashion* (Detroit: Saint James, 1995).

6.   Richard Martin and Harold Koda, *Jocks and Nerds: Men's Style in the Twentieth Century* (New York: Rizzoli, 1989).

7.   Judith Thurman, "A Cut Above: Giorgio Armani's Cool, Cool Elegance," *Connoisseur* (August 1988), p. 92.

8.   Giovanna Grignaffini, "A Question of Performance," in Gloria Bianchino, Grazietta Butazzi, et al., eds., *Italian Fashion: From Anti-Fashion to Stylism* (Milan: Electa, 1987), p. 24.

9.   Richard Martin and Harold Koda, *Giorgio Armani: Images of Man* (New York: Rizzoli, 1990), pp. 9–10.

10. Quoted in "Armani: On the Loose," *Gentleman's Quarterly* (September 1979), p. 120.

11. See Jay Cocks, "Suiting Up for Easy Street: Giorgio Armani Defines the New Shape of Style," *Time*, April 5, 1982, p. 60.

12. Thurman, p. 92

13. Valerie Steele, "The Italian Look," in Giannino Malossi, ed., *Volare: The Icon of Italy in Global Pop Culture* (New York: The Monacelli Press and Pitti Immagine, 1999), p. 91.

14. Martin and Koda, *Giorgio Armani*, pp. 9–10.

MADE IN MILAN: NOTES FOR A SCREENPLAY

Martin Scorsese and Jay Cocks

When the idea of making a short movie about Armani first came up in 1990, we had already spent a fair amount of time on the general subject of clothes. Although we knew nothing at all about design, we were aware that we liked to wear the results, and talk about them, too. Along with considering the finer points of mise-en-scène in, say, Carol Reed's *The Third Man* (1949), we also admired Joseph Cotten's suit and Trevor Howard's long dark overcoat, which we could never positively identify as either a belted rubber slicker or a black leather trench. For us, there was a romance connected with clothes that had much to do with movies, and nearly as much with our own fantasies of escape.

Made in Milan, as the Armani movie soon came to be called, was a chance to ground our own fantasies in reality, and then to establish a kind of alternative fantasy that had some basis in fact as well as in our imagination. The movie would try to chronicle our learning the fundamentals of a design process that ended in such offhandedly beautiful clothes. We hoped also to impart a sense of the mystery of the process, make a cameo portrait of our friend Giorgio, and try, as well, to get some incidental notion of the place he works in and the past he works from.

A tall order. We started to write, however, before any doubts could daunt us. The script that follows is the result. It differs significantly, even substantially, from the finished film, but re-reading this text we worked from, and subsequently revised, we think it has the merits of freshness and enthusiasm. It conveys—rather naively, in some cases—our subjective sense of how Giorgio creates. We were not after technical accuracy here, not at first, and, to anyone at all familiar with the demands and intricacies of a design studio, that will be abundantly clear. We wanted to give a sense of the difficulty of his creative process, as well as the sensuality of the creation, and in the unguarded rush to get all our thoughts and feelings down first on paper, we caught, it seems now, an impression that still surprises us of the feeling of the clothes, some fleeting sense of purpose and soft enigma of their special beauty.

We had Armani's own words to guide us. All his dialogue in the pages that follow comes from notes we made of conversations we'd had with him from years past, or, in a few cases, from unused interview material compiled originally for various articles in *Time* and elsewhere. With those words, we could roam at will and free associate. We thought repeatedly of some of Alain Resnais's early nonfiction films, especially *Toute la mémoire du monde* (1956), and perhaps you will sense the delicate shadow of that great filmmaker here and there, alongside Armani's own vigorous and skillful hands. We could never succeed in definitively showing, or even suggesting, how those hands finally form and shape his work, but we may have taken a step or two toward suggesting what keeps them moving.

AN ART GALLERY NIGHT

A large painting. Traditional. Covering a whole wall. TRACK along the painting on the wall. We see small groups of mannequins, looking at the painting, and other paintings near it. CAMERA moves with a young man (MALE MODEL 1), walking past the paintings and the mannequins (who may be part of the exhibit, or part of the public).

GA (VOICE OVER)

I thought there must be a way of refining the freedom I saw everywhere. I had to reject convention. But I didn't want to discard everything that was good in the past. I wanted to find a way to make and wear clothes for a time that was less formal but that still yearned for style. I had to start from the foundation.

CAMERA moves off MALE MODEL 1 as he passes GROUP of mannequins. MOVES IN to mannequin wearing very distinctive Armani jacket.

GA (VOICE OVER)

And, for me, the foundation was the jacket.

RESEARCH ROOM

A jacket. Literally being deconstructed in a SERIES OF DISSOLVES. Lining is removed. Inner lining is yanked away. Sudden, quick SOUNDS of tearing.

GA (VOICE OVER)

Taking the structure out of a man's jacket was a way of loosening the form. And finding a new one. Looking for elegance in ease. The style had to be almost surreptitious. I developed a way of buttoning and hanging which made the lapels fall a little bit forward, in a relaxed way. Not well-pressed. Not perfect. Not rigid.

DISSOLVES end on image of beautiful new Armani jacket.

MIRROR ROOM

Close on the same jacket, being shrugged on by a very beautiful MODEL 1. MOVE IN to her face.

GA (VOICE OVER)

My first jackets for women were in fact men's jackets in women's sizes. I'd noticed that when women were with their brothers or boyfriends, they were always trying on men's clothes . . . their jackets, their sweaters, and their trench coats.

Move back now to reveal: the jacket.

GA (VOICE OVER)

Once they put my jacket on, though, women could see they weren't really dressed like men. There was a very subtle proportion in the tailoring that made it different. But I kept the ease of the man's jacket.

Close on a hand moving (slow motion?) toward jacket pocket, finally resting there easily.

> GA (VOICE OVER)
>
> The jacket gave the same sense of comfort and security. She could put her hands in her pockets.

GA comes into frame. He removes MODEL 1's jacket, then helps MALE MODEL 1 into it.

> GA (VOICE OVER)
>
> But, for men, I also borrowed something from women. I wanted to give men some of the sensuality and suppleness in construction and fabric that were found only in women's clothes.

As GA continues to speak, in two-shot, young man finishes putting on jacket. Then he starts to leave. CAMERA unexpectedly PANS WITH MALE MODEL 1 as he picks up a SMALL VIDEO CAMERA and leaves the room. CAMERA follows.

HALLWAY

. . . as we FOLLOW MALE MODEL 1. MUSIC up; something like the Melodians singing "By the Rivers of Babylon." MALE MODEL 1 turns straight to camera.

> GA (VOICE OVER)
>
> Think of the way a man dresses. Think of it. It's totally irrational.

He aims the Sony Video 8 straight at the camera.

HALLWAY VIDEO

OUR MOVIE CREW: on VIDEO.

TRATTORIA

MALE MODEL 1, holding the Sony. Aiming right at us. Somebody takes the video camera from his hand, starts to shoot all the people sitting at the table.

ON VIDEO. MALE MODEL 1. And a group of friends. And waiters. And other diners, waving at the camera. And food. A full bounty of regional food on the table.

> GA (VOICE OVER)
>
> Sometimes beautiful. But irrational. Lapels on jackets, which serve no purpose. They're just decorative, like the collar and cuffs of a shirt. And the tie . . . a ribbon of tissue that dangles from your throat . . . it's just comical. How can we take ties seriously? We can't, really. But we do. Why? Probably because they're beautiful.

VIDEO shot ends on MODEL 1. She looks in the camera. Suddenly she grabs a jacket and tosses it over the lens. Screen goes BLACK.

MALE MODEL 1'S APARTMENT NIGHT

MALE MODEL 1 enters. Loosens his tie. Hangs up his jacket.

GA (VOICE OVER)

My jackets change all the time. The shape, the line, the detail. But always I want them to look as if they had hung in your closet for years. Like something that you'd owned forever.

Hold on jacket, as it hangs in closet, DISSOLVING TO . . .

MEN'S RESEARCH ROOM

. . . Drawing. Of a jacket.

Then we see: many sketches of designs. The drawings are part of a huge pile of fashion drawings and rough sketches.

GA (VOICE OVER)

Men's clothes are almost easy for me. A welcome routine. I do a men's collection the way a pianist might practice scales. But there's more to do with women's clothes. More shapes to try. More ideas more combinations. More anxiety. And more adventure.

ADVERTISING STILLS

by Karole Vail

Reflecting his longtime fascination with the cinema, Armani's fashion-advertising campaigns are infused with cinematic elements and atmospheres. A blurry image of a desolate car brings to mind the Italian neorealist cinema of the 1940s, and humorous echoes of Federico Fellini's 1970 film *I Clowns* (*The Clowns*) can be traced in the spring/summer 1981 men's Circus collection, photographed by Aldo Fallai. While postwar European cinema has inspired Armani throughout his career, it is the glamour, beauty, luxury, and illusory magic of Hollywood—and, in particular, its stars of the 1930s and 1940s—that have had the greatest impact on the designer's vision and the presentation of his image.

The fall/winter 1987–88 women's collection campaign, photographed by Fallai, features dramatically lit, seductive close-up portraits, recalling publicity shots of stars like Greta Garbo and Veronica Lake by studio photographers such as George Hurrell. The spring/summer 1991 campaign, again shot by Fallai, is similarly reminiscent of Hollywood photography. It also recalls the purposeful mystery of German-born photographer Horst's famed early formal studio shots of fashion models, photographed with meticulous precision against austere and often geometric backgrounds.

The nonchalant, cocky couple in the fall/winter 1993–94 campaign evokes the mythical bank robbers Bonnie and Clyde, with a sense of freedom elicited by the models' loose and comfortable clothing. A man sporting a tough-looking unzipped jacket, white T-shirt, and sneakers from the spring/summer 1997 men's collection recalls such legendary macho film stars as James Dean or Marlon Brando, while another wearing loose white trousers from the spring/summer 1996 collection brings to mind the legendary and elegant dancer and actor Gene Kelly. All three campaigns were shot by Peter Lindbergh, one of the first contemporary fashion photographers to appropriate cinematic lighting techniques to re-create the atmosphere of the film still.

Perhaps most influential on Armani has been the immaculately dressed star persona of Marlene Dietrich, the femme fatale par excellence. Her androgynous glamour and sexual ambiguity are conveyed in a collection of photographs by Lindbergh featuring model Amber Valletta wearing Armani. Significantly, in 1995, at the Martin-Gropius-Bau in Berlin, Armani curated an exhibition entitled *Armani vis-à-vis Dietrich*, which incorporated Dietrich's restored clothing as well as his own designs. The leitmotif of the exhibition was androgyny, exemplified by the tuxedo, suit jacket, and wide trousers, elements that have defined Armani's look for women throughout the years just as they characterized Dietrich's personal style.

Fall/Winter 1987–88

261

Spring/Summer 1981

Fall/Winter 1993–94

facing page: Fall/Winter 1993–94; above: Spring/Summer 1997;

right: Spring/Summer 1996

265

Spring/Summer 1991

Special project, Amber Valletta

photographed by Peter Lindbergh, 1995

ARMANI AND FILM COSTUME: CREATING CHARACTER

by Catherine Perry

Armani has provided wardrobes or costumes for over one hundred films internationally. But although the influence of the cinema on his own collections has often been considered, there is a converse relationship that is less explored yet equally enticing: What do Armani's designs represent, literally or symbolically, in a film? And further, how is a character defined by wearing Armani?

There is a saying among wardrobe designers: "The first thing to know about a character is how much money they make a year, then you will know how they dress." Certainly, Armani's "designer value" confers a certain economic status on those who can afford his clothes. But beyond the obvious attributes of wealth and luxury, there are personal qualities that are associated with them as well. His clothes imply an erotic subtext, an almost casual sensuality that is echoed in his relaxed structures and tactile fabrics. And, equally important, there is an inherent suggestion of class and taste. His clothes represent not just expensive designer wear, but they require a certain knowledge and refinement, a true appreciation of quality and beauty rather than ostentatious show.

In Armani's first film project, *American Gigolo* (1980), director Paul Schrader employed the designer to help define Richard Gere's character, an elite male escort to privileged status-discerning clients in Beverly Hills. The character's preference for Armani revealed a young, urban sophistication. As Gere's portrayal became the epitome of sleek sensuality in pursuit of money and power, Armani, already defined as "cool and sexy," became synonymous with seductive elegance. Soon after, 1980s icon Don Johnson, as a charming detective on television's *Miami Vice*, sealed Armani's fate as *the* designer for the charismatic, sexy male protagonist.

In films ever since, Armani has continued to represent beauty, taste, and subtle eroticism. In *The Comfort of Strangers* (1990), Schrader again used Armani to demonstrate wealth and power, this time portraying a more mysterious, menacing sexuality in the character of Robert, a dangerously sadistic Italian businessman played by Christopher Walken. Robert, obsessed by an English couple on holiday in Venice, is driven by a need for power and a quest to reclaim the sexual authority he feels has been lost by men of his generation. A sort of armor, his square-shouldered suits with soft-moving fabrics and clean lines embody the character's aspirations.

Armani's clothes have been used in films that cross worlds and times. In Brian De Palma's *The Untouchables* (1987), his "roguish," broad-shouldered interpretation of 1920s Chicago dress added panache and drama to the story, set in an era restrained by prohibition. Ten years later, in Andrew Niccol's *Gattaca* (1997), his designs embodied a vision of perfection and triumph in a futuristic, genetically enhanced world. And characters in the high-powered realms of Hollywood film and sports agency wore him like a banner of their driving ambition in Anthony Drazan's *Hurlyburly* (1998) and Cameron Crowe's *Jerry Maguire* (1996).

Even in comedies and lighter fare, placing characters in Armani can lend credibility to their causes and help to illustrate their struggles and aspirations. Here, Armani's role as the consummate standard of excellence and unparalleled good taste is often most clearly defined. In Michael Lindsay-Hogg's *The Object of Beauty* (1991), Armani was the choice for characters with faultless style and extravagant lifestyles, while in John Patrick Shanley's *Joe Versus the Volcano* (1990), Armani symbolized the modern American ideal of accomplishment: when Tom Hanks's character, Joe Banks, a depressed clerk with little in life, is offered a brief chance to live like a king, the first stop on his shopping spree is inevitably a Giorgio Armani store.

Paul Schrader, *American Gigolo*, 1980

Paul Schrader, *American Gigolo*, 1980

274

Brian De Palma, *The Untouchables*, 1987

Andrew Niccol, *Gattaca*, 1997

Anthony Drazan, *Hurlyburly*, 1998

Stephen Frears, *The Grifters*, 1990

John Patrick Shanley, *Joe Versus the Volcano*, 1990

Paul Schrader, *The Comfort of Strangers*, 1990

Walter Hill, *Streets of Fire*, 1984

John Singleton, *Shaft*, 2000

279

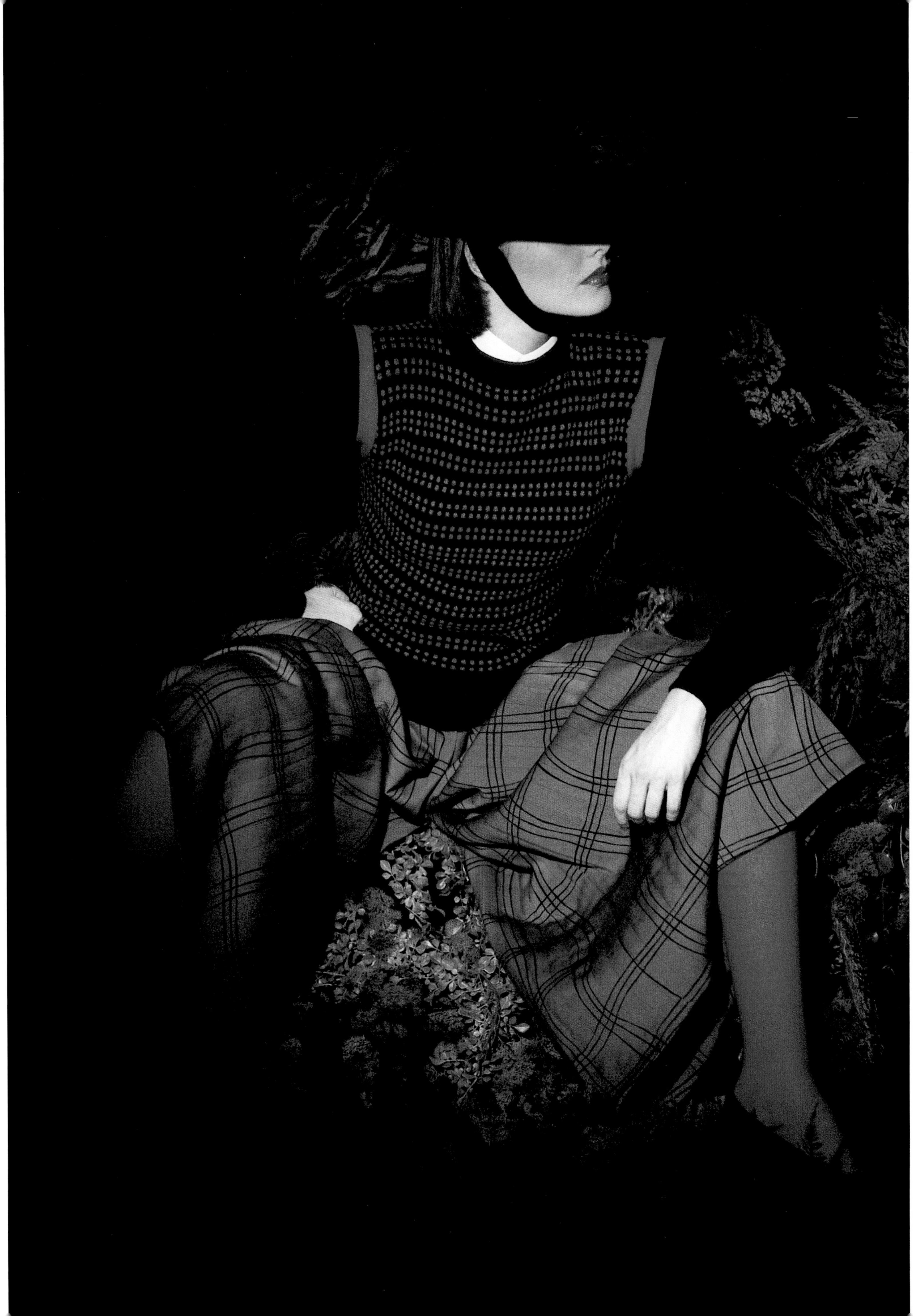

280

MOVING IMAGES

by Karole Vail

Armani has been influenced by the world of cinema ever since he was a small child in his native Piacenza. His father gently used to tease Armani and his older brother by promising that they might go to the cinema, the uncertainty enfolded in that very word "might" being quite unbearable to the youngsters. In fact, the boys were often taken to the local cinema on Sunday afternoons. Upon their return home, they would continue their cinematic experience with a multitude of invented stories that they related and acted out to their parents.

Armani's great fascination with the cinema has been brought to bear throughout his design career. Not only has he participated in the creation of films by designing wardrobes for an array of different movies, but this passion has also surfaced in his own collections. Often, his designs allude to cinematic memories of films he has seen by evoking their mood or costuming. One of Armani's earliest film memories, for example, is elicited in his spring/summer 1990 collection, in which tops with heraldic-looking motifs appear to hark back to the first feature film that Armani saw as a small boy: Alessandro Blasetti's *La Corona di ferro* (*The Iron Crown*, 1941), a kind of Wagneresque Nibelungen saga with highly decorative and extravagant costumes.

Some of Armani's favorite films are the Hollywood movies from the 1940s and 1950s, including Alfred Hitchcock's *Notorious* (1946) and Billy Wilder's *Witness for the Prosecution* (1957), whose glamorous female and male casts have stimulated his evening collections. The designer has also found inspiration in some of the works of the great directors of the latter part of the twentieth century, including Akira Kurosawa, Bernardo Bertolucci, and Martin Scorsese. The shimmering bustiers composed of compressed panels in Armani's impressive and critically acclaimed fall/winter 1981–82 women's collection can be traced to the *oyoroi*, protective armor worn by high-stationed Japanese warriors, seen in Kurosawa's warrior saga *Kagemusha* (1980). Ten years later, in his elegant spring/summer 1992 women's eveningwear collection, which included long dresses with generous décolletages and high frontal slits, and again in spring/summer 1996, Armani translated the chilling long, sleek, black and white evening gowns worn by Stefania Sandrelli and Dominique Sanda in Bertolucci's politically wrought *Il Conformista* (*The Conformist*, 1970). At the other extreme, in his light spring/summer 1995 women's collection, which included tiny beaded shorts and matching boleros, he adopted the sexy and playful ultrashort hot pants worn by Jodie Foster in Scorsese's tale of urban alienation, *Taxi Driver* (1976). And the following year he incorporated the tight white T-shirt worn by Harvey Keitel in the same movie into his minimalist spring/summer women's collection.

Fall/Winter 1981–82

above: Martin Scorsese, *Taxi Driver*, 1976

facing page: Spring/Summer 1995

284

facing page: Spring/Summer 1996

above: Martin Scorsese, *Taxi Driver*, 1976

286

above: Akira Kurosawa, *Kagemusha*, 1980

facing page: Fall/Winter 1981–82

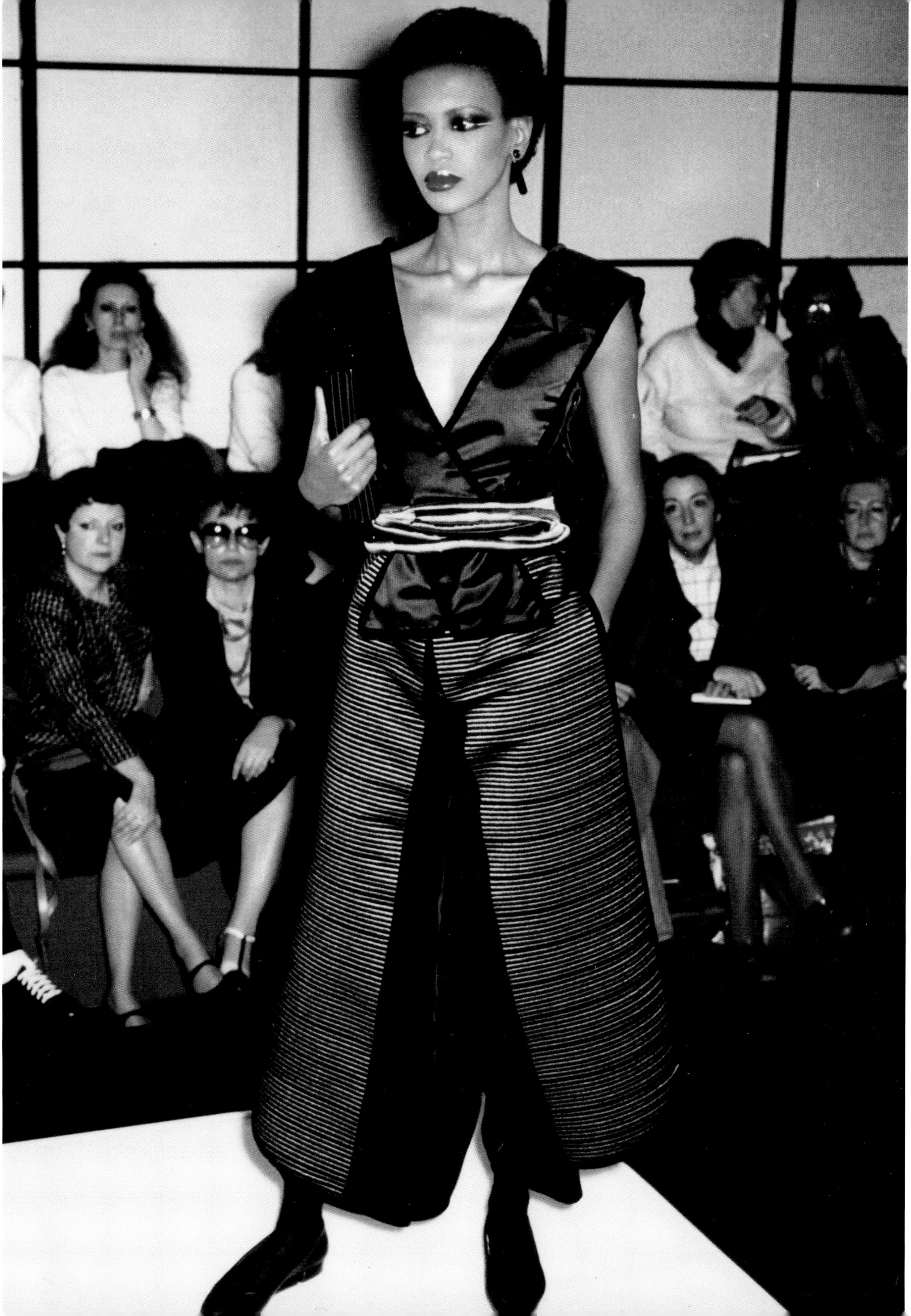

288

facing page: Spring/Summer 1990

above: Alessandro Blasetti, *La Corona di ferro*, 1941

above: Bernardo Bertolucci, *Il Conformista*, 1970

facing page, left: Spring/Summer 1996

facing page, right: Spring/Summer 1992

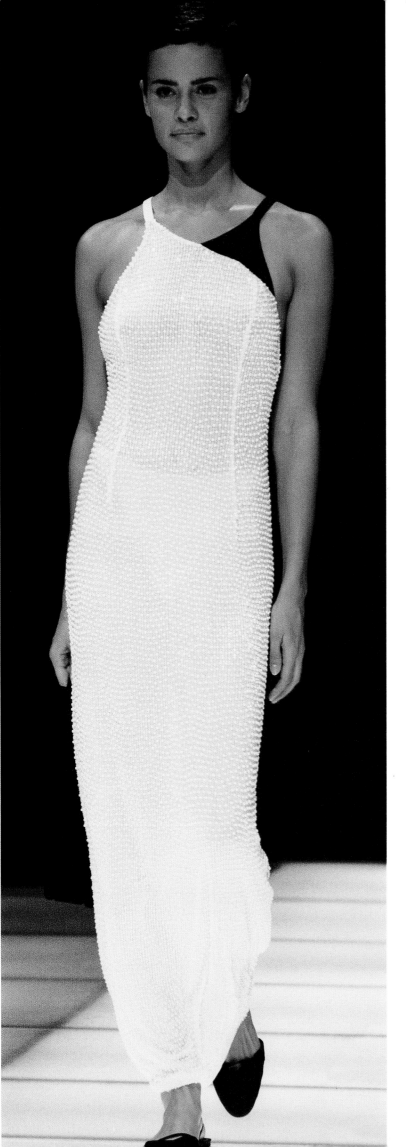

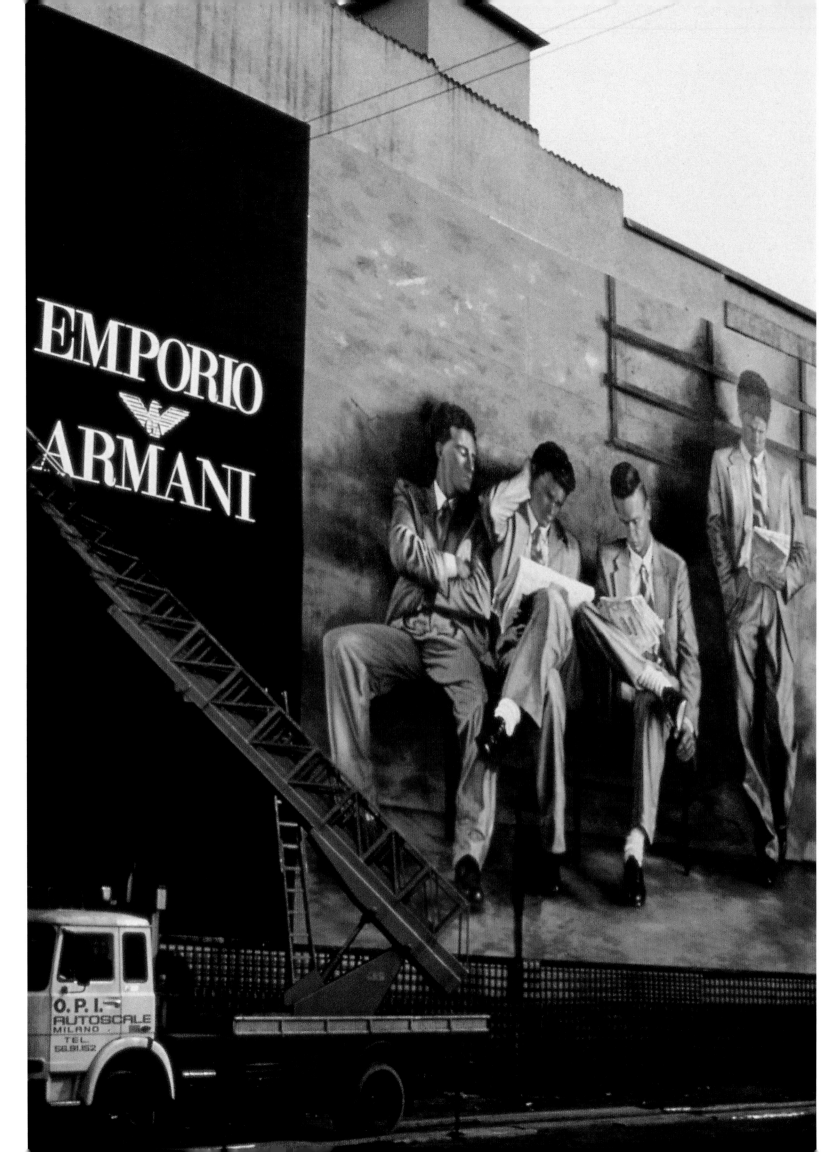

SNAPSHOTS OF MILAN: EMPORIO ARMANI BILLBOARDS

by Alberto Abruzzese

In 1984 a large wall on Via Broletto in Milan became both visible and invisible, when Armani installed the first in an ongoing series of vast, wall-sized images there. Though ostensibly advertisements for Emporio Armani, the images also revealed to the city Armani's dream: to have the eye, rather than bricks, bring forth the metropolis that had always been missing, not only from the Lombard capital, but from Italian culture as a whole. Via Broletto provides the best clue for interpreting Armani's wider aesthetic project, which extends well beyond the exceptional artistic and entrepreneurial success of a great designer.

Armani's metropolitan dream fit perfectly within certain fundamental coordinates of Italy in the 1980s. During these years the entry of private television into the old Italian media system (which tended to be monocultural) marked a quantitative leap in collective consumption, as the new television system fostered the rapid development of a mass-consumer audience. But the effect was qualitative, too: a process was set in motion whereby everyday life became metropolitan, modern, and the world of fashion offered a culture that was *different* from the forms and strategies of the market.[1]

Like Benetton, which was developing its corporate image during the same period, the Armani label was identified by a clear and strongly innovative marketing plan that rejected all preestablished boundaries between nationalities, genders, generations.[2] Yet while Benetton's advertising used the world of Benetton products for social critique, overturning their usual meaning, the world of Armani products, instead, was used to construct—in selective, indeed stylistic, fashion—an alternative for the mass-consumer imagination. Armani worked with the substance of dreams, with the temporality of myths, with comfort. He sought the extreme possibility that modern development still allowed for the transformation of the classical into experience, into present time, into use.

Exposed, the Via Broletto wall was transformed into a gigantic screen depicting Milan and its history. This was the Milan of consumers (*Milano da bere* [Milan, drink it in], as the well-known slogan for Ramazzotti by Marco Mignani said)—the industrial city where Italian modernity expressed both its aspirations and its endemic limits, without the alibi of being impeded by historical and bureaucratic ruins, as in Rome, or by a cityscape with a rich cultural patrimony but no mass of humanity or industry, as in Florence, or by a regal but expropriated grandeur, as in Naples.

Thus Armani exploited—in an utterly innovative way with regard to fashion-advertising strategies—the living medium of a city without equal within the Italian panorama. Milan straddles the static and dynamic worlds, a condition embodied in the urban landscape of Via Broletto, which can be read as a fracture between slowness and speed, city and metropolis, community and society. It is *here*, in this double nature, that Armani's images have not only their roots, but also their generative power.

The language of Armani's images, which is suspended between the casualness of graffiti and the predetermination of painting, was chosen by the designer in order to have the city speak about itself, about the life it has experienced, but also about something other than itself and thus of the metropolis. The images are characterized by a movement between the visible—pure and simple commercial advertising, its explicit writings, its simple posters—and what goes beyond the visible, what Armani, from the beginning, more than twenty years ago, saw in the "abyss between what people were beginning to want and what the industry was offering."[3] His billboard represented the definitive surfacing, after years of gestation, of a new subjectivity: the living body of the consumer, ever freer from the constrictions of high fashion, but also from the trivialities of mass production. Not only were they a sort of emotionally inventive graffiti, but they were also images of reality.

Year after year, Armani's Via Broletto site has celebrated both the expectation and the presence of another way of living: a sense of things and people, of places and experiences freed from the bonds of physical territory and tradition, depicted through a metropolitan dream. The dream is always the same and yet always different, just as the spirit of Armani's fashions, from the start, alternated between imagination and repetition. Within this rhythm, Armani created his casualness and freedom, qualities that sociologist Georg Simmel, in his 1905 essay "Philosophie der Mode," had seen in the manners of the metropolitan individual. Casualness and freedom distinguish the Armani jacket from all others. It has become the sign of an *Italian* sensibility of the metropolis, a sign so vivid that it has become a sort of logo recognized around the world.

In 1980, for the film *American Gigolo*, Armani dressed Richard Gere's character, whose frenzied meticulousness for his wardrobe would become—and this is no accident—the psychological cipher of the serial killer in *American Psycho*, the hyper-metropolitan 1991 novel by Bret Easton Ellis. So even prior to his murals, Armani had worked for Hollywood, a place that exists somewhere between the past (New York) and the future (Los Angeles). Armani knows the meanings of these great metropolises and he experiences their spaces. That world—where the realms of the imaginary and the real are so strongly integrated—forms his mental matrix and the matrix of what he wants to create. This causes him to go beyond being a mere creator of clothing and fashion shows, to become the designer and producer of a more ambitious undertaking. He creates the metropolis beyond the metropolis itself, even where it isn't, where it hasn't been, and where it never will be.

Armani began at La Rinascente, an Italian department store without the metropolitan quality of comparable stores in Paris or London. He delved into this cultural gap, finally recreating the metropolitan substance of Hollywood when he opened his own Emporio, a selling place where the object under the spotlight is a lifestyle, not a piece of clothing per se. This is the Armani who made the Via Broletto images possible.

Armani's images are an immaterial, abstract screen, but one that is inseparable from its physical, concrete site. They are a metaphor, not only of the spirit of fashion, but also of what is most profound about fashion, what nurtures it, the wellspring from which it draws: life. In the first billboard of 1984, four young, well-dressed young men appeared. Their ties said it was no longer the 1970s, but the new time of a more mature, mass democracy. They seemed to have been photographed in secret—that is, as if they weren't actors but real people, casual figures existing for themselves and not for the glances of those who, passing by, saw them in all the alienation of their gigantic dimensions.

This Gulliver effect, this distance/closeness between the everyday nature of the spectator and the artificial magnitude of the images, produced an amazement, a Benjamin-like shock that forced the passerby to observe in a mode of suspension or interval that could be called the mode of the sublime. One of the four youths, more relaxed than the others, takes care of himself rather than of his status. It was the first sign of a long dialogue between the simulacra of fantasy and the truth of things. From that time on, Armani's images have described the variations and nuances with which a quality suit—the idea of a suit, its sentiment—recounts the activities of the group and the clan, the sense of belonging and flight, closeness and detachment.

Translated from the Italian by Marguerite Shore.

Notes

1. On the television revolution of the 1980s in Italy, see Alberto Abruzzese, *Lo splendore della TV* (Genoa: Costa & Nolan, 1995).

2. On Toscani and Benetton, see Alberto Abruzzese, "Toscani: A Neo-Modern in a Post-Industrial World," in Leonardo Arte, ed., *Oliviero Toscani al muro/Visual Art in United Colors of Benetton Communication*, exh. cat. (Rome: Museo Nazionale delle Arti e Tradizioni Popolari, 1999), pp. 8–13. In Italian and English.

3. Armani, quoted in Linda Gobbi, Francesco Morace, Roberto Brognara, and Fabrizio Valente, "Emporio Armani: il boom dello stile trasversale," in their *I Boom. Società e prodotti degli anni '80* (Milan: Lupetti, 1990), pp. 119–47.

following eighteen pages: Fall/Winter 1998–99, Spring/Summer 1988, Spring/Summer 1990, Fall/Winter 1994–95, Fall/Winter 1997–98, Fall/Winter 1985–86, Spring/Summer 2000, Spring/Summer 1991, Fall/Winter 1992–93

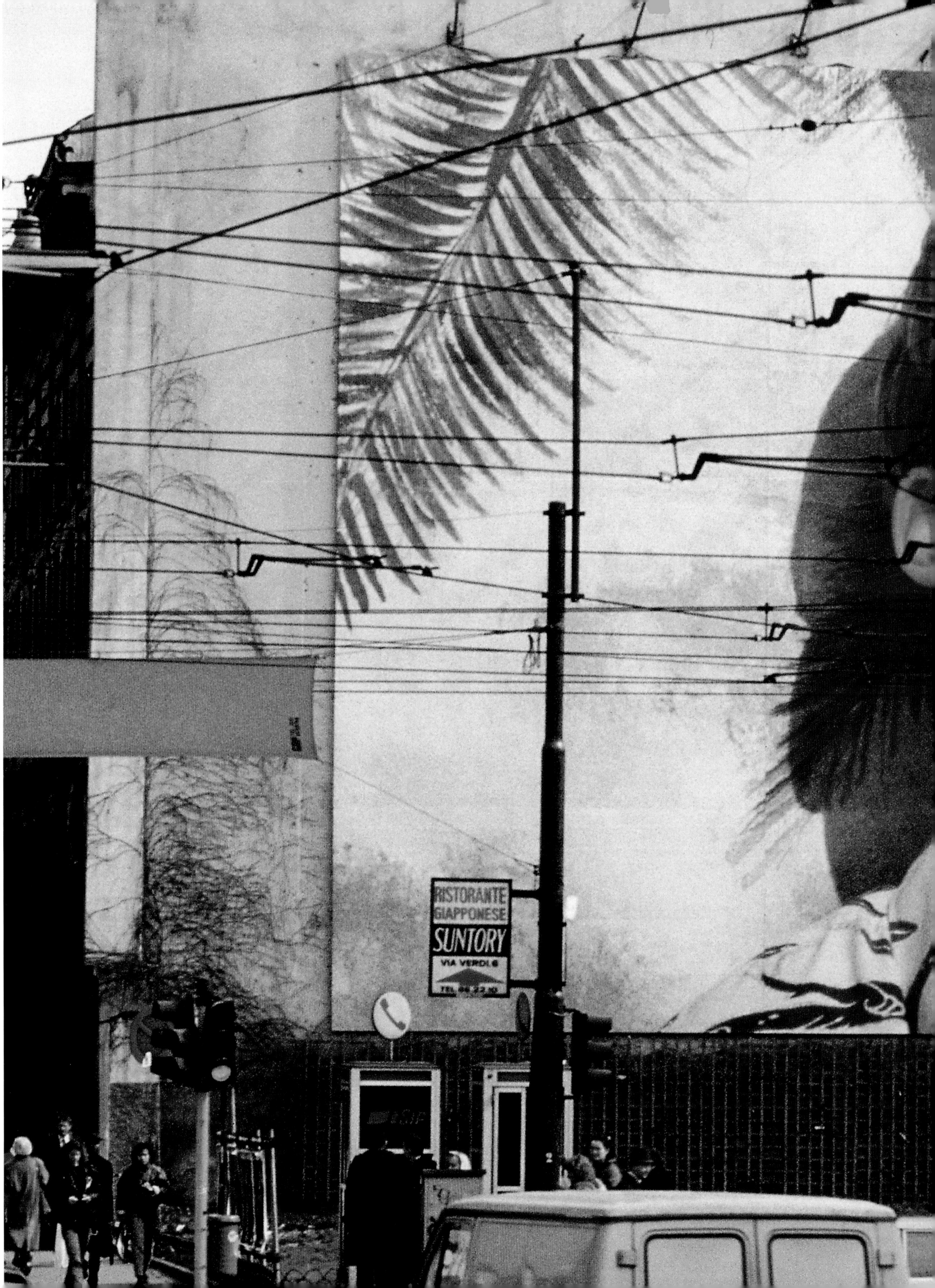
RISTORANTE
GIAPPONESE
SUNTORY
VIA VERDI 6

302

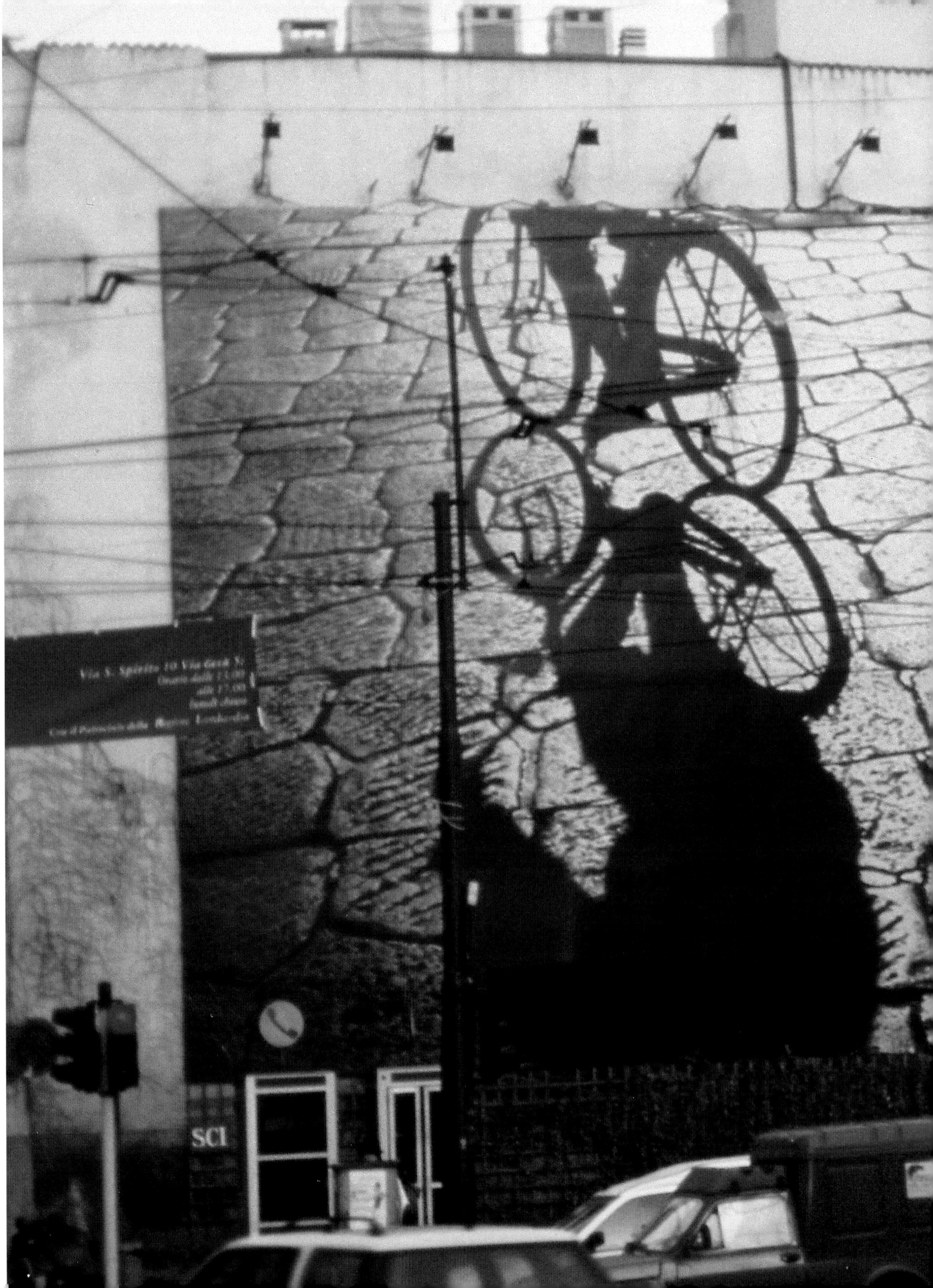

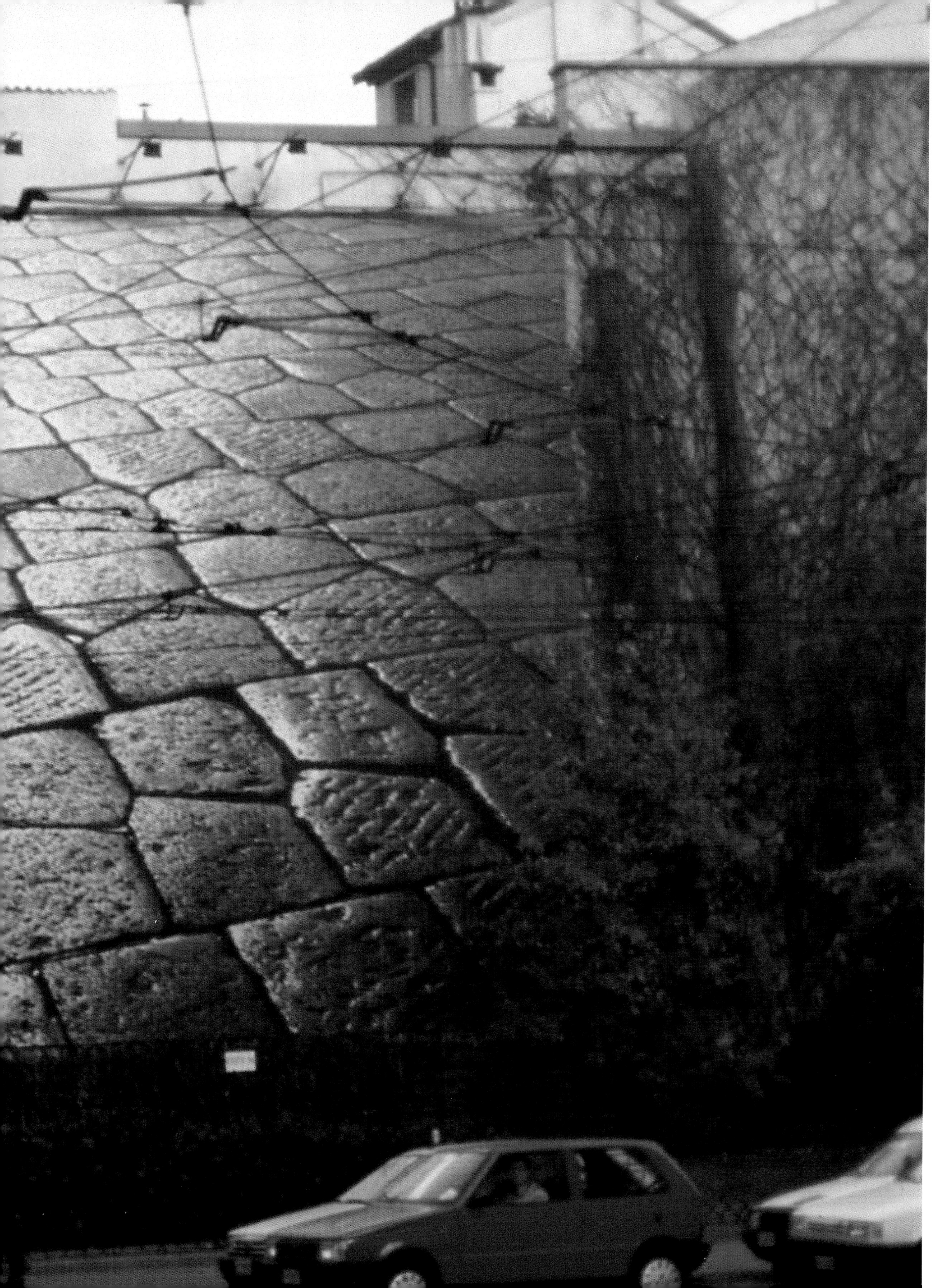

304

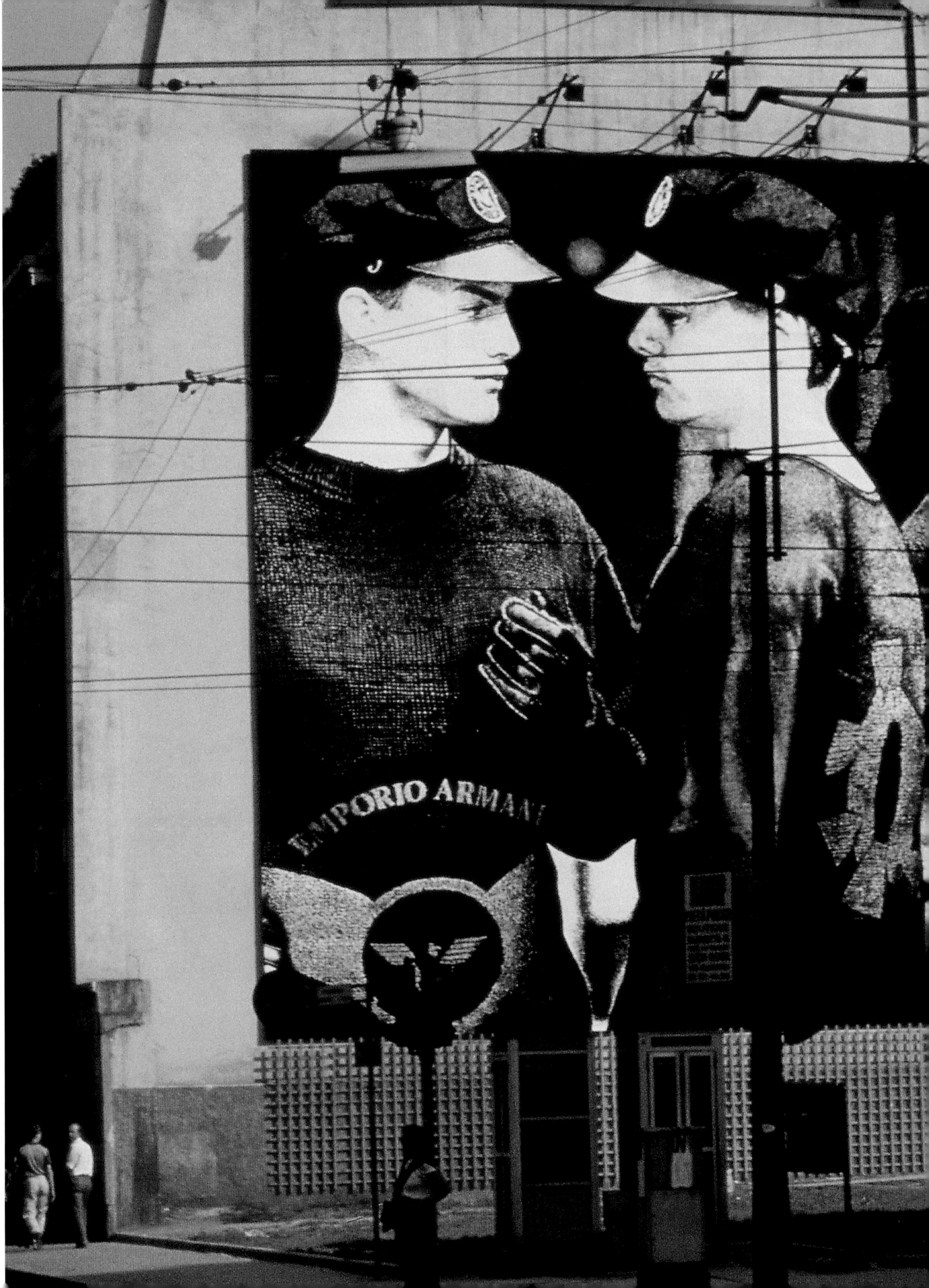
EMPORIO ARMANI

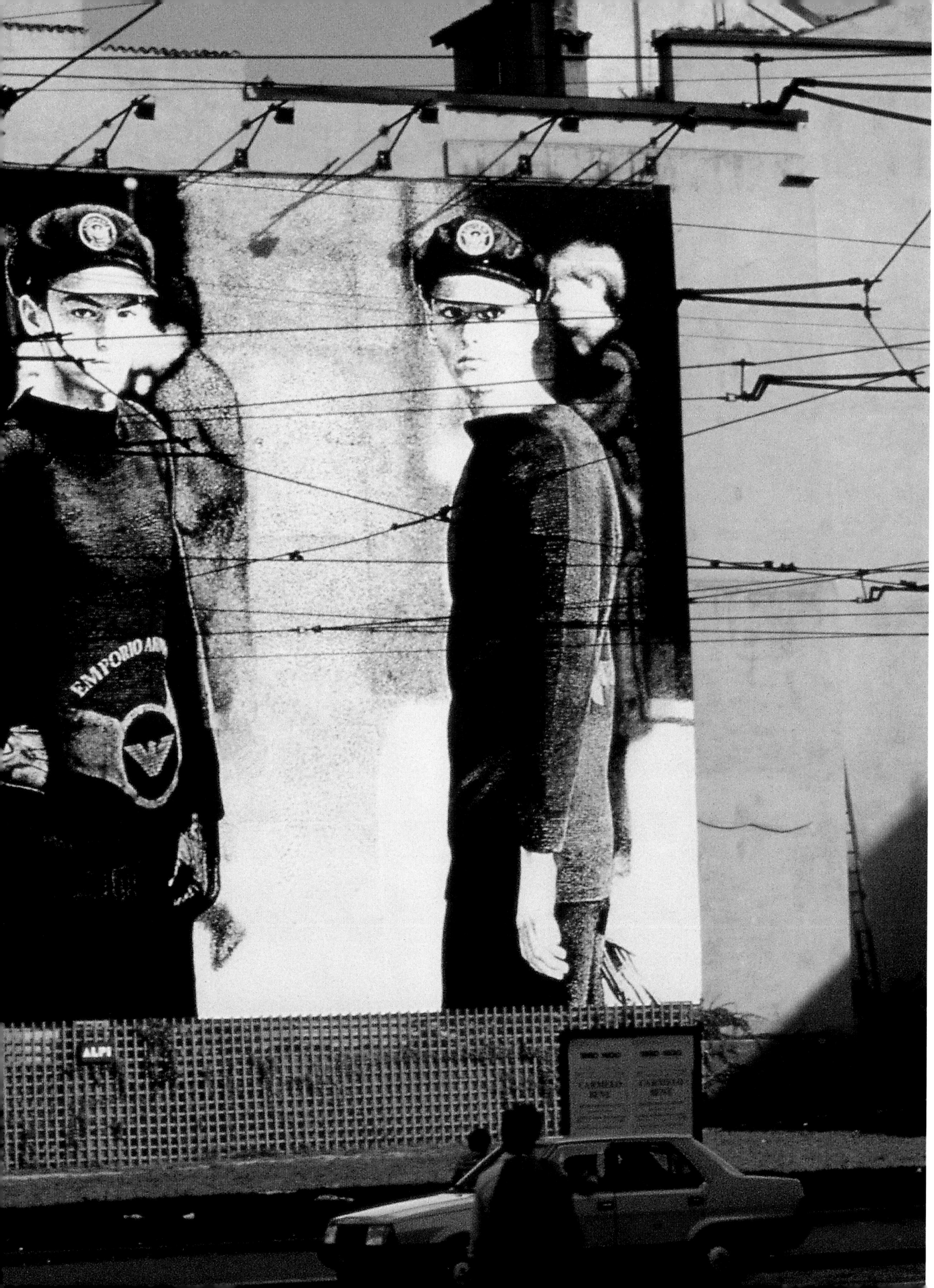
EMPORIO
ALPI

308

EMPORIO ARM
La Milano del Giovin Signore
Le arti nel Settecento di Parini
INTERCOOLER TURBO

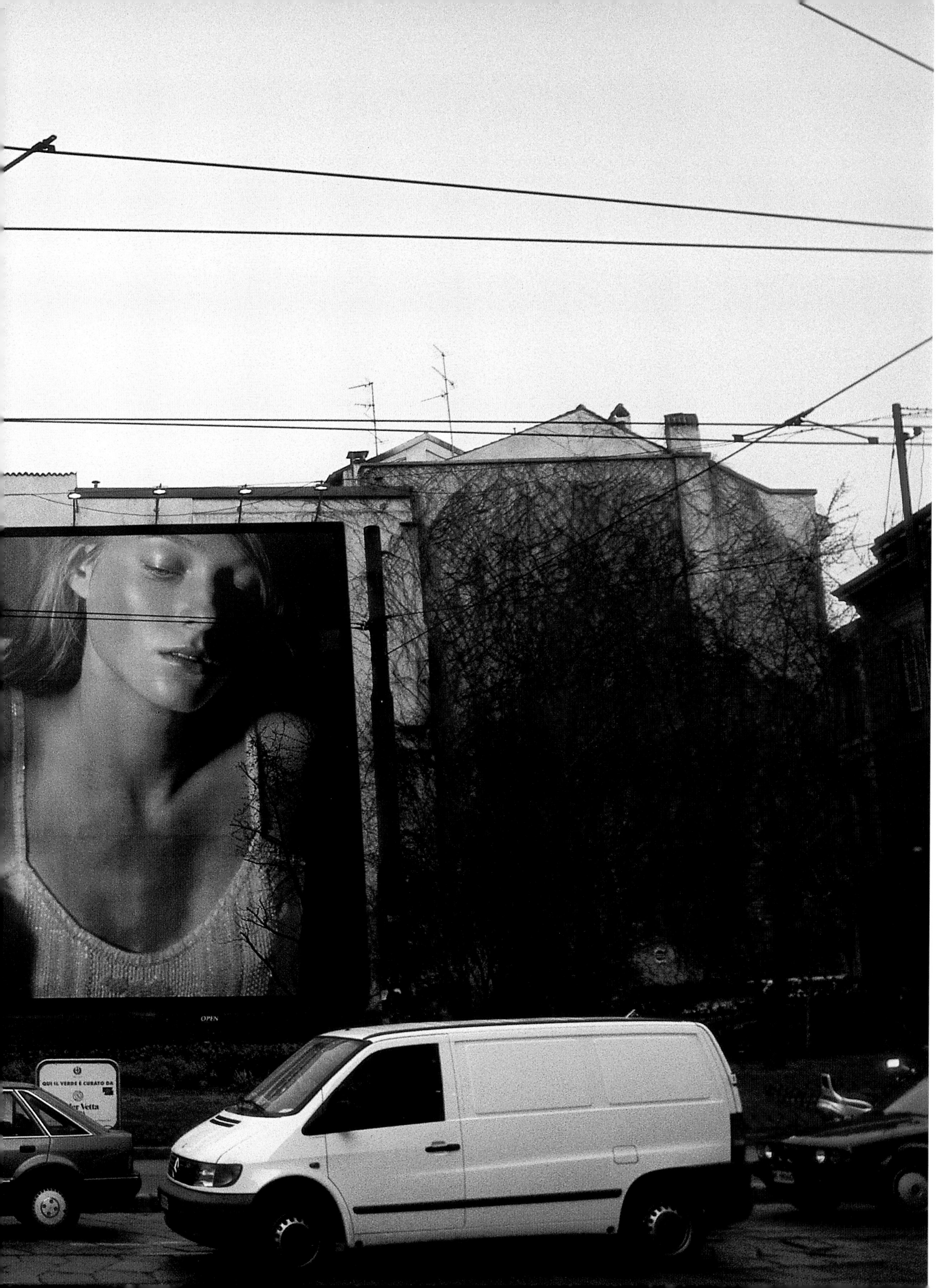
OPEN
QUI IL VERDE È CURATO DA

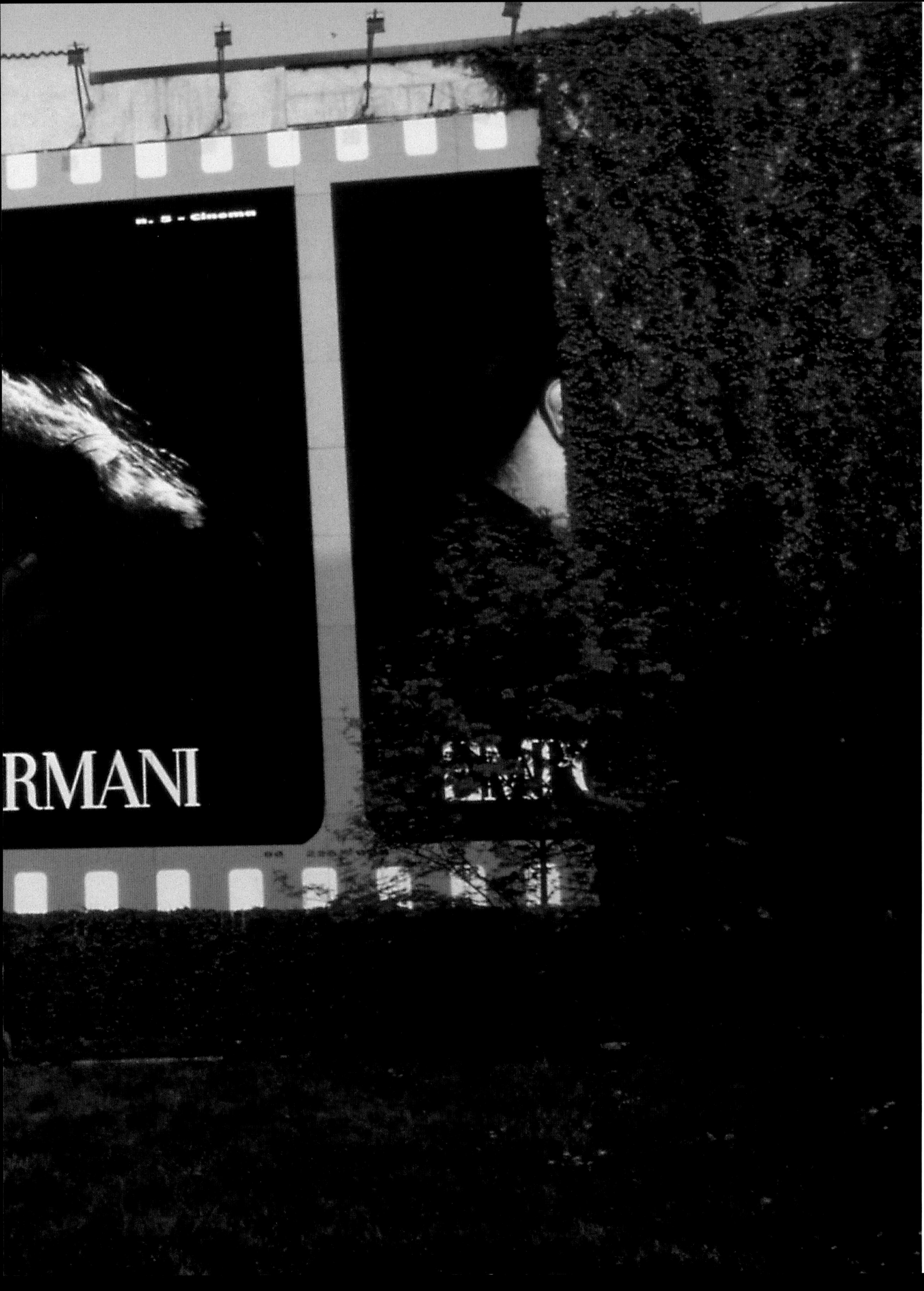
RMANI

127

128

127. Woman's evening tunic and pants ensemble, fall/winter 1994–95. **128. Woman's evening vest coat and pants ensemble,** fall/winter 1994–95. **129. Woman's evening jacket and skirt,** fall/winter 1989–90. **130. Woman's evening jacket and pants ensemble,** fall/winter 1989–90. Armani's historicism has the selective and synthesized character of cinema costume. Essential signs of an era—a fretwork of beads on a black vest

129

130

coat, a pointed waist on a velvet bodice, or a trompe-l'oeil kerchief with Jesuitical motives—are intertwined with elements of contemporaneity. If a character and era are evoked, it may be as specific as a widowed grande dame of the Belle Epoque and as esoteric as a proselytizing Catholic missionary of the late sixteenth or early seventeenth century.

131

131. Woman's evening tunic and pants ensemble, fall/winter 1994–95. **132. Woman's evening bodice and skirt,** spring/summer 1990. **133. Woman's evening jacket, overskirt, and pants ensemble,** spring/summer 1990. **134. Woman's evening bandeau and pants ensemble,** spring/summer 1990.   Narratives in Armani's collections are often the result of his rarified allusions. Faithful interpretations are rare, but they do

132

133

134

occur in his oeuvre, as in the Léon Bakst and Ballets Russes–inspired orientalist evening ensembles on the right. In other instances, it is difficult to ascribe a source or sources to his extraordinary conflations. The ensemble on the left, for example, suggests a chimerical mix of a Renaissance page painted by Domenico Ghirlandaio with Louis XIV costumed as Apollo.

135

136

137

135. **Woman's evening gown,** spring/summer 1989. 136. **Woman's off-the-shoulder evening bifurcated gown,** fall/winter 1989–90. 137. **Woman's halter-neck evening gown,** spring/summer 1990. 138. **Woman's evening sweater and skirt,** fall/winter 1998–99. In the eveningwear illustrated above, Armani conjures early Renaissance nobility, 1930s Hollywood glamour, and fin-de-siècle propriety in silhouettes of surprising similarity. References are established through one compelling detail drawn from each period, with the success of his simulation based on his extrapolation of

138

that single telling aspect. Here a gathered fullness of a skirt front suggests the belly of a bride in a painting by Jan van Eyck, a bias-twist neckline evokes Carole Lombard or Jean Harlow, and a long sweep of train alludes to the dashing society women depicted by John Singer Sargent and Giovanni Boldini.

139

139. Woman's evening bustier and skirt ensemble, spring/summer 1993. **140. Woman's evening bodice and skirt,** spring/summer 1996.
141. Woman's evening scarf top and skirt ensemble, spring/summer 1999. **142. Woman's strapless evening gown,** spring/summer 1999.
A sportswear-like ease informs Armani's eveningwear, whether inspired by the 1950s, 1960s, or 1970s, even gowns that allude to the pleated

140

141

142

masterpieces of Jean Desses or jewel-bodiced confections of Hubert de Givenchy are constructed as separates. Siren dresses are simple tubes cinched like a sarong at the torso. While the elegant, form-fitting effects of earlier styles are maintained, understructure and interfacings have almost completely disappeared.

A SELECTION OF ARMANI:
ENTRIES BY HAROLD KODA

MEN'S AND WOMEN'S COLLECTIONS,
1976–2001

CHRONOLOGY

SELECTED BIBLIOGRAPHY

1

Woman's evening dress, spring/summer 1997
Taupe silk chiffon with bugle beads, rhinestones, sequins, and metallic silver
thread embroidery
Giorgio Armani Archives, Milan
An Armani evening dress is often a manifestation of the contradictory
impulses to bare and conceal. This slip dress of sheer "nude" chiffon is
invested with a modicum of modesty through the doubling of its layers.
Reflective appliqués of silvered beading and sequining contribute an
additional form of concealment for erogenous zones. These gestures of
modesty, however, are subverted by the low-buttoning camisole closure
and the high center-front slit hem, which provide opportunities for further
bust and leg exposure.

2 and 4

Woman's evening pants ensemble, fall/winter 1995–96
Bodysuit: nude nylon knit mesh with appliqué of micro seed beads, bugle beads,
mini sequins, cabochon stones, rhinestones, and faceted beads secured with
micro seed beads; pants: multicolor floral-printed silk satin
Giorgio Armani Archives, Milan

Woman's evening pants ensemble, fall/winter 1995–96
Bodysuit: nude nylon knit mesh with appliqué of micro seed beads, bugle beads,
mini sequins, cabochon stones, rhinestones, and faceted beads secured with
micro seed beads; pants: multicolor floral-printed silk satin
Giorgio Armani Archives, Milan
In these two ensembles, pants evocative of 1920s lounging pajama
bottoms establish the watercolor palette of the jeweled plastron and cuffs
of the sheer net bodysuits. A foliate beaded relief that seems to have
migrated and expanded into three dimensions from the scrolling chinoiserie
patterns of the silk pants provides camouflage to the wearer rather than
true coverage. But though the torso is, in fact, exposed, it is with the
sense of the nudity of the tattooed: the tattooed body is never quite naked
to the eye.

3

Woman's evening pants ensemble, fall/winter 1995–96
Bodysuit: nude nylon knit mesh with raised floral appliqué of micro seed beads,
bugle beads, and mini sequins secured with micro seed beads; pants: gold
micro-pleated rayon/acetate blend satin
Giorgio Armani Archives, Milan
The crimped satin of these pants recalls the hand pleating of Mariano
Fortuny's Delphos dresses, suggesting that the pants—like Fortuny's tea
gowns before them—might be appropriate attire for intimate entertainment.
In a typical Armani synesthetic coordination, the bois-de-rose satin is
juxtaposed with the beaded rose motif of the bodysuit and a three-
dimensional rose-petaled neckpiece. Chromatic essence becomes
beaded pattern, which is transformed into sculpted form.

5

Woman's evening shorts ensemble, spring/summer 1995
"Corset" top: black rayon jacquard with raised floral appliqué of sequins,
rhinestones, and seed beads; shorts: black silk organza
Giorgio Armani Archives, Milan
While the beaded bustier derives its structure from eighteenth- and
nineteenth-century corsetry, its heavily encrusted form alludes to the
breastplates of Teutonic heroines seen in the movie of Armani's earliest
memory, Alessandro Blasetti's *La Corona di ferro* (1941). Carapacelike,
it protects and shields the fragile jacquard- and organza-enclosed body.

6

Woman's evening bustier and skirt ensemble, spring/summer 1988

Bustier: navy blue silk organza with sequins, navy blue silk chiffon shirring, and gray rayon braiding; skirt: black silk chiffon and light blue-green foliate-patterned silk organza

Giorgio Armani Archives, Milan

By the end of the nineteenth century, even corsets had covers. The layers of underpinnings—from chemise to camisole, corset, corset cover, petticoat, and overpetticoat—generally progressed from less to increasingly more adorned. Armani takes elements of these layers and submits them to a postmodernist jumble. But while they are inspired by a renewal of the layers of historical underpinnings, certain details establish other references. The hitched gypsy skirt and outer corselette with a Northern African–style passementerie edge combine to suggest the Islam-influenced forms of Andalusia.

7

Woman's evening bodice and skirt ensemble, spring/summer 1988

Bodice: navy blue silk organza with sequins, shirred navy blue silk chiffon, and gray silk braiding; skirt: dark blue silk chiffon and light blue floral-printed silk organza

Giorgio Armani Archives, Milan

Joining evocations of gypsies dancing and the hiked-up, petticoated skirts of peasants in the fields to the appearance of an odalisque's silk-bandaged torso, this ensemble combines the styles of Spain and its Northern African neighbors. By doing so, Armani blends the wildly expressive emotion of gypsy dances with the languorous restraint of the seraglio.

8

Woman's evening jacket and skirt, spring/summer 1988

Jacket: navy blue and gray floral-patterned, discharge-printed silk/viscose/cotton blend chiffon with handmade French knot silk buttons; skirt: black nylon tulle, black nylon "horsehair" braid, and blue silk braid

Giorgio Armani Archives, Milan

Here, as Armani reverses the order of crinoline and skirt, the skirt becomes a kind of lining while the exposed petticoat reveals the nature of its structure in bands of stiffened "horsehair" braid. The tightly fitted Turkish-style jacket plays against the petticoat's unfinished effect.

9

Woman's evening gown, spring/summer 1997

Gown: charcoal gray nylon knit mesh; pants (not visible in photograph): black silk satin

Giorgio Armani Archives, Milan

While beading's reflective properties are invariably eye-catching, Armani often subverts this effect. By beading giant peonylike floral clusters in midnight blue on black net, and then backing the ensemble from waist down with black satin pants, the graphic quality of the appliqué is compromised. This deliberate muting of the pattern's capacity to be read is then offset by the one cluster blooming across the bust that is dramatically silhouetted against the torso's pallor.

10

Woman's evening pants ensemble, spring/summer 1997

Top: Black nylon knit mesh with faceted jet and seed beads; overskirt: light green nylon tulle with micro seed beads and black rayon velvet appliqué; pants: light blue nylon knit mesh with bugle beads and sequins

Giorgio Armani Archives, Milan

Much of Armani's beading operates with a self-nullifying agenda. Pants with horizontal bands of subtly colored bugle beads and sequins are overlaid with a sheer net scrim embellished with a graduated foliate pattern of jet beads. Yet even in this instance, where one layer of beading is

activated against a background of another more luminous layer, the faint haze of supporting net veils the underlayer.

11

Woman's strapless evening gown, spring/summer 1999

Nude nylon knit mesh with clear sequins and seed beads secured with orange, red, and turquoise thread, and off-white nylon tulle overlay

Giorgio Armani Archives, Milan

The beaded banding of this gown is comprised of clear sequins and seed beads infused with the colors of their anchoring threads. The effect is a frosty rendering of the flame-stitched knit patterns of the early 1970s. But in its organic irregularity and crusty relief, the banding also implies the stratified layering of agate and other striated geologic forms. As in so many other examples of the designer's work, the glint of the beading is obscured by a veil of tulle.

12

Woman's strapless evening gown, spring/summer 1999

Orange silk organza with seed beads, sequins, and rhinestones, and pale mauve nylon tulle overlay

Giorgio Armani Archives, Milan

The juxtaposition of saturated colors in this gown produces a vivid optical conflict, as the small clusters of blue beads contrast with the orange silk against which they are laid. As in the late paintings of Claude Monet, the fibrillation of the violent chromatic contrast seems opposed to what preceded it, yet an overview of Armani's work reveals that this strategy has an extended history within his oeuvre—the only difference here being one of wattage.

13

Woman's strapless evening gown, spring/summer 1999

Two-tone gray silk/rayon blend chiffon with gray silk satin appliqué, seed beads, rhinestones, and cupped sequins, and steel gray nylon tulle overlay

Giorgio Armani Archives, Milan

The directional beading and overlay of dark net do not simply mute the highlights of this gown's embroidered patches. Rather, the overlay lends depth to the beading's shadowed areas. A smoldering iridescence comes from this careful modulation of the reflective effects of the beads. Further, their unified orientation results in a blurred grain to the edges of the highlights, not unlike the feathered boundaries within a Mark Rothko painting.

14

Man's blouson jacket ensemble; jacket: ca. fall/winter 1978–79; pants: ca. fall/winter 1982–83

Jacket with detachable vest: brown cotton plain weave; pants: taupe wool sateen

Giorgio Armani Archives, Milan, Gift of Verna and Jay Cocks

Armani's menswear develops out of traditional components of male dress, much of it from the functional apparel associated with labor, sport, and the military. While this does not differ broadly from the pool of design inspiration of many menswear designers, Armani's efforts have certain hallmarks, including a transformative adaptability. Detachable liners, vests, collar latches, and shoulder yokes in his jackets upholster and insulate the wearer in inclemency, but then may be shed in good weather. The mutability of the jacket shown here—which has a detachable vest—is especially apparent when it is reduced to a shell, for it is then that the success of the designer's combination of cut and fabric is seen in the jacket's lank, dégagé hang.

15

Man's shirtjacket ensemble; shirtjacket: ca. fall/winter 1982–83;
pants: ca. 1980–85
Shirtjacket: light beige suede; pants: taupe and khaki brushed wool twill
Giorgio Armani Archives, Milan, Gift of Verna and Jay Cocks

Armani's confident use of leather in its various weights and textures—
and his surprising application of it in garments such as pleated trousers,
T-shirts, and pullovers—are founded in his many years of experience as
the designer of leatherwear for Sicons. In this suede shirtjacket, the
Armani touch is evident in the placement of the buttons, which serve
as a sign of merged paradigms: on the one hand, they reflect a shirtlike
positioning, but on the other, they are omitted from the waist down as
they would be in a jacket.

16

Man's sports jacket and sweater vest ensemble, fall/winter 1994–95
Jacket: green wool/polyamide blend plain weave; vest: brown alpaca knit;
pants: mustard brown wool/viscose/polyamide/acetate blend novelty weave
Giorgio Armani Archives, Milan

The thick layering of textures and unexpected colors in this ensemble
suggests the wardrobe of a professor, writer, or country gentleman.
However, Armani introduces an informal suavity to the tweedy rusticity
by easing the fit of the components and by exaggerating traditional
patterns and applying them in unconventional ways. Any primness expires
in the soft, but straight drop of the jacket front from the shoulders, and,
when teamed with supple trousers that also drape loosely, this produces
an effect of barrel-chested vigor rather than academic restraint.

17

Woman's jacket and skirt ensemble, spring/summer 1987
Jacket: gray cotton/nylon blend glen plaid; blouse: off-white silk organza;
skirt: gray wool striped novelty weave
Giorgio Armani Archives, Milan

This tailored ensemble for women is reminiscent of mens' sports jacket
and slacks combinations. Interpreted for women, the jacket has been
shorn of lapels and pockets and reduced to a proportion intermediate to
jacket and waistcoat. This is combined with emphatically feminizing details
that are somewhat atypical for the designer: a scallop-embroidered hem
on the skirt and a Peter Pan collar on the shirt. Expressed in materials
with masculine associations, these flourishes suggest an ironic intent.

18

Man's vest ensemble, fall/winter 1994–95
Vest: brown cotton velvet; shirt: pale green cotton poplin; pants: brown wool
novelty weave
Giorgio Armani Archives, Milan

On the runway, as here, the Armani man is endowed with a disheveled
nonchalance: shirts are unbuttoned, sometimes to the waist, and
waistcoats are commonly anchored by only one of their buttons. This
casual, diffident effect plays against the precision of the garments' cut
and their carefully controlled drape. After creating an ensemble of tonal,
textural, and proportional balance, the designer disrupts this sartorial
order with an entropic chic.

19

Man's jacket and sweater vest ensemble, fall/winter 1993–94
Jacket: dark brown cotton corduroy; vest: brown wool knit with gray wool knit trim;
pants: brown and light gray wool/polymide/elastan blend ribbed novelty weave
Giorgio Armani Archives, Milan

Since the Edwardian era, the stocky male, if properly attired, has enjoyed
a physical authority not shared by his feminine counterpart, and here

Armani conjures the prepossessing bulk of a bear of a man by piling layer
upon sensual layer. The leather buttons and piped pocket trimming of this
corduroy jacket suggest sources in regional Austrian dress.

20

Man's sports jacket ensemble, fall/winter 1992–93
Jacket: black, beige, and white wool houndstooth; pants: gray wool/
polyamide/elastan blend twill
Giorgio Armani Archives, Milan

Although the Armani silhouette has witnessed innumerable
transformations in the past twenty-five years, a relatively stable
component in his proportioning of male attire is the fixing of the trouser
waist at a point slightly higher than is seen in traditional menswear.
Over this faintly truncated torso and elongated legs, Armani juxtaposes
his more mutable jacket designs. The alignment of this jacket's top
button with its elevated waistline is rather rare.

21

Woman's suit, fall/winter 1979–80
Gray wool bouclé tweed
The Museum at the Fashion Institute of Technology, New York, Gift of Jay Cocks

Every haute-couture house has two separate ateliers, one for the *tailleur*
and one for the *flou*. This distinction between the skills of tailoring and
dressmaking is fundamental to the thinking of most designers. Yet Armani,
schooled in the ranks of a different mechanism of production—pret-à-
porter rather than couture—mixes the techniques of both in a chimerical
simultaneity of forms. Here, suggesting a total mastery of both methods,
a man's suit jacket is gathered in a waist-cinching drape.

22

Man's three-piece suit, fall/winter 1990–91
Dark brown and beige wool/cotton/linen blend herringbone-patterned twill
Giorgio Armani Archives, Milan

The three-piece suit—that dressiest form of male business attire—evolved
in the late nineteenth century, when jacket, vest, and trousers were first
cut from the same cloth. The sportswear-like ease of Armani's rendering
here is more a consequence of the suit's supple fabric and loose cut than
it is of the collarless shirt. The jacket is exaggerated in its length, but
because of the designer's reconfiguration of button stance and gorge, a
Zoot suit mannerism is averted.

23

Woman's pantsuit, fall/winter 1998–99
Gray and off-white wool mini-checked novelty weave
Giorgio Armani Archives, Milan

This pantsuit for women—conceived as a Eurasian mix, according to
Armani—combines Western textile and suit references with the stand-
collar styling that recalls the classless and genderless uniforms of Maoist
China. From the perspective of costume history, the ensemble also revives
an eighteenth- and nineteenth-century style found in military uniforms.
In a time when sabers were as much a part of warfare as guns, a double-
layered jacket front with quilted interfacings provided some small
protection to the wearer.

24

Man's suit, fall/winter 1990–91
Gray wool striped novelty weave
Giorgio Armani Archives, Milan

Armani's tailoring for men incorporates certain body-enhancing strategies
used by the great Spanish couturier Cristóbal Balenciaga. For Balenciaga—
at a time when Christian Dior's New Look had reintroduced the nineteenth-

century primacy of the waist—the critical point of suspension for any garment was the shoulder. In this jacket for men, deflated shoulder pads, placed in a slightly different position than usual, allow the sleeves and chest pieces to fall without collapsing or constricting. In addition, the textile has been cut to hang slightly away from the body at the waist, only to cleave to the back haunches at hip level. Like a Balenciaga gown, which was said to accommodate "a little belly," the Armani jacket invests the less-than-ideal torso with a largely illusional V-shaped taper.

25

Woman's jacket and pants, fall/winter 1994–95
Jacket: gray and tan tussah silk/rayon blend plaid novelty weave;
pants: gray silk satin
Giorgio Armani Archives, Milan
The scaled-down man's jacket applied to womenswear is an idea that appeared in Armani's earliest collections. But unlike his earlier efforts, in which the transposition of men's tailoring to women's sportswear seemed to occur without any alterations, here Armani has excised much of the jacket's collar and eliminated the chest pocket. The result is an unarticulated and supple expanse of fabric left to register subtly the topography of the bust. Combined with trousers widened to the fullness of a skirt, the jacket forms part of an ensemble of capacious, minimalist ease.

26

Woman's pantsuit, fall/winter 1995–96
Beige and black viscose/nylon/wool blend shadow-striped compound weave
Giorgio Armani Archives, Milan
This pantsuit merges two silhouettes from contiguous decades. Its mannish shoulders are straightened and extended with pronounced sleeve caps in the manner of the late 1930s and early 1940s, when fashionable women sported a broad-shouldered trunk that tapered into a narrowed, girdled hipline. Here, however, the waist is suppressed and the hips have a distinct curvature: the silhouette of the war years merges with the hourglass silhouette of Dior's New Look. While most suits have a fish dart concealed under the jacket's lapels to accommodate the chest or bust, Armani's shaping is accomplished simply by the extension of the shoulder line and the darting of the waistline. No vertical collapse occurs at the juncture of shoulder and chest, as is observable in most menswear styles for women.

27

Woman's three-piece pantsuit, fall/winter 1993–94
Suit: gray and beige wool novelty weave; shirt: white silk chiffon
Giorgio Armani Archives, Milan
Since the nineteenth century, the three-piece suit has been the uniform of the Establishment male. But with relatively small modifications—lightweight fabric, boxy-cut waistcoat, and drawstring pants—Armani accomplishes such profound transgressions that this suit could never be confused with its masculine precedents. Cut without regard to conventional fit, it repudiates the very basis of tailoring, and the padded and buttoned-up corporate armor of the businessman is transformed into a new paradigm for the professional woman.

28

Woman's jacket and pants, fall/winter 1993–94
Jacket: brown and black wool/cashmere blend houndstooth; pants: dark green, tan, and maroon silk/acetate/rayon blend novelty weave
Giorgio Armani Archives, Milan
Balancing the masculine with the feminine, Armani combines the widened shoulders of this double-breasted jacket with a suppressed waist and rounded hipline. Although the resulting silhouette is inarguably feminine,

there is a further sartorial manipulation that confirms its gender: the collar with a lowered notch is constructed like a peaked lapel, but with the outline of a shawl collar. An inventive form outside the codified parameters of traditional menswear, the collar is thus ascribed to women, who are given a broader range of expressive devices in dress.

29

Woman's pantsuit, ca. fall/winter 1985–86
Tan silk herringbone
Giorgio Armani Archives, Milan, Gift of Verna and Jay Cocks
It is inevitable that Armani would envision a suit pared of all but the most elemental parts. What remain are trousers paired with a jacket shorn of collar and lapels. Interestingly, the jacket front is overlapped, as in a double-breasted suit or perhaps a kimono. Thus the jacket alludes to a modernism that prizes asymmetry and the elimination of ornament, while also recalling the simplicity of regional styles and untailored traditions.

30

Woman's suit, fall/winter 1994–95
Light olive silk/wool blend novelty twill
Giorgio Armani Archives, Milan, Gift of Verna and Jay Cocks
Armani's impulse toward minimalism is not at the expense of visual or conceptual complexity. This suit jacket is based on the draping of a double-breasted front panel, but its collarpiece has been eliminated and what would normally be the fabric for a conventional lapel has been folded back on itself to form an origami-like rever. The rigorous balance of the skirt, cut to fall with a flattened center panel and deep flutes at the sides, anchors the asymmetry of the jacket.

31

Man's suit, fall/winter 1982–83
Navy blue wool pinstriped novelty weave
The Museum at the Fashion Institute of Technology, New York,
Gift of Jay Cocks

In the construction of the earliest of Armani's power suits for men, a crisp faintly linear silhouette conformed to prevailing ideas of professional dress. Where Armani departed from the standard, however, was in his use of textiles with a springier, more supple hand than the stiff traditional worsted wools. Also, by eliminating, famously, much of the interlinings, and excessive padding seen in conventional tailoring, his apparel enhanced the bodies of a generation of men who prized a new, elevated standard of physical fitness.

32

Man's suit, fall/winter 1978–79
Navy blue wool gabardine
The Museum at the Fashion Institute of Technology, New York,
Gift of Robert L. Turner
At the time of Armani's entry into the field, tailored menswear was a calcified collection of conventions. Good suits were made from a standard repertoire of textiles, with a limited range of cuts and a checklist of certain details, such as pocket flaps, interfacings, and shoulder and chest padding. Armani pared away much of this for a sleeker line and enhanced comfort. Compensating for the absence of hidden structural supports entailed a reconsideration of the very shape of the pattern pieces. What is masterful about an Armani suit is that its form is almost exclusively a consequence of its cut and the body of its textile, not the hidden prosthesis of padding.

33

Woman's pants ensemble with overskirt, fall/winter 1996–97
Shirtjacket and shirt: off-white silk crepe; overskirt: black, off-white, and brown
floral-printed silk organza; pants: off-white nylon ottoman; tie: black silk satin
Giorgio Armani Archives, Milan
When pants with overskirts first appeared in the 1950s, the overskirt generally suggested an informal at-home dressiness, comfortable luxury, and (open at the front to reveal skintight capri pants beneath) modest coquetry. In Armani's iterations, the earliest examples of which date to his spring/summer 1977 collection, the overskirt is less a marker of decorum or sexuality than it is one of issues of gender. Here, an unstructured white suit with shirt, tie, and boutonniere—explicitly transgender and decidedly not for wearing at home—is securely appropriated to the feminine by the overskirt.

34

Man's suit, ca. fall/winter 1995–96
Blue wool pinstriped crepe
Giorgio Armani Archives, Milan, Gift of Verna and Jay Cocks
Here, Armani revives the stylish double-breasted suits of the 1930s, but with his characteristic alteration of proportion. By dropping the skirt of the jacket, the waist-thickening double-breasted front is compensated for by a slimming attenuation. After this gentle reproportioning, the style—not generally recommended for the stout—is available and flattering to all. Further, the designer's evisceration of traditional tailoring depends upon accommodating materials. Wool crepe, with its lightness and springy hand, provides Armani with his ideal medium.

35

Woman's jacket and pants, spring/summer 1998
Jacket: charcoal gray rayon twill; pants: dark blue-gray and blue-green striped
silk/rayon blend satin
Giorgio Armani Archives, Milan
Faintly Chaplinesque, with its torso-cleaving jacket and straight-cut pants, this ensemble was presented on the runway with a narrow tie and no shirt. Although Armani has always criticized the excessive use of nudity in fashion, he does not shy from controlled exposure of the body. Here the flash of bare torso is less a proposal than a prop: the vulnerability of the body to exposure underscores the validity of the jacket, even when reduced to a chic if meager line that precludes its closure.

36

Woman's jacket and pants, fall/winter 1995–96
Jacket: black wool twill; pants: gray wool/rayon blend chalkstriped compound weave
Giorgio Armani Archives, Milan
Unlike Armani's analogous pieces for men, his jackets for women frequently evidence radical departures from the stylistic conventions of tailoring. In this piece, the angled breaking of the lapel from the collarpiece creates a portrait neckline—albeit a restrained one, with roots in the styles of the late 1930s and early 1940s. What is essentially a man's jacket endowed with a woman's neckline is then paired with trousers with contradictory gender signals: the chalkstriped fabric is typical of menswear, but their uncreased and wide-cut pajama-like fluidity situates the pants more ambiguously. Like a Surrealist *corps exquis*, the ensemble unfolds in parts, from the transformed, feminized neckline to the masculine, tailored, double-breasted waist, and finally to the androgynous legs.

37

Woman's "Bermuda" suit, spring/summer 1992
Jacket and shorts: orange silk crepe; shawl: orange silk chiffon
Giorgio Armani Archives, Milan
Like Balenciaga—who also designed shorts ensembles, despite his reputation for decorous formality—Armani plays with line-attenuating strategies in this "Bermuda" suit. By pairing a jacket with Bermuda shorts, Armani allows a longer expanse of leg to be exposed without self-consciousness than would be possible with a similarly short skirt. He also imbues the neck with a swanlike grace by eliminating the jacket's collarpiece. Strong color—an arresting traffic-cone hue—and design adjustments calculated to create the gangly proportions of youth might allude to Balenciaga, but the supple ply of the suit's textile can only be Armani.

38

Woman's suit, fall/winter 1980–81
Olive wool/rayon blend twill
Giorgio Armani Archives, Milan, Gift of Verna and Jay Cocks
Unlike many Armani tailored ensembles, which are endowed with the interchangeability of sportswear, this suit jacket is proportioned to be worn to best advantage with its skirt. The jacket is cut long, and serves as a mechanism to control the opening of the skirt. More importantly, the lowered button stance, centered between shoulder and hemline rather than at the natural waist, not only deepens the jacket's neckline, but also serves as a proportional mechanism to unify jacket and skirt into a merged whole.

39

Woman's "muscle tee" top and skirt, fall/winter 1998–99
Top: gray mohair knit; skirt: gray wool/rayon blend novelty twill
Giorgio Armani Archives, Milan
Armani utilizes a variety of strategies in his appropriation of male dress for women. Here, a sleeveless, beefcake "muscle tee" is dematerialized, its ostentatious torso-hugging qualities replaced by the more elusive disclosures of a smoky, loosely worked mohair. A floor-grazing skirt with belt loops and a fly-front closure assumes an equally Tiresian whimsy, as if pants in the process of transformation into a skirt were frozen in mid-conversion.

40

Woman's cowl top and pants, fall/winter 1998–99
Top: pink silk/elastomer blend crepe; pants: pink, light blue, and gray
angora/cashmere/rayon blend crepe
Giorgio Armani Archives, Milan
In an example of the extraordinary technical mastery required to accomplish the simplest of effects, a sophisticated manipulation of the bias cut endows this silk blend blouse with the ease of a hooded sweatshirt. An elliptical seam discloses a conical construction that results in the fluid release and collapse of folds at the cowl neckline and the shoulder-cleaving tautness that holds the top in place. Redolent of the glamorous gowns of the Hollywood designer Adrian, the top is the yin to the yang of the full-cut 1940s hipster pants.

41

Woman's jacket and pants, fall/winter 1998–99
Jacket: gray and ocher wool/nylon blend mini-checked novelty twill;
hooded bodysuit: pink nylon knit; pants: pink wool/rayon blend crepe
Giorgio Armani Archives, Milan
A men's fashion editorial spread of the early 1980s presented athletic young models wearing richly textured and patterned tweed jackets by Armani over hooded gray fleece sweatshirts. The feature captured the designer's love of unexpected juxtaposition together with the adaptable ease of his soft jackets. While jackets and sweatshirts are hardly of the

formality one expects of eveningwear, Armani reprised this idea in a group of evening ensembles for women in his fall/winter 1998–99 collection. Here, the basic elements are elevated a notch from their original example: the jacket, in a fine-striped wool blend, appears to have been a part of a business suit, while the sweatshirt is a body-clinging fine-gauge jersey.

42

Woman's evening gown and coat, fall/winter 1998–99
Coat: steel gray wool/elastomer blend plain weave; gown: sage green silk crepe
Giorgio Armani Archives, Milan
In this evening ensemble, the Armani twist is found in his rendering of the coat in a gray wool-blend suiting. Despite its tailored sleeves, the coat has the ease of a lounging robe or kimono, attributable to the narrow shawl collar and unconstrained shape, as well as to the presence of elastomer in the fabric, which contributes body and bounce to its soft fluting.

43

Woman's evening gown and jacket, fall/winter 1998–99
Jacket: gray wool/rayon blend pinstriped compound weave; gown: pink silk twill
Giorgio Armani Archives, Milan
Any other designer might show an evening gown with a tuxedo or a smoking jacket, repudiating gender proscriptions but still conforming to rules of formality. Armani, however, goes further. Pairing this minimalist evening gown with a spare, but traditionally styled suit jacket, he plays not only with the idea of gender transposition, but with the inversion of conventions of daywear and eveningwear.

44

Woman's evening jacket and pants, fall/winter 1991–92
Jacket: black silk/rayon blend velvet; pants with attached scarf: black silk chiffon pavé-embroidered with sequins, seed beads, and faceted stones; cummerbund: black silk satin
Giorgio Armani Archives, Milan
Among the most explicit semaphors of Establishment male attire, club- and school-tie stripes have come to be associated with white button-down shirts, blue blazers, and chinos: the informal attire of preppie and post-preppie alike. Here, Armani takes these vivid stripings and renders them in pavé beading for an evening ensemble. With characteristic aplomb, he merges this albeit glamorized signal of informality with more traditional elements of formalwear—the tuxedo jacket and cummerbund.

45

Woman's evening suit, fall/winter 1991–92
Brown silk chiffon pavé-embroidered in a herringbone pattern with seed beads, bugle beads, and sequins
Giorgio Armani Archives, Milan
Daisy Fellowes is credited with inventing during the 1930s the sequined evening jacket cut like a man's tuxedo, and for being the first to wear a wool dress as evening apparel. Similar "*épater la bourgeoisie*" notions recur in Armani's work. Here, the hearty herringbone pattern associated with men's suiting is rendered in seed and bugle beads and sequins. Arranged in alternating, angled rows, they capture light from a number of directions, resulting in an especially animated shimmer.

46

Woman's evening ensemble, fall/winter 1985–86
Jacket: black silk/rayon blend velvet with jet bead openwork; skirt: black and white plaid-printed silk damask with clear sequins; shawl: off-white cashmere knit
Giorgio Armani Archives, Milan
Incorporating surprising elements of daywear and more conventional eveningwear components, this sportswear-styled evening ensemble is

quintessentially Armani. The black velvet jacket with jet-beaded cuffs and plunging neckline conforms to expectations of evening glamour, but the beret and wool shawl mute its drama. The ankle-length skirt also embodies the contradictions that Armani prizes: sedately pleated and with a glen-plaid pattern, it is formalized by a uniform application of transparent sequins.

47

Woman's evening gown, fall/winter 1986–87
Gown: black silk/rayon blend velvet; collar and tie: white silk plain weave and black silk satin
Giorgio Armani Archives, Milan
In his fall/winter 1986–87 collection, Armani accessorized a number of his day ensembles with a decorative neckpiece in the form of a man's shirt collar, which he placed under suits worn with supple silk blouses or without a blouse altogether as a talismanic vestige of male professional dress. Paradoxically, the collars emphasized the very femininity of these suits, which had otherwise completely usurped all aspects of the menswear paradigm. For evening, this sign of the appropriation of male power took the form of a collar and four-in-hand tie, as it has in this gown. Interestingly, despite this whimsical reference to gender parity—a contemporary issue—the long velvet evening gown with its trim, shirtwaist details recalls nothing so much as the elegance of the 1930s and the lithe, slim-hipped dresses designed by Mainbocher for the Duchess of Windsor.

48

Woman's evening ensemble, fall/winter 1992–93
Bustier: off-white silk satin with black rayon velvet "bow tie" trim; skirt: off-white silk satin
Giorgio Armani Archives, Milan
The crisp linearity of a man's tuxedo shirt, with its textured piqué bib front, is conveyed here in the stiffened ribbed silk of a ball gown. But the rigid constraints of the conventional tuxedo are otherwise inverted: the undone black tie is actually trompe l'oeil, functioning as a halter that secures the unboned bodice, even when it is unbuttoned for less discreet exposure.

49

Woman's evening gown, fall/winter 1992–93
Black triacetate/rayon blend crepe with white silk satin and faceted jet
Giorgio Armani Archives, Milan
The columnar form of this gown and the cut-away curve of its hem suggest a tuxedo sleeve detached from its jacket. The bodice, a Brobdingnagian French cuff barely secured with jet cuff links, completes the illusion. But the joke may equally be about sleevelessness: tiny black gloves are furnished with small white gauntlets that seem to complete sleeves that are not there.

50

Woman's evening gown, fall/winter 1992–93
Black rayon crepe with black silk satin trim
Giorgio Armani Archives, Milan
Of all the tuxedo gowns that have resulted from Armani's extensive exploration of the form, this minimalist example introduces the sparest signifiers of the genre. The tuxedo's lapels, waistcoat, cummerbund, and trouser side stripes—which by convention are in silk satin or gros grain to contrast against the black wool of the suit—are evoked by the gown's juxtaposition of matte and shine. As in the gown that takes the sleeve as its starting point, here the tuxedo pant leg is an opportunity for surreal play.

51

Woman's halter-top evening gown, fall/winter 1997–98

Black silk/rayon blend velvet and black nylon/elastomer blend organza with mini sequins, seed beads, and bugle beads

Giorgio Armani Archives, Milan

This halter dress is an expansion on the theme of the tuxedo's black tie undone, seen in the fall/winter 1992–93 evening ensemble (cat. no. 48) in which a trompe l'oeil tie serves as a means of support for the bodice. Here, the tie is expanded to ascot size and wraps around the bust. What was a small decorative device with disguised functions in the earlier piece has evolved into a form that is less directly referential (the ascot is not a traditional eveningwear form) and more responsive to the structure of apparel. The overt allusion to the tuxedo has been subsumed to a more obliquely witty expression.

52

Man's tuxedo, spring/summer 2000

Black wool/silk blend crepe

Giorgio Armani Archives, Milan

Like a military uniform, the tuxedo is a garment whose power resides in its conformity to the rules. Armani's achievement with regard to this iconic garment has been to improve it in the most subtle but fundamental ways. As with his suits and jackets, he has imbued it with sexiness by removing any quality of stiffness or constraint. By constructing it for comfort, and by selecting textiles that are of a weight that discloses more of the body beneath, Armani has appeared to follow all the rules while surreptitiously changing the game.

53

Woman's pants ensemble, fall/winter 1998–99

Heather gray wool/nylon/elastomer blend knit

Giorgio Armani Archives, Milan

By taking the visual qualities of gray flannel and transposing them to a sheer stretch fabric, Armani upends our expectations. In its incarnation as *the* 1950s businessman's suit fabric, gray flannel was endowed with a certain symbolism, both positive and pejorative. But here Armani introduces a new sensuality that subverts the cloth's associations of conformity, propriety, and functionality without sacrificing other allusive aspects of the textile, such as warmth, comfort, and security.

54

Woman's overshirt and pants, spring/summer 1994

Eggshell silk novelty weave

Giorgio Armani Archives, Milan

Here, Armani has combined components separated by geography, culture, and time to create a convincing, though mythic, regional style. The voluminous collarless shirt worn as a tunic is typical of the clothing of Punjabi men, and the wrapping construction of the pants alludes to the diaper-like dhoti of the region. More Central Asian than Indian, however, is the vestlike effect over the shirt. Furthermore the shirt's bib front suggests the form of the nineteenth-century European collar-band dress shirt.

55

Woman's shirt and skirt, spring/summer 1994

Shirt: light brown silk/rayon blend novelty weave; skirt: light brown rayon twill

Giorgio Armani Archives, Milan

This open-weave shirt and wide, ballooning skirt have the airy insubstantiality of clothing designed for the heat. Easily animated by movement and the breeze, their aerated gauze catches every gust, just as its transparency captures the eye. The horizontally seamed construction of the skirt creates the barrel-shaped silhouette of harem pants.

56

Woman's evening pantsuit, spring/summer 1994

Off-white silk satin-striped novelty weave with bugle beads

Giorgio Armani Archives, Milan

In his novel *The Sheltering Sky* (1949), Paul Bowles distinguishes the tourist from the traveler: tourists have only a short time for their visits, whereas travelers, characterized by leisurely and open-ended peregrinations, have neither calendar nor itinerary to address. In reality, Armani's excursions abroad are of a touristic duration, but his imagination settles and persists in certain places for years and his intuitive grasp of the telling form comes from the cultural assimilation of the traveler. This Tunisian striped evening pajama is an example of his evocation of the dress of a region through the citing of local dress traditions as they might be translated by someone who lives in but is not of a place.

57

Woman's pants ensemble, fall/winter 1994–95

Black and gray "Fortuny"-printed silk chiffon

Giorgio Armani Archives, Milan

A richly historical layering of references is applied to this pants ensemble in silk chiffon. The custom of men on the Indian subcontinent to wear a full tunic shirt over narrow pants of the same fabric has inspired Armani to a number of interpretations, though the precise region and time period of their origins are never directly identifiable. Rather, the elements are sifted and recombined in the designer's memory to form an improbable, but undeniably romantic, expression. Here, Armani takes a print pattern from aesthete and designer Mariano Fortuny, who himself had adopted it from Islamic sources.

58

Man's sports jacket ensemble, spring/summer 1991

Jacket: beige linen novelty twill; pants: beige linen plain weave

Giorgio Armani Archives, Milan

Armani's references are rarely literal or unabridged, but are communicated obliquely—in this instance through a sand- and dust-colored palette and a graduated range of textured linens. He has used the word *scavo* (excavation) to describe such summer ensembles, and though the outfit evokes the image of an archeologist on a desert dig, any historicism is only a convincing projection. Without the subliminal narrative cues that emerge out of the designer's coordination of the parts, each element of the ensemble is indisputably of our time.

59

Man's suit, spring/summer 1990

Beige linen plain weave

Giorgio Armani Archives, Milan

In the 1910s and 1920s, summer resort wear for men included suits stripped of much of the linings and paddings of the period's city attire to create a lighter, cooler garment, and yet the tailors and their clients of the period were unwilling to negotiate certain aesthetic qualities of the suit even for comfort. They replicated the crisp contours of professional dress with textiles of a stiff-fibered and, sometimes, heavy weave. Armani has proposed that the very style of the suit should be relaxed along with the excision of its interior stiffenings. The jacket of this suit, therefore, has a crumpled nonchalance, and the pants are worn uncreased, like pajama bottoms.

60

Woman's jacket and pants, spring/summer 1993
Jacket: off-white silk damask; overskirt: beige silk organza; pants: yellow silk/linen blend plain weave
Giorgio Armani Archives, Milan

This pantsuit for women is imbued with a poetic exoticism by the addition of a short overskirt, which synthesizes imagery from at least two regions, Central and Southeast Asia. Worn under a jacket and over narrow pants, the skirt has the immediate effect of the long, tunic-length shirttails of men in Pakistan and other northern parts of the Indian subcontinent. This juxtaposition of jacket and skirt can also be seen as a reference to the Indonesian practice of pairing a Western-style tailored jacket with a native sarong.

61

Woman's jacket and sarong pants, spring/summer 1994
Jacket: tan rayon/acetate blend herringbone; bodysuit: gray silk knit; pants: gray rayon/polyester blend knit
Giorgio Armani Archives, Milan

This collarless jacket retains vestiges of a collar piece and lapels in the double-curved undulation of its neckline, the sharply contoured edges of which contrast with the soft drape of the wrap-effect pants. Reminiscent of a sarong or a dhoti—both spiraling forms that anchor to the body with firm knots—the pants introduce an undeniable sensuality to the cool propriety of the neatly fitted jacket.

62

Woman's pants ensemble, fall/winter 1994–95
Overshirt and pants: light gray silk crepe; bodysuit: gray wool/cotton blend knit mesh; shawl: light gray rayon/angora/mohair/nylon blend chenille pile on gray nylon knit mesh
Giorgio Armani Archives, Milan

Although cut and draped in a seemingly loose and uncontrolled flare, the jacket of this ensemble has been carefully fitted at the shoulders. It is typical of Armani not to showcase his technique, and here his mastery has been hidden under a luxurious chenille mesh shawl. A view of the perfectly tailored shoulder from which this ostensibly unconstructed garment is suspended is less important to the designer than the sophisticated assembling of tonally related textiles.

63

Woman's jacket and dress, spring/summer 1994
Jacket: taupe linen gauze; dress: beige rayon/nylon blend knit
Giorgio Armani Archives, Milan

The dense layering of thin fabrics as insulation against the desert sun inspired Armani to create this ensemble, which consists of parts that assemble and disassemble according to the caprice of the wearer, the climate, or perhaps the cultural codes of different environments such as the mosque or the street. Armani adds a ruffle to a regional apparel tradition notably absent of such forms, in the semicircular pattern pieces in graduated layers that create the cascade front of the jacket.

64

Woman's jacket and pants, fall/winter 1994–95
Jacket: light gray alpaca twill; bodysuit (not visible in photograph): gray-green wool/cotton blend knit; pants: gray wool/rayon blend knit
Giorgio Armani Archives, Milan

Regional garments are often shaped to maximize the efficient use of textiles, resulting, commonly, in rectilinear pattern pieces. The loose, untailored fit of this jacket suggests this practice, but in fact its semicircular shape necessitates a dramatic contouring accomplished by the assembling of a surprising number of pattern pieces. Its edges are finished using a conventionally industrial technique, which precludes the unraveling of the loose alpaca cloth while giving the effect of a simple double-stitched border.

65

Woman's evening gown, fall/winter 1994–95
Brown wool/angora/viscose/nylon blend chenille pile on brown nylon knit mesh
Giorgio Armani Archives, Milan

This dress of acetic simplicity recalls both the silhouette of a dervish and Claire McCardell's "monastic" dress of the late 1930s. It is rendered in a textile that appears to be a crocheted chenille, but is actually an unusual voided mesh with chenille pile. Because the textile is made with a flesh-toned ground, the effect is of an open-worked and elastic crochet or wool lace. Here, Armani's allusions to other cultures are subtle, residing in the rolled "harem" hem of the dress, a blanketlike shawl, and a bold amber bead necklace.

66

Woman's floor-length dress, fall/winter 1994–95
Taupe rayon/mohair/nylon/wool blend knit
Giorgio Armani Archives, Milan

Armani's references to other cultures are often clearest in the context of a runway show or advertising campaign, where a compilation of visual imagery begins to constitute a sense of place or time. Without this context, the references are more elusive; this dress, for example, accompanied by a diagonally worn shoulder bag, points broadly to the Islamic world. Its high neckline, long sleeves, and floor-length skirt evoke simultaneously the modesty of the *chador* and the protective coverage of the djellabah. The allusion might equally be to the long cotton gowns worn with vests by men in Palestine.

333

67

Woman's evening vest and pants, spring/summer 1994
Vest: off-white silk and metallic gold thread plain weave with faux pearls, rhinestones, sequins, and seed beads; shirt: white silk organza with sequins secured with seed beads; pants: off-white silk organza with off-white linen plain weave appliqué
Giorgio Armani Archives, Milan

Vests worn over untucked shirts are a common form of everyday attire for men across a varied cultural and geographic terrain, from the Near East to Central Asia. But in Armani's reinvention of the form as woman's eveningwear, the evocation is of a world more physically circumscribed—that of the seraglio, a place of sybaritic indulgence in the Western imagination. Armani coopts Islamic forms of dress in the manner of the early suffragettes and feminists, as appropriate expressions of independence and equality.

68 and 69

Woman's evening dress, spring/summer 1995
Dress: metallic gold silk organza with sequins, cupped sequins, micro seed beads, and seed beads; shorts (not visible in photograph): off-white foliate-printed silk charmeuse
Giorgio Armani Archives, Milan

Woman's evening dress, spring/summer 1995
Dress: metallic gold silk organza with micro seed beads, bugle beads, sequins, and seed beads; shorts (not visible in photograph): off-white silk foliate-printed charmeuse
Giorgio Armani Archives, Milan

The caftan appears from Northern Africa to the Ivory Coast with a number of local variations. While most are characterized by narrow passementerie or metallic embroidered bands edging the neckline slit, all are modestly floor-length. In this interpretation, Armani not only crops the robe to mid-thigh, he beads the whole of the garment and substitutes the neckline embroidery with an expanded field of floral beading across the chest. Decontextualizing and dramatically reconfiguring his precedents, Armani deliberately deprives them of their original meanings and requirements, investing them with the desires and fantasies of his own world.

70

Woman's evening vest, overskirt, and pants, spring/summer 1993
Vest: beige cotton/nylon blend lace and beige silk gauze with mini sequins and faceted stones; overskirt: off-white cotton/nylon blend lace; pants: taupe silk organza
Giorgio Armani Archives, Milan
The persistence and stylistic consistency of regional forms underscores the radical manipulations of Armani's interpretations. The bib-fronted robe worn by a peasant woman in William Holman Hunt's *The Afterglow in Egypt* (1860–63), for example, is not dissimilar to embroidered dresses still made in the Near and Middle East and available in shops from London's Camden Passage to New York's East Village. Armani's amalgamation of materials in this evening ensemble—including lace, beige silk gauze, and frosted stones and sequins—alone describes the magnitude of his imaginary departure.

71

Woman's evening tunic coat and pants, fall/winter 1990–91
Coat: iridescent metallic gold silk taffeta with rhinestones and metallic gold thread embroidery; pants: gold silk satin
Giorgio Armani Archives, Milan
According to the designer, this evening coat was inspired by India. His attribution is not unreasonable, but in seeking out specific sources it becomes clear that Armani's references are not to details or specific precedents, but to a broader sensibility. The beaded lace pattern that edges the coat suggests, faintly, the swirling effect of paisley. The asymmetrical, triangulated neckline border might be derived from a Mughal *jama*, but its continuation into a cutaway skirt and the garment's lithe, body-conscious silhouette deviates from the Indian model. Further, the ensemble is accessorized by a *topi*, a cylindrical cap worn in Nepal, although similar shapes can also be found in Afghanistan.

72

Woman's evening pants ensemble, spring/summer 1990
Top: black nylon knit mesh with seed and bugle beads; pants: turquoise, white, and amber cloud-printed silk/rayon blend plain weave with black silk/nylon blend tulle overlay
Giorgio Armani Archives, Milan
As with many of Armani's ethnic designs, this ensemble is a simulacra, a convincing copy of an original that never existed. It melds a number of cultural sources. In the top, gold bugle beads delineate a trompe l'oeil vest with matching cuffs, which is paired with narrow, Chinese cloud-patterned pants covered by a draped overlay. In Armani's hands the pants are transformed into a credible visual facsimile of a dhoti.

73

Woman's evening dress and pants, fall/winter 1994–95
Dress: light gray printed silk/rayon blend tulle with silk embroidery and rhinestones; pants: light gray silk/rayon blend knit mesh with bugle beads and cupped sequins
Giorgio Armani Archives, Milan
Armani plays with body disclosure in this layered evening ensemble. A plastron of dense embroidery covers the front of the lightly patterned

dress. Fitted pants in a pattern related to that of the dress intensify the ensemble's richness through layering and the compression of patterning in the folds of the overskirt. As in other of his designs, Armani uses a single sheer textile in different configurations to accrue an intensified effect of richness.

74 and 75

Woman's evening jacket and skirt, spring/summer 1995
Jacket: beige silk organza pavé-embroidered in an oriental-carpet pattern with floral cupped sequins and seed beads; skirt: beige silk organza
Giorgio Armani Archives, Milan

Woman's evening jacket and divided skirt, spring/summer 1995
Jacket: beige silk organza pavé-embroidered in an oriental-carpet pattern with floral cupped sequins and seed beads; skirt: beige silk organza
Giorgio Armani Archives, Milan
In these evening ensembles, Armani interprets oriental-carpet patterns in densely beaded embroidery. The small, tight jackets vaguely suggest the snug bodices of the elaborately embroidered formal coats for women found in Iran. But in this instance, unusual for the designer, the inspiration appears to be restricted primarily to a simple and direct interpretation of a surface pattern rather than a reformulation of a structural component derived from an exotic item of dress.

76

Woman's evening "polonaise" ensemble, spring/summer 1988
Jacket: multicolor floral-printed silk georgette pavé-embroidered with clear sequins, and silk braid; skirt: multicolor silk/polyester blend plaid chine taffeta overskirt with pale green and peach floral-printed silk organza and peach silk chiffon underskirts
Giorgio Armani Archives, Milan
Among Armani's more complex conflations of culture and time is this evening ensemble, which blends the silhouette of an eighteenth-century *robe à la polonaise* with imagery of the Near East. With a *mille-fleurs* pattern similar to Persian illuminations and Zouave-like braid closures, the sequined jacket suggests a nineteenth-century Turkish genealogy. In broad strokes the ensemble resembles one place and time, and in finer details another.

77

Woman's evening vest, overskirt, and pants, spring/summer 1994
Vest: gold silk organza with seed beads and sequins; bandeau: gray, beige, and white printed silk organza; overskirt: gray, beige, and white printed silk chiffon; pants: green silk organza
Giorgio Armani Archives, Milan
Two clues unravel the tangled lineage of this ensemble: the chinoiserie pattern of the silk chiffon and the apronlike construction of the overskirt. As with any mystery, there are red herrings—Armani complicates the costume historian's search by adding a sequined vest, structured bandeau, and dhoti-styled pants. Furthermore, the more easily discernable references are not left untouched: the floral pattern of the fabric is more Eurasian than Chinese, even twentieth-century Chinese, and the hundred-knife pleated folds of the paired panels of the Manchu apron skirt have been suggested here by soft gathers.

78

Woman's evening jacket and pants, spring/summer 1994
Jacket: gray, beige, and white printed silk chiffon with seed beads and sequins; pants: gray, beige, and white printed silk chiffon
Giorgio Armani Archives, Milan
Beginning in the late nineteenth century, Chinese clothing was, like some

forms of Turkish dress, adopted with little modification in the West as negligee and at-home wear. However, the trend for Chinese silk pajama lounging sets—which were especially in vogue during the period between the two world wars—was of a mixed parentage. The pajama was a form with its roots in India, and more distantly in Persia, rather than in China. With this ensemble, then, Armani begins with a precedent of combined cultural heritage, but in his disposition of elements he asserts its Chinese lineage: a rondel appears where an embroidered ranking badge would be, and band borders along the sides and hem of the legs are placed precisely where they would fall on a *shuangqun* or "paired apron" skirt.

79

Woman's evening pantsuit, fall/winter 1990–91
Copper silk knit pavé-embroidered with micro seed beads and sequins
Giorgio Armani Archives, Milan
In this pantsuit, seed beads and sequins are aligned in a vertical fish-scale embroidery, deviating only at the center-front hem of the jacket to form opposing rondels. By changing the grain of the beading, the rondels expand its range of light-catching effects. With these comblike lines and spiraling rondels, the pantsuit represents the designer's interest in Shang dynasty metalwork.

80

Woman's evening jacket and pants, fall/winter 1995–96
Jacket: gold silk charmeuse pavé-embroidered with seed beads and cupped sequins; vest: gold bugle bead openwork; pants: gold silk/polyester blend satin
Giorgio Armani Archives, Milan
Precedents for the scrolling floral pattern of the extraordinarily complex beaded embroidery on this evening jacket can be seen in Chinese black-and-white reserve-glaze porcelains. However, Armani has muted the strong graphic effect of these porcelains by rendering a textural rather than tonal definition of forms. The bugle-bead vest is constructed like ancient Chinese undershirts, which were a mesh of tiny bamboo segments joined in a fine fretwork intended to protect the wearer's silk robes from the body. In Armani's version, this mundane undergarment is transfigured into elegant body jewelry.

81

Woman's evening jacket and pants, fall/winter 1990–91
Jacket: brown silk/rayon blend velvet, floral-embroidered with French knots, metallic gold coil, sequins, and seed beads, and black silk tulle overlay; pants: brown silk/rayon blend velvet
Giorgio Armani Archives, Milan
The success of Armani's assimilation of the traditional dress of other cultures is in his retention of the allusive power of the forms while transforming them to conform to his uncompromised credo of comfort and modernity. In this evening jacket, the radiating pin tucks that shape the neckline and shoulders are a structural application of the pieced segments that comprise a Manchu cloud collar. The elaborate floral-and-sprig pattern originates in *kousu* tapestry weaves and silk-thread embroideries.

82

Woman's evening gown, fall/winter 1995–96
Multicolor chinoiserie-printed silk satin with seed beads, bugle beads, and micro sequins
Giorgio Armani Archives, Milan
In Bernardo Bertolucci's *The Last Emperor* (1987), changes in China's cultural and political climate are manifested most clearly in the costumes, when Manchu robes are exchanged for tennis whites. The reality of social and political transformation is, of course, more complex, and those accompanying ambiguities of intercultural accommodation were as manifested in Chinese fashion as they were in music and the visual arts. The floral design of this evening gown suggests a Westernized Chinese pattern, alluding to the assimilation of Western aesthetic conventions by traditional Chinese painting. To this, Armani adds a rainbow border, a characteristic feature of Chinese court dress; however, he has inverted his forms, placing what would be the hem of a venerable court robe across the bodice of the strapless evening gown. Like the chiffon velvet cheongsams of the 1930s, Armani's gown expresses the merging of Eastern and Western aesthetics.

83

Woman's evening dress with overshirt, spring/summer 1998
Overshirt: off-white silk organza; dress: gray and taupe silk chiffon, embroidered in a dragonfly pattern with metallic silver coil, rhinestones, and bugle beads
Giorgio Armani Archives, Milan
The poetic evocation of ephemerality, the fragile and transient nature of life, is prized by the Japanese. A fascination with the natural world and its beauty is paired with a recognition of its temporality. Dragonflies, for example, with their darting insubstantiality, frequently appear on screens and pottery. Armani intuits this Japanese sensibility in this translucent evening dress, in which a swarm of beaded dragonflies, clearly visible near the neckline, disappear as faint and elusive flickers at the shadowed hem.

84

Woman's evening ensemble with wrap skirt, spring/summer 1998
Top: off-white silk chiffon pavé-embroidered with sequins, and taupe silk chiffon overlay; skirt: beige and green printed silk plain weave with sequins, seed beads, and bugle beads
Giorgio Armani Archives, Milan
A motif of pines and abstracted clumps of grass decorates the wrap skirt in this ensemble. The print is similar to those commonly found on Japanese kimonos, where they are sometimes delineated and augmented by couched gold threads and silk floss, but here Armani articulates the printed pattern with a more assertive overlay of seed and bugle beads interspersed with sequins. Unlike a kimono, which suppresses the bust and pads the waist to achieve a narrow, columnar silhouette, this evening ensemble conforms to the body. In fact, the tank-style top exaggerates the body's shape with its metallic, light-contouring surface of sequins. Whereas a kimono is overlaid by an obi, Armani presents his ensemble uncinched, but the eye is nonetheless engaged by the midriff since the tank's chiffon overlay and the waist of the skirt do not meet, creating a fissured view of the top's mercurial sequined surface.

85

Woman's evening jacket and culottes, fall/winter 1982–83
Jacket: taupe silk satin with trapunto; culottes: black silk satin with sequins
Giorgio Armani Archives, Milan
All armor has an uncanny beauty. The simultaneous requirements of mobility and protection result in an interpretation of the body that is specific and non-negotiable in parts (as in the positioning of joints) and subject to generalization and abstraction in others (the contours of the chest or shoulders). Japanese armor, perhaps because it originates from a nontailored clothing tradition, is composed of segmented planes, sheets of flattened steel rods connected by brilliant-colored cording. This form of armor is interpreted by Armani in this evening ensemble as a corded trapunto satin that replicates the channeled effect of the original, but in applying the technique to the sleeves, the designer transforms the flat platelets into the curved shaping of a tailored garment.

86

Woman's evening jacket and pants, fall/winter 1990–91
Dark blue silk satin with royal blue silk satin trapunto
Giorgio Armani Archives, Milan

A decade after his first Japanese collection in 1980–81, Armani continued to experiment with shapes and techniques he had introduced at that time. By the 1990s, however, another conceptual strand intersected with the designer's application of the rectilinear pattern pieces of Japanese dress, when the Russian Constructivists' planar fields of rectangles and arcs asserted themselves as color blocks and semicircular pattern pieces. These designs are a 180-degree departure from the supple, body-disclosing fit associated with the designer, but in their exploration of reductive shaping and luxurious, minimally ornamented materials, they are typical of Armani.

87

Woman's jacket and culottes, fall/winter 1980–81
Jacket: light brown, black, and white wool checked novelty weave;
culottes: charcoal gray and gray-green printed wool plain weave
The Museum at the Fashion Institute of Technology, New York,
Gift of Mrs. James Levy

In a collection inspired by Akira Kurosawa's *Kagemusha* (1980), a movie set in feudal Japan, Armani focuses as much on the rustic costumes of the peasants as on the regalia of the Shogun and his samurai. The result is daywear that combines elements of historical Japanese dress with an uncompromised contemporary Milanese sportswear sensibility. In this example, the application of the banded kimono collar to an impeccably tailored jacket contributes a stripped-down modernity as well as an ethnographic reference.

88

Woman's evening shirt and floor-length skirt, spring/summer 1997
Shirt: white silk chiffon with metallic gold coil, seed beads, and rhinestones;
skirt: white silk tulle with metallic gold coil, seed beads, and rhinestones
Giorgio Armani Archives, Milan

The Javanese practice of wearing a tightly fitted shirt or jacket over a long sarong is interpreted here by Armani as eveningwear. Made of heavily beaded white silk chiffon, the shirt suggests transparency, but in fact is of a density that is more modest than nude. The sexiness of the piece, which has been shrunk to reveal sternum and midriff, ultimately resides in its bursting-at-the-seams fit.

89

Woman's evening shirt and pants, fall/winter 1997–98
Shirt: black polyester tulle with bugle beads, rhinestones, cupped sequins, seed beads, pearls, and metallic silver thread embroidery; pants: black silk chiffon and black silk tulle with seed beads, cupped sequins, bugle beads, rhinestones, silk cordonnet couching, and metallic silver thread embroidery
Giorgio Armani Archives, Milan

Armani takes an ensemble of sensual fit and intensifies its provocation with transparency. But, as with Yves Saint Laurent's transparent effects, the sheer beauty of materials and elegance of line in Armani's see-through pieces preclude any sense of prurience or vulgarity. Here the beading on black tulle and chiffon appears more like a speckling of light than it does embroidery.

90

Woman's evening jacket and pants, spring/summer 1997
Jacket: celadon and silver polyester blend plain weave pavé-embroidered with seed beads, bugle beads, sequins, and rhinestones; pants: iridescent bronze polyester satin

Giorgio Armani Archives, Milan

In many areas of Southeast Asia, fitted shirtjackets are often worn with a cummerbund or waist sash. In other parts of the region, sashes are wrapped around the bust as bustiers or used to secure the drape of long skirt cloths. In this evening jacket, Armani superimposes one regional style over another. Although the bust panel is a recollection of a traditional clothing detail, it no longer has any true structural purpose; rather, it serves to frame but obscure the bust, presenting it while constraining it. Like so many of Armani's design syntheses, the pleasure of the work resides in the richness of its ambiguity.

91

Woman's evening tunic coat and pants, fall/winter 1990–91
Coat: multicolor floral-printed silk/rayon blend plain weave with metallic gold bullion and coil and multicolor silk thread embroidery; pants: light green silk satin
Giorgio Armani Archives, Milan

The style of this evening coat is derived from India, and harks back to ancient Mughal court jackets. The originals had fabric tie closings at the neck and mid-chest, a sashed waist, and a strongly defined, A-line skirt—details that have been eliminated by Armani. But though the silhouette has been tapered and the embroidered fabric has motifs that are more Southeast Asian than Indian, the designer has retained the narrow-sleeved, chest-hugging courtly fit and rich textile heritage of the jacket's source.

92

Woman's evening jacket and pants, fall/winter 1990–91
Jacket: white silk cloque; pants: multicolor floral-printed silk/rayon blend compound weave
Giorgio Armani Archives, Milan

The mismatched coordination of jacket and sarong seen in Java and Bali is alluded to in this pairing of a pristine white silk cloque jacket with richly toned, batik-printed silk pants. Even in the original, the body-hugging fit of the jacket juxtaposed with the loose wrap of the sarong creates a silhouette of sensual provocation; here Armani tightens the jacket's fit until it breaches, presenting a crescent of fissured nudity. Its textured surface references traditional quilting techniques, used to reinforce the durability and insulating qualities of the textile.

93

Woman's strapless evening ensemble, spring/summer 1993
Multicolor tropical-printed silk plain weave with sequins, micro seed beads, bugle beads, and micro rhinestones
Giorgio Armani Archives, Milan

A sarong may be wrapped in a number of ways, depending on tribal and regional custom. Although this ensemble is comprised of a separate top and skirt, it retains the effect of a unified and continuous textile. The top, with its asymmetrical, scarflike drape, alludes to the practice of Southeast Asian tribal women displaying the border design of their skirt cloths across their chest.

94

Woman's evening vest, overskirt, and pants, spring/summer 1993
Vest: purple, green, orange, and yellow striped polyester pin-tucked-effect novelty weave; skirt: rose polyester gauze with clear sequins and orange and mauve floral-printed silk crepe de chine underlay; pants: multicolor tropical-printed silk organza
Giorgio Armani Archives, Milan

Here, Armani adopts the essentially male tradition of donning a short vest over a tunic or robe, seen from the west coast of Africa to the far reaches of Southeast Asia. Part of a collection with Malaysian and Indonesian references, this ensemble also suggests a use of textiles that dates to nineteenth-century Western clothing, when colorfully patterned calicos were used to line more sumptuous dress fabrics. In Armani's interpretation, layers of uniformly sequined, plain-patterned fabrics cover an elaborately printed underskirt in an equally luxurious silk.

95

Woman's one-shouldered evening ensemble, spring/summer 1993
Top: green and bordeaux silk plain weave with seed beads and silk floss embroidery; skirt: multicolor tropical-printed silk plain weave
Giorgio Armani Archives, Milan

The wrapping of rectangles of cloth in different lengths and proportions has provided an infinite variety of clothing types around the world; bandeaus, bustiers, skirts, gowns, and even pants have emerged from the topologies of these twist-and-knot practices. The one-shouldered wrap top of this ensemble alludes to the neckline of the sari, but it also suggests the evolving form of a fitted bodice in the process of being draped on a dressmaker's dummy.

96

Woman's evening blouse, pareo, and skirt, spring/summer 1990
Blouse: predominantly beige tropical-printed silk chiffon; pareo: navy blue and off-white paisley-printed silk chiffon with pearls and gold cord embroidery; skirt: predominantly green tropical-printed silk chiffon with pearls, faceted stones, micro seed beads, and gold cord and silk floss embroidery
Giorgio Armani Archives, Milan

A fluttering blouse redolent of the 1930s is worn here with a pareo. In this ethereal ensemble, Armani does not so much merge cultures as he poises them in an elegant and unexpected balance. Like a photograph faded by the sun, the wild mix of tropical prints is leached of color until only a tinted grisaille remains.

97

Woman's strapless evening ensemble, spring/summer 1990
Bustier: metallic gold lace on black silk/rayon blend organza with sequins; skirt: drab green silk chiffon with foliate-patterned silk floss embroidery
Giorgio Armani Archives, Milan

Though the elements of this ensemble can be found in much of the Malay Peninsula and in parts of Indonesia, their rich embroidery suggests artisanal traditions particularly associated with the Philippines. Again, Armani has created a historical conundrum, an ensemble of multiple referents but no source, for Philippine lace and embroidered garments appear to be an evolved, localized form of European models, arguably derived from nineteenth-century Spain.

98

Woman's evening tank top and skirt, spring/summer 1993
Predominantly sage green Gauguin-inspired printed silk organza with bugle beads, micro rhinestones secured with micro seed beads, and metallic silver thread embroidery
Giorgio Armani Archives, Milan

In a collection based on overembroidered fabrics with prints inspired by Paul Gauguin's Tahitian paintings, Armani illustrates the sportswear strategy that informs many of his designs for evening. In this ensemble, the humble and sporty tank top, rendered in silk organza, is transformed into an evening bodice, which is worn over wide-cut pants with the billow and movement of a skirt. A corona of silk petals is worn on the head like a *hakalei*, the traditional garland of flowers worn in Polynesia.

99

Woman's evening jacket, overskirt, and pants, spring/summer 1993
Jacket: gold and off-white linen twill; overskirt: predominantly sage green

Gauguin-inspired printed silk plain weave; pants: light green silk novelty basket weave with metallic silver thread embroidery
Giorgio Armani Archives, Milan

Here, a signature Armani jacket-and-pants ensemble is transported to the South Pacific by its accessorization with a lei and the introduction of an overskirt. With the vertical fall of the softly tailored pants, the skirt's scarflike drape suggests a border-patterned pareo or sarong. Although the wearing of a jacket with a pareo is not unknown in the South Pacific, it is more typical of Southeast Asia. Again, Armani has created a design that is a cross-fertilization of cultural forms and practices with a certifiable reality, if only distantly recalled.

100

Woman's evening dress and pants, spring/summer 1993
Dress: predominantly beige Gauguin-inspired printed silk plain weave with clear sequins, bugle beads, and micro rhinestones; pants: light green silk novelty basket weave
Giorgio Armani Archives, Milan

Armani has invested this evening dress, inspired by the simple wrap of a sarong, with greater structural complexity without sacrificing the elegant line of the original. Spiraling around the body, the dress ends at the front with two deep pleats, which create the regular, fanlike fall of fabric emphasized by the curved cut of the cloth. In movement, this fullness encourages the light fabric to billow open to expose the narrow, tapered pants worn beneath.

101

Woman's evening jacket, over skirt and pants, spring/summer 1993
Jacket: predominantly sage green Gauguin-inspired printed silk plain weave with cupped sequins, bugle beads, and clear sequins secured with green thread and micro seed beads; skirt and pants: predominantly gray Gauguin-inspired printed silk organza
Giorgio Armani Archives, Milan

When working with light fabrics, Armani typically plays with the effects of layering. Here, the illusion of transparency invests the ensemble with a palpable eroticism. Sheer pants are seen as a narrow, shadowed outline beneath an equally sheer overskirt, and a silk jacket worn without a blouse has only slightly more opacity than the layered overskirt and pants, but potentially more opportunity for body disclosure. Armani exploits the susceptibility of the imagination to suggestion, where the implied is often more powerful than the overt.

102, 103, and 104

Woman's strapless evening gown, spring/summer 1993
Charcoal gray silk organza with micro seed beads and bugle beads and sage green silk chiffon underlay
Giorgio Armani Archives, Milan

Woman's strapless evening gown, spring/summer 1993
Gray-green silk crepe
Giorgio Armani Archives, Milan

Woman's strapless evening gown, spring/summer 1993
Charcoal gray silk organza with micro seed beads and bugle beads and sage green silk chiffon underlay
Giorgio Armani Archives, Milan

These three pareo-style evening gowns, all cut identically, appeared in Armani's spring/summer 1993 défilé in single file. In a modular approach that resonates with the influence of Minimalist art, Armani frequently sends down the runway in quick succession identical designs made of different fabrics, or designs with only subtle variations in identical fabrics, inducing a faintly uncanny and incantatory serenity. The two gowns with beading shown here reference, improbably, both tapa-cloth patterns and the richly gilded graphic language of Gustav Klimt and the Wiener Werkstätte.

105

Woman's pants ensemble, fall/winter 1993–94
Jacket: light gray wool herringbone; vest: sage green silk crepe-back satin;
pants: sage green wool/rayon/nylon blend twill
Giorgio Armani Archives, Milan

A spencer appears to have been the point of origin for this pared-down jacket's stylistic transformation. Collar and lapels have been reduced to tiny crescent lappets at the throat, with the fine seams used in the construction of a conventional collar remaining as vestigial marks. In their angled disposition, these seams also appear to be *pentimenti* of the fish darts that mark the tailor's shaping of the jacketfront around the neckline, across the collarbone, and to the shoulder. Elsewhere, seams and darts are treated with typical tailored finishes, except for the welt at the jacket's hipline, which marks a short, shirttail-like extension of the jacket. The join is a cicatrix, a demarcation of the annexing of one form to another.

106

Woman's pantsuit, spring/summer 1995
Beige cotton/rayon blend jacquard
Giorgio Armani Archives, Milan

The importance of materials and finishing details in Modernist architecture derives in part from the expression of structure, a strategy that foregrounds previously hidden elements. In this soft suit, Armani creates a single-ply jacket without linings and—more importantly—without self-facings; the revers are simply the underside of the cloth, with the reversal of the tiny jacquard pattern's zones of matte and shine the only indication that the jacket front has not been self-lined. A merrow machine, which cuts and overstitches the edge of a fabric—typically an industrial finishing technique—has been used to outline the garment. By doing so, Armani not only elevates the mundane mechanisms of production to ornamental status, but is also able to create a tailored jacket with the lightness of a silk blouse.

107

Woman's pantsuit, fall/winter 1993–94
Beige silk jacquard
Giorgio Armani Archives, Milan

By conscripting delicate, dress-weight fabrics for tailored jackets, Armani virtually precludes the use of shoulder pads and interfacings, which not only would show through in relief, but, more importantly, would change the character of the cloth. Armani exploits the natural drape of the fabric to produce a body-molding shape, which is clearly facilitated by the cloth's flexibility and suppleness—characteristics not found in traditional suitings. Despite this lack of any stiffness, Armani maintains a crisp line, compensating for any of the disadvantages inherent in the lightness of the fabric through his unprecedented understanding of tailoring in his unconventional medium. The shrinking of the collar, for example, is made possible by the elimination of the shoulder darts.

108

Woman's suit, fall/winter 1995–96
Black wool crepe
Giorgio Armani Archives, Milan

Charles James, the great American designer of the mid-twentieth century, and Balenciaga can be seen as the extremes of the practices of tailoring and dressmaking. James constructed his designs using padding,

"horsehair" braid, whalebone, heavily sized net, and a number of interfacings. So elaborately supported were the taut skins of his garments that it was said they could virtually stand on their own. Balenciaga, on the other hand, attempted to achieve shape with his choice of cloth and seaming alone. Often the full effect of a garment's silhouette could only be glimpsed when the wearer was walking and movement inflated the piece. In a suit that recalls the heavily structured, shoulder-, bust-, and hip-padded shaping of the James method, Armani has—with the slight exception of thin flannel pads at the jacket's shoulders—opted for the light touch of Balenciaga.

109

Woman's evening pants ensemble, spring/summer 1999
Jacket: teal blue silk crinkle crepe; pants: steel gray silk/nylon blend satin with
black nylon/rayon blend tulle overlay
Giorgio Armani Archives, Milan

From his earliest collections for women, Armani has explored the idea of a tailored jacket that wraps at the waist, thus merging, sphynxlike, the parts of two distinct species. Gradually, the bunched drape of his earlier designs has given way to a vestigial cluster of radiating ripples. The gathered cloth no longer appears to allude to cummerbunds, sashes, and ethnic traditions, but instead communicates a self-reflective Modernist assertion: the folds now represent no more than the essential characteristics of the cloth itself. As dress-weight fabric is manipulated into a jacket, its feminized essence—its suppleness and drape—appears out of the masculinized conditions of tailoring as in a palimpsest.

110

Woman's evening pants ensemble, spring/summer 1998
Jacket: dark gray silk/cotton blend crepe; pants: blue-black silk satin
Giorgio Armani Archives, Milan

As if to destabilize the effortless elegance that is the result of his mastery of fit and present himself with new tailoring challenges, Armani creates here a series of ripples at the waist of an otherwise uninflected torso-skimming jacket. The consequence of this small detail is its introduction of excess fabric that must be accommodated elsewhere. The fabric's grain must be balanced so that the hem of the jacket falls without ripples, the waist does not bag, and the jacket closure does not shift off-angle, and Armani accomplishes this by introducing only so much additional fabric as to create a legible drape, but not so much that it cannot be taken up by the contours of the bust and hips.

111

Man's leather coat ensemble, fall/winter 1999–2000
Coat: dark brown leather; pants: gray wool twill
Giorgio Armani Archives, Milan

Like architect Sigrid Leweretz's sophisticated treatment of glass and brick or sculptor Carl Andre's virtuoso piecing of plywood to achieve seemingly simple effects, Armani celebrates the inherent beauty of materials in this ensemble with a deliberate avoidance of extraneous intervention. The crisp edge of the coat achieves its perfection through the weight and quality of the leather—no edges have been backed or bound, but rather they have been left raw. Here, the raw is the more refined.

112

Man's suit, fall/winter 1991–92
Black and charcoal wool blend pinstriped novelty twill
Giorgio Armani Archives, Milan

The navy blue pin- or chalkstriped suit has undergone a number of permutations in Armani's hands over the last quarter century. Most notable is the designer's relaxing of the fit of men's tailoring and his introduction of new materials as suitings. But his interventions are also a fundamental reconsideration of masculinity and its signs. Although an Armani suit from one period of the designer's work is inevitably differentiated from that of another, there is an uncompromised consistency in his tailored creations: they are never stiff. The ease that Armani has introduced to the suit is nowhere better represented than in his advocacy of uncreased pants with pooling cuffs, creating business dress with the relaxed feel of nightclothes.

113

Man's raincoat and suit, ca. fall/winter 1984–85
Raincoat: dark blue wool gabardine with detachable tan wool flannel lining;
suit: navy blue wool twill
Giorgio Armani Archives, Milan, Gift of Verna and Jay Cocks
Like the unconstructed blazer, the raincoat has become a signature Armani item. In this example, the traditional form of the balmacaan is given a worn-in suppleness: shoulders are rounded, the neckline is opened up, and the body of the coat is expanded, not in an exaggerated conventional A-line, but with a fullness that is more equally distributed. The result is a coat with a loose swagger, comfortably capacious and with a sense of movement. As in all of Armani's garments, the coat has been designed to give a sense of weight and play against the body, but not so much as to introduce an insupportably ostentatious theatricality.

114

Woman's evening dress and pants, spring/summer 1993
Dress: navy blue viscose/rayon blend plain weave; pants: navy blue acetate/rayon blend knit
Giorgio Armani Archives, Milan
While rufflelike ornament occurs in Armani's oeuvre, it is likely to be a fluted fall of excess fabric that is the consequence of a structural necessity, or the finished edge of a shirred or smocked expanse. Armani prefers the more architectonic tiered band, an exaggerated tuck, pleat, or fold that is more in keeping with his interest in introducing sensuality and femininity to the rigorous orthogonality of Modernism.

115

Man's coat and suit, fall/winter 1999–2000
Coat: dark blue wool novelty twill; suit: black cotton plain weave
Giorgio Armani Archives, Milan
In Armani's fall/winter 1999–2000 collection, the razor-sharp details of the 1950s introduced previously unreferenced imagery to the designer's tailoring. While communicating a more honed linearity, the collection's suits and coats maintained the elegance and *gravitas* inherent to Armani's sensibility. Here, the high-notched, narrowed lapels and cropped length of the coat have been balanced by its widened shoulders and straight drop. The result is a proportion that is reduced but not shrunken, closer to the body but not constricting.

116

Man's suit, fall/winter 1999–2000
Black wool twill
Giorgio Armani Archives, Milan
For almost 150 years, tailored menswear has relied on a number of conventions that, though occasionally broken and slowly evolving, continue to inform recent experiments. Even Armani's deliberate transgressions have expressed themselves primarily through innovations in fabrics and cut and have generally incorporated much of tailoring's historical language. Because that language is so codified, changes—no matter how nuanced—carry a dramatic weight. Here, the hidden closure of the double-breasted jacket effaces the buttons that normally define

and reinforce that garment's identity, and the omission is so notable as to become a surreal zone that is the focus of the suit.

117

Woman's evening jacket and shorts, spring/summer 1992
Jacket: gold silk organza pavé-embroidered with micro rhinestones, seed beads, and bugle beads, and zipper closing; shorts: taupe cotton/rayon blend faille
Giorgio Armani Archives, Milan
Taking its prime motif from asymmetrically closing motorcycle jackets, and with a chain-mail effect produced by its bead- and rhinestone-encrusted surface, this jacket suggests protective armor while also projecting an aura of evening glamour. Paired with cropped Bermuda shorts that offer freedom of mobility and a level of modesty not possible with a skirt of the same length, the ensemble is typically Armani in its simultaneous embodiment of contradictions.

118

Woman's evening mini dress and shorts ensemble, spring/summer 1991
Dress: gold silk chiffon pavé-embroidered with rhinestones and seed beads; shorts: gold silk/acetate blend satin
Giorgio Armani Archives, Milan
Here, Armani exploits the slippery, mercurial effect of pavé-embroidered silk. By anchoring the heavily beaded textile at the side seams, Armani causes a liquid drape to fall, apronlike, across the pelvis. Even the revers at the plunging neckline collapse under the weight of the surface embellishment. While the ensemble, with its glimmer and heft, is reminiscent of chain mail, Armani's draping of the material is more closely aligned to that of the glamorous, chiffon-weight gold-lamé gowns of the 1930s.

119

Woman's evening gown, fall/winter 1994–95
Gray-green silk/nylon/spandex blend knit
Giorgio Armani Archives, Milan
Armani has claimed that each of his designs originates in a consideration of the textile. Here, the addition of nylon and spandex to silk has resulted in a gossamer-weight fabric with strength and elasticity. Specifically because of the fabric's blend, the sleeves of the gown can be tautly fitted and its bodice tightly shirred without shaping seams or darts. The fabric's give has encouraged and enabled a design freed of the constraints of fit lines.

120

Woman's one-shouldered evening gown, spring/summer 1994
Gown: silver gray silk plain weave with seed beads and rayon floss embroidery; pants (not visible in photograph): celadon silk organza
Giorgio Armani Archives, Milan
Armani has introduced designs with the effect of chain mail in several of his collections. In some instances, the effect is produced by a woven mesh of metallic thread, but more frequently it arises from the uniform and overall application of beading. Armani rarely exploits the effect for direct historical reference; rather, it becomes the basis for designs of an industrial sleekness, at once atavistic and futuristic.

121

Woman's evening gown, spring/summer 1992
Celadon silk crepe
Giorgio Armani Archives, Milan
The curved edges at the neckline and plunging armholes of this gown lap the torso as it moves, but they are so anchored by the weight of the gown that inadvertent exposure is precluded. The rounded edges of the center-front opening at the hem collapse together to conceal the break, but in mid-stride the skirt plays against the legs in a more exaggerated version of the shifting revelations of the bodice.

122

Woman's one-shouldered evening gown, spring/summer 1997
Electric blue silk crepe
Giorgio Armani Archives, Milan

Saturated colors are not generally associated with Armani, yet they recur consistently in his collections, in which ultramarine blues, emerald greens, and reds often appear either alone or in combination. In this gown, a biomorphic neckline describes the concavities and convexities of the wearer's poitrine. But, like the splash of blue paint on a naked Yves Klein model, the skin-tight cut of Armani's gown only appears to disclose more than it reveals.

123

Woman's evening gown, spring/summer 1997
Nude nylon knit mesh pavé-embroidered with rhinestones, seed beads,
and bugle beads, and linen twill tape
Giorgio Armani Archives, Milan

Costume historian Richard Martin often cited Claude Lévi-Strauss's cultural metaphor of "the raw and the cooked" to describe the strategy of contemporary designers to juxtapose the crude with the refined. This impulse is manifested in Armani's unapologetic use of the most mundane, if functionally suited, materials in his work. The beading of this gown is fixed to an elastic flesh-toned mesh, producing a sirenlike fit, but to control the stretch and deformity that is inevitable when such an elastic material is encumbered by the weight of beads, the designer finishes the gown's neckline and armholes with twill binding tape. The rough-and-fine play of industrial tape and silver-lined glass beads is typical of Armani's tempering of even the most formal effects with the casual and the everyday.

124

Woman's evening gown, spring/summer 1997
Pale peach nylon knit mesh with sequins and seed beads
Giorgio Armani Archives, Milan

The glazed body shimmer of this translucent, glove-tight evening gown harks back to the concert wardrobe of Marlene Dietrich and to the incandescent dress worn by Marilyn Monroe in celebration of President Kennedy's birthday. In contrast to the more worldly, theatrical designs worn by the two blonde sex icons, however, Armani's version is infused with a classicizing innocence. This gown has its progenitors in the simple cotton mull chemises worn by *merveilleuses* during the Directoire period; the chemises, it is said, were doused with water to dry clinging to the body. By introducing the casual cut of the T-shirt to the "naked" evening gown, Armani infuses it with simplicity and historical allusion without eroding any of its sensual appeal.

125

Woman's one-shouldered evening dress, spring/summer 1998
Nude nylon organza with faceted stones, seed beads, and bugle beads
Giorgio Armani Archives, Milan

The narrow straps of this one-shouldered evening dress suggest the quiver harnesses worn by the goddess Diana and her attendants over their chitons. Beyond this mechanism for support, the dress's primary ornament is its allover beading. Armani adds lines of faceted stones and seed beads to the matrix of directionally laid bugle beads. The subtlety of the resulting "striped" pattern is appreciated only in close proximity, or when light is fixed on the dress in movement and lightninglike flashes of brilliance are conducted by the rhinestones up and down the dress.

126

Woman's evening gown, spring/summer 1989
Black silk crepe with silk floss embroidery
Giorgio Armani Archives, Milan

This gown evokes disparate references, from Pre-Raphaelite medievalized costume to Northern African robes, but its most salient characteristic is the dressmaking skill required to construct it. The pattern pieces outlined by floss embroidery suggest a rigorous orthogonality, and to maintain that right-angled projection onto the contours of the female form requires a virtuosic handling of the flat pattern, for grains, the lines of warp and weft, must align and be balanced.

127

Woman's evening tunic and pants ensemble, fall/winter 1994–95
Tunic and pants: black nylon tulle with seed beads and bugle beads;
bodysuit: black nylon/elastomer blend knit mesh with black sequins
Giorgio Armani Archives, Milan

This evening ensemble with flared tunic has the proportions of a day suit from 1910, but is paired with pants rather than a skirt. Surprisingly, this does not dilute the allusion. As with some anachronisms encountered in the theater and cinema, the liberties taken in Armani's work are often the very elements that reinforce the historical effect. The trousers, wide for pants but narrower than most skirts, convey the taper of the period hobble skirt. Like his evocations of foreign lands, Armani's designs that refer to other times have a deceptive, epigrammatic clarity. Transformed by his imagination, the elusive and imprecise sources for his designs appear convincingly historical.

128

Woman's evening vest coat and pants ensemble, fall/winter 1994–95
Vest coat: black cotton/nylon blend lace and black nylon tulle with seed beads,
bugle beads, and sequins; bodysuit: black nylon knit mesh; pants: black nylon knit
mesh with bugle beads and rayon floss embroidery
Giorgio Armani Archives, Milan

With dark humor, Armani merges the embellished propriety of the late-nineteenth-century mourning dress with the black beret and turtlenecked bohemianism of the Apache dancer of Paris in the 1950s. The etiquette of mourning from Victorian into Edwardian times required that many people were clothed in some sartorial expression of grief for much of their lives; black dresses became a uniform of the times. Given the irrepressible impulse to fashion, however, various socially acceptable means evolved to dress up mourning apparel. Jet embroidery and lace were favored forms of elaboration, and they are cited here in Armani's recontextualizing of "*autre temps, autre moeurs.*"

129

Woman's evening jacket and skirt, fall/winter 1989–90
Jacket: black rayon velvet; skirt: black silk chiffon with faceted stones and sequins
and white silk satin underlay
Giorgio Armani Archives, Milan

Here, Armani's rendering of historical dress—inspired by depictions of Portuguese traders on Japanese screens of the late Momoyama and early Tokugawa periods—is filtered through the transformative lens of his imagination. While the jacket retains the high band collar and pointed waist of the original, its sleeves have been narrowed. More drastically, the ballooning breeches of the time have been replaced by a long skirt, although this does not shatter the illusion: by weighting the hem of the chiffon overlayer with beading, and by cutting the skirt in a slight peg, Armani re-creates the silhouette of seventeenth-century pantaloons.

130

Woman's evening jacket and pants ensemble, fall/winter 1989–90
Jacket: black rayon velvet and trompe l'oeil black silk organza neckerchief with
metallic silver thread embroidery and bugle beads; pants: black rayon velvet
and black silk satin
Giorgio Armani Archives, Milan

In perhaps his most academic and esoteric reference, Armani details
this evening ensemble with elements derived from the dress of late-
sixteenth–early seventeenth-century Jesuit missionaries. Because of the
full cut of the pants, the ensemble has the silhouette of a clerical robe,
an allusion that is reinforced by the trompe l'oeil neckerchief with a
pattern of jet beaded crosses.

131

Woman's evening tunic and pants ensemble, fall/winter 1994–95
Tunic: beige silk chiffon with bugle beads and sequins; bodysuit and
pants: nude nylon tulle with bugle beads and cupped sequins
Giorgio Armani Archives, Milan

The tunics and tights of late-fifteenth-century Renaissance nobles
and the gilded Apollo costume made in 1653 for Louis XIV
(the Sun King) are both, arguably, sources for this evening ensemble.
As always, the appropriation is not a plagiarizing of historical fact,
but rather a fabulist's interpretation. Enough abides of the original to
establish the narratives, but the final expression is an almost total,
albeit convincing, invention.

132

Woman's evening bodice and skirt, spring/summer 1990
Bodice: charcoal gray silk chiffon with round and tear-shaped pearls and metallic
gold cord; skirt: multicolor floral-printed silk chiffon
Giorgio Armani Archives, Milan

In his spring/summer 1990 collection, Armani presented a series of
evening ensembles inspired by Sergei Diaghilev's Ballets Russes.
Precipitated by the company's performance of *Scheherazade* in 1910, an
orientalist rage persisted into the 1920s, abetted in no small way by the
production's opulent costumes, designed by Léon Bakst. In this evening
ensemble, Armani has mined not only the orientalist imagery and densely
encrusted components of Bakst's costumes, but the structural
components that accommodated the explosive dance technique of the
Russian dancers: sleeves cut high and tight (counter-intuitively, this allows
for a greater freedom of rotation of the arm) and legs that are barely
constrained by silk chiffon.

133

Woman's evening jacket, overskirt, and pants ensemble, spring/summer 1990
Jacket: multicolor printed silk chiffon with bugle beads, mini sequins, silk floss
embroidery, seed beads, and pearls; overskirt: multicolor printed silk organza with
black silk knit and multicolor printed silk chiffon; pants: multicolor printed cotton
tulle; sash: gold net with multicolor filet embroidery and sequins
Giorgio Armani Archives, Milan

This pagoda-skirted tunic conveys the rich and restrictive formality of
the court, but like a costume worn for the part of a Persian prince in a
ballet, the tunic's skirt—actually a separate element—can be removed in
the second scene to leave the short, fitted jacket and narrow pants, the
better to see the *grandes jettées* of the principal. The theatrical
costume's ability to evolve is a feature shared by sportswear. Even in
this most exotic expression of fantasy, Armani does not abandon his
convictions about dress: beauty never entails the sacrifice of comfort,
and true elegance can only exist in physical ease.

134

Woman's evening bandeau and pants ensemble, spring/summer 1990
Bandeau: black silk tulle with pearls, bugle beads, and metallic gold bullion,
thread, and coil; pants: black polyester chiffon with sequins, black nylon tulle with
sequins, and multicolor printed silk tulle
Giorgio Armani Archives, Milan

Among the Ballets Russes's most recognized costumes was the shoulder-
baring ensemble worn by Vaslav Nijinsky as the wildly acrobatic slave in
Scheherazade. Photographs by Baron Adolf de Meyer captured Nijinsky's
animalistic charisma, enhanced in no small way by the oriental splendor
of his jeweled girdle, fluffed waist sash, and gold harem pants. In
Armani's interpretation, the girdle shrinks to a midriff-baring brassiere, an
article of clothing not invented at the time, and the highly sculptural lamé
waist sash and pants are rendered in transparent layers of chiffon and
tulle. The male slave is transformed into an equally resplendent
odalisque, dressed not in the stiff ornamental textiles of ceremonial livery,
but in the seductive and filmy lounging pajamas of the harem.

135

Woman's evening gown, spring/summer 1989
Gown: black silk chiffon; stole: black silk chiffon and white silk chiffon
Giorgio Armani Archives, Milan

Unlike most of Armani's work, which is resolutely nonreferential, certain
of his designs elicit a recognitory response that suggests a precedent—
no matter how elusive—for the garment. This evening gown, which has
certain characteristics of Jan van Eyck's Arnolfini bride's costume, may
in fact allude to the cotton mull dresses of the Directoire and Empire
periods. The raised waistline, open neckline, and short, tight sleeves
conform to styles of the period, as does that vestige of *ancien régime*
court dress, the center-front slit that reveals an underskirt. Even the
accessorizing of the gown with a long, rectangular scarf has a counterpart
in the coordinated sheer mull wraps of the time. Still, like Cecil Beaton's
costumes for Audrey Hepburn in *My Fair Lady* (1964) that alluded to the
Directoire revival of 1910, Armani's evocation is informed more by his
own very contemporary aesthetic sensibility than any historical precedent.

136

Woman's off-the-shoulder evening bifurcated gown, fall/winter 1989–90
Brown silk/rayon blend velvet with off-white silk satin
Giorgio Armani Archives, Milan

This gown with a nonchalant, off-the-shoulder neckline evokes the
languorous elegance of the 1930s. But, by bifurcating the skirt, Armani
contemporizes the historical allusion and balances the overtly feminine
with the covertly masculine: gendered associations are still attached
to pants, even when the pants are cut to the width of a full skirt. The
wearer is freed to experience the liberation of movement made possible
by pants, even as she projects an uncompromised femininity.

137

Woman's halter-neck evening gown, spring/summer 1990
Gown: dark mustard silk crepe with seed beads, bugle beads, and faceted
stones; pants (not visible in photograph): dark mustard silk crepe
Giorgio Armani Archives, Milan

The cut of this gown is similar to others created by Armani over the
years, but here its uninterrupted flow is supported by a twist-effect halter
neckline. This is the graphic marker of a style of saronglike draping found
in the Belgian Congo, in which two corners of a large rectangle of fabric
are overlapped, twisted around the neck, and tied in back. The spare
elegance of the gown also recalls the bias-cut dresses of the 1930s,
with their Art Moderne–inspired streamlining.

138

Woman's evening sweater and skirt, fall/winter 1998–99
Sweater: midnight blue wool/cashmere blend knit;
skirt: midnight blue silk satin
Giorgio Armani Archives, Milan

Although Mainbocher is credited with creating the first evening sweater during World War II, his design was actually a coordinated jewel-embroidered pullover and cardigan. Since Mainbocher's enlistment of the knitted top to evening dress, other designers, most of them American, have explored the possibilities of the strategy. Armani's contribution to the genre in this ensemble is characteristically minimalist, but unabashedly luxurious as well. Although its unrelenting spareness can only be seen as contemporary, the full sweep of the skirt's train evokes Belle Epoque grandeur.

139

Woman's evening bustier and skirt ensemble, spring/summer 1993
Off-white silk chiffon
Giorgio Armani Archives, Milan

In homage to the impeccable craft of post–World War II couturier Jean Desses, Armani pleats this bustier in the French designer's signature style. Armani makes it his own, however. First, he separates the bodice from the skirt, introducing a sportswear-like ease. (In contrast, the pleats of the bodice in Desses's original released at the waist to become the continuous panels of the gown's skirt.) Second, a stiffly boned corset would have supported the pleated skin of the original dress, whereas Armani's structuring is unboned, flexible, and elastic. In a final signature touch, Armani introduces an element of the exotic in the form of a corded waist tie redolent of the passementeries of the Near East.

140

Woman's evening bodice and skirt, spring/summer 1996
Bodice: gray silk organza with bugle beads and metallic gold thread embroidery;
skirt: blue, yellow, and white silk organza
Giorgio Armani Archives, Milan

The late 1950s and early 1960s witnessed a style of ball gown that was universally adopted. Characterized by a jeweled bodice attached to a voluminous bell-shaped skirt, the style was endorsed by Balenciaga and Hubert de Givenchy. In his version, Armani detaches the bodice from the skirt to reveal the contemporary zone of erogeny, the toned abdomen. A thin black patent-leather belt introduces a quality of informality to the ensemble and emphasizes the disjointed condition of the gown. Because the belt is not anchored to the skirt's waistband, it shifts, riding up into the sliver-exposed midriff.

141

Woman's evening scarf top and skirt ensemble, spring/summer 1999
Scarf top: gray silk organza; skirt: gray silk tulle with bugle beads, cupped sequins,
and rhinestones, gray silk tulle overlay, and taupe silk chiffon lining
Giorgio Armani Archives, Milan

A softening of the structure of eveningwear occurred in the 1970s, particularly in the work of Italian and American designers, who endowed dresses with a body-conscious ease reminiscent of the 1930s, but without that period's complications of cut. In his spring/summer 1999 collection, Armani appeared to hark back to the lithe glamour of the time with a series of evening gowns based on the wrap of a scarf. The informal practice of knotting a scarf top as a cover-up, most frequently encountered on the beach, is the central element of this "gown" (actually a skirt and top).

142

Woman's strapless evening gown, spring/summer 1999
Scarf: light gray silk chiffon; gown: light gray silk organza with cupped sequins
and dark silver gray silk tulle overlay
Giorgio Armani Archives, Milan

The layering of a variety of materials of barely shifting hues and sheen is characteristic of Armani, as is a casual, sportswear approach to dress, even for eveningwear. This ethereal evening gown is composed of a body-hugging patterned and sequined underdress overlaid with a wide cage of silk mesh. The iridescent silk bodice is actually a scarf wrapped tightly around the bust, securing the strapless neckline. Using richly oscillating optical effects in difficult-to-define chromatic mixes, Armani renders a design of elegant simplicity and subtle complexity.

In July 1975 Giorgio Armani registered his trademark. That October he presented his men's collection for spring/summer 1976, the first under his own name.

The following descriptions of his collections for men and women are not intended to be comprehensive, but rather to outline the most significant innovations of each season. Information has been compiled from Giorgio Armani press releases, reviews and articles in fashion magazines and newspapers, and Richard Martin and Harold Koda's *Giorgio Armani: Images of Man* (New York: Rizzoli, 1990).

344

SPRING/SUMMER 1976

Menswear Double-breasted suits that are softer and have a contemporary look, worn with wide ties; collars inspired by work clothing and the Chinese "Mao" jacket; and natural-colored separates. Fabrics: linen and light suedes. Advertising campaign: photographs by Aldo Fallai.

Womenswear Jackets made with traditional menswear fabrics that are simple and soft and scaled down in size, worn over casual separates; terry blousons in tobacco, purple, blue, fuchsia, raspberry, and lilac, worn with matching giant terry shoulder bags; suede sweatshirts in white with pale blue stripes and vice versa; front-pleated pants (a first in women's fashions); straight skirts slightly gathered at the waist, worn with cotton T-shirts; very long skirts, worn with shirts without fastenings but closed by a button on the shoulder; and below-the-calf skirts with contrasting linen tops inspired by India. Fabrics: natural, including "fake poor fabrics" such as coarse linens, Indian cottons, canvas-type hemp, velour terry, and very soft suede. Advertising campaign: photographs by Aldo Fallai.

FALL/WINTER 1976–77

Menswear Suits in low-relief ribbed wools; single-breasted jackets with squared shoulders and narrowed sleeves worn with button-down-collar, flap-pocket shirts, plain wool challis ties, and long cashmere scarves; jackets with shaped lapels and straight hems, cut in narrower silhouettes; pants with flat fronts and straight legs; overalls; fine-gauge sweaters in geometric jacquard knits; leather bomber jackets with high necks; cloth blousons and car coats with military details; and outerwear with zippered pocket closures. Fabrics: cotton piques and striped poplins, fine-ribbed wools, corduroy, pinstriped and bird's-eye wools, velvet, and jacquard jersey knits. Colors: stone gray, charcoal, chestnut, and dark chocolate brown. Advertising campaign: photographs by Aldo Fallai.

Womenswear Tweed suits; suits with printed velvet vests and brown-and-white wool bouclé skirts; masculine jackets, worn with feminine pleated skirts; jackets with long, running lapels and single-button closures; cloth shirtjackets; Scottish wool flannel blouses; brown velvet dusters; chevron coats; peckary suede trench coats; and waterproof taffeta coats. Fabrics: wide-ribbed velvet, leather, and wool plaids. Colors: sporty and rustic, sometimes austere, referring to English country ladies' fashions. Advertising campaign: photographs by Aldo Fallai.

SPRING/SUMMER 1977

Menswear Unconstructed suits comprised of unlined jackets with a lower button stance, straight, lightly padded shoulders, patch pockets, and loose pants; sportswear defined by a rumpled look; and leather vests and coats. Fabrics: cotton toiles, slubbed silk, textured wool crepes (traditionally used in womenswear), solid seersucker, and linen in basket-weave effects. Colors: natural tones from off-white to ecru and sand, with blue, rust, and black. Advertising campaign: photographs by Aldo Fallai.

Womenswear Soft, unconstructed jackets; double-layered skirts (the second one held loosely at the hips by a belt); rolled-up pants and shorts; and V-neck and collarless shirts. The collection features a classic and elegant, nonchalant style. Accessories: small bag-shaped pockets lightly secured on belts. Fabrics: raw silks, linens, checked gauzy cottons, and leather sewn like patchwork. Advertising campaign: photographs by Aldo Fallai.

SPRING/SUMMER 1978

Menswear Unconstructed double-breasted suits in mud and earth colors, worn with two-inch ties; shorts suits with cowl-neck shirts; pants with gathered waistbands, worn with sunburst-seamed tops; military-look tapered pants with drawstring or elasticized waists and large bellow pockets; relaxed-necked shirts; plain or textured casual knit tops; boat-neck shirts; and smocked leather jackets, worn with T-shirts with tire tracks printed across the chest. Colors: mostly olive green and khaki. Advertising campaign: photographs by Aldo Fallai.

Womenswear Jackets and blazers to be worn by day or night or even over a swimsuit; short silk crepe de chine jackets that close at the waist like boleros; softly tailored dresses and skirts with a deep slit down the front; and, for evening, crepe de chine blazers worn over matching strapless dresses. Fabrics: damask with a palm-leaf motif and linen with flannel-like pinstripes. Colors: green, bronze, brown, pink, orange, olive green worn with red, and gray tones. Advertising campaign: photographs by Bob Krieger.

FALL/WINTER 1977–78

Menswear Classic double-breasted cashmere blazers with long, running lapels and single-button closures; vests worn over jackets; flat-front pants; turtleneck shirts and sweaters; unusual shirt collars; high-collar rainwear; and coats and vests with cotton/wool fleece linings. Fabrics: patterned suitings, mohair, tweed, wool, corduroy, and glove leather. Colors: softer and more feminine, including blanket checks in bordeaux, pink, and camel. Advertising campaign: photographs by Aldo Fallai.

Womenswear Layered jackets: knit jackets over tweed blazers, mottled cloth jackets over leather blousons, fabric jackets over leather jackets; llama-wool blazers with long, running lapels and single-button closures; innovative drawstring-closure blazers; tweed wool blazers and blousons; shirtjackets and flannel "British officer" shirts; straight-cut pants; long, flowing wrap skirts; skirts with yoke detailing at the hips; skirts with rolled waistbands; masculine-cut shirts with lace cuffs and collars; traditionally styled and military-inspired sportswear; shearlings; and zipper-front coats with cotton/wool fleece linings and leather trim. Accessories: faux fur boas worn around the shoulders. Fabrics: feather-printed velvets, mohair gauze, corduroy, flannel, suede, leather, plaids, and Harris tweed. Colors: burgundy, pink, olive, and camel. Advertising campaign: photographs by Aldo Fallai.

FALL/WINTER 1978–79

Menswear V-shaped proportions (broad shoulders to tapered waist and hips); double-breasted suits with wide peaked lapels; suit and sports jackets with martingales; leather jackets worn with ties; military-style Eisenhower jackets with epaulets; leather pants; overalls; and cowl-neck knits. The collection—inspired by American actors of the 1930s and 1940s, such as Cary Grant and Gregory Peck—introduces the "Armani slouch," which appeals to the youth market. Fabrics: corduroy and innovative wools. Colors: earth tones—neutral, clay, and ocher—accented with wine red. Advertising campaign: photographs by Aldo Fallai.

Womenswear Prince of Wales suits with slim wrap skirts or full, pleated skirts; square-shouldered jackets with pleats around a single button; tapered, lean-cut jackets with varied lapels and tiny pockets; jackets with martingales; pants that are narrow at the calf and very tight around the ankle; wide, pleated pants; Bermuda shorts in lamé and velvet to be worn day or night; crepe shirts with fabric roses at the throat; lamé mini dresses with silk kimono jackets; high-collar, crocodile-print raincoats; leather jackets; and furs, including sheared mink coats. Accessories: boas thrown over jackets and coats. Fabrics: flannel, bird's-eye, and tweed. Colors: pewter, black, mustard, lilac, apricot, teal, raspberry, plum, and chestnut. Advertising campaign: photographs by Bob Krieger.

SPRING/SUMMER 1979

Menswear Double-breasted suits with two-button closures, long lapels, and padded shoulders; single-breasted jackets with a narrow cut, narrow lapels, single-button closure, and a wide, sharp but sloping shoulder line; comfortable jackets with raglan sleeves; overalls; white pants; pants with tapered legs; and raincoats. Military details are eliminated and looks are more romantic. Fabrics: suede, terry, cotton, sheer linen, and velour. Colors: iridescent blues, purples, and mustard with white, Bordeaux, and rust. Advertising campaign: photographs by Aldo Fallai.

Womenswear Suits; soft blazers with narrow lapels; loose-fitting jackets and blazers with broad, squared shoulders; shirts with brief roll collars and patch pockets; V-neck cotton blouses; short, wide pants; wrap skirts with cascading ruffles in silk and cotton; linen apron skirts; draped dresses that fall just below the knee; and silk trench coats. Accessories: colored boas and high heels. Fabrics: chevron tweed, crepe de chine, fine silks, and black chiffon. Advertising campaign: photographs by Aldo Fallai.

SPRING/SUMMER 1980

Menswear Jackets with notched and peaked lapels, a low gorge, and slight waist suppression; slightly longer jackets; full-cut, pleated pants; collarless shirts with thin rolled piping around the neckband, worn with sportswear as well as tailored clothing; polo-collar shirts; wide ties with a blue-and-white polka-dot and other patterns; harlequin-patterned sweaters; and earth-tone quilted leather jackets. The collection is inspired by American cinema of the 1930s, especially by Clark Gable. Colors: beige, light blue, and dark blue. Advertising campaign: photographs by Aldo Fallai.

Womenswear Tailored pantsuits; round-shouldered, single-button jackets with truncated lapels and tailored bustiers in cotton, linen, or lightweight wool, some with bold horizontal stripes, worn over ankle-length skirts or culottes; close-fitting knickers; linen pants; roomy, wide, short pants; blouses with ruffles pulled over the jacket neckline; four-color T-shirts (blue, violet, sage green, and toast) with shirred-linen cap sleeves; and violet and gold cotton fan-shaped strapless tops, worn over violet shorts. Eveningwear: strapless "tuxedo" dresses. Advertising campaign: photographs by Aldo Fallai.

346

FALL/WINTER 1979–80

Menswear "Clark Gable" jackets with wide, low lapels and the gorge at mid-breast, worn with wider ties; vests in tie-pattern knitted fabrics; pointed shirt collars; fuller, draping pants; high-waisted pleated pants with fabric belts; leather jackets, bomber jackets, and trench coats; tuxedos; and double-breasted formalwear. The collection returns to a more classic style, with broad shoulders and a slim silhouette. Fabrics: soft flannels, pure cashmeres, vicuña and alpaca, rough tweeds, smooth velvets, corduroys, fine silks, pinstripes, and fur. Colors: neutral, including tobacco, brown, slate gray, ocher, olive green, black, and dark blue. Advertising campaign: photographs by Aldo Fallai.

Womenswear Tailored suits comprised of wide-shouldered, gathered jackets with single-button closures; asymmetrical jackets—longer at the back—with a single button at the bottom and a low gorge; cardigans; wide pants with pleats at the waist; straight, knee-length skirts; striped silk shirts tied at the neck with a fabric rose; rain jackets with four small zippers in place of pockets; and black crocodile-print coats and jackets with high, slightly gathered collars. Accessories: felt hats and high heels. Fabrics: bird's-eye tweeds and Prince of Wales plaids. Colors: lacquer red, emerald green, blue, violet, black, orange, and gray. Advertising campaign: photographs by Aldo Fallai.

FALL/WINTER 1980–81

Menswear Leaner cut, with more distinct waist suppression, narrow hips, sloping shoulder line, low gorge, and wide lapels; asymmetrical details, especially in shirts and outerwear; sweaters with jacquard designs; straight pants, tapered toward the cuff; long trench coats, short blousons, and belted car coats in cashmere and camel hair; and raincoats with fur collars. Fabrics: two-tone twills, miniature patterns, bird's-eye, four-tone twists, and muted plaids. Colors: brown and tan for outerwear and accessories. Eveningwear: soft pants worn with classic jackets, vests, shirts, and bow ties. Advertising campaign: photographs by Aldo Fallai.

Womenswear Large jackets with asymmetrical lapels, worn over knickers in suede, velvet, or nubby wool; close-fitting, linear leather jackets with asymmetrical closings; classic tapered pants; side-pleated pants; cuffed skirts; and sheared furs, including a slim, asymmetrical coat in amethyst sheared mink and a sleek belted trench coat in graphite-colored sheared beaver. Fabrics: geometric mega stripes, diagonals, checks, and tweeds. Colors: saffron, persimmon, jade, cinnamon, and china blue, along with black and white, neutral grays, and earth tones. Eveningwear: fitted black jackets with one-sided closings; black-and-white-striped skirts gathered at the waist; and soft pants worn with classic jackets, vests, shirts, and bow ties. Advertising campaign: photographs by Aldo Fallai.

SPRING/SUMMER 1981

Menswear Suits with a less sharply defined waist, trimmer tailoring, and bold patterns, such as herringbone in two-tone combinations; dress shirts with strong stripes; cotton baseball-style shirts; kimono-sleeve shirts with full back yokes in both short- and long-sleeve styles; colored suede polo-neck shirts with knit collars and cuffs; jodhpur-style and side-buckled pants in cotton or colored leather; boxer-type shorts with self-belt and elasticized cinch-waist treatments; knitwear in bold patterns and graphic stripings; belted blousons in both leather and cotton with flat epaulets and the new GA eagle logo; outerwear strongly influenced by military styles. Advertising campaign: photographs by Aldo Fallai.

Womenswear Very long jackets worn with wide, corsetlike belts; shorter, boxy, collarless jackets with no buttons; jackets with kimonolike sleeves, slightly lower shoulders, and short Chinese collars; few skirts, and many types of pants, including bloomers, drawstring Bermuda shorts, culottes, knickers, jodhpurs, and Zouave and harem pants. Fabrics: wide stripes; rich weaves; tapestrylike prints; cotton moiré; printed wool gabardine; linen in gray and havana; and ribbed and chalkstriped kid leather in gray, oxblood, emerald green, periwinkle, golden yellow, and terra-cotta. Advertising campaign: photographs by Aldo Fallai.

SPRING/SUMMER 1982

Menswear Elongated jackets; pants cut close to the leg; pants and shorts with rolled-over waists; gaucho-style pants gathered at mid-calf or just below the knee; geometrically patterned sweaters; hooded sweatshirts in flyweight suede; tunic-length shirts worn with vests; and an Australian stockman–style caped raincoat. The collection features Indian, Australian, and American influences, favoring functionality and simplicity. Details: asymmetrical closings, dropped armholes, and stand-up collars. Accessories: brightly colored felt hats. Fabrics: linen; and leather and suede combinations. Colors: vivid or deadened. Advertising campaign: photographs by Aldo Fallai.

Womenswear Long classic and cardiganlike jackets with wide shoulders softened by shirring and gathering; square, waist-length jackets with soft shoulders and a vest pattern in front; gathered, pleated, or tubular pants; short Bermuda shorts; long or short gathered or pleated skirts; and wide, low-waisted shirts with sashes that tie at the hips. Colors: bright: geranium pink with mint green and black, vermilion red with turquoise and jade green, lacquer red with black and salmon pink, sunflower yellow with steel gray, indigo blue with red and turquoise, peacock green with fuchsia. Advertising campaign: photographs by Bob Krieger.

FALL/WINTER 1981–82

Menswear Suits with defined shoulders, wide lapels, and a lower button stance, in bold three-dimensional chalkstriped twill, worn with patterned shirts and ties; plaid sports jackets in neutral colors (beige, brown, and gray with mustard, forest green, and blue-gray); uncreased pants with narrow hips, full thighs, and narrow legs (as in flight pants and jodhpurs) in heavy cotton twill, corduroy, gabardine, and leather; shirts with band collars; and military-influenced hooded vests, parkas with parachute straps, and duffel coats with asymmetrical closures, button throat latches, and quilting. Advertising campaign: photographs by Aldo Fallai.

Womenswear Japanese-style line of silk and leather garments; long black velvet blazers with slits at the hips and cotton satin fronts; jackets with rounded shoulders and parallel double stitching; pencil-cut pants; large, rounded-hem culottes; short pleated skirts; shirt dresses with straight shoulders; and three-quarter-length Andean-style coats made of two large rectangles of fabric, one of which is thrown over the shoulder like a shawl. Fabrics: wide-wale corduroy, jacquard tweed chiné with patch designs, wool satin, silks, trompe-l'oeil prints, and Scottish plaids. Colors: lacquer red, bright yellow, and China blue. Eveningwear: quilted and stitched satin and velvet robes with kimono necklines, worn with obi-like sashes and short culottes. Advertising campaign: photographs by Aldo Fallai.

FALL/WINTER 1982–83

Menswear High-waisted pants; sports pants in poplin and canvas; shirts in heavier-weight double cotton, flannel-like cotton, jacquard fabrics, and gabardine; balmacaan raincoats; bomber jackets, toggle coats, blousons, and parkas in distressed leather with mottled surfaces; and synthetic teddy-bear-pile anoraks and blousons. The collection is influenced by Steven Spielberg's *Raiders of the Lost Ark*. Shapes are boxy with big shoulders. Fabrics: heavy upholstery-style suitings, novelty wools, and macro tweeds. Advertising campaign: photographs by Aldo Fallai.

Womenswear Suits comprised of long jackets and ankle-length pants, broad-shouldered, wide-striped jackets and ankle-length pants, or vestlike jackets with gathered stripes on the shoulders and gathered skirts; brightly colored hooded sweatshirts in lightweight suede; gaucho-style pants gathered at mid-calf or just below the knee; and long-sleeve blouses that wrap diagonally at the front. Fabrics: wool velvet, padded linen, silk, and cotton sateen. Eveningwear: black silk pants and matching collarless shirts with lamé fronts and gold lamé jackets; eveningwear accessories: flat boots, hats, and high heels. Advertising campaign: photographs by Aldo Fallai.

SPRING/SUMMER 1983

Menswear Broad-shouldered jackets; fishermen's jackets and vests worn with narrow, cropped ties; dress shirts with rolling and reversing collars; lumberjack plaid camp shirts; narrower plain-front, box-pleated, or single-pleated pants; belted blousons with large horizontal and vertical zippers; and outerwear with camping-style details such as flap and bellow pockets, zipper-closing pockets, and snap and placket zipper closings. Fabrics: polished cotton, wool crepe in lumberjack plaids, poplins, doeskin cotton, linen, and micro-pinwale corduroy. Colors: gray/brown and chamois/charcoal combinations, with black, white, tan, blue gray, and chocolate brown predominating. Advertising campaign: photographs by Aldo Fallai.

Womenswear Elegant day suits with below-the-knee and calf-length skirts; single- and double-breasted crew-neck jackets cropped at the waist, with slightly rounded shoulders; tapered pants, front-pleated or with three pleats on each side, front and back; and simple shirts. Fabrics: traditional English, including Prince of Wales plaid, bird's-eye, camel hair, cashmere, alpaca, vicuña, and leather. Colors: red, white, black, tans, beiges, and sand, with turquoise, pink, ivory, and peacock green. Eveningwear: black velvet, embroidered satin, and tiger prints; deep, low-cut necklines; and amphora-shaped skirts. Advertising campaign: photographs by Aldo Fallai.

SPRING/SUMMER 1984

Menswear Single- and double-breasted suits; tapered jackets with side vents, wide lapels, and broad, sloping shoulders; wide-collar plaid blousons; striped sweaters; vests; leather blousons worn with colored leather pants; blousons worn with Bermuda shorts; pants worn with suspenders; pants rolled up to the knee; oversized shirts, some with tab collars, some collarless (including baseball shirts); long, loose raincoats; and striated ties. The collection is inspired by the 1940s. Fabrics: linens, cottons, and lightweight wool. Patterns: mixed plaids; small checks; and heathered, striated, and chiné effects. Colors: gray, brown, light blue, and yellow. Advertising campaign: photographs by Aldo Fallai.

Womenswear Casual, masculine jackets with loose-falling lapels; side-buttoned linen jackets with hip panels; polka-dot jackets worn with pants and long overskirts; silk bomber jackets with matching skirts worn over black pants; full, striped pants; black-and-white quilted cotton checkerboard pants; long, wrap-front skirts; collarless blouses; midriff-baring bra tops; dresses with side drapings; and light coats with a draped single lapel. Fabrics: moiré organza, satins, cottons, and linens. Colors: smoky tones mixed with beige and gray; dark blue; and black. Advertising campaign: photographs by Gianpaolo Barbieri.

FALL/WINTER 1983–84

Menswear Jackets with a higher gorge and notably higher notch placement; loose-fitting pants with single- and double-inverted and sewn-down pleats; patterned sweaters; brushed cotton shirts; printed leather jackets; and ties with large-scale patterns. Outerwear is big-collared and beefy, influenced by steamer and balmacaan coats, including leather or heavy cotton jackets with fur collars. Fabrics: velvet, broken-twill patterns, and bird's-eye tweed for jackets and coats; flannel and brilliantine for shirts; and damask for ties. Advertising campaign: photographs by Aldo Fallai.

Womenswear Suits with loose, oversized jackets and straight or bias-cut skirts; suits with wide-shouldered, tuniclike, collarless jackets, buttoned at the back, and slim, straight skirts or short, softly tapered pants; single-breasted white jackets; loose knitwear jackets; wide, classic pants; full, checked dresses; gray-and-black-checked coats; and long, wide-shouldered trench and duster coats. Accessories: high heels. Eveningwear: long, collarless, V-shaped shirts, long straight skirts, vests, and undershirts in fine crepe silk, panne velvet, satin, chiffon, organza, and flocked tulle. Advertising campaign: photographs by Gianpaolo Barbieri.

FALL/WINTER 1984–85

Menswear Scaled-up, baggier suits and jackets with wider peaked lapels and padded shoulders; pants with an updated Zoot-suit look; slouchy sweaters; box-pleated pants with wide, unpressed legs; collarless shearling blousons; and bold-textured overcoats with dropped armholes. Fabrics: herringbones in different scales with either high-contrast or low-contrast yarns, basket-weave and window-pane plaids, bold twills, and ombréed stripes; contrasting textures are used together. Colors: gray, black, and white mixed in subtle Nordic patterns. Advertising campaign: photographs by Aldo Fallai.

Womenswear Loose, comfortable suits comprised of oversized jackets worn with exaggeratedly full pants; traditional jackets with very flat lapels; overalls worn under jackets; knee-length skirts with soft side ties; clean, flat-collar shirts, often with snap closures; knit tops; embossed leather coats; sheepskin jackets and reptile-print coats with velvet collars; and brightly colored coats. Fabrics: natural and casual, with an emphasis on pattern and texture, including stripes, jacquard prints with floral motifs, and herringbone velvet. Colors: slate, stone, brown, metal gray, and occasional bright tones. Advertising campaign: photographs by Aldo Fallai.

SPRING/SUMMER 1985

Menswear Low-gorge, high-notch, four-button single- and double-breasted suits, worn with wide ties and sneakers; droopy, crumpled long jackets with single-button closures and side vents; blousons tucked into pants; tailored sports jackets and blazers worn with shorts; Bermuda and very short shorts worn with long white socks; beach pants; and leather jackets. Fabrics: wool and cotton crepes; striated linens; and small-scale and tonally patterned wools. Colors: neutral, with accents of sea blue, purple, and apricot. Advertising campaign: photographs by Aldo Fallai.

Womenswear Long, collarless, cuffed jackets with strong shoulders and hip-hugging men's jackets, worn over shaped skirts or crepe, linen, or silk pants tailored like jeans; detachable collars; vests; loose pants; short skirts, including wrap skirts; boxer shorts; sarongs tied over Bermuda shorts; long, slightly military-style coats; and trench coats. Accessories: high-heeled shoes with plastic sides and leather points. Fabrics: cottons, silks (including Thai silks screened with vegetable dyes), and Prince of Wales and Scottish plaid. Colors: inspired by Henri Matisse, with tones of ruby and brown, ruby and blue, purples, shamrock green, and cobalt blue. Eveningwear: sequined sweaters. Advertising campaign: photographs by Aldo Fallai.

SPRING/SUMMER 1986

Menswear Sports jackets in semi-crepe linen, wool crepe, or crepon; pale tan suede shirtjackets; knitwear in two-tone marled yarns; band-collar shirts in homespun jacquard; square-collar, pajama-style shirts in cotton jacquard; brightly colored silk crepe and cotton/viscose knit T-shirts; and bell-collar spring coats in black and white viscose crepe. Fabrics: denim blue and marron brown batik patterns printed on jersey for T-shirts and on woven cotton for pants and shorts. Colors: low-contrast palette, including charcoal, manilla, black, white, and olive. Advertising campaign: photographs by Aldo Fallai.

Womenswear Wide-shouldered masculine jackets, single-button blazers with stitched notched collars, and curve-shaped jackets, all worn over T-shirts; Bermuda suits with round-collar, concealed-closure jackets; long wrap and layered organza and chiffon skirts; full crinoline skirts; collarless, V-shaped shirts; and long coats. Fabrics: crepon, cashmere, silks, linen, and chiffon, with batik prints. Colors: grays, beige, pink, fuchsia, dark blue, and black. Eveningwear: sequined and embroidered padded jackets; collarless sequined jackets with square pockets and concealed closures; and black 1930s-style skirts with apron construction; all worn with high heels. Advertising campaign: photographs by Aldo Fallai.

FALL/WINTER 1985–86

Menswear Tight-fitting silhouette, with wide, sharp shoulders and extremely tapered chest and hips; high-notch tailored jackets with knit cuffs; easy-fitting, black-belted, shirred-yoke jackets; roll-collar and wide-collar sweaters; sports pants with elasticized waists, inspired by 1930s ski wear; gathered jodhpurs with lacing; long plaid shirts reminiscent of nineteenth-century nightshirts; blousons in Shetland plaids; leather blousons with very wide waistbands; duster coats in crinkled nylon; pile overcoats; belted navy gabardine coats; car coats; and cropped trench coats. Fabrics: Shetland wools, wools in marled solids, complex tweeds, and tan leather. Advertising campaign: photographs by Aldo Fallai.

Womenswear Jackets with strong, square shoulders, cropped and fitted at the waist; long, single-button blazers without lapels; double-breasted jackets, cropped at the waist, with wide lapels; four-pocket safari jackets with or without collars; shirt-style blousons with soft, rounded shoulders; sweater jackets; cavalry-style pants in featherweight cotton gabardine; loose, double-pleated pants; full, knee-length skirts worn with buttonless padded tops, tapered at the waist; and blouses that are draped in front or "scarfed" around the neck. Fabrics: tweed, plaids, gabardine, cashmere, silks, and lace. Colors: pink, black, white, and brown. Advertising campaign: photographs by Aldo Fallai.

FALL/WINTER 1986–87

Menswear Marled wool crepe suits worn with wool terry sweatshirts; full-cut pants; polo-collar sweaters; hooded bomber jackets in silver-colored viscose; and taupe viscose double-breasted coats. Fabrics: Prince of Wales plaid crepes, herringbones, and cavalry twill. Advertising campaign: photographs by Aldo Fallai.

Womenswear Single-button blazers with stitched, notched collars; curve-shaped jackets worn over longer matching T-shirts; short, close-fitting jackets; cardiganlike or oversized jackets worn over calf-length wrap skirts or crepon pants; wrap skirts in printed silk; full-flaring dresses; camel-hair coats worn over calf-length dresses or short tunics; checked or Scotch plaid housecoats and long trench coats; and soft, oversized coats worn over slim wool pants. Fabrics: geometric-printed silks, jacquard wools, and crepes. Eveningwear: long, slender, loose-fitting gowns and pants and cardigans; fabrics include silks printed with Chinese designs, black wool dotted with black beads, tooled lace, and prints overlaid with rhinestone-studded tulle. Advertising campaign: photographs by Aldo Fallai.

SPRING/SUMMER 1987

Menswear Suits with padded but not exaggerated shoulders and roomy pants, worn with scarflike ties; and sportswear with a "back to basics" feel, including knitwear with classic jacquard designs in bold but faded colors. Fabrics: silk or cotton woven with glossy fibers, raw silk, linen/viscose blends, wool crepe, washed cottons with surface patterns, Prince of Wales plaid wools, and worsteds. Colors: cool mineral shades, such as sand and ferrous tones. Advertising campaign: photographs by Aldo Fallai.

Womenswear Loose, masculine jackets worn over body-tight lingerie; jackets with a more traditional shaping; and full-flare and semicircular skirts. Details: overlock trimmings, scalloped hems, grosgrain borders, silk cord edging, and satin lapels. Accessories: short mesh gloves. Fabrics: paper-weight tweeds, soft wool gauzes, downy silks, and prints. Eveningwear: veiled lace skirts; short white organdy jackets; long, robelike gowns; and silk jumpsuits and pajamas. Advertising campaign: photographs by Aldo Fallai.

SPRING/SUMMER 1988

Menswear Single-breasted jackets with wide peaked lapels and a looser silhouette; fitted jackets; broad-shouldered jackets worn with drawstring pants; full, high-waisted pants; and knee-length Bermuda shorts. Fabrics: solid or patterned, in traditional weaves using blended fibers, such as silk and linen with a viscose thread. Colors: pastels, tans, grays, beige, musky browns, and neutrals. Advertising campaign: photographs by Aldo Fallai.

Womenswear Jackets with delicately padded shoulders; short jackets nipped at the waist and flaired at the hips; jackets with curved lapels; high-waisted pants; classic pants worn with polo shirts; short and floor-length divided skirts; tulip-shaped skirts; long Bermuda shorts; scallop-neck and high-neck blouses; and V-neck shirts with side closures emphasized by large flowers. Accessories: silk flower belts. Fabrics: silk tweed, silk chiffon, linen, rayon crepe, silk and rayon knits, silk crepe, crepon, chiffon, jacquard, tulle, and taffeta. Patterns: country florals, tartans, and gypsy-inspired prints. Eveningwear: full skirts with elasticized waists; sheaths knotted in the back; and pouf-skirt dresses worn with full-length skirts beneath. Advertising campaign: photographs by Aldo Fallai.

FALL/WINTER 1987–88

Menswear High-gorge, mid-notch, four- and six-button pinstriped suits with broader lapels; tapered jackets; single-pleated pants; monochromatic suit ensembles; funnel-neck collars worn under suits; zipper-neck and loose-roll turtlenecks; long leather jackets; full, A-line topcoats with no shoulder pads; broad-shouldered topcoats with tapering bodies; and shearling coats. Advertising campaign: photographs by Aldo Fallai.

Womenswear Soft-shouldered, figure-molding jackets worn with long, double-faced crepe georgette skirts; deep-gorged vests worn under matching jackets; knee-length skirts and pants with unpressed, turned-under hems; soft, high-neck blouses with grosgrain edges; blouses with flat, bias-cut collars; and single- and double-breasted coats that simulate overlong jackets or are seamed at the waist and slightly flared at the bottom. Details: rolled piping, braided closures, matching-fabric buttons, and thinly bellowed pockets. Colors: beiges and grays, eggplant, brown, military green, and, for evening, dark brown. Advertising campaign: photographs by Aldo Fallai.

FALL/WINTER 1988–89

Menswear Suits with shortened jackets and very full pants; formal suits worn with waistcoats, suspenders, and/or colorful shirts with bold patterns; drapey, elongated jackets worn over pencil-thin pants; double-breasted blazers; double-breasted sports jackets worn unbuttoned; plaid suits and sports jackets worn with plaid flannel work shirts; slim leather jackets; short sweaters with velvet finishes in indistinct colors; piled-fleece athletic pants; and solid-color wool velvet overcoats with large, rounded lapels and checkered linings. Fabrics: knitwear for suits; wool tweeds; brushed cottons; napped and plushed wools; camel hair; cotton chamois; corduroy; and crinkled wools. Tweeds are layered with brushed and solid suitings. Advertising campaign: photographs by Aldo Fallai.

Womenswear Draped-neck and cropped jackets, nipped at the waist; vests; band-hemmed pants; full, mid-calf-length skirts with draped sashes at the waist; and beaded bustiers worn with contrasting, paperbag-waisted, full-length skirts. Eveningwear, inspired by India and the Middle East: short, beaded Zouave jackets; knee-length skirts with matching sashes; and pants worn with quilted funnel-collar jackets tucked into sashes. Advertising campaign: photographs by Aldo Fallai.

SPRING/SUMMER 1989

Menswear Soft suits, including shorts suits with long, three-button jackets and full-cut shorts (many in knits); cropped jackets; short-sleeve polo-neck sweaters; silk shirts with jockey stripes; and short, wide ties with subtle patterns. Details: rounded pockets, unstarched collars, and oversized buttons. Fabrics: slightly iridescent silks; linens and linen blends; washed silks; cotton and silk gabardine; wool crepes; and knits. Colors: faded tones, hazy blues, and frosty grays, with mismatched suits in retro grays and tans. Advertising campaign: photographs by Aldo Fallai.

Womenswear Double-breasted pinstriped jackets with matching pants; light, collarless jackets with unpadded shoulders; wider, rounded pants (a homage to couturier Paul Poiret); longer skirts; and simple blouses. Accessories: woven shawls; fabric slippers strapped at the back; and hats. Fabrics: traditional and exotic fabrics worn together—such as viscose and shantung, or checked linen tweeds and Turkish prints. Colors: off-whites, muted blues, and grays. Advertising campaign: photographs by Aldo Fallai.

SPRING/SUMMER 1990

Menswear Jackets that are longer than fingertip length, with long shawl collars and rounded, unpadded shoulders; Chinese brocade jackets; knit vests; sarongs; hooded shirts; polka-dot shirts; short, narrow pants; and striped shorts. The collection is more fitted throughout, with narrowed shoulders giving an elongated, cylindrical silhouette. Fabrics: richly patterned (including tie-dyed and camouflage patterns) and softly woven, with strong colors and unusual matches. Advertising campaign: photographs by Aldo Fallai.

Womenswear Long and extra-long jackets, double-breasted or with three buttons, some with concealed button closures; wide, full pants; simple skirts; and loose-cut blouses. Fabrics: raw silk, featherweight wools, silk etamines, georgette, and grosgrain. Colors: spicy tones, as well as solid ivory, amethyst, and emerald green. Eveningwear: lavishly adorned dresses, embroidered and beaded with stones and pearls, reminiscent of Russian designer Léon Bakst's costumes for the Ballets Russes. Advertising campaign: photographs by Jacques Olivar.

FALL/WINTER 1989–90

Menswear Sack suits with three-button, single-breasted jackets and fuller, looser pants; two- and six-button double-breasted jackets; full-cut, pleated pants with tapered cuffs; funnel-neck shirts and shirtlike sweaters with patterns in tone-on-tone colorings; cashmere sweaters; vests and cardigans in soft, textured fabrics with diffused patterns; trench coats in velour and tweed; leopard-print pile jackets; and loose-fitting coats with large collars. Fabrics: corduroy, velveteen, camel hair, chevron, hard-finished silk, true velvets, jacquards, soft wools, and doeskin-like cotton. Colors: off-whites, grays, brown, tan, and rust tones, with rich burgundy, blue, and green. Advertising campaign: photographs by Aldo Fallai.

Womenswear Narrow, wrapped jackets with small shoulders and defined waists; blazers with patch pockets, either oversized and masculine and cut like cardigans, or ultrashort and fitted; straight and loose pants; overalls; short and calf-length skirts; light chiffon blouses; and long, soft coats. Fabrics: houndstooth, doeskin-looking silk, old-fashioned goffered silks, padded and quilted linen, heavy wool, wool/silk blends, velvet, grisaille, flannel, and cashmere. Colors: amethyst, fuchsia, dark blue, rosewood, eggplant, tangerine, sage, and mustard yellow, as well as grays and neutral sandy and earth tones. Eveningwear: velvet, silk, chiffon, and embroideries. Advertising campaign: photographs by Aldo Fallai.

FALL/WINTER 1990–91

Menswear Double-breasted sack suits with narrow shawl collars; tonally coordinated jackets and patterned shirts, worn without ties; longer jackets, fitted at the waist, with unpadded shoulders; square-cut vests; basket-weave sweaters worn over velveteen pants; leather blousons; four- and six-button coats with lance lapels; trench coats with luxurious linings; tapered camel-hair coats; and narrow ties. Fabrics: velour, velvets, wool bouclé, lambs'-wool crepes, brushed cottons, chenille, cashmere, suede treated to look like denim, and corduroy. Colors: gray, dark green, and bronze. Advertising campaign: photographs by Aldo Fallai.

Womenswear "Avant-garde" line: unstructured jackets with small shoulders, raglan sleeves, and a soft, round shape at the base; short, straight skirts; masculine shirts with mandarin collars; and wild-mink furs; fabrics include twilled wool and tie-patterned jacquards. "Mongolian" line: jackets in jacquards and quilted textiles, worn with slim or rounded pants with matching fabric boots; full, cinched coats with draping on the shoulder and neckline; and, for evening, coats and tunics with damask satin linings with quilted gold inlays. "Chinese" line: longer jackets with rounded hems, worn with matching pants; details include embroidery, braid belts, and lamé insets; fabrics include silver- and gold-printed off-white silk, and lace. Advertising campaign: photographs by Aldo Fallai.

SPRING/SUMMER 1991

Menswear Single- and double-breasted suits made of natural fibers, such as wools, linens, and silks in neutral colors; jackets without shoulder pads; loose pants; Bermuda shorts; full-cut shirts; and leather bomber and bush jackets. The collection takes its inspiration from clothing of the 1920s, 1930s, and 1940s. Fabrics: linen, rag-like Indian cotton, silk, and striped ramie in rough textures and open weaves. Advertising campaign: photographs by Aldo Fallai.

Womenswear Hip-length jackets with deep rounded vents and lapels that are extensions of the garment; long, slim pants, often without tucks or pleats; men's pants cropped into shorts in lengths from six inches above the knee and up; draped dresses; and tank-top and T-shirt-shaped dresses. Fabrics: jacquard linens and crepes, with eveningwear characterized by thick embroidery. Advertising campaign: photographs by Aldo Fallai.

SPRING/SUMMER 1992

Menswear Jackets with narrower lapels, a slightly lower notch, and a loosened, boxier silhouette; stitched cotton round-neck sweaters; double-buttoned band-collar shirts; scarves and vests worn without shirts; comfortable, slim pants with inverted box pleats; and overalls. Fabrics: natural and crisp, including bird's-eye, pinstripes, twills, micro checks, gabardine, etamine, reed-matted cottons, crepelle, and grisaille. Colors: cool and dyed naturally, including deep faded blue, gray, and burgundy. Eveningwear: shawl-collar white dinner jackets worn with black shorts. Advertising campaign: photographs by Aldo Fallai.

Womenswear Slender, simple jackets with high kimono sleeves, softened shoulders, and concealed closures; jackets worn over matching dresses; pants; short skirts; folkloric bodices and vest tops; and voluminous dresses with ruched necklines. Accessories: straw hats. Fabrics: tightly woven, light, and brightly colored, with embroidery and exotic batik patterns. Colors: natural, such as taupe, gray, and off-white. Advertising campaign: photographs by Aldo Fallai.

FALL/WINTER 1991–92

Menswear Lightweight suits in body-conscious cuts; slightly elongated jackets with lightly padded shoulders, a higher notch, and smaller lapels; pants that are fuller at the thigh and taper to the ankles; quilted-satin vests and linings; shirts in antique bold and thin striping, polka dots, and tablecloth checks, in rosewood, pink, wet sand, neutral beiges, browns, charcoal grays, and blues; hooded sweaters worn with overcoats; and Navaho Indian blanket–patterned outerwear. Fabrics: weightier, naturally brushed and textured cloths, including Oxfords, assorted twills, and spongy, wrinkled crepes. Patterns: mini checks, classic chevron, and muted Prince of Wales plaids; some ensembles combine tartan with blanket stripes. Eveningwear: tuxedos, including one with a burgundy jacket. Advertising campaign: photographs by Aldo Fallai.

Womenswear Long, fitted jackets, some with high collars, some collarless with a high button stance; short, discreetly slit skirts; dresses worn over shorts or short skirts, or worn as coats; and voluminous coats with attached scarves. Fabrics: camel hair, double-faced crepe, gabardine, baby alpaca, and soft etamines. Colors: taupe, caramel, cocoa brown, navy, wisteria, amethyst, rosewood, coral rose, jade green, shocking pink, geranium red, and indigo blue. Eveningwear: tuxedos with feminine fabrics and details. Advertising campaign: photographs by Aldo Fallai.

FALL/WINTER 1992–93

Menswear Suits with long, single- and double-breasted jackets with wide lapels; band-collar jackets; sweaters; vests; long cardigans; hooded cotton and leather blousons with small zippers; loose pants, both full-cut and more tapered; wide-collar shirts; car coats, raincoats and long coats with ultrawide brown and burgundy stripes; and plaid and striped ties. Fabrics: tweeds and woolens. Colors: fuchsia, burgundy, dark and light gray, blue, and taupe. Advertising campaign: photographs by Aldo Fallai.

Womenswear Well-tailored, constructed jackets with soft shoulders; cashmere twin sets with the outer piece cut like a man's cardigan; pants; knee-length and mid-calf skirts; long, wide, richly colored coats in embossed tricot; and mid-calf-length coats. Colors: cream, light and dark camel, gray, white, and black. Eveningwear: black-tie touches, including a long dress with a pleated bodice recalling a man's formal shirt, an off-white bodice supported by a trompe l-oeil undone bow tie, and a gown based on the form of a tuxedo sleeve, with white satin edging framing the décolletage to resemble a giant cuff finished with formal cuff links; a jeweled bodice worn under a waistcoat and knitted cardigan; and tops worn over pants with a sash. Advertising campaign: photographs by Peter Lindbergh.

SPRING/SUMMER 1993

Menswear Double-breasted jackets with lightly padded shoulders and double vents; monochromatic suit, shirt, and tie combinations; smock jackets; long caftans worn over tailored pants and jackets; full-cut pants; Nehru-collar shirts; and rug-patterned ties. Accessories: bandanas and berets. Fabrics: seersucker, treated linen, silk blends, reed-matting cottons, paisley-printed cottons, embossed crepons, striped silk gauze, checked homespun linens, striped jacquards twills, and novelty weaves. Patterns: batiks and Senegalese geometric motifs. Colors: natural beige tones, stone gray, and slate mixed with black and blue shades from indigo to navy with accents of faded green, garnet, and mustard. Eveningwear: white jackets with satin shawl collars worn over black pants. Advertising campaign: photographs by Peter Lindbergh.

Womenswear Menswear-inspired jackets worn over striped silk pajama pants; jewel-trimmed, tapered pants or long carousel skirts worn with shirts or vests in soft, caftanlike fabrics; and apronlike skirts worn over pencil-thin pants with colorful Northern African trimmings. Eveningwear: strong colors and precious fabrics reminiscent of traditional Turkish and Moroccan clothing; Oriental and Polynesian prints; and sarong-inspired dresses. Advertising campaign: photographs by Peter Lindbergh.

SPRING/SUMMER 1994

Menswear Suits with soft, slouchy, broad-shouldered jackets with a high notch and wide lapels, and full, double-pleated pants; six-buttoned double-breasted suits with a wasp-waisted silhouette; single-breasted jackets with unpadded shoulders; long, Chinese-collar jackets worn with loose pants; Mao-collar jackets; printed vests worn instead of shirts; long fine-gauge knit tops; high-colored paisley tunics worn with vests and sweaters over sarongs or pajama pants; football pants; linen Bermuda shorts; leather jackets; and duster coats. Fabrics: fluid linens and cottons with sophisticated weaved patterns. Colors: gray, burgundy, navy, beige, white, and natural tones. Eveningwear: white tuxedo jackets with shawl collars. Advertising campaign: photographs by Peter Lindbergh.

Womenswear Suits with long, loose jackets like soft, drawstring cardigans, or pajama vests with buttoned Chinese collars, or coats with vestlike overlays; wide pants; long skirts with stitched horizontal stripes; and peplum dresses and sarongs worn over pants. Fabrics: raw silk, waffled gauffré, jacquards, gauze, doubled chiffon, and knit meshes. Colors: range from white to sky gray, flintstone beige to bronze browns. Advertising campaign: photographs by Peter Lindbergh.

FALL/WINTER 1993–94

Menswear Lean, six-button Mao-collar jackets; slim jackets with notched collars and small armholes; wide pants; striped shirts; and herringbone and checked knitwear. The collection features a silhouette that is trim on top and full at the bottom. Fabrics: soft and full, including textured wools, low-pile velours, and surfaced crepes. Colors: blues, grays, and natural tones. Advertising campaign: photographs by Peter Lindbergh.

Womenswear Menswear-inspired pencil-striped suits worn with vests in contrasting fabrics and colors; fitted single- and three-button jackets; spencer-style jackets worn over austere coats reminiscent of friars' habits; brightly colored double-faced wool jackets worn with ultrawide pants and scarves; flat-flounce sheath jackets worn with shawls and fringed shirts; and sweaters worn with long skirts trimmed with fringes and large scarves. Colors, inspired by Henri Matisse: beige, jade green, fuchsia, oranges, reds, and violets. Eveningwear: large skirts, fitted bodices, and baggy pajamas; also features the influence of Matisse in its patterns, prints, and embroideries. Advertising campaign: photographs by Peter Lindbergh.

FALL/WINTER 1994–95

Menswear Straight-shouldered jackets with a high button stance, even on the double-breasted silhouette; three-piece suits with loose-hanging vests; long, comfortable jackets with Chinese collars and dropped shoulders; jackets with band collars, rounded shoulders, no vents, and smaller lapels, worn with cropped vests; tapered pants with angled seams; and 1940s-inspired overcoats, fitted at the chest and flaring below. Fabrics: ribbed and barklike wool crepe, tone-on-tone bouclé and twilled wools, Prince of Wales plaid, pied-de-poule, knitted-look wools, strié jersey, smooth velvets and corduroys, and washed and aged leather. Colors: slate, asphalt, indigo, rope, bronze brown, and dark green. Eveningwear: dark brown or green velvet single-breasted jackets with peaked lapels or shawl collars, worn with crepe de chine shirts in the same color and black pants. Advertising campaign: photographs by Peter Lindbergh.

Womenswear Soft jackets like long sweaters or shirts, with a gentle A-line from the shoulder, draped in front or hemmed in handkerchief points; slim pants, slightly bunched on the shoe; zipper-front blouses; long dresses; and leather jackets. Fabrics: distressed velvets, chenille, gossamer silks, waffle-weave mohairs, and gauzy wools. Colors: warm and mellow, reminiscent of the colors used by painter Balthus. Advertising campaign: photographs by Peter Lindbergh.

SPRING/SUMMER 1995

Menswear Three-piece suits with Nehru, collarless, or very narrow band-collar single-button, wasp-waisted jackets worn without shirts; pinstriped suits worn with Nehru-collar vests; trench-coat-like jackets; full, tapered pants; flat-front, high-waisted pants; large, untucked shirts with comfortable collars; cardiganlike shirts with drawstring waists; sarongs; and unusually shaped, unlined, fluid ties. Fabrics: wool, linen, and silk blended with acetates, and colored suedes and leathers. Colors: cool tonalities of asphalt gray, lead, steel, blue-gray, and deep and very dark blue. Advertising campaign: photographs by Peter Lindbergh.

Womenswear Gently flaring Empire-line jackets worn with split-side shorts; fitted jackets; jackets with bow closures; semitransparent chiffon or rayon pants; short, filmy skirts; and organza or georgette smock dresses. The collection has a more traditionally feminine look. Accessories: high heels. Fabrics: light. Colors: soft and luminous. Eveningwear: characterized by glittering beaded embroideries, exposed in the form of halter-neck bodice tops or veiled as a sheath layer worn under organza tunics and skirts. Advertising campaign: photographs by Peter Lindbergh.

SPRING/SUMMER 1996

Menswear Single-breasted suits with broad-shouldered, wasp-waisted jackets; broad-shouldered, double-breasted suits with tapered waists; safari jackets; gathered and cropped vests; sweaters worn with narrow belts and 1940s-style scarves; 1940s-style double-pleated, full pants; long raincoats; and wide ties. Fabrics: suitings with ribbed textures and cotton/crepe/viscose mixes for shirts. Colors: pale yellow, cream, earthy greens, khaki, moss, and grays. Eveningwear: Nehru shirts; and elongated hourglass, shawl-collar, double-breasted jackets. Advertising campaign: photographs by Peter Lindbergh and Neil Kirk.

Womenswear Short jackets with fitted waists fastened by invisible zippers or large buttons; long jackets; jackets structured only in the shoulders; wide, straight pants with or without pleats; and long and knee-length black and white dresses. Fabrics: wool/silk and silk/viscose blends; wool crepe; silk jacquard; and jersey. Colors: black, blue, ivory, and beige tones ranging from banana or very light pink to apricot and powdered rose. Eveningwear: two-piece gowns with skirts in organza with colored inlays, sequins, and embroidered floral designs worn with small T-shirts in black jersey or rigid tops with plunging necklines. Advertising campaign: photographs by Peter Lindbergh and Neil Kirk.

FALL/WINTER 1995–96

Menswear Suits with jackets with pronounced, padded shoulders, precisely cut lapels, and tapered waists (often accentuated by a belt), and straight-cut pants; sporty suit jackets; masculine, narrow-cut blousons; close-fitting knitwear; wide-collar shirts; slim, ankle-length pants; knee-length or short-cut coats; and wide ties. Accessories: low-laced boots. Fabrics: solid with novel textures and weaves. Colors: shades of gray from asphalt and lead to slate and fog. Advertising campaign: photographs by Peter Lindbergh.

Womenswear Short, straight-shouldered jackets, fitted at the waist and hips, with a slight flare below; bias-cut pants without pleats; long skirts with high slits; and fitted ankle-length coats with velvet lapels, high collars, and quilted silk linings. Fabrics: smooth-surfaced wools, silk velvet, damask, crinkled silks, wool crepe, cady, and satin. Colors: grayish beige, slate, gun-metal gray, dark brown, and black. Eveningwear: a tuxedo with a Mao-collar jacket worn over a low-cut bustier; body-hugging sheaths in black or skin-tone stretch tulle with embroidery appliqués; and long dresses and jackets in jacquard silk, embroidered with Chinese floral motifs in pearls, sequins, and beads, all in evanescent pastel shades. Advertising campaign: photographs by Peter Lindbergh.

FALL/WINTER 1996–97

Menswear Fitted, constructed, double-breasted jackets with wide peaked lapels; sweater jackets; rope-shouldered jackets; ski-style jackets with zippered closings; cigarette-cut, cuffed pants; zippered vests and shirts; waisted shirts with small or large collars; leather jackets and coats with fur collars; minimalist camel-hair car coats with zippered closings; slim coats with well-defined waists; and Directoire-style long, narrow coats. Fabrics: crisp and smooth-surfaced. Patterns: chevron, pied-de-poule, pinstripes, checks, and Prince of Wales plaids. Colors: black, slate gray, taupe, sand, earthy Siena brown, rosewood, aquamarine, green, teal, and red. Advertising campaign: photographs by Peter Lindbergh.

Womenswear Shapely jackets with geometric cuts; short, fitted jackets; shirtjackets like kimonos; slim silk pants; full-length skirts; short, flared skirts; men's shirts and ties; lightweight coats cut like long jackets; and short, flared coats. Fabrics: plissé wools, quilted matelassé velvet, double crepes, lace, and prints on black backgrounds. Eveningwear: short black dresses; small cardigans with ivory and ebony embroideries; black velvet gowns with appliquéd red roses; and black-and-white-striped satin dresses. Advertising campaign: photographs by Peter Lindbergh.

SPRING/SUMMER 1997

Menswear Closely fitted jackets with sloping shoulders, fitted "tailor-made" sleeves, and narrow, high lapels; gabardine suits with cardigan-style jackets; zippered vests and jackets; ski-like sweaters; pants with inverted pleats or no pleats, often with slash pockets; fitted shirts; light leather jackets; and narrow, light ties. Fabrics: natural fibers such as wool, silk, cotton, and "beaten" linen. Colors: luminous grays, putty, slate, coffee-bean brown, and black, as well as red, fuchsia, sage green, aquamarine, and yellow. Eveningwear: black and white double-breasted evening jackets with shawl collars, and tuxedos worn with black neck bands instead of ties. Advertising campaign: photographs by Peter Lindbergh and Paolo Roversi.

Womenswear Buttonless jackets; fluid kimono-cut jackets; duster-length shirtjackets; straight, cropped pants; deeply slit skirts; and dresses with knitted details, discreet transparencies, and spaghetti-strap shoulders. Fabrics: linen and silk knits, feather-light shantung, satin, double organza, quilted matelassé, and linen cady. Colors: gray and brown tones, as well as coral, indigo blue, turquoise, and violet (inspired by Anish Kapoor). Eveningwear: day shapes in embroidered tulle, organza, and georgette. Advertising campaign: photographs by Peter Lindbergh and Paolo Roversi.

SPRING/SUMMER 1998

Menswear Longer jackets with lightly padded shoulders, concealed closures, and pockets in the side seams; slim-fitting sweaters cut low at the front or at the nape of the neck, some sleeveless; straight, unpleated pants that fall with the crease pressed into the turn-ups; fitted shirts worn with ties; and snug or loose shirts with single-button closings at the neck or on the chest, contrasting trims, and stylized prints. Fabrics: light, pinstriped jacquard crepes, honeycomb weaves, and chevrons. Colors: dark, with an emphasis on navy, brown, indigo, slate gray, and racing green. Advertising campaign: photographs by Aldo Fallai.

Womenswear Jackets with lightly padded shoulders; jackets with pronounced shoulders, elongated lapels or thin shawl collars, and a single button at the waist; wide, unpleated pants; and knotted scarves or ties worn over bare skin or bodysuits. Fabrics: opaque silk shantung, silks with printed stripes, and iridescent silks. Colors: gold, brown, blue, and green, and icy hues ranging from pearl to aquamarine. Eveningwear: calf-length décolleté dresses; transparent shirtjackets; and short embroidered jackets; fabrics include embroidered stylized flower or dragonfly patterns, and organza, solid-color double chiffon, and jacquard organza with tone-on-tone stripes. Advertising campaign: photographs by Paolo Roversi.

FALL/WINTER 1997–98

Menswear Skinny three-button suits; five- and six-button, high-gorge jackets; single-button, low-gorge jackets; short, form-fitting jackets with lightly padded shoulders, narrow lapels, and concealed closures or single-button fastenings; form-fitting sweaters; pencil-thin cuffed pants with shallow pressed pleats; shirts with pronounced collars or French collars; leather blousons and jackets; suede anoraks; double-breasted coats with concealed closures; Directoire-style coats; ties made from the same wool as the jacket; and scarves. Fabrics: cashmere, camel hair, frosted wool, stretch jersey, and velvet. Colors: black, navy blue, musk green, and gray, with touches of gold and China blue. Eveningwear: velvet jackets and coats with velvet lapels, and velvet tuxedos worn over black shirts. Advertising campaign: photographs by Paolo Roversi.

Womenswear Pinstriped suits and long wool topcoats lined with gold velvet; long jackets; straight, ankle-length pants with pressed pleats; tracksuits worn with shawls and capes; midi skirts; and silk jersey dresses. Fabrics: wool and silk, with embossed surfaces and geometric motifs. Colors: dark jewel tones and saturated neutrals. Eveningwear: long black velvet dresses with narrow embroidered borders; scaled-down jackets worn with nothing underneath; tops cut like T-shirts; and floor-length duster coats. Advertising campaign: photographs by Paolo Roversi.

FALL/WINTER 1998–99

Menswear Classic and minimal suits with traditional patterns from checks to pinstripes; woven jersey jackets and blousons with small lapels and dropped shoulders; shawl-collar, knee-length coats worn with matching worsted pants; funnel-collar coats with concealed placket fronts worn with full-cut, wide pants; shirts with concealed closures, stand-up or polo collars, and velvet edgings; leather jackets and coats; and long, military-style trench coats and reefer jackets. Fabrics: luxury wool and cashmere, with complex stitches and optical-effect ribbing. Eveningwear: spencers worn over tucked and untucked shirts with cummerbunds and pegged pants. Advertising campaign: photographs by Aldo Fallai.

Womenswear Slim, lapel-less jackets with concealed side fastenings; short, structured jackets with defined waists and straight shoulders; lightweight knitwear with voluminous shapes; wide, low-waisted pants; long, straight skirts; long dresses; duster coats; and long overcoats cut like jackets. Colors: rosewood, cloud gray, eggshell, slate gray, black, and green. Eveningwear: sweaters with Lurex threads; embroidered dresses in soft and luminous colors; simply cut jackets with embroidered black or black-and-white beading; and long skirts with trains or narrow hems, finished with fine embroidery and worn with skimpy tops. Advertising campaign: photographs by Paolo Roversi.

SPRING/SUMMER 1999

Menswear Lightweight, unlined, high-notch jackets with soft shoulders, funnel or raised collars, and narrow lapels; drop-waisted pants; Chinese cropped shirts and pajamas; shirts with snap closures and concealed placket fronts; sheer, band-collar, widely cut, short shirts; sheer shirts cut like T-shirts with a draped neckline and hood; Nehru dusters; and minimal leather jackets. Fabrics: frosted crepe de chine, linens, double-faced silks and wools in dusty shades, ramie, jersey-effect silks, and jacquard crepon. Colors: gray, green, blue, and brown, with lilac, jade, and aquamarine. Advertising campaign: photographs by Albert Watson.

Womenswear Double georgette jackets with close-fitting bodices; light, deconstructed shirtjackets worn like cardigans; cigarette-shaped pants; and ankle-length skirts. Fabrics: silk, linen, shantung, organza, and georgette. Colors: pale, pastel, and powdery shades: neutral tones and grays are coordinated with powdery blues, wisteria green, and light purple. Eveningwear: long dresses embroidered with glass beads; tube shapes; deep décolletés with bare shoulders; and fabrics including prints on white, gray, and aquamarine silk gauze, with iridescent shocking pink, mango, and orange-red sequins embroidered in Chinese-style patterns. Advertising campaign: photographs by Albert Watson.

SPRING/SUMMER 2000

Menswear Lean, lightweight, unconstructed, single-breasted jackets with slim shoulders, narrow lapels, and split pockets fastened by concealed zippers; shirtjackets with Velcro fastenings at the neck and short zippers hidden at the waist; "tracksuit" suits comprised of shirts and drawstring pants; blouson-style knit shirts in lightweight yarns, cashmere, or hemp; wide-legged pants; and duster coats with waterproof pockets or very fine hoods lined in net. Sportswear fabrics: polyester, cotton, and silk, some with tie-dyed patterns. Colors: wisteria and rose-gray, with steel gray predominating. Advertising campaign: photographs by Ellen Von Unwerth.

Womenswear Small, waist-length jackets; extra-long jackets without fastenings or with mini fastenings at the waist; shirtjackets with Velcro fastenings at the neck; transparent quilted vests; tracksuit pants with elasticized waists; slender, low-waisted pants worn under very light skirts shaped like flowers; short and calf-length asymmetrical skirts with zippers; sarongs; and minimalist bustiers in black varnish. Fabrics: patterns inspired by Vasily Kandinsky; superfine hemp knitwear; and light, luminous shining silks, plastered cottons, polished linens, and wet-look chiffons. Colors: mauve, lemon yellow, fuchsia, pale blue, ice, cloud gray, and black. Advertising campaign: photographs by Ellen Von Unwerth.

356

FALL/WINTER 1999–2000

Menswear Sober, simple jackets with straight-cut fronts; full-length jackets with miniature lapels; straight-cut pants; full, low-rider hip-hop pants; snap closings and concealed placket fronts; shirts cut like sweaters, with high collars and raglan sleeves; minimal leather jackets; knee-length down coats; hooded Chinese car coats; hooded sweater coats; and zipper-closure leather overcoats. Fabrics: double-face textiles in wool and innovate blends. Colors: grays, mud, earth brown, and moss green as well as red, white, and yellow. Eveningwear: black silk velvet garments. Advertising campaign: photographs by Ellen Von Unwerth.

Womenswear Short jackets with large kimono sleeves; jackets cut like Mughal shirts; hooded sweaters; tops in masculine fabrics worn in place of jackets and sweaters; tunics worn over slim pants; men's cotton shirts worn over oversized pants; ultramini tops worn with pants pleated below the knee; ankle-length skirts with low waistbands; and duster coats in double-face fabrics. Fabrics: high-tech fiber combinations and weaves. Colors: English pastels; bright green, turquoise, and ruby; neutrals such as putty, mud, dove gray, and cold brown; and black. Eveningwear: long dresses with neat necklines; pants and jackets highlighted with light-catching embroidery applied to net or tulle backgrounds with a spider-web finish. Advertising campaign: photographs by Ellen Von Unwerth.

FALL/WINTER 2000–2001

Menswear Tailored single and double-breasted suits; tapered, high-gorge, narrow-lapel jackets; jackets with concealed closures or zippers; jackets with asymmetrical hook-and-eye closures; gathered, ribbed sweaters; fur vests; sleek, narrow pants; sports shirts; narrow, square-shouldered, textured leather jackets; and knee-length coats. Fabrics: iridescent patterned velvets, tone-on-tone printed velvets with relief effects, and high-tech wool/polyester blends with a washed effect. Colors: iceberg gray, polar blue, aquamarine, frosted lilac, fog white, deep sea blue, and reds. Eveningwear: velvet tuxedos with concealed Velcro-tab closures. Advertising campaign: photographs by Peter Lindbergh.

Womenswear Shaped jackets with various necklines from collarless to novelty lapels; blouses in cut, pleated, or folded leather; full pants, undarted but snug over the hips. The collection features sculpted tailoring and an elongated silhouette. Fabrics: floral- and geometric-printed silk satin, cashmere knits, velvets, crocodile-embossed leather, and wool and silk crepes. Colors: black, midnight blue, and forest green with accents of aquamarine, amethyst, jade, and garnet. Eveningwear: bead-embroidered mesh bodysuits worn under light shirts and beaded satin trench coats; and mosaic-patterned jackets worn with embroidered and beaded pants. Advertising campaign: photographs by Peter Lindbergh.

SPRING/SUMMER 2001

Menswear Slim-waisted jackets with braid-type; asymmetrical fastenings with double-tab zips; deconstructed jackets with hand-sewn finishes; lightweight shirts with leather inserts; shirt-jackets with pockets with double or slanted fastenings; and draped jackets with small horn loop fastenings and collars. Fabrics: lightweight soft nappa leather; etched knitwear in deluxe yarn; cashmere/silk embossed knitwear; pinstripes with denim effect; cotton/silk with metallic thread; silk/tactel for shiny/matte pullovers; and natural linen. Colors: wet-sand gray, deep green, jasper green, summer-corn yellow, Tuareg azure, and Dogon red. Advertising campaign: photographs by Peter Lindbergh.

Womenswear Men's-style trousers with wide braces; unstructured jackets with constructed shoulders; shirts and blouses; knee-length skirts; ultralight lace dresses with patterns on sheer backgrounds; and short jackets, tops, and shirts. Fabrics: jacquard wool and silk; semisheer viscose; and honey-colored leather and suede. Colors: black and brown with burned and blue-tinted touches, tobacco tones, water shades, and black illuminated by small shiny pearls, encrusted stones, and crystals. Eveningwear: small embroidered tops and short skirts; and crystal-covered trousers. Advertising campaign: photographs by Peter Lindbergh.

SPRING/SUMMER 2002

Menswear Close-fitted, elegant suits; jackets with peaked lapels; jackets well-set on shoulders with vents and side parts; double-breasted jackets; "Royal Air Force pilot's" jackets; colonial straight jackets; straight trousers widened moderately by darts; sports trousers and activewear pants fastened at the waist by a drawstring; shirts with upright collars and stitched shoulders; long frock coats; ties, pullovers, and jerseys. Fabrics: silk; knit-effect silk with cotton; silk and linen; silk and wool; silk with tonal graphic motifs; silk in classic weaves; and leather. Colors: gray, lichen green, Baltic blue, and wet-sand beige, with a touch of brilliant blue. Advertising campaign: photographs by Peter Lindbergh.

Womenswear Slightly square, short, and structured jackets; asymmetrical trousers fastened at the waist by an internal drawstring belt; knotted, calibrated, or scooped tops; and asymmetrical dresses and skirts. Accessories: bags, broaches, and bracelets made of textile and jet; and rolled and shaped hats and veils. Fabrics: threaded jersey with Lurex shimmers. Colors: black and white, jet black with sparks of red. Eveningwear: gathered and sumptuously embroidered skirts and trousers; tulle evening gowns; and tops with thin printed or embroidered straps. Advertising campaign: photographs by Peter Lindbergh.

FALL/WINTER 2001–02

Menswear Tailored gauged shoulders, with elongated and open lapels; slim trousers, many featuring turn-ups; high-collared shirts with concealed buttons or mother-of-pearl buttons and embroidered buttonholes; four- or six-button coats with military-style pocket details; jackets, blousons, and dufflecoats; urbanlike sportswear in luxury fabrics and relaxed shapes. Fabrics: wool/silk; stretch wool and wool/nylon; "rainsystem-treated" cashmere flannel; silk and silk/nylon velvet; cashmere cloth; rabbit-fur- and kangaroo-fur-lined cotton; plissé leathers; matelassé and washed leather; and suede deerskin. Colors: deep and matte. Eveningwear: polo tuxedo shirt with starched shirtfront and raised matte/gloss stripe or polka-dot effects. Advertising campaign: photographs by Peter Lindbergh.

Womenswear Suits with short jackets, or straight, Nureyev-style jackets with braided loop fastenings; overcoats and duster coats cut off the shoulder; bodices paired with full skirts; and billowing dress coats in black velvet or double satin. Fabrics: micro patterns, checks, and stripes. Colors: gray, from gravel to putty to dawn gray, with shades of azure blue. Eveningwear: ruched and flounced skirts; loose pleated skirts with raised embroidery; sequins; and beads and crystals under layers of tulle. Advertising campaign: photographs by Peter Lindbergh.

FALL/WINTER 2002–03

Menswear Fitted and loose suits with impeccably detailed straight coats and jackets; striped shirts; fine and fitted knitwear with turtle or polo necks, fastened with buttons; jersey sets and short jacket-lie cardigans; and denim jackets. Fabrics: knitwear, flannel-effect jersey, chunky wool, weather-proofed cotton, and ultrabeaten gabardine. Colors: gray with shades of sand, Reseda green, burgundy, and brandy brown. Eveningwear: formal suits in black wool crepe with satin edgings and fastenings. Advertising campaign: photographs by Paolo Roversi.

Womenswear Shaped and fitted jackets with slightly pointed shoulders; wide trousers gathered at the bottom with foot straps and tight trousers gathered at the knees with small pleats; generous skirts constructed as trousers; knee-length overcoats and trenches, as well as long coats; and leather flying jackets. Accessories: small leather helmets; goggles; and satin stocking boots. Fabrics: chiffon, silk, and satin, with matte and textured wools and gabardine. Colors: flesh pink and powder blush, gray/black, and black/brown/taupe. Eveningwear: stylized geometric knitwear and pearls and allover embroidery. Advertising campaign: photographs by Paolo Roversi.

SPRING/SUMMER 2003

Menswear Double-breasted streamlined jackets as well as shirt-jackets, small blousons, and leather jackets; Nehru-collar shirts and kimono shirts; narrow trousers; and trousers with high floral turn-ups. Fabrics: coarse linen, silk and linen, sablé linen, and textured gauze. Colors: velvet gray, shades of cobalt and ultradark blue, greens, and reds. Advertising campaign: photographs by Paolo Roversi.

Womenswear Long jackets over soft skirts; short jackets over straight skirts with tiny pleats at the knee; ultraslim jackets over lightweight trousers rolled over at the waist; asymmetrical tops and strapless bodices; lightweight jerseys worn with jackets; and long parachute skirts. Fabrics: jacquard silk with washed finish or glazed with a coating of powder, and multilayered wool gauze. Colors: beige, gray quartz, sandy gray, gold, orange, blue, fuchsia, and enamel greens. Eveningwear: evening dresses contrasted with ethnic jackets; light and airy taffetas worn like pinafores; and light tunics and trousers with maxi stripes with embroidered tops. Advertising campaign: photographs by Paolo Roversi.

FALL/WINTER 2002–03

Menswear Close-fitting and compact jackets, sometimes with a military dash with patch pockets; jackets with slim shawl collars; jackets worn with coats featuring belts, stitched pleats on the back, and raised collars; trench-coat and dress-style shirts; fitted leather parkas with straight Nehru-type collars (as featured throughout the collection); and light unlined, double-breasted, zip-fastened or assymetrically fastened trench coats. Sportswear: duffel-style coats in eco leather; and blousons with natural, T-shirt-style arm fitting. Eveningwear: unstructured jackets worn over white shirts with dress collars and cravats and trousers without satin stripes; and long jersey coats with pleats. Fabrics: shiny mercerized cotton; knitwear with large stitching in relief; matte wool; chenille jersey; techno fabrics; futuristic textiles with waffled herringbone; and bold patterns. Colors: wine, bilberry, green/gray, and black. Advertising campaign: photographs by Mert and Marcus.

Womenswear Strikingly short constructed jackets, obliquely cut to fit closely around the bust, worn with flared miniskirts with a layer of silk tussore and mini-patterned tights. Fabrics: shiny techno fabrics; bias-cut ciré; heavy wool/cashmere; lace netting; and thickly tiered organza. Colors: variations of black, black and white, and silver with graphics. Advertising campaign: photographs by Mert and Marcus.

1934–50

Born July 11, 1934, on Via Colombo in the Lupa neighborhood of Piacenza, a small town in the Pianura Padana, a vast misty plain near Milan, Giorgio Armani is the second child and second son of Ugo and Maria Raimondi Armani. He is the middle brother of Sergio and Rosanna, who, at age seventeen, would be the cover girl of the Italian magazine *Arianna*; a second sister dies when she is three months old. Raised in a humble, but close-knit family, Armani attends the local public school in Piacenza, the Liceo Ottorino Respighi. His father, a theater and cinema aficionado and a soccer player on his home team, is an employee of the Fascist party in Piacenza. His mother, an attractive woman with an innate sense of style, makes her children well-tailored clothes from parachute material and military uniforms; she is a constant inspiration to her son. Armani's maternal grandfather is a cabinetmaker, and his paternal grandfather makes wigs for the Piacenza city theater. The wig shop fascinates Armani and introduces him to the world of design, color, and fantasy. His love for the theater develops while he is still a boy, and he and his brother stage puppet shows and plays together. His passion for the cinema also begins when he is young; the first film he sees is Alessandro Blasetti's *La Corona di ferro* (*The Iron Crown*, 1941), a fascist film saga in the style of Richard Wagner's *Nibelungenlied*. Over the years, he would count among his favorite films Roberto Rossellini's *Roma città aperta* (*Rome, Open City*, 1946), Alfred Hitchcock's *Notorious* (1946), Vittorio De Sica's *Ladri di Biciclette* (*The Bicycle Thief*, 1948), Billy Wilder's *Witness for the Prosecution* (1957), Bernardo Bertolucci's *Il Conformista* (*The Conformist*, 1970), and Martin Scorsese's *Taxi Driver* (1976), as well as Gene Kelly's musicals, Danny Kaye's comedies, and Luchino Visconti's movies. At age eleven, he is badly burned by gunpowder that he and some friends are playing with, but recovers quickly. At the end of World War II, Armani's father becomes an accountant in a transport company and commutes between Piacenza and Milan, until the family moves permanently to Milan, having found a house in the university area of Città Studi. Armani attends the Liceo Scientifico Leonardo da Vinci in the hopes of becoming a country doctor, in the spirit of the hero of A. J. Cronin's novel *The Citadel* (1937). He attends medical school at the Università di Milano, but his studies are interrupted in his third year, when he leaves to do his military service at the military hospital in Verona, where he works in the infirmary for invalid civilians. In Verona, he rarely misses the operas performed in the town's Roman amphitheater, including Giuseppe Verdi's *Aïda*. Deciding that a medical career is not well suited to his personality and in need of earning a living, he gives up his studies.

1951–56

Modern Italian fashion is born in Florence, due to the efforts of the aristocrat Giovan Battista Giorgini, who successfully introduces the first fashion presentations by such designers as the Fontana sisters, Emilio Pucci, and Simonetta Visconti, among others, to American buyers in his home. As Italy emerges from the devastation of World War II, remarkable creativity is manifested in fashion—as well as in cinema and industrial design. In terms of fashion, the country begins to usurp France, which had monopolized haute couture up until then. The tradition of Italian tailoring and excellent handicraft is already familiar to the American public, which favors practicality and simplicity of cut. Giorgini encourages the young Italian fashion houses to create not only *alta moda* (high fashion) collections, but also boutique and prêt-à-porter garments that are "more appropriate to everyday elegance and the sensibilities of modern women, especially American women, who [are] understood as active and working. It is these collections that represent a truly new departure in the understanding of fashion and of how women dress."[1] In 1952, the runway presentations are held in the Sala Bianca at the Palazzo Pitti, where they will continue to be held until the early 1970s. At the end of the 1950s, Rome will begin to vie with Florence for the role of primary podium for Italian *alta moda,* and Milan will start to fortify its position too, due to the influence of its weekly fashion magazine *Novità* (which will become *Vogue Italia* in 1966). Eventually, Milan will eclipse its Southern rivals.

1957–63

Armani accepts a job as an assistant photographer at the department store La Rinascente in Milan. At the time, the store is not just a business establishment, but also a space dedicated to cultural initiatives. He becomes an assistant to the Milanese architects (including Giancarlo Ortelli) employed by La Rinascente to travel the world in order to select quality products from India, Japan, and the United States—countries still unfamiliar to the ordinary Italian—and exhibit them in the store. Armani takes on a more creative role in the display office of the store, dressing the windows in a beautiful and imaginative way. This reminds him of his boyhood theatrical exploits with his brother. His enthusiasm and accomplishments are such that he is transferred to the Stile Moda Ufficio (Office of Fashion and Style), where he coordinates and oversees the different roles of the menswear buyers. He learns to appreciate the importance of the relationship between salespeople and customers. His first suggestion is to import popular yellow English sweaters that can only be found in London, whose fashion scene favors the younger generation. This success encourages him to import other unusual items. As manufacturing costs rise, he begins to look for clothes that are not as costly as custom-tailored garments, but which at the same time do not look machine-made. While visiting a manufacturer, he meets the eminent designer Nino Cerruti.

360

He travels abroad for the first time, visiting Spain and France; in particular, he enjoys Antoni Gaudí's church of Sagrada Familia in Barcelona and the atmosphere in Avignon.

1964–65

Interested in hiring Armani, Cerruti asks him to choose some fabric as a test. Armani passes inspection, opting for the same pinstripe that Cerruti favors, and he begins to learn about fabrics and the craft of tailoring from the designer. Without any formal training, he begins to design a new line of knit- and shirtwear for Hitman, Cerruti's new menswear line. He creates perfect, industrially tailored garments, a paradox in the 1960s, the age of social revolution, at which time "Giorgini—and with him the majority of Italian dressmakers—sensed that haute couture, at least as they had always known it, was doomed."[2]

1966–69

Armani meets Sergio Galeotti at La Capannina, a club at the fashionable seaside resort of Forte dei Marmi on the Tuscan coast. Galeotti, an energetic and flamboyant younger man from Pietrasanta, a small town on the coast, becomes his collaborator and partner in life and work. A designer and architectural draftsman who works for the Milanese architectural firm BBPR, Galeotti persuades Armani to start designing on his own. He proves to be exceptionally talented in understanding and marketing Armani's clothes.

1970–72

At the Sala Bianca, Armani presents his bomber jackets made of leather, treated as though it is fabric. They are a great success and begin to reverse the image of leather that has been held until this time.

To Armani, leather is *una seconda pelle* (a second skin—although *pelle* is also the Italian word for leather) that should be a stable and lasting element in every wardrobe. Encouraged by Galeotti and his business acumen, Armani leaves his stable position with Cerruti and becomes a freelance fashion designer and consultant for companies such as Allegri (sportswear and raincoats), Bagutta (shirts), Boulevard (shirts), Hilton (men's suits), Sicons (leatherwear), and Spirito (knitwear), as well as continuing to consult for Hitman.

1973–74

Armani and Galeotti move into a small office at Corso Venezia 37, in the heart of Milan. They sell everything they can—including Armani's old Volkswagen, in order to buy a table and a few lamps as well as paint for the new office. There are just two rooms, one for business and management matters handled by Galeotti, and one for Armani's designing. They employ a young student, Irene Pantone, to help them out; she is still with the company today. Besides designing for several manufacturers, Armani styles their runway shows at the Sala Bianca. For Hitman, Armani juxtaposes dissimilar garments that somehow blend together and play with a newfound freedom. He creates a voluntarily disordered style, with the shirt unbuttoned at the collar, the blazer left open, and the sweater tucked inside the pants.

1975

Together, Galeotti and Armani establish their own company, registering the trademark Giorgio Armani S.p.A. on July 24, 1975. For several years, however, Armani continues to design for Allegri, Bagutta, Gibò, Hilton, Hitman, Loewe, Montedoro, Sicons, Spirito, Ungaro, and Ermenegildo Zegna, as well as for Loewe, a Spanish house. Dissatisfied with the traditional men's jacket, which he feels does not flatter the male body, Armani creates his first sartorial innovation, an unlined and unconstructed jacket, which is relaxed, loose, and informal, allowing sensual hints of the body to surface casually and elegantly. He is one of the very few designers to begin with menswear instead of womenswear. The unconstructed jacket marks a major departure, a revolution of sorts, from the stuffy jacket popular in the 1970s, which had left the strange sartorial legacies of hippie nonchalance and over-dressy clothes. Armani senses that something that looks already worn and not absolutely perfect is urgently needed in fashion. His unconstructed jacket conveys a way of dressing up that looks rather like dressing down, as if it had been miraculously rescued from an old suitcase. Buttons are moved down, the lapels are given a lower notch, the shoulders are sloped, and the inner structure is modified. A new breed of tailoring is born, with a different appearance and a comfortable elegance, which Italian men quickly adopt.

Armani shows his first men's collection under his own name (for spring/summer 1976) in July. Three months later he shows his first women's collection (also for spring/summer 1976) at the Hotel Palace in Milan. Responding to the burgeoning feminist movement and inspired by his sister Rosanna and her girlfriends, who like to wear their brothers' jackets, Armani creates a women's jacket that proves to be an immense success; made with traditional menswear fabrics, it is as simple and soft as the one Armani has already created for men, but scaled down in size and bearing a certain masculine authority. Armani advocates an easy and fluid elegance in women as well as in men. He emancipates women's fashion, just as Paul Poiret did by eliminating corsets and constrictive clothing from women's wardrobes, and as Gabrielle "Coco" Chanel did by rendering clothing more comfortable, by shortening skirts to the knee, and by translating menswear elements to women's clothing. Armani initiates a new chapter in contemporary fashion, introducing a style for women that is decidedly masculine, and a style for men that is rather more feminine. Characteristic of his approach is his use of traditionally feminine fabrics for menswear and menswear fabrics for women.

Armani discovers the tiny, rugged volcanic island of Pantelleria, situated in the Mediterranean sea between Sicily and Tunisia, and purchases a small vacation house there.

1976–77
Armani moves temporarily to an office in Via Santa Cecilia before settling into Palazzo Durini Caproni di Taliedo, a handsome seventeenth-century building designed by architect Francesco Maria Richini and located in the heart of Milan, at via Durini 24. The principal rooms are decorated with mythological and allegorical frescoes by Nuvoloni, Giuseppe Maria Crespi, and Schusters.

The Giorgio Armani label is introduced to the U.S. market by an enthusiastic Fred Pressman, president of the luxury department store Barney's New York.

Spurred on by an invitation from *L'Uomo Vogue*, Armani designs hypothetical uniforms for the Italian military based on comfortable sportswear. The collection is photographed in military barracks with the collaboration of military staff and presented in *L'Uomo Vogue* in June/July 1977.

Armani's fall/winter 1977–78 women's collection is considered revolutionary in the way that the outfits are presented, with one jacket worn over another: a wool jacket over a tweed blazer, a leather jacket over a canvas jacket, or a fabric jacket over a leather jacket, for example. The men's collection is equally revolutionary, featuring men's pants constructed without pleats and waistcoats worn over jackets.

Armani travels to the island of Martinique.

1978
A licensing agreement is established with Gruppo Finanziario Tessile (GFT), which manufactures and distributes the Giorgio Armani collections.

Giorgio Armani Le Collezioni, a less expensive line for men, is launched.

Introduced in the fall/winter 1978–79 men's collection, the Armani slouch—with wide-wale corduroy and baggy bottom pockets—penetrates the youth market. In womenswear, Armani's second sartorial innovation is presented: tapered and leanly cut jackets with varied lapels and tiny pockets, giving a broad-shouldered and slim-hipped glamour to the "power suit." The look is still casual, but less rumpled, with a nonchalance suggesting an easy assurance.

At the Academy Awards, Diane Keaton wears an Armani blazer to collect her Best Actress award for her performance in Woody Allen's film *Annie Hall*.

Armani buys a house in the seaside Tuscan resort of Forte dei Marmi.

1979
The Giorgio Armani Men's Wear Corporation USA is established.

Gabriella Forte joins Giorgio Armani S.p.A. as vice president; she is responsible for U.S. operations, the company's image, press, and marketing, and events held in Armani's name.

Giorgio Armani Le Collezioni for women is launched. Mani, also a more affordable line, is launched. The Mani men's line is exclusive to the U.S. and Canadian markets, while the women's line is available in the rest of the world.

Armani is awarded the Neiman Marcus Fashion Award; other Italians to have been presented with the award are Missoni in 1973 and, before that, Emilio Pucci and Roberta di Camerino in the 1950s.

1980
A licensing agreement is signed with L'Oréal (formerly Helena Rubinstein) for the creation of fragrances.

Armani decides to show his spring/summer 1981 collections in his palazzo, rather than at the traditional fashion fair in Milan.

Armani wins the Cutty Sark Award for the International Top Men's Fashion Designer.

He designs shirts, suits, and ties for Italian-American dancer and choreographer Louis Falco's ballet *Service Compris* at theaters in Milan and Rome, and costumes for two operas directed by Luca Ronconi at La Scala in Milan: Arnold Schönberg's *Erwartung* and Richard Strauss's *Elektra*.

Following the success of his films *Grease* and *Saturday Night Fever*, John Travolta visits Armani to choose some forty suits from the designer's collections for his role in Paul Schrader's forthcoming film *American Gigolo*—but it is instead Richard Gere who appears in the film, which also stars model and actress Lauren Hutton. *American Gigolo* ensures Armani's fame, and his clothes become a status symbol for any young—or not so young—man who wants to seduce.

Armani takes Manhattan by storm, hosting the White Party at Studio 54 to celebrate his fall/winter 1980–81 collections. In the April issue of *L'Uomo Vogue*, Mat Serra, general merchandise manager of department store Saks Fifth Avenue, hails Armani as the "Michelangelo of fashion," claiming that he has created a perfect silhouette that everyone wishes to emulate. Italy is recognized as a new and dynamic country on the world's stage, its position symbolized by the easy, elegant, and sober style of Armani, who understands the sociological significance of fashion and its power of communication. As the 1980s progress, the booming, materialistic era comes to be symbolized by the somewhat austere tailored Armani power suit for men and women, defined by broad padded shoulders and wider lapels, inspired by the 1940s Hollywood look.

Andy Warhol, whose novel cable-television programs cover everything from haute couture to punk, features an interview with Armani by Italian journalist Daniela Morera in episode three of his *Andy Warhol's T.V.* series.

1981
Armani Junior, Emporio Armani, and Armani Jeans are launched in Italy and subsequently in the U.S. Emporio Armani clothing is based on the same stylistic criteria as the Giorgio Armani line, but is more affordably priced. A new trademark logo for jeans and T-shirts, shoes, and sportswear—an imperial eagle with Armani's initials—is introduced to distinguish and protect his products from copies.

The first Emporio Armani boutique opens in Milan, on Via Durini.

The fall/winter 1981–82 women's collection features a Japanese-style line inspired by Akira Kurosawa's 1980 film *Kagemusha*, including shimmering bustiers influenced by the protective armor worn by high-stationed warriors in the Heian period (ninth–tenth centuries) and by samurai as late as the end of the nineteenth century. A general interest in things Japanese—including Kabuki theater, traditional Japanese prints, and modern television cartoons—pervades Europe and New York.

Armani wins *Gentleman's Quarterly* magazine's Men's Style Award for Best Fashion Designer and the Cutty Sark Award for the International Top Men's Fashion Designer.

Warhol paints a portrait of Armani.

Armani buys land on Pantelleria, at Cala Gadir, a small fishing port. His property encompasses six houses in a style typical of the island; known as *dammusi*, the houses are made of volcanic rock laid with earth and water and have white cupola roofs. After being refurbished by architect Gabriella Giuntoli, they comprise guest quarters, a living/dining complex, and Armani's own simple and elegant villa. Palm trees, capers, oleanders, lavender and rosemary bushes, cacti, hibiscus, roses, and pomegranate, orange, and olive trees on the property produce a wonderful array of color and scent.

1982

In April, Armani becomes the first fashion designer since Christian Dior in the 1940s—and the only other Italian besides Nobel Prize–winning playwright Luigi Pirandello—to appear on the cover of *Time* magazine. Inside is an eight-page color spread with text by screenwriter Jay Cocks. The piece is published during the same week that the prêt-à-porter collections are presented in Paris, which the French take as a personal affront to their sartorial prestige. Cocks lightly rebuffs Pierre Bergé, partner and protector of Yves Saint Laurent, who challenges, "Give me one piece of clothing, one fashion statement that Armani has made that has truly influenced the world," by listing Armani's achievements: "The unstructured jacket. An easeful elegance without stricture. Tailoring of a kind thought possible only when done by hand. The layering of fabrics by pattern, texture and color. Surprising combinations of garments— leather pants as part of a suit, a long jacket over foreshortened slacks, a vest worn over a coat—that scramble clichés and conventions into a new and effortless redefinition of a style. A functional celebration of fabric. A reshaping of traditional geometry with witty contours, sudden symmetries and startling vectors. A new sort of freedom in clothes. An ease, the Armani ease."[3] He quotes Grace Mirabella, editor of *Vogue*, who describes Armani's approach as "style without excessive design," and American designer Bill Blass, who calls him a "genius for his time."[4]

Armani moves his offices to Via Borgonuovo 21 in Milan. From this time, most of his runway shows will be presented in a theater located here.

During French fashion week in Paris, Armani attends a launch party for his first women's fragrance, simply named Armani Donna.

Emporio Armani underwear, swimwear, and accessories for men and women are launched.

Armani is awarded the Fil d'Or at the Festival International du Lin in Paris; the Ambrogino d'Oro from the municipality of Milan; and the Leone d'Oro from the Lions' Club in Piacenza, his native city.

Armani's work is included in *Intimate Architecture: Contemporary Clothing Design*, an exhibition at M.I.T. in Cambridge, Massachusetts, that presents historical and aesthetic forms interpreted by fashion designers. The exhibition represents a broader interest in fashion as a metaphorical eye for scrutinizing contemporary culture.

Milanese publisher Franco Maria Ricci issues a handsome volume on Armani, with biographical texts by Arturo Carlo Quintavalle, Richard de Combray, and Anna Piaggi. The book includes over one hundred hand-colored drawings on black paper by Armani that document his collections to that time; together, they record the development of his style and the growth of his identity through the fashion seasons.

Armani donates a collection of his drawings to the Università di Parma, whose fashion archives contains over 50,000 original drawings by major Italian designers.

Armani acquires Villa Rivara, a country house built in the 1950s in an eighteenth-century style, located in Cigognola near Broni in the province of Pavia. Armani hires Giancarlo Ortelli, who has designed many of Armani's boutiques around the world, to renovate the house.

1983

The Giorgio Armani Fashion Corporation is created in order to oversee the distribution of all Giorgio Armani products in the U.S. (superceding the Giorgio Armani Men's Wear Corporation U.S.A.).

The first Giorgio Armani boutique opens, on Via Sant'Andrea in Milan.

Armani is honored with a gold medal from the municipality of Piacenza; the Fil d'Or at the Festival International du Lin in Paris; and the Council of Fashion Designers of America Award for Best International Designer.

1984

The first Emporio Armani advertising billboard makes its appearance in Milan, at the crossroads of Via Broletto, Via Cusani, Via dell'Orso, and Via Ponte Vetero. The first image features four slouching young men wearing similar unconstructed suits, casually reading newspapers. Subsequent images include landscapes and scenes of everyday life in Milan, workmen, Armani's Volkswagen, Africa and the tropics, and young couples. Another billboard greets passengers at Milan's Linate Airport, welcoming visitors to the Italian fashion capital.

A Giorgio Armani boutique opens in New York, at 815 Madison Avenue and 68th Street.

Armani, the designer's first fragrance for men, is launched.

Armani wins the Occhio d'Oro for Best Designer, Spring/Summer Collections; and the Cutty Sark Award for the International Top Men's Fashion Designer.

He contributes the wardrobe for actors Willem Dafoe in Walter Hill's film *Streets of Fire* and most of the wardrobe for Don Johnson and Philip Thomas in the television show *Miami Vice*.

Armani designs the uniforms for Italy's top American-style football teams, the Frogs and the Seamen.

1985

Together with fashion designers Emanuel Ungaro and Valentino, Armani presents his fall/winter 1985–86 women's collection at a benefit for the Italian Red Cross at the Castello di Rivoli, near Turin.

He becomes the first Designer Laureate of the Cutty Sark Men's Fashion Awards and is awarded the Commendatore dell'Ordine al Merito della Repubblica by the Italian government.

Giorgio Armani clothing is worn by Patrick Bauchau, Jennifer Connelly, and Donald Pleasence in Dario Argento's film *Phenomena* (*Creepers*); Catherine Deneuve in Mario Monicelli's *Speriamo che sia femmina* (*Let's Hope It's a Girl*); and Ariane in Michael Cimino's *Year of the Dragon*.

Armani participates in Fashion Aid, a benefit against hunger organized by Bob Geldorf in London. (He is the only Italian fashion designer invited to do so.)

Several of Armani's jackets are included in *Italia: Il Genio della Moda*, an exhibition that narrates the story of Italian fashion from the 1950s to the 1980s, presented during the Milanese trade fair Grande Fiera di Aprile.

After a few years of ill health, Galeotti dies of cancer in August. Contrary to all expectations, Armani not only continues to design all of his collections, but successfully takes over the business side of the company as well.

American architect Peter Marino designs Armani's home at Via Borgonuovo 21, with furnishings by French designer Jean-Michel Frank.

1986

A Giorgio Armani boutique opens in Paris.

Armani hires socialite Lee Radziwill as his special events coordinator.

Armani is honored with the Grand'Ufficiale dell'Ordine al Merito della Repubblica, Italy's highest government award. He also wins the Cutty Sark Award for the International Top Men's Fashion Designer; the

Occhio d'Oro for Best Designer, Spring/Summer Collections; and the Occhiolino d'Oro for Best Designer, Fall/Winter Collections.

Giorgio Armani clothing is worn by Maruschka Detmers in Marco Bellocchio's film *Il diavolo in corpo* (*Devil in the Flesh*) and by Harvey Keitel, Stefania Sandrelli, and Trudie Styler in Giovanni Soldati's *La Sposa Americana*.

He designs the uniforms for the players of the soccer team from Foggia, a small town south of Rome, and for the Italian national soccer team, the Azzurri, for the World Cup, which is played in Mexico.

He designs the Notturno, a stylish new electronic telephone commissioned by Italtel Telematica, a private Italian telephone company.

At the Rufino Tamayo Museum in Mexico City, Armani is included in *Italia 1946–1986*, an exhibition featuring fashion and industrial and graphic design from Italy.

1987
In order to enter the Japanese market, Armani establishes a joint venture with the group Itochu to promote the Giorgio Armani brand and opens three Giorgio Armani boutiques in Tokyo.

Giorgio Armani Calze (hosiery) and Occhiali (eyewear) are launched.

Armani is awarded the Gran Cavaliere della Repubblica by the Italian government. He also receives the Fil d'Or at the Festival International du Lin in Paris; the Council of Fashion Designers of America's Lifetime Achievement Award for his menswear; the Occhio d'Oro for Best Designer, Spring/Summer Collections; and the Cutty Sark Award for the International Top Men's Fashion Designer.

Pope John Paul II commissions Armani to design a new cover for the evangelistary, which is used in cathedrals during pontifical celebrations. Armani is granted an audience with the Pope on this occasion.

Taking his cue from the 1930s, but remaining faithful to his own vision, Armani designs selected costumes for actors Sean Connery, Kevin Costner, Billy Drago, Andy Garcia, and Charles Martin Smith in Brian De Palma's film *The Untouchables*, dressing the character of killer Frank Nitti (Al Capone's right-hand man, played by Drago) in brilliant shades of white, ice, and cream. The film wins an Oscar for Best Costumes.

Armani participates in *Una vetrina per l'arte*, a collaboration between art and fashion in Milan's Via Sant'Andrea, in which designers are asked to exhibit paintings in their store windows. Armani chooses Cesare Viazzi's *Valchiria, omaggio a Wagner*, a homage to German composer Richard Wagner.

Photographs of Armani's work are included in *Fotografia: Immagine della Moda Italiana*, presented during the Salone Internazionale Cine Ottica Fotografia in Milan. The exhibition explores the relationship between photography and the cultural politics of fashion, through the work of some of the most important Italian fashion designers photographed by Richard Avedon, Aldo Fallai, Antonio Mulas, and Oliviero Toscani, among others. His work is also included in *Moda Italia*, an exhibition promoting the "Made in Italy" label, presented at Pier 88 in New York; and in *Lo stilista e i suoi fotografi*, which features fashion shots by photographers such as Avedon, David Bailey, Fallai, and Bob Krieger, held at the Galleria Civica in Suzzara, near Parma.

Martin Scorsese shoots the first television commercial for the Emporio Armani line.

1988
Emporio Armani boutiques open in New York's Flatiron district and in Florence. Giorgio Armani boutiques open in Turin, Paris, London, Zürich, Saint Moritz, and Nagoya, Japan, and another in Tokyo. Armani also opens a Giorgio Armani boutique on Rodeo Drive in Los Angeles, in conjunction with a gala at the Museum of Contemporary Art. He invites Pat Riley, the high-profile coach of the Los Angeles Lakers basketball team and an Armani devotee, to wear Giorgio Armani clothing constantly in the public eye. Just as Italian and French movie stars wore clothes by famous fashion designers in the 1950s, Hollywood actors are wooed to wear Armani's clothes at the Academy Awards; Michelle Pfeiffer wears a long, simple skirt and jacket with silver buttons, and the rest of Hollywood will soon follow suit by wearing Armani designs to the ceremonies.

Armani wins the Occhio d'Oro for Best Designer, Spring/Summer and Fall/Winter Collections; the Cristóbal Balenciaga award for best international designer, presented by King Juan Carlos of Spain; and the Media Key Award for an Armani fragrance commercial directed by Martin Scorsese.

Giorgio Armani clothing is worn by Anouk Aimée and Ricky Tognazzi in Giorgio Capitani's film *Arrivederci e grazie*.

Giorgio Armani clothing is also worn by the Korean musical orchestra performing at the Seoul Olympics, and by Italian conductor Claudio Abbado and the musicians of the Gustav Mahler Jugendorchester and the European Community Youth Orchestra during a summer European tour.

Armani designs the new uniforms for the Carabinieri, the Italian police force with military and civil duties.

1989
The Emporio Armani Gift Collection, comprised of fine items for the home, is launched.

The French fashion house Lanvin asks Armani to become its creative director, a position he declines.

Armani receives the Woolmark Award in New York; the Senken Award in Japan; and the Pubblicità e Successo in Italy for an Armani Jeans commercial.

Giorgio Armani clothing is worn by Michael Keaton as the Bruce Wayne character in Tim Burton's film *Batman*.

Armani e il Cinema, an exhibition exploring Armani's relationship with the cinema, is presented in Modena's town hall.

Armani travels to Kenya.

1990
A Giorgio Armani boutique opens in Palm Beach, Florida.

Armani presents his fall/winter 1991–92 women's collection at the Museum of Contemporary Art in Los Angeles.

Giorgio Armani clothing is worn by Tom Hanks in John Patrick Shanley's film *Joe Versus the Volcano*; Rupert Everett, Helen Mirren, Natasha Richardson, and Christoper Walken in Paul Schrader's *The Comfort of Strangers*; Mickey Rourke in Michael Cimino's *Desperate Hours*; Robin Williams in Roger Donaldson's *Cadillac Man*; John Cusack in Stephen Frears's *The Grifters*; Tom Cruise, Nicole Kidman, and Randy Quaid in Tony Scott's *Days of Thunder*; Joanne Whalley in Lewis Teague's *Navy SEALS*; and Lauren Bacall in Rob Reiner's *Misery*. Armani also contributes the wardrobes for Martin Scorsese's *Goodfellas*.

He designs the uniforms for the Italian national soccer team for the World Cup, which is played in Italy. He also designs T-shirts for taxi drivers in Milan, and clothing for Milan's voluntary ecological officers.

Armani designs the Pierrot figure for events associated with the Carnevale Ambrosiano, the annual carnival honoring Milan's patron saint.

Giorgio Armani: Images of Man, curated by Richard Martin and Harold Koda, is presented at the Museum of the Fashion Institute of Technology in New York.

1991

The first A/X Armani Exchange store opens, in SoHo in New York, offering a less expensive line of clothing. Giorgio Armani boutiques open in Florence, Barcelona, Madrid, Düsseldorf, Munich, and Boston.

Armani is awarded an honorary doctorate by the Royal College of Art in London in a ceremony at the Royal Albert Hall.

Giorgio Armani clothing is worn by Steve Martin and Diane Keaton in Charles Shyer's film *Father of the Bride*; Veronica Hamel in Arthur Hiller's *Taking Care of Business*; Marisa Paredes in Pedro Almodóvar's *Tacones Lejanos* (*High Heels*); Andie MacDowell and John Malkovich in Michael Lindsay-Hogg's *The Object of Beauty*; and Dianne Wiest in Jodie Foster's *Little Man Tate*.

Armani designs the uniforms for Alitalia's female flight attendants and ground staff.

Martin Scorsese and Jay Cocks make *Made in Milan*, a documentary on Armani and his work. The film premieres at the Venice Film Festival.

Armani travels to Morocco.

1992

Giorgio Armani boutiques open in Rome, Brussels, Osaka, Taipei, and Manhasset, New York.

Giò, a new women's fragrance, is launched with a party at Villa Rivara. A black-and-white commercial for the new perfume is shot by David Lynch.

He presents his women's and men's spring/summer 1993 Le Collezioni line at the newly renovated Solomon R. Guggenheim Museum in New York, where a retrospective of work by Minimalist artist Dan Flavin is on view.

In Florence, on the fortieth anniversary of the inauguration of the Sala Bianca fashion shows, Armani is awarded the Fiorino d'Oro by mayor Giorgio Morales for promoting the Made in Italy image throughout the world. Some seventy womenswear and twenty-five menswear items are presented in a special exhibition designed by Gae Aulenti in the Sala Bianca—the same place that Armani showed his designs in the late 1960s.

Armani receives the Woolmark Award for Best New International Men's Collection for his A/X line; the Occhio d'Oro for Best Italian Designer of the Year; and the Accademia del Profumo award for the best Italian print and television advertising campaign in 1992.

Giorgio Armani clothing is worn by Richard Gere in Phil Joanou's film *Final Analysis*; Helen Hunt in Billy Crystal's *Mr. Saturday Night*; Andy Garcia in Bruce Robinson's *Jennifer Eight*; Nick Nolte and Susan Sarandon in George Miller's *Lorenzo's Oil*; Robert De Niro in Barry Primus's *Mistress*; and Kevin Costner in Mick Jackson's *The Bodyguard*.

Armani acquires a country house in the hills of Saint-Tropez, on the French Riviera.

1993

Armani receives an Honorary Nomination from the Accademia di Brera in Milan; a Golden Effie for the advertising campaign used to launch his jeans line in the U.S.; the Aguja de Oro Award for Best Designer of the Year; and the Telva Triunfador Award for the Best International Designer of the Year.

On the occasion of the sixtieth birthday of cartoon character Donald Duck, Armani designs several outfits directed to a younger audience, including a classic double-breasted suit, slouchy trousers with a brightly colored waistcoat, a grunge-inspired outfit, and a guru-collar shirt and pants.

Giorgio Armani clothing is worn by Lena Olin and Richard Gere in Mike Figgis's film *Mr. Jones*; Roberto Benigni, Claudia Cardinale, and

Deborah Farentino in Blake Edwards's *The Son of the Pink Panther*; Timothy Hutton in Tom Holland's *The Temp*; Peter Coyote in Pedro Almodóvar's *Las Una del Asesino*; Sean Connery in Philip Kaufman's *Rising Sun*; Rene Russo in Wolfgang Petersen's *In the Line of Fire*; Alessandra Martine in Claude Lelouch's *Tout ça . . . pour ça!* (*All That . . . for This?!*); and Christian Slater in Tony Scott's *True Romance*.

Armani designs the clothes for several events associated with the Todi Festival, a summer dance and music festival in Todi, Italy.

He underwrites *La Nuova Pittura Cinese*, *Passaggio ad Oriente*, an exhibition of contemporary Chinese painting at the Venice *Biennale*.

He makes a guest appearance on the NBC television show *Saturday Night Live*.

1994

Giorgio Armani boutiques open in Bologna, Geneva, Dubai, Seoul, and Singapore. An Emporio Armani boutique opens in Brussels.

Gabriella Forte, who has been Armani's right hand for over fifteen years, leaves the company. Lee Radziwill resigns as Armani's special events coordinator.

Armani hosts the annual Fire and Ice Ball in Los Angeles, which benefits the Revlon/UCLA Women's Cancer Research Program, and presents his spring/summer 1995 women's collection there.

Armani receives the Lifetime Achievement Award for the Arts and Fashion given by the National Italian American Foundation in Washington, D.C., and the Occhio d'Oro for Best Italian Designer of the Year.

Giorgio Armani clothing is worn by Lauren Bacall in Robert Altman's film *Prêt-à-Porter*; Donald Sutherland in Stuart Orme's *The Puppet Masters*; Sylvester Stallone in Luis Llosa's *The Specialist*; Bruce Willis in Richard Rush's *Color of Night*; Nick Nolte in Charles Shyer's *I Love Trouble*; and Richard Gere in Mark Rydell's *Intersection*. Emporio Armani clothing is worn by Tom Sizemore in Oliver Stone's *Natural Born Killers*; Uma Thurman and Ving Rhames in Quentin Tarantino's *Pulp Fiction*; and Patrick Bruel in Claude Zidi's *Profil Bas* (*Low Profile*).

Emporio Armani clothing is also worn by the cast of Jonathan Miller's production of Mozart's *Così fan' tutte* at the Royal Opera House in London.

Armani designs white cotton shirts and navy wool pants for the waiters at the Gramercy Park Tavern in New York, and a formal wardrobe for the Italian national soccer team on the occasion of the World Cup, which is played in the U.S.

Four garments created by Armani between 1990 and 1994 are included in *Orientalism: Visions of the East in Western Dress*, an exhibition at the Costume Institute of the Metropolitan Museum of Art, New York. The exhibition illustrates Eastern influences on Western fashion trends over several centuries.

1995

Acqua di Giò, a fragrance for women, is launched. Giorgio Armani Neve (skiwear) and Giorgio Armani Golf are also launched.

The first Armani Junior boutique opens, in Milan. Giorgio Armani boutiques open in Sydney and Riyadh, Saudi Arabia, and another in Tokyo.

Armani shows his fall/winter 1995–96 women's collection in a former factory in the Ansaldo, Milan, an industrial area that is taking on a more commercial and cultural character.

Armani receives the Together for Peace Foundation Cultural Award in Rome; the Maschera d'Oro, Campione d'Italia award; and the Telva Triunfador de Belleza Award for his Acqua di Giò fragrance. He is also named Designer of the Year, Best Modern Classics, by *Marie Claire UK*.

As part of *Kino, Movie, Cinema* at the Martin-Gropius-Bau, Berlin,

Armani curates *Armani vis-à-vis Dietrich*, an exhibition that includes the actress's clothes—restored by Armani—as well as Armani's own designs. The exhibition highlights the androgynous aspects of their styles, focusing on the tuxedo, suit jacket, and wide trousers, which have defined Armani's look through the years.

Giorgio Armani clothing is worn by Enrica Antonioni, John Malkovich, and Sophie Marceau in Michelangelo Antonioni and Wim Wenders's film *Par-Delà les nuages* (*Beneath the Clouds*); Nicole Garcia and Marie Trintignant in Nadine Trintignant's *Une Fille Galante*; Andy Garcia in Andrew Davis's *Steal Big, Steal Little* and in Gary Fleder's *Things to Do in Denver When You're Dead*; Christian Slater in Marc Rocco's *Murder in the First;* Christopher Lambert in J. F. Lawton's *The Hunted*; Antonio Banderas and Sylvester Stallone in Richard Donner's *Assassins*; Margherita Buy in Mario Monicelli's *Facciamo Paradiso*; Tom Arnold in Chris Columbus's *Nine Months*; Al Pacino in Michael Mann's *Heat*; Annette Bening in Rob Reiner's *The American President*, Anjelica Huston in Sean Penn's *The Crossing Guard*; Debra Winger in Billy Crystal's *Forget Paris*; and Gabriel Byrne in Bryan Singer's *The Usual Suspects*. Emporio Armani clothing is worn by Hugh Grant and Julianne Moore in *Nine Months*. Both Giorgio Armani and Emporio Armani clothing is worn by Steve Martin in Charles Shyer's *Father of the Bride Part II*.

A long beaded dress from Armani's spring/summer 1994 women's collection is included in a runway show at the Roman amphitheater in Caesaria, Israel, as part of a special fashion event to promote peace.

1996
Armani moves his press and styling offices to Palazzo Orsini, at Via Borgonuovo 11, Milan. The Palazzo Orsini was built at the end of the sixteenth century and maintains most of its original structure, though the original front doors are kept at the Museo Civico in Milan. The oval-shaped dressing room on the *piano nobile* was decorated by Andrea Appiani in the second half of the eighteenth century, and architect Luigi Clerichetti designed the façade in the mid-nineteenth century. The Renaissance courtyard is exceptionally beautiful, and the small garden is contiguous with the botanical gardens on Via Brera. Armani's administrative offices are located across the street at number 18. He retains his home at Via Borgonuovo 21, where the runway theater and studio also remain.

Armani's new flagship store, designed by Peter Marino & Associates, opens in New York, on Madison Avenue at Sixty-fifth Street. Three times the size of the original store, it is finished in French limestone and ebonized wood, with big leather and suede club chairs and private sitting rooms for personal-shopping appointments. Merchandise includes the Giorgio Armani, Classico, and Le Collezioni lines, as well as new ski and golf clothing lines. To celebrate the opening, he hosts a party, An Evening of Music and Style, at the Twenty-sixth Street Armory, at which singer Eric Clapton, flamenco dancer Joaquin Cortes, and the bands the Fugees and the Wallflowers give a concert. Giorgio Armani boutiques also open in San Francisco, Venice, Brussels, Jakarta, and Hong Kong. Emporio Armani boutiques open in Barcelona and Lisbon.

Giorgio Armani Classico, a classical line that features such items as crepe suits for women and conservative suits for men, and Acqua di Giò, a fragrance for men, are launched.

The spring/summer 1997 men's collection is presented at the Palazzo del Senato in Milan.

Armani receives the Man of the Year Award from *GQ USA*, based on votes cast by magazine readers.

As fashion enters the realm of official culture, Armani is included in the Italian encyclopedia *Treccani*, which is akin to the Encyclopedia Britannica.

On the occasion of the annual Pitti Immagine fashion events in Florence, Robert Wilson creates *GA Story*, a ninety-minute performance comprised of separate tableaux, presented in the Leopolda, a renovated nineteenth-century train station. The performance includes music, video, dance, special lighting, and a nontraditional fashion show featuring the designer's spring/summer 1997 men's collection. Certain guests wear garments from Armani's personal archives, and models and dancers wear his clothes both in the performance and as part of the audience.

Giorgio Armani clothing is worn by Jean Marais and Liv Tyler in Bernardo Bertolucci's film *Stealing Beauty*; Richard Gere and Laura Linney in Gregory Hoblit's *Primal Fear*; Mel Gibson and Rene Russo in Ron Howard's *Ransom*; Michael J. Fox and Jack Nicholson in Tim Burton's *Mars Attacks!*; Ana Belén in Manuel Gómez Pereira's *El amor perjudica seriamente la salud*; Woody Harrelson in Michael Cimino's *The Sunchaser*; Christopher Lambert in Jeannot Szwarc's *Hercule et Sherlock*; and Sally Field in John Schlesinger's *Eye for an Eye*.

Armani is featured in *La regola estrosa, cent'anni di eleganza maschile*, an exhibition curated by Luigi Settembrini at the Leopolda station. It includes photographs, objects, clothes, and accessories from the wardrobes of seventy of some of the most elegant Italian men of the twentieth century.

Armani participates in the *Biennale di Firenze*, which explores the intimate relationship between art and fashion. His work is included in the exhibition sections *New Person*, *New Universe*, curated by Germano Celant, and *Visitors*, curated by Settembrini.

With the Italian publisher Leonardo Mondadori, Armani underwrites *Da Monet à Picasso*, an exhibition of Impressionist and Post-Impressionist paintings, watercolors, and drawings from the Pushkin Museum in Moscow, presented at the Palazzo Reale in Milan.

Armani participates in a fund-raising effort for the Rehabilitation for Addicted Prisoners program. Requesting prisoners to produce drawings, he selects the three best and has them printed on T-shirts, which he sells in all Emporio Armani boutiques in Great Britain with the proceeds benefiting RAPT.

1997
Emporio Armani Orologi (watches) is launched.

Giorgio Armani boutiques open in Hamburg; San Francisco; Kaohsiung, Taiwan; and Melbourne. The first Collezioni Giorgio Armani boutiques open, in Milan, London, and Tokyo, featuring the Mani line for women and the Giorgio Armani Le Collezioni line for men. The first Armani Jeans boutique opens, in Rome. Emporio Armani boutiques open in Istanbul; São Paolo; Pesaro and Cosenza, Italy; Nagoya, Japan; and Pusan, South Korea. A new Emporio Armani boutique also opens in New York, on Madison Avenue between Fifty-seventh and Fifty-eighth streets. Designed by Thomas O'Brien, the multilevel store features more youthful clothes, accessories, home objects, and a café.

The spring/summer 1998 men's and women's collections are presented in Tokyo, fifteen years after Armani's last visit to Japan.

Armani is named Designer of the Year, Best Modern Classics, by *Marie Claire USA*.

Giorgio Armani clothing is worn by Tom Hanks in Rob Reiner's film *I am Your Child*; Wesley Snipes in Mike Figgis's *One Night Stand* (a scene within the film also depicts an Emporio Armani commercial being shot); Ethan Hawke in Andrew Niccol's *Gattaca*; Gina Gershon in Paul Schrader's *Touch*; Francesca Neri in Pedro Almodóvar's *Carne Trémula* (*Live Flesh*); Diego Abatantuono, Christopher Lambert, and Emmanuelle Seigner in Gabriele Salvatores's *Nirvana*; Christopher Lambert in Claude Zidi's *Arlette*; Bruce Willis in Michael Caton-Jones's *The Jackal*; Dustin Hoffman in Costa-Gavras's *Mad City*; Glenn Close in Wolfgang Petersen's *Air Force One*; Mira Sorvino in Guillermo del Toro's

Mimic; Dustin Hoffman in Barry Levinson's *Wag the Dog*; Jack Nicholson and Greg Kinnear in James L. Brooks's *As Good As It Gets*; and Billy Crystal in Ivan Reitman's *Fathers' Day* (in which a scene is shot at an Emporio Armani boutique in San Francisco). Emporio Armani clothing is worn by Claudia Gerini and Leonardo Pieraccioni in Pieraccioni's *Fuochi d'Artificio*.

Armani designs the costumes for flamenco dancer Joaquin Cortes and his company for Cortes's ballet *Pasión Gitana*, performed at New York's City Center.

On the occasion of the Italian Ecological Party's annual meeting, which is held in Milan, Armani designs a line of hemp clothing for his Emporio Armani collection.

As a tribute to Princess Diana, a presentation of Giorgio Armani clothing takes place at the AIDS Charity Gala in Singapore.

1998

Emporio Armani, a fragrance for men and women, is launched.

The world's largest A/X Armani Exchange store opens in New York, on Fifth Avenue at Fifty-first Street. Designed by English architect Keith Hobbs of United Designers, the store is inspired by Italian open-air markets. A 32-foot stainless steel door seals the store like a vault when it is closed and a 20-foot-wide billboard showing several images from the A/X campaigns hangs behind the cashiers' counter. An Emporio Armani boutique opens on the Boulevard St-Germain in Paris. Giorgio Armani boutiques open in Las Vegas and Kobe, Japan.

An Emporio Armani runway show planned for the Place Saint-Sulpice in Paris is canceled by the French authorities. Armani decides to show the collection in New York instead, at the Cipriani Wall Street, which is transformed into a runway theater similar to the one in his Milan palazzo.

Armani receives the Bambi Award for Best International Fashion Designer from Burda Editions in Karlsruhe, Germany; the Risultati Bocconi award from the Italian financial newspaper *Il Sole 24 Ore* for best financial results in Italy; and the Pitti Immagine Uomo award in Florence.

Giorgio Armani clothing is worn by Melanie Griffith in Randal Kleiser's film *Shadow of Doubt*; Alessandra Martines in Claude Lelouch's *Hasards ou coïncidences*; Kevin Spacey and Robin Wright in Anthony Drazan's *Hurlyburly*; and Bruce Greenwood and Ashley Judd in Bruce Beresford's *Double Jeopardy* (in which a scene is filmed in a Giorgio Armani boutique). Emporio Armani clothing is worn by Claudia Gerini in Franco Bernini's *Sotto la Luna*.

Armani designs the wardrobe for the musicians of the Verdi Orchestra on the occasion of director Giorgio Strehler's production of Mozart's opera *Così fan' tutte* at the Piccolo Teatro in Milan, and for the dancers and musicians performing in choreographer John Neumeier's ballet *Bernstein Dances*, which celebrates the life of Leonard Bernstein, at the Hamburg State Opera Theater, the Baden-Baden Festival, and the Lincoln Center Festival in New York. He also designs costumes for Robert Wilson's *La Donna del Mare* (*Lady from the Sea*) at the municipal theater in Ferrara.

Armani designs a dress for Barbie, which is auctioned at Christie's in New York to benefit the fight against breast cancer.

1999

Armani acquires the former Nestlé factory at Via Bergognone 59/61, near the Ansaldo in Milan, for his new headquarters. Once renovations are complete in 2000, the complex will house the commercial, administrative, and marketing offices, show rooms for each product line, and a theater for runway shows and other events. The press offices will remain at Borgonuovo 11. The spring/summer 2000 women's collection

is shown in the factory. Looking for a more contemporary attitude, Armani features color prominently in the advertising campaign, which is photographed by Ellen von Unwerth.

The Giorgio Armani boutique in Place Vendôme in Paris is renovated by architect Claudio Silvestrin. While the façade of the store respects the historical architecture of Place Vendôme, the interior has the simplicity and beauty of other flagship stores around the world.

Giorgio Armani clothing is worn by Sean Connery and Catherine Zeta-Jones in Jon Amiel's film *Entrapment* and by Dermot Mulroney in Roland Joffé's *Goodbye Lover*. Emporio Armani clothing is worn by Patricia Arquette in *Goodbye Lover*.

Armani designs the uniforms for the Newcastle United soccer team for the British Cup Final.

He produces and collaborates on Martin Scorsese's *Il Dolce Cinema*, a documentary recounting the history of Italian cinema between 1914 and 1962. A shorter version of the final documentary premieres at the Fifty-sixth Venice Film Festival.

2000

Armani Collezioni is launched in Europe, Asia, and the United States. In Europe and Asia, the new label encompasses the already existing Giorgio Armani Le Collezioni men's and Mani women's lines. In the U.S., it replaces the Giorgio Armani Le Collezioni men's and women's lines (but not the Mani men's line).

Mania, a women's fragrance, is launched, as well as Giorgio Armani Cosmetics and an accessories line that includes bags, shoes, and belts.

The Giorgio Armani web site is launched, with pages devoted to each of the company's five lifestyle brands—Giorgio Armani, Armani Collezioni, Emporio Armani, Armani Jeans, and A/X Armani Exchange—that are designed to reflect their individual attitudes and styles.

Under an agreement with Holding di Partecipazioni Industriali, the Armani Group assumes control of certain production facilities at two factories owned by GFT, ensuring that all production is brought under Armani's management and expertise. The agreement also returns responsibility for sales and distribution of the Armani Collezioni and Mani labels in the U.S.—formerly undertaken by the GFT America Fashion Group—to Armani.

A joint venture with Ermenegildo Zegna—one of the world's leaders in luxury fabric and men's clothing—is established for the production and distribution of the Armani Collezioni and Mani men's lines.

In the former Assicurazioni Generali building on Via Manzoni, Milan, designed by Enrico Griffini in 1937 and acquired by Armani in 1999, Armani opens Armani/Via Manzoni 31. Renovated in collaboration with architect Michael Gabellini of Studio Gabellini Associates, the building comprises three floors with a courtyard and a rotunda—reminiscent of Milan's Galleria Vittorio Emanuele—that disperse natural daylight throughout. Around these atriums are arranged separate boutiques: The lower level houses Armani/Sony Style, which offers innovative Sony audio, video, and technology products; the ground level houses Emporio Armani, Armani Jeans, Armani Profumi (perfume), Armani Fiori (flowers), a café, and a sushi bar; and the upper level houses Armani Casa (the new home collection comprising decorative objects, fabric furnishings, and table settings, as well as sofas, tables, chairs and beds), Armani Libri (books), and Mediterranean and Japanese restaurants. The building will provide an ongoing showcase for young Italian artists, who will be able to exhibit their work throughout the store.

The spring/summer 2000 women's collection is presented at the Royal Albert Hall, London.

An exhibition of architectural models from the Milan Politecnico's collection, cohosted by *Wallpaper* magazine and Armani Casa, is shown at Via Bergognone, Milan.

In collaboration with *Dazed and Confused* magazine, Armani hosts an exhibition dedicated to young artists at the Emporio Armani store in St-Germain-des-Prés, Paris.

The book *Espresso*, a study of contemporary art, is presented at Armani/Via Manzoni 31, Milan.

Armani receives the David di Donatello (the Italian equivalent of an Oscar) for his contribution to film and cinema. The award is presented to him at the ceremony by Lauren Hutton.

Armani receives the Man of the Year Award from *GQ USA*.

The twenty-fifth anniversary of Giorgio Armani S.p.A. is marked by a major exhibition at the Solomon R. Guggenheim Museum in New York.

Armani designs the costumes for the principal characters of Giuseppe Verdi's *Rigoletto*, performed at the Los Angeles Opera.

Giorgio Armani clothing is worn by Samuel L. Jackson and Vanessa Williams in John Singleton's film *Shaft*; Glenn Close in Rodrigo Garcia's *Things You Can Tell Just by Looking at Her*; and Bruce Willis in Jon Turteltaub's *The Kid*.

Giorgio Armani and Emporio Armani clothing is worn by Ben Affleck in Don Roos's film *Bounce*.

Emporio Armani clothing is worn by Toni Collette in *Shaft* and by Gwyneth Paltrow in *Bounce*.

Armani dresses George Michael and Biagio Antonacci for the "Pavarotti and Friends" concert in Modena.

He designs the uniforms for the Chelsea soccer team for the British Cup Final.

2001

Armani establishes a joint-venture company with Vestimenta S.p.A. for the production and distribution of the Giorgio Armani men's and women's lines.

He acquires the apparel-manufacturing company SIMINT.

Emporio Armani White, a fragrance for men and women, is launched.

The first Giorgio Armani Accessori boutique (selling accessories including handbags, shoes, and luxurious leather items for men and women) opens at Via della Spiga 19, Milan. Designed in collaboration with the architect Claudio Silvestrin, the single-level store mirrors the newly refurbished Giorgio Armani store on Via Sant'Andrea, Milan.

Armani/Teatro opens in the new headquarters at Via Bergognone, Milan. Designed by Tadao Ando as an arresting fusion of concrete, water, and light, the theater is conceived as a site for various diverse events, including fashion shows, showroom presentations, conferences, and art installations. Adjacent to the theater is a dining room seating up to five hundred people.

The opening of the new Emporio Armani store in the Tokyo Forum is celebrated with an Emporio Armani fashion show.

The books *Achille Castiglioni* and *Uniforms: Order and Disorder* are presented at Armani/Via Manzoni 31, Milan (the latter in collaboration with Pitti Immagine and *Esquire* magazine). *H()ME*, an exhibition of photographs of sculpture by Loris Cecchini, and the new commercial for the Fondo per l'Ambiente Italiano are also presented at the store during the year.

The Guggenheim exhibition marking the twenty-fifth anniversary of Giorgio Armani S.p.a. travels to the Guggenheim Museum Bilbao, Spain.

Armani sponsors *Smile*, an exhibition of photographs celebrating the twenty-fifth anniversary of *i-D* magazine, held at the Wapping Hydraulic Power Station, London.

Armani hosts a charity concert by Russell Crowe's band 30 Odd Foot of Grunts in Milan.

Armani launches a project in Korea to save the Korean tiger and

contributes to building a modern breeding facility for the tiger within the Everland Zoo, Seoul.

Armani receives a "FiFi" (Fragrance Foundation Recognition Award) for Best Women's Packaging for his fragrance Mania.

Armani designs suits for Vince Vaughn in Jon Favreau's film *Made*. Giorgio Armani clothing is worn by Sean Penn in Jessie Nelson's film *I Am Sam*; Billy Crystal and Seth Green in Joe Roth's *America's Sweethearts*; Jennifer Lopez in Adam Shankman's *The Wedding Planner*; Jackie Chan in Brett Ratner's *Rush Hour 2*; and Tom Cruise in Cameron Crowe's *Vanilla Sky*.

Giorgio Armani and Emporio Armani clothing is worn by Michelle Pfeiffer in *I Am Sam*; Eddie Murphy in Steve Carr III's film *Dr. Dolittle 2*; Chris Tucker in *Rush Hour 2*; and Penélope Cruz in *Vanilla Sky*.

Emporio Armani clothing is worn by Gwyneth Paltrow and Jack Black in Peter and Bobby Farrelly's film *Shallow Hal*.

Giorgio Armani clothing is worn by Wyclef Jean and his band for a concert at Carnegie Hall, New York.

Armani Jeans clothing is worn by Craig David on his North American tour debut.

2002

Armani acquires the highly respected knitwear manufacturer Miss Deanna S.p.A., as well as share control of Guardi S.p.A., a factory specializing in the production of women's and men's shoes.

Armani Mania, a fragrance for men, is launched.
Emporio Armani Gioielli, featuring jewelry for men and women; Armani Dolci, a range of pralines, chocolates, teas, coffees, and desserts; and Sensi, a fragrance for women, are launched.

Armani Jeans collections for men and women are launched in department stores in the United States.

Emporio Armani Orologi is launched on the Armani site in the United States.

Armani/Chater House opens in Hong Kong. The store includes Emporio Armani, Armani Jeans, Emporio Armani Caffè, Armani Libri, Armani Fiori, and Giorgio Armani Cosmetics boutiques. Massimiliano Fuksas's design for the store is presented at the Venice *Architecture Biennale*.

Giorgio Armani boutiques open in Florence (with an inaugural party at Palazzo Strozzi) and in Moscow, where an Armani Casa store also opens. An Armani Collezioni boutique opens in Paris with a Giorgio Armani fashion show and a party at Renoma Café.

Pieces from the fall/winter 2002–03 Armani Casa collection are shown at Abitare il Tempo, an international fair of interior design and decor in Verona.

The exhibition and book *Armani Backstage*, featuring behind-the-scenes images of Armani during the final preparations for one of his women's fashion shows, are presented at Armani/Teatro, Milan. The exhibition travels to Armani boutiques in Antwerp, Düsseldorf, London, Madrid, Paris, and Hong Kong.

Armani and *Domus* present *The View from Domus*, an exhibition featuring photographs from the architecture magazine, at Armani/Teatro.

Armani presents a video installation by Sam Samore at the Emporio Armani store in Saint-Germain, Paris, as part of the exhibition *Parcours* organized by the Saint-Germain Committee.

Armani presents Edoardo Ponti's film *Between Strangers* at Armani/Teatro, Milan.

Armani and Fedele Confalonieri, President of Mediaset, cohost the Milan premiere of *Il Mio Viaggio in Italia*, a documentary on the history of Italian cinema directed by Martin Scorsese.

Armani and Mediaset cohost "Cinema Forever," a screening of four newly restored Italian films: Antonio Pietrangeli's *Adua e le compagne*

(Adua and Company, 1960); Pietro Germi's Un maledetto imbroglio (Diledetto Imbroglio, 1959); Bernardo Bertolucci's La Commare secca (The Grim Reaper, 1962); and Federico Fellini's I Vitelloni (The Young and the Passionate, 1953).

Armani sponsors a concert by Solisti Veneti organized by the Friends of the Fondo per l'Ambiente Italiano, performed at the Italian embassy in Washington, D.C.

Armani presents *Desplazados*, a documentary produced by the United Nations High Commission for Refugees (UNHCR) to raise awareness and funds for their Colombia emergency campaign, at Armani/Teatro. Christmas Shopping Days, during which a portion of sales is donated to the UNHCR's Afghanistan fund, are held at Giorgio Armani and Emporio Armani stores throughout Europe. Armani is named Goodwill Ambassador by the UNHCR in recognition of his work for the fund and for his ongoing partnership with the agency to protect and assist the world's refugees.

Armani supports Children in Crisis through the sale of Giorgio Armani T-shirts enclosed in the December issue of *ELLE Italy*.

Armani Fiori creates the decoration for a charity dinner for AMFAR (American Foundation for Aids Research) during the Venice Film Festival.

Armani receives an award from the region of Emilia Romagna for "entrepreneurship" and "research and development" related to hemp.

As part of a series dedicated to Italian fashion, the Italian postal service issues a stamp showing a Giorgio Armani sketch.

Giorgio Armani clothing is worn by Francesca Neri and Cliff Curtis in Andrew Davis's film *Collateral Damage*; Cuba Gooding, Jr., in Brian Levant's *Snow Dogs*; Jennifer Lopez in Michael Apted's *Enough*; Lena Olin in Jaume Balagueró's *Darkness*; Tom Cruise in Steven Spielberg's *Minority Report*; Anthony Hopkins in Brett Ratner's *Red Dragon*; Kate Bosworth in John Stockwell's *Blue Crush*; Jackie Chan in Kevin Donovan III's *The Tuxedo*; Samuel L. Jackson in Rob Cohen's *XXX*; Ben Affleck and Morgan Freeman in Phil Alden Robinson's *The Sum of All Fears*; Jodie Foster in David Fincher's *Panic Room*; and Taye Diggs in Rob Marshall's *Chicago*.

Both Giorgio Armani and Emporio Armani clothing is worn by Jennifer Love Hewitt in *The Tuxedo*; George Clooney in Steven Soderbergh's film *Solaris*; Ashley Judd in Carl Franklin's *High Crimes*; and Tobey Maguire and Willem Dafoe in Sam Raimi's *Spider-Man*.

Emporio Armani clothing is worn by James Franco in *Spider-Man*.

Armani dresses Vittoria Belvedere as presenter at the Fifty-second San Remo Music Festival and singers Nelly Furtado and Lucio Dalla for their respective tours.

Emporio Armani clothing is worn by Miguel Bosé, presenter of the Italian TV show *Operazione Trionfo*, and by Biagio Antonacci, Ronan Keating and his band, Pino Daniele, Tiziano Ferro, and Articolo 31 on their respective tours.

Models in the Italian tire manufacturer Pirelli's 2002 calendar, photographed by Peter Lindbergh, are dressed exclusively in designs by Giorgio Armani.

2003

Armani presents *Athlete*, an exhibition of photographs of the human body and sportsmen by Howard Shatz, at Armani/Via Manzoni 31, Milan.

Giorgio Armani clothing is worn by Mark Wahlberg in F. Gary Gray's film *The Italian Job*; John Travolta in John McTiernan's *Basic*; Josh Hartnett in Ron Shelton's *Hollywood Homicide*; Sam Elliott in Ang Lee's *The Hulk*; Samuel L. Jackson and Ashley Judd in Philip Kaufman's *Blackout*; and Liam Neeson in Richard Curtis's *Love Actually*.

Both Giorgio Armani and Emporio Armani clothing are worn by Charlize Theron in *The Italian Job*.

Giorgio Armani clothing is worn by singer Ashanti during the Soul Train of Soul Awards in London and by Britney Spears at the Neil Bogart Cancer Event.

Armani is the first to be honored on the Rodeo Drive Walk of Style in Beverly Hills, California. A permanent plaque celebrating his contributions to the world of fashion and entertainment is placed in the sidewalk along the famous street.

Notes

1.   Luigi Settembrini, "From Haute Couture to Prêt-à-porter," in *The Italian Metamorphosis, 1943–1968* (New York: Guggenheim Museum, 1994), pp. 486–47.

2.   Ibid., p. 492.

3.   Jay Cocks, "Suiting Up for Easy Street," *Time*, April 5, 1982, pp. 60–62.

4.   Ibid., p. 62.

SELECTED BIBLIOGRAPHY

by Ilaria Dupré

Selected Books and Catalogues:

Agins, Teri. *The End of Fashion: The Mass Marketing of the Clothing Business*. New York: William Morrow & Co., 1999.

Alfonsi, Maria Vittoria. "Giorgio Armani. Giorgio's Gorgeous Style." In *Leaders in Fashion: I grandi personaggi della moda*. Bologna: Cappelli Editore, 1983.

Aspesi, Natalia. "Giorgio Armani." In *Perchè loro. Armani, Baudo, Berlusconi, Biagi, Dalla, De Benedetti, Eco, Falcao, Forattini, Nicolini, Pertini, Scalfari*. Bari: Editori Laterza, 1984, pp. 33–57.

Astori, Antonia. "Una problema di cultura." In Silvia Giacomoni, *L'Italia della moda*. Milan: Gabriele Mazzotta Editore, 1984.

Bascapè, Giacomo C. *Il Palazzo Durini Caproni di Taliedo a Milano, note di storia e d'arte*. Milan: Istituto Editoriale Cisalpino La Goliardica, 1980.

Bianco, Giovanni and Susanna Cucco. *Pipoca Instant Fashion*. Milan: Self-Published by Bianco and Cucco, 1996.

Blonsky, Marshall. *American Mythologies*. New York: Oxford University Press, 1992.

Bocca, Giorgio. *Metropolis*. Milan: Arnaldo Mondadori Editore, 1993.

Borioli, Gisella. *Dieci anni di moda 1980–1990. Cronache tendenze protagonisti*. Milan: Edizione Edimoda, 1990.

Butazzi, Grazietta and Alessandra Molfino Mottola. *La moda italiana. Dall'antimoda allo stilismo*. Milan: Electa, 1987.

Caoasibetta, Charlotte. *Fairchild's Dictionary of Fashion*. New York: Fairchild, 1988. 2nd ed.

Carnegy, Vicky. *Fashions of a Decade: The Eighties*. New York: Facts on File, 1990.

Celant, Germano, ed. *The Italian Metamorphosis, 1943–1968*. New York: Guggenheim Museum Publications, 1994.

Celant, Germano, Luigi Settembrini and Ingrid Sischy. *Biennale di Firenze. Looking at Fashion*. Florence: Skira Editore, 1996

Chenoune, Farid. *A History of Men's Fashion*. Paris: Flammarion, 1993.

Costantino, Maria. *Men's Fashion in the Twentieth Century: From Frock Coats to Intelligent Fibers*. New York: Costume and Fashion Press, 1997.

Davis, Fred. *Fashion, Culture and Identity*. Chicago: University of Chicago Press, 1992.

De Combray, Richard. *Armani*. Milan: Franco Maria Ricci Editore, 1982.

Fraser, Kennedy. *The Fashionable Mind*. New York: Alfred A. Knopf, 1981.

Gobbi, Linda, Francesco Morace, Roberto Brognara, and Fabrizio Valente. *Emporio Armani: Il boom dello stile trasversale*. In *I Boom. Società e prodotti degli anni '80*. Milan: Lupetti, 1990.

Hartman, Rose. *Bird of Paradise: An Intimate View of the New York Fashion World*. New York: Delta, 1980.

Hollander, Anne. *Sex and Suits*. New York: Alfred A. Knopf, 1994.

Italian Fashion. New York: Rizzoli International, 1987.

Jacobsen, Wolfgang, Hans Helmut Prinzler, and Werner Sudendorf, eds. "Armani vis-à-vis Dietrich." In *Kino, Movie, Cinema*. exh. cat., Berlin: Stiftung Deutsche Kinemathek und Argon Verlag GmbH., 1995.

Khornak, Lucille. *Fashion 2001*. New York: Viking, 1982.

Malossi, Giannino, ed. *The Style Engine*. New York: The Monacelli Press, 1998.

Martin, Richard and Harold Koda. *Giorgio Armani. Images of Man*. New York: Rizzoli, 1990.

Martin, Richard and Harold Koda, eds. *Designers History Ten Years: Giorgio Armani, 1985–1995*. Texts by Junko Ouchi and Akiko Fukai. Tokyo: Gap Japan, 1997.

Martin, Richard. *Contemporary Fashion*. New York: St. James Press, 1995.

Martin, Richard, ed. *The St. James Fashion Encyclopedia: A Survey of Style from 1945 to the Present*. Detroit: Visible Ink, 1997.

McDowell, Colin. *The Man of Fashion: Peacock Males and Perfect Gentlemen*. New York: Thames and Hudson, 1977.

—————. *McDowell's Directory of Twentieth Century Fashion*. London: F. Muller, 1984.

Milbank, Caroline Rennolds. *Couture: The Great Designers*. New York: Stewart, Tabori & Chang, 1985.

Mulassano, Adriana. *I Mass-Moda. Fatti e personaggi dell'Italian Look*. Florence: Edizioni G. Spinelli, 1979.

Polan, Brenda. *Fashion 84*. New York: St. Martin's Press, 1984.

Sidlauskas, Susan. *Intimate Architecture: Contemporary Clothing Design*. Cambridge, Mass.: MIT Press, 1982.

Steele, Valerie. *Fetish: Fashion, Sex and Power*. New York: Oxford University Press, 1996.

—————. *Fifty Years of Fashion: New Look to Now*. New Haven, Conn.: Yale University Press, 1997.

Stegemeyer, Anne. *Who's Who in Fashion*. 3rd ed. New York: Fairchild, 1996.

The Fashion Book. London: Phaidon Press, 1998.

The Fashion Guide, International Designer Directory (1996–1997). New York: The Fashion Guide International.

Vergani, Guido. *Dizionario della moda*. Milan: Baldini & Castoldi, 1999. pp. 30–34.

White, Emily. *Fashion 85: The Must Have Book for Fashion Insiders*. New York: St. Martin's Press, 1985.

Articles and Essays

Alphandery, Annalisa. "American Gigolo veste alta moda." *Il Tirreno* (Livorno), October 31, 1980.

Ansaloni, Gian Marco. "Armani, in vista casa e accessori." *Milano Finanza* (Milan), September 30, 1999, p. 16.

"Armani in America." *Harper's Bazaar* (New York), September 1, 1996, p. 418.

"Armani Inc." *Esquire* (New York), October 1, 1997, p. 84.

Arnet, Alison. "Bars, Not Food, Now Make the Scene." *The Boston Globe* (Boston), June 2, 1994, p. 130.

Arosio, Paola. "A piedi o in auto non vederlo è impossibile." *L'Unità* (Rome), November 1985.

Aspesi, Natalia. "Basta anteprime sui miei abiti, ordino il black out." *La Repubblica* (Rome), February 1982.

—————. "Quel candido collo luogo del desidero e la moda diventa rifugio." *La Repubblica* (Rome), March 1984.

Barbieri, Giampolo. "La moda diventa arte." *Amica* (Milan), December 1982.

Beckett, Kathleen. "Giorgio Armani." *Fashion Almanac* (New York) 71, April 1997, pp. 32–37.

Berti, Paola. "Armani: una nuova filosofia per una moda che non vuole abbellire." *La Gazzetta di Mantova*, March 1984.

—————. "Sarà di nuovo corta la gonna nella moda del prossimo inverno." *Il Messaggero Veneto* (Udine), March 1984.

Boccardi, Luciana. "Armani decreta il top secret sulla sua collezione di moda." *Il Gazzettino* (Venice), March 1982.

Bocconi, Susanna. "Stilisti: un potente vola nelle mani dell'industria." *Il Sole 24 Ore* (Milan), July 1984.

Brampton, Sally. "Armani's Island." *Elle Decor* (London), Autumn 1989.

Brantley, Ben. "The Armani Mystique." *Vanity Fair* (New York), June 1988.

—————. "The Emperor of New Clothes." *The Daily Telegraph Weekend Magazine* (London), December 17, 1988.

Brodsky, Renatt. "The Designer Decade 1980s." *Daily News Record* (New York), May 14, 1999, p. 91.

Bruzzi, Stella. "F for fashion." *Sight and Sound* (London) 6, November 1996.

Bucchi, Massimo. "È urgente attendere." *La Repubblica* (Rome), October 1985.

Bulbarelli, Paola. "Una nuova maison per Armani." *Il Giornale* (Milan), June 22, 1999.

Capitta, Gianfranco. "Gere, gigolo e gentiluomo." *La Nazione* (Florence), December 9, 1983.

Carloni, Maria Vittoria. "Comprare è di moda." *Panorama* (Milan), March 1984.

Cavalletti, Lavinia. "Il gran rifiuto di Armani." *Il Mattino di Napoli* (Naples), March 1982.

Christy, George. "The Great Life." *Hollywood Reporter*, December 1994, p. 71.

Cianfanelli, Renzo. "Armani, ambasciatore della moda a Londra. Cosi vorrei vestire la principessa Diana." *Corriere della Sera* (Milan), November 1985.

Cianfanelli, Renzo. "Londra, per combattere la fame scende in campo anche la moda." *Corriere della Sera* (Milan), November 1985.

Cocks, Jay. "Armani's Place in the Sun." *Vanity Fair* (New York), January 1994, p. 100.

Cohen, Eddie Lee. "Giorgio Armani." *Interior Design* (New York), April 1989.

—————. "Emporio Armani." *Interior Design* (New York), September 1989.

Colasanti, Livio. "Made in Italy sigla di bellezza." *Il Tempo* (Rome), November 1985.

Conti, Samantha and Luisa Zargani. "Busy Day at Armani: Admits LVMH Talks, Revises GFT License." *Women's Wear Daily* (New York), February 11, 1999.

Conti, Samantha. "Eyes on the Future." *Women's Wear Daily* (New York), June 1, 1999.

—————. "Exclusive: The New Armani." *Women's Wear Daily* (New York), June 18, 1999.

Cosi, Marina. "La donna Armani è viva." *Il Giorno* (Milan), March 1982.

—————. "Mezzogiorno di fuoco tra Armani e Versace." *Il Giorno* (Milan), March 1982.

—————. "Pratica di giorno ma sexy di sera la donna di Armani." *Il Giorno* (Milan), March 1984.

—————. "Signore e signorine ecco a voi le cravatte." *Il Giorno (*Milan), March 1984.

—————. "Milano è scoppiata dalla moda." *Il Giorno* (Milan), March 1984.

Cremonesi, Marco. "Armani firma via Manzoni." *Corriere della Sera* (Milan), September 17, 1999.

Christensen, Anne. "The Swing Set." *Vogue* (New York), September 1995, pp. 572–78.

Danelian, Stephen. "Designer Jeans: The Sequel." *Esquire* (New York), June 1, 1997, p. 84.

De Alcahud, Victoria. "Giorgio e Roberta Armani in privato." *Chi* (Milan), July 19, 2000.

Dean, Syahmedi. "Maestro from Milano." *Harper's Bazaar* (New York), June 2000.

Del Buono, Oreste. "Di morale in murales." *Panorama* (Milan), January 3, 1988.

Della Torre, Paolo Filo. "Sarti, principi e modelle tutti a Fashion Aid." *La Repubblica* (Rome), November 1985.

Dombrowicz, Laurent. "Armani For Ever." *La Libre Essentielle* (Brussels) 10, September 1999.

Donally, Trish. "The Master Designer Speaks." *San Francisco Chronicle*, February 1, 1996.

Doyle, Kevin. "Armani's True Confessions." *Women's Wear Daily* (New York), June 25, 1992.

Fallaci, Paola. "In mutande sei alla moda." *Oggi* (Milan), August 1984.

Feltri, Vittorio. "Armani re triste della moda." *Corriere della Sera* (Milan), November 1985.

Ferrè, Giusi. "La nuova natura del piacere. Più seducente la donna, più attraente l'uomo. Giorgio Armani percorre l'erotismo. E promette nuovi peccati." *Amica* (Milan), March 2000, pp. 182–89.

Fiori, Pamela. "The Quiet Man." *Town & Country* (London), January 1, 1998, p. 70.

Forden, Sara Gay. "Giorgio Armani, The World's Most Successful Designer, Still Isn't Satisfied." *Women's Wear Daily* (New York), October 26, 1994, pp. 4–8.

—————. "According to Armani." *Daily News Record* (New York), January 19, 1995.

Fratelloni, Cristina. "I grandi sarti scoprono la bellezza del grigio." *L'Ora* (Palermo), March 1984.

Fressola, Peter and Alexander Lobrano. "Armani's Array Arresting." *Daily News Record* (New York), July 10, 1987.

Friend, Ted. "The Armani Edge." *Vogue* (New York), March 1992.

Furness, Janine. "Alluring Armani." *Interior Design* (London), May 1989.

Galeotti, Adele. "Mariel Hemingway: amo i libri del nonno e Armani." *La Gazzetta del Mezzogiorno*, November 1985.

Gerrie, Anthea. "Giorgio Armani." *Clothes Show* (London), June 1991.

Giacomini, Silvia. "Che bello, l'uomo in smoking, è così che piace alla moglie." *La Repubblica* (Rome), January 1982.

—————. "Non è sexy, ne esibizionista la donna Armani per il 1983." *La Repubblica* (Rome), May 1982.

Goodman, Tonne. "Armani at Night." *Harper's Bazaar* (New York), November 1, 1998, p. 228.

Gordon, Maryellen. "Armani in New York." *Elle* (New York), September 1, 1996, p. 360.

Grazzini, Filippo. "Italiani, emigrati di lusso." *Il Giornale di Napoli* (Naples), October 1985.

Griffo, Laura. "Armani, il re che incanta Cardin, presenta la collezione inverno." *La Nazione* (Florence), May 1982.

——————. "E al terzo giorno sfilò Armani." *La Nazione* (Florence), March 1984.

——————. "Moda, un bagliore." *Il Resto del Carlino* (Bologna), March 1984.

Guarneri, Luisa. "Ora c'è anche il Fashion Aid." *Reporter* (Florence), November 1985.

Guatterini, Marinella. "Falcao tifa Armani." *L'Unità* (Rome), March 1984.

Hamilton, Rita. "Giorgio Armani's Fine Italian Hand." *Esquire* (New York), May 22, 1979.

Henno, Martine. "L'art armanien." *Le Figaro* (Paris), September 9, 1998.

Holley, Bandon. "Bravo, Giorgio!" *GQ* (New York) 4 (April 2000), pp. 231–33.

Hoschswender, Woody. "Armani Classico. Corporate Chic." *Esquire* (New York), February 1, 1996, p. 101.

Howell, Georgina. "Armani: The Man Who Fell to Earth." *The Sunday Times Magazine* (London), February 18, 1990.

Hublet, Marianne. "Armani et la nouvelle ère." *Weekend Le Vif /L'Express* (Paris) 8 (February 25, 2000), pp. 96–97.

Hutton, Lauren. "Giorgio Armani." *Interview* (New York), April 1993.

Invernici, Elisabetta. "Cara moda parliamoci chiaro." *Bella* (Milan) 41 (October 1984).

Kirk, Neil. "Armani and the Woman." *Vogue* (London), February 21, 1995, pp. 101–03.

Jacaud, Dany. "Giorgio Armani accueille le tout Hollywood pour une des plus belles soirées du monde." *Match* (Paris), December 1994, pp. 42–43.

Jones, Nick. "Eagle's Spread." *Building Design* (London), April 28, 1989.

Jovinell, Paola Valeria. "Tutta la luce del mega-Armani." *Corriere Economia* (Milan), March 20, 2000.

Keers, Paul. "The Emporio of Style." *GQ* (London), February/March 1989.

Kostner, Kevin. "The Emperor Strikes Back." *Sky* (London), March 1989.

LaFerla, Ruth. "Sizing Up Giorgio Armani." *New York Times Magazine*, October 21, 1990.

Lannelongue, Marie-Pierre. "Giorgissimo." *Elle* (Paris) April 2000.

Lane, Mara. "Take the Armani and Run." *Absolute Marbella* (Málaga), April 2000, pp. 48–51.

Lanza, Attilia. "Semplice di giorno scintillante di sera." *L'Ora* (Palermo), March 1984.

Laurenzi, Laura. "Nella storia grazie a una giacca." *La Repubblica* (Rome), December, 12, 1999, p. 28.

Lobrano, Alexander. "Armani's America." *Daily News Record* (New York), June 19, 1989.

Lobrano, Alexander and Kevin Doyle. "Giorgio Continues His Reign in Milan." *Daily News Record* (New York), January 12, 1989.

Lytle, Lisa. "Benefits Is Just Like Armani." *Accent* (New York), December 1994, p. 2.

Maclasaac, Heather Smith. "Milan by Armani." *Travel & Leisure* (New York), October 1, 1996, p. 160.

Magni, Tiziano. "Music to the Eyes." *Interview* (New York), August 1995, p. 52.

Mardore, Lucienne. "La storia di Giorgio Armani." *Marie Claire* (Paris), May 1990.

Mari, Lucia. "Una camicia-pullover per l'uomo moda '82." *Paese Sera* (Rome), January 1982.

——————. "E la giacca con i revers torna regina." *Paese Sera* (Rome), March 1984.

Martin, Richard. "What Is Man! The Imagery of Male Style of J. C. Leyendecker and Giorgio Armani." *Textile & Text, Fashion Institute of Technology* (New York) 13, 1 (1990), pp. 3–27.

——————. "Giorgio Armani's Encyclopedia of Man in 1986." *Textile & Text, Fashion Institute of Technology* (New York) 13, 2 (1990), pp. 3–13.

——————. "Fashion and a Sense of Place: Emporio Armani's European Grand Tour." *Textile & Text, Fashion Institute of Technology* (New York) 13, 2 (1990), pp. 14–21.

——————. "Cine-mode: Fashion and the Movie Metaphor in the Art of Giorgio Armani." *Textile & Text,* Fashion Institute of Technology (New York) 14, 2 (1991), pp. 22–31.

——————. "Dress and Democracy." *Emporio Armani Magazine* (Milan) 14 (September 1995–February 1996), pp. 10–11.

Mascolo, Anna. "La guerra è gonna." *La Notte* (Milan), October 1984.

Masera, Anna. "Al Fashion Institute of Technology una mostra sui 35 anni del design italiano. Il genio del vestito." *Il Progresso*, November 1985.

Mather, John. "Master Class." *Esquire* (New York), Aug. 1, 1996, p. 112.

McDowell, Colin. "Armani for All Seasons." *The Australian Magazine* (Sydney), September 26, 1999.

Mead, Rebecca. "Body of Work." *New York*, September 16, 1996, p. 26.

Mendoza, Deirdre. "The Marketing Jackpot. Placing a Product in a Hit Movie Translates to 'Big Box Office' on Seventh Avenue." *Women's Wear Daily California* (Los Angeles), August 22, 1999.

Menkes, Suzy. "Armani's Off-the-Rack Mozart." *International Herald Tribune* (Paris), January 17, 1995.

——————. "World Class Armani Show Wraps Up Italian Season." *International Herald Tribune* (Paris), March 11–12, 1995.

——————. "Armani? Si!" *Deutsche Vogue* (Munich) 11 (June 2000), pp. 142–49.

Michaels, James. "To Give And to Take Away." *Forbes* (New York), October 28, 1991.

Morris, Bernardine. "Armani Triumphant: Italy Crowns Its Fashion King." *New York Times* (New York), October 6, 1979.

Mosca, Antonello. "Il grande fascino di Giorgio Armani entra nella casa." *Il Giornale* (Milan), April 16, 2000, p. 32.

Mower, Sarah. "Giorgio Armani: A Man for All Seasons." *Woman's Journal* (London), April 1986.

——————. "Emperor Armani." *Vogue* (London), January 1989.

Mulassano, Adriana. "A Firenze la moda italiana per uomo riconferma il suo primato mondiale." *Corriere della Sera* (Milan), January 1982.

——————. "La donna '85: annoiata con eleganza." *Corriere della Sera* (Milan), 1984

——————. "Io, l'uomo, la donna. L'abito maschile e femminile secondo Giorgio Armani." *A.D.* (Milan), February 1984.

——————. "La moda italiana dal cinquanta a oggi in una grande rassegna a Villa Borghese." *Corriere della Sera* (Milan), April 1984.

Mundy, Michael. "Doing Milan with Giorgio Armani." *Travel & Leisure* (New York) 10 (October 1996), pp. 20–23.

Municchi, Anna. "Giorgio Armani: l'eleganza della semplicità." *Il Giornale* (Milan), March 1984.

——————. "A New York il genio italiano della moda." *Il Giornale d'Italia* (Rome), November 1985.

Neuman, Nicolaus. "Rostreui und Sinnlich." *Stern* (Hamburg) 38 (September 1994), pp. 136–42.

O'Donnel, Brooke. "Giorgio Armani." *Elle Australia* (Sydney), June 2000.

Omelianuk, Scott. "Matt Meets Giorgio." *GQ* (New York), March 1, 1996, p. 224.

Oppo, Maria Novella. "Quello scialle che sa di ideologia." *Reporter* (Florence), November 1985.

Pacoda, Pierfrancesco. "Londra, percorsi e incontri." *Reporter* (Florence), 1985.

Paltrinieri, Anita. "Vado, sistemo l'America e torno." *Donna* (Milan), July–August 1984.

——————. "Madison Avenue che parla italiano." *Mondo Uomo* (Milan), September 1984.

Panza, Stefania. "Giorgio Armani: magister elegantiae." *Malpensa Express* (Milan) 3 (March 2000), pp. 20–23.

Pericoli, Lea. "Gonna corta e giacca lunga: ecco la ricetta per la donna elegante del prossimo inverno." *Il Giornale Nuovo* (Rome), March 1984.

Pericoli, Lea. "Per la donna essere sexy è un obbligo." *Il Giornale* (Milan), November 1985.

Pezzi, Maria. "Sessant'anni di debolezze maschili." *Donna* (Milan), May 1984.

Pisa, Paola. "Tra i tanti pezzi da museo anche gli abiti di Jacqueline." *Il Messaggero* (Rome), April 1984.

—————. "Giacca e bermuda per i 50 anni di Giorgio Armani.".*Il Messaggero* (Rome), July 1984.

—————. "Comodi pullover." *Il Messaggero* (Rome), November 1985.

Polan, Brenda. "The Genius of Giorgio Armani." *Options* (London), December 1989.

Pisa, Paola. "Armani propone: via i completi, torniamo ai pantaloni." *Il Messaggero* (Rome), May 1982.

—————. "La gonna è spaccata (fin dove si può) e ritorna il colore." *Il Messaggero* (Rome), March 1984.

—————."Cappotto avvolgente." *Il Messaggero* (Rome), November 1985.

Polan, Brenda. "Armani Aura." *Friday* (Tokyo), August 21, 1999.

Polese, Ranieri. "Ritratto di gattopardo in un interno." *La Nazione* (Florence), December 9, 1983.

Prince, Bill. "Giorgio Armani." *GQ* (New York), March 2000, pp. 116–27.

Quintini, Roberto. "Questione di stile." *Linea Italiana* (Milan), February 1982.

Redomdo, Maite. "Armani 'viste' al Guggenheim." *Deia* (Bilbao), March 24, 2000.

Ricca, Giuliana. "Pantaloni abbondanti e giacchi colorate." *Il Mattino* (Naples), March 1984.

Richard, Aline. "Giorgio Armani designer. Le Patricien de la mode italienne." *La Tribune* (Quebec), December 30, 1996, p. 26.

Romanelli, Marco. "Giorgio Armani: Il progetto dell'abito 1988." *Domus* (Milan), January 1988.

Rossetti, Elsa. "Ma che bella quella donna, pare un uomo." *Stampa Sera* (Turin), March 1984.

Sacchi, Maria Silvia. "Armani cambia pelle." *Corriere Economia* (Milan), May 8, 2000, p. 22.

Sajbel, Maureen. "Deconstructing the Labels That Are Armani." *Los Angeles Times*, October 1994, p. 3.

Schiff, Stephen. "Lunch with Mr. Armani, Tea with Mr. Versace, Dinner with Mr. Valentino." *The New Yorker*, November 7, 1994.

Sharkey, Alix. "Es war der reinste Wahn." *Stern* (Hamburg) 19 (2000), pp. 162–66.

—————. "Grand Design." *South China Morning Post* (Hong Kong), May 13, 2000.

Schiavi, Marta. "Rivedremo l'uomo vestito di pelle." *Vogue Pelle* (Milan), August 1984.

"Social Study: The Proust Questionnaire Suits Giorgio Armani." *Vanity Fair* (New York), May 1995, p. 174.

Soli, Pia. "Come somiglia a un uomo questa donna di Armani." *Il Tempo* (Rome), March 1984.

—————. "Lo spirito creativo di trent'anni di moda italiana sbarca a New York." *Il Tempo* (Rome), November 1985.

—————. "Il genio antipatico cambia titolo e vola a New York." *Il Tempo* (Rome), November 1985.

—————. "Ora si chiama Italia il genio del fascino." *Il Tempo* (Rome), November 1985.

Sollazzo, Lucia. "Incontro con il sarto (famoso in USA) che ha vestito Gere nel film 'Quelle giacche di Armani che fan' la gloria di gigolo." *La Stampa* (Turin), September 21, 1980.

—————. "Pensando al prossimo inverno: torna di moda l'uomo in grigio." *La Stampa* (Turin), January 1982.

—————. "Com' è elegante vestita da uomo." *La Stampa* (Turin), March 1984.

—————. "Ecco come la grazia e la femminilità si nascondono in un cappotto maschile." *La Stampa* (Turin), March 1984.

Soppelsa, Moreno. "I falsi Armani. Quasi un'industria." *L'Unità* (Rome), November 1985.

Spindler, Amy M. "Armani and Ferré: A Study in Contrast." *New York Times*, March 11, 1995.

—————. "Sensuality, Not Practicality." *New York Times*, October 22, 1996.

Sullivan, Ruth Tailor. "Armani Invests to Save Blue Jeans." *The European* (London), December 1994, p. 28.

Taino, Danilo. "Ministro e operatori a consulto sull'Italian Style." *Reporter* (Florence), November 1985.

Teston, E. "Architectural Digest Visits Giorgio Armani." *Architectural Digest* (Los Angeles), May 1983.

Toussai, Ginevra. "Armani trionferà anche con Falcao." *La Provincia Pavese* (Pavia), March 1984.

Thurman, Judith. "A Cut Above." *Connoisseur* (New York), April 1986.

Tyrrel, Rebecca. "Guida ragionata al profumo per gentiluomo." *La Stampa* (Turin), November 1985.

Vacalebre, Rosanna. "Alla corte della moda contro la fame nel mondo." *Avvenire* (Rome), November 1985.

Wayne, George. "Ten Questions You Thought We'd Never Ask—What Does Giorgio Armani Think about Fashion Now?" *Vogue* (New York), August 1996, pp. 256–57.

Webb, Iain R. "Mover and Shaper." *The Times Magazine* (London), December 16, 1995, pp. 49–51.

West, Carinthia. "Giorgio Armani." *Marie Claire* (London), April 1989.

Wilson, Catherine. "My Deft Cut: Clothes You'd Give Your Right Armani For." *Harper's & Queen* (London), July 1994, p. 88.

Interviews

"Un casual look, il gusto della dissonanza e dei rapporti difficili." *L'Uomo Vogue* (Milan), February 1971.

Bernasconi, Silvana. "Giorgio Armani. Avant-première de la collection masculine printemps-été 1976". *Vogue Hommes* (Paris), Winter 1975–76.

"Giorgio Armani: uomini e donne stile country." *Oggi* (Milan), November 11, 1976.

Soli, Pia. "First, Viva La Moda." *The Times* (London), February 21, 1978.

Bevilacqua, Maria Grazia and Franca Zambonini. "Moda? Armani conserva ancora un suo pubblico." *Famiglia Cristiana* (Milan), February 18, 1979, p. 31.

"Giorgio Armani." *Panorama* (Milan), August 1979, pp. 10–11.

Giachetti, Romano. "Giorgio I, re a New York." *Epoca* (Milan) 1533 (February 23, 1980), pp. 38–41.

Mercoli, Laura. "Armani: un genio tranquillo." *Gioia* (Milan), March 10, 1980, pp. 53–59.

Alfonsi, Maria Vittoria. "Giorgio Armani: di stagione in stagione l'immagine della moda oggi." *L'InformazioneTessile* 3 (April 1980), pp. 24–25.

Del Freo, Marco. "Giorgio Armani." *La Repubblica* (Rome), April 9–10, 1980, p. 9.

Gervaso, Roberto. "È più facile vestire le donne." *Corriere della Sera* (Milan), August 20, 1980.

Sistro, Maddalena. "Giorgio Armani e Sergio Galeotti." *Lei* (Milano), September 1980, pp. 168–238.

Zaina, Caterina. "Giorgio Armani: nel vestito ci dovrete ballare." *Domenica del Corriere* (Milan), September 20, 1980, pp. 58–60.

Alfonsi, Maria Vittoria. "I veronesi? Bella gente ci adula Giorgio Armani." *L'Arena di Verona* (Verona), October 25, 1981.

Gabriele, Salvatore. "Gli ozi panteschi di Armani." *L'Ora* (Palermo), June 20, 1981.

Guatterini, Marinella. "La moda è un lavoro, non uno spettacolo." *L'Unitá* (Rome), January 3, 1982, p. 13.

Mosca, Paolo. "Made in Armani." *La Notte* (Milan), February 1982.

Noceto, Maddalena. "Armani." *Amica* (Milan) 6 (February 9, 1982), p. 70.

Ferrè, Giusi. "Moda uomo." *Epoca* (Milan) 1642 (March 26, 1982), pp. 67–73.

Cocks, Jay and Georgia Harbison. "Suiting Up for Easy Street: Giorgio Armani Defines the New Shape of Style." *Time* (New York) 14 (April 5, 1982), pp. 50–57.

Antonelli, Isa. "Si' sono un'aquila, ma in gabbia." *Amica* (Milan) 18 (May 4, 1982), pp. 132–35.

Castellani, Claudio. "Eleganza è giurare fedeltà a se stessi." *Annabella* (Milan), May 15, 1982, pp. 84–88.

Fallaci, Paola. "Da ragazzo, Giorgio voleva fare il dottore." *Annabella* (Milan) 30–31 (July 31, 1982), pp. 54–57.

Vergani, Guido. "Tutto a misura d'uomo." *L'Uomo Vogue* (Milan), July–August 1983.

Micali, Gianfranco. "Gli devo un certo stile." *Oggi* (Milan) 49 (December 7, 1983), pp. 49–53.

Barneschi, Gheri Alfa. "Vogue è la Bibbia." *Ulisse 2000* (Milan), 1984, p. 53.

Enriquez, Rachele. "In giacca oltre la moda." *Vogue Italia* (Milan) 406 (January 1984), pp. 292–99.

Minetti, Maria Giulia. "Ma che razza di sesso stai mettendo addosso?" *Europeo* (Milan) 13 (March 31, 1984), pp. 57–60.

De Cesco, Myriam. "Vesto la donna che amo." *Il Mattino di Padova* (Padua), July 1984.

Righetti, Donata. "La vita è più bella a 50 anni." *Il Giorno* (Milano), July 12, 1984, p. 3.

Pensotti, Anita. "Per vestire il mondo ho reso spoglia la mia vita." *Oggi* (Milan) 29 (July 18, 1984), pp. 28–31.

Mulassano, Adriana. "Incontro straordinario con Giorgio Armani." *Annabella* (Milan) 38 (September 22, 1984), pp. 20–25.

Castrovilli, Mariangiola. "I piaceri di un uomo tranquillo." *Sorrisi e Canzoni TV* (Milan) 43 (October 21, 1984), pp. 60–63.

Rea, Ermanno. "Lui e il suo doppio, o soltanto lui?" *Il Giorno* (Milano) 302 (December 29, 1984), p. 3.

Gerosa, Guido. "Lo stilista del mese Giorgio Armani." *Max* (Milan) 48 (March 1985), pp. 56–59.

Maza, Cristina. "Armani un mito giovane." *Gioia* (Milan) 11 (March 19, 1985), pp. 12–17.

Bertoldi, Cecilia. "Armani Armani." *Amica* (Milan) 12/13 (March 26, 1985).

Enriquez, Rachele. "Milano nuova alta moda: Giorgio Armani." *Vogue Italia* (Milan), September 1985, pp. 351–52.

Mazzucca, Alberto. "Continueró da solo." *Il Sole 24 ore* (Milan) 201 (September 10, 1985), p. 3.

Massaia, Susanna. "I ragazzi dell'Emporio." *Moda* (Milan), November 1985, pp. 9–18.

Piccinino, Bianca Maria. "Giorgio Armani: il personaggio giacca e rigore." *Taxi* (Milan), December 1985, pp. 140–44.

Pietroni Storace, Elisa. "Un piacentino milanese al 100 percentuale." *Gazzetta di Parma* (Parma), December 1, 1985, p. 3.

Forti, Luisa. "Faccio moda ma con stile." *Il Secolo XIX* (Genoa), December 18, 1985, p. 3.

Aloi, Andrea. "E forse nel 1999 i giovani sogneranno." *L'Unità* (Rome), 1986, pp. 91–96.

Borzicchi, Florido. "Tutto il patriottismo del nuovo look." *Il Resto del Carlino* (Bologna), January 24, 1986.

Enriquez, Rachele. "Gran sera a Milano." *Vogue Italia* (Milan), March 1986, pp. 388–90.

Rizzo, Maristella. "Non credo alle invenioni." *Business* (Milan) 3 (March 1986), pp. 58–60.

Beria, Chiara. "La presa dei conti." *Panorama* (Milan) 1039 (March 16, 1986), pp. 154–61.

Oliva, Gian Guido. "Armani dalla moda a Wall Street." *Il Giornale* (Milan), April 19, 1986, p. 13.

Minetti, Maria Giulia. "Come i primi più dei primi—Armani Jeans." *Uomo Vogue* (Milan), June 1986, pp. 126–27.

Enriquez, Rachele. "Tailleurs lineari morbidi." *Vogue Italia* (Milan), July 1986, pp. 183–90.

Castellacci, Claudio. "Giorgio racconta come fa moda." *Max* (Milan), August 1986.

Soli, Pia. "Giorgio Armani—dieci anni dopo." *Grandhair* 8 (August 1986).

Ferrari, Davide. "Paninari." *Wild Boys* (Milan), August 8, 1986, pp. 15–17.

Cattaneo, Antonio. "Armani: ecco il look finanziario con cui voglio andare in borsa." *Il Giornale* (Milan), November 25, 1986.

Santini, Aldo. "E la borsa vestirà Giorgio Armani?" *Il Tirreno* (Livorno), November 30, 1986, p. 13.

Ferri, Edgarda. "Ho il successo ma sono un uomo solo." *Gente* (Milano) 49 (December 5, 1986), pp. 108–15.

Carloni, Maria Vittoria. "S'io fossi Armani." *Panorama* (Milan) 1077 (December 7, 1986), pp. 125–27.

Di Caro, Fabrizio. "Diamoci una regolata." *L'Espresso* (Rome) 48 (December 7, 1986), pp. 30–31.

Galdo, Antonio. "Armani, un impero di rigore." *Il Mattino* (Naples), March 27, 1987.

Kasam, Viviana. "E Armani conferma: sono tradizionalista e un po' provinciali." *Corriere della Sera* (Milan), April 24, 1987.

Cenatiempo, Ciro. "Quei fusti spendono troppo." *Il Mattino* (Naples), July 16, 1987.

Papi, Donatella. "La mia donna." *Gioia* (Milan) 39 (September 28, 1987), pp. 17–22.

Del Buono, Oreste. "Giorgio il calvinista." *L'Uomo Vogue* (Milan) 178 (October 1987), p. 194.

Carretta, Raffaela. "Il gran circo moda." *Epoca* (Milan) 1932 (October 15, 1987), pp. 96–101.

Pericoli, Lea. "Essere alla moda? Non è di moda." *Il Meglio* (Foggia), February 1987, pp. 58–61.

Pisa, Paola. "Armani: le mie donne difficili." *Il Messaggero* (Rome), March 7, 1987, p. 28.

Di Piazza, Giuseppe. "1988, guarda il look, quant'è bello." *Il Messaggero* (Rome), January 10, 1988, p. 7.

Ferrè, Giusi. "Il re è solo." *Europeo* (Milan) 6 (February 5, 1988), pp. 92–95.

"Ma il passepartout è la giacca." *Mondo Uomo* (Milan) 43 (March 1988), p. 95.

Testori, Matteo. "Tutto ok. Parola di Armani." *Espansione* (Milan) 216 (May 1988), pp. 30–31.

Maza, Cristina. "Una moda da Oscar." *Gioia* (Milan), June 6, 1988, pp. 20–24.

Villa, Nora. "Lo stile di Milano." *Ulisse 2000* (Rome), August 1988, pp. 66–69.

Castagna, Lucia. "Giorgio Armani." *Ciak* (Milan), September 1988, p. 96.

Alfonsi, Maria Vittoria. "Armani: la moda come coerenza e onestà." *L'Arena di Verona*, September 19, 1988.

Russo, Maria Rosa. "Sexy ma in modo innocente." *Giornale di Sicilia* (Palermo). November 16, 1988, p. 29.

Lo Vetro, Gianluca. "Tutte le occasioni di moda." *L'Unitá* (Rome), November 17, 1988, p. 24.

Maza, Cristina. "Armani oltre frontiera." *Gioia* (Milan) 3 (January 16, 1989), pp. 30–32, 132.

Nicolao, Fernanda. "Vestendo gli incorruttibili." *Caravel America* (Milan) 5 (April 1989), pp. 30–37.

Alfonsi, Maria Vittoria. "Ristorante Doney." *A Tavola Con Stile* (Milan) 3 (May/June 1989), pp. 83–84.

Pisa, Paola. "Armani, giacche da 460 miliardi." *Il Messaggero* (Rome), June 26, 1989.

Mastromo, Paolo. "Lasciate al creativo l'illusione di essere diverso." *Mondo Economico* (Milan), July 1, 1989, p.103.

Oddo, Giuseppe. "Un'impresa tagliata su misura." *Mondo Economico* (Milan), July 8, 1989, pp. 64–66.

Ranni, Loredana. "Fascino orientale in corpo di donna." *Corriere Adriatico* (Ancona), August 6, 1989.

Dubini, Laura. "L'uomo nuovo secondo Armani." *Corriere della Sera* (Milan), August 31, 1989, p.7.

Lauro, Ausilia. "Raffinatezza nuova era della moda." *Il Mattino* (Naples), September 17, 1989.

Premoli, Aldo. "Razionale e funzionale." *Vogue Pelle* (Milan) 50 (September/October 1989).

Cosi, Marina. "Con naturalezza aiuto gli altri a vestirsi." *Italia Oggi* (Milan), January 16, 1990, pp. 8–9.

Arpaia, Bruno. "Rigore e sogno." *Grazia* (Milan) 2559 (March 18, 1990), pp. 134–35.

Grignaffini, Giovanna and Patrizia Polacco. "E quel *forse* ci faceva soffrire. Intervista a Giorgio Armani." *Cinema & Cinema. L'arte della scena. Cinema e moda* (Bologna), May/August 1990, pp.15–21.

Sannelli, Rosetta. "La donna del terzo millennio." *Allure* (Bologna) 6 (June 1990), pp. 115–19.

Soli, Pia. "L'orso di Pantelleria." *Il Resto del Carlino* (Bologna), August 18, 1990.

Borioli, Gisella. "Il vero Giorgio, raccontato da Armani." *Donna* (Milan) 8 (October 1990), pp. 90–94.

Dubini, Laura. "Adesso la griffe ha bisogno di solide fabbriche." *Corriere della Sera* (Milan), October 3, 1990

Carloni, Maria Vittoria. "Meglio fa l'americano." *Europeo* (Milan), November 11, 1990, pp. 173–75.

Pisa, Paola. "Droga, figlia di cattivi modelli." *Il Messaggero* (Rome), December 18, 1990, p. 35.

Ferrè, Giusi. "Io, vittima della moda." *Europeo* (Milan) 1–2 (January 10, 1991), pp. 52–56.

Iozzia, Giovanni. "Milanese in tre D." *Class* (Milan) 3 (March 1991), pp. 16–22.

Setta, Monica. "Armani riveste l'Alitalia." *Milano Finanza* (Milan), April 18, 1991, p. 16.

Quagliaroli, Stefano. "La Piacenza di Giorgio Armani." *La Gazzetta di Piacenza* (Italy) 18 (May 3, 1991), p. 9.

Giacomoni, Silvia. "La moda non è finita?" *La Repubblica* (Rome), July 7, 1991, p. 25.

Colonna, Francesco. "Nella moda sono entrati troppi faciloni." *La Nazione* (Florence), July 21, 1991.

Taverna, Salvatore. "Una vacanza in stile." *Il Messaggero* (Rome), July 21, 1991, p. 35.

Ciuti, Ilaria. "L'Armani furioso—Vi amo, vi odio." *La Repubblica* (Rome), August 20, 1991, p. 5.

Giordana, Marco Tullio. "Sogni paralleli." *Lei* (Milan), October 1991, pp. 76–80.

Dubini, Laura. "Così la moda non va." *Corriere della Sera* (Milan), October 4, 1991, p. 18.

Elkan, Alain. "Armani, stilista per caso." *La Stampa* (Turin), November 8, 1991, p. 16.

Mascolo, Anna. "Conquisterò L'America con l'abito per tutte le tasche." *La Notte* (Milan), January 27, 1992.

Elkann, Alain. "Diamanti a colazione." *Amica* (Milan) 6 (February 1992), pp. 68–71.

Casasco, Annamaria. "Made in Armani." *Sorrisi e Canzoni TV* (Milan) 13 (April 1992), pp. 74–86.

Marzullo, Gigi. "A tu per tu con Giorgio Armani." *Il Giornale d'Italia* (Rome), May 4, 1992, p. 6.

Desiderio, Eva. "La Sala Bianca per Armani." *La Nazione* (Florence), May 12, 1992.

Municchi, Anna. "Per Giorgio Armani si riaprono le porte della Sala Bianca." *Il Giornale d'Italia* (Rome), May 13, 1992.

Rusconi, Marisa. "Pornosfilate? No, grazie." *L'Espresso* (Rome), May 24, 1992, p. 67.

Palomba, Aura. "Armani preferisce Wall Street." *Il Messaggero* (Rome), May 25, 1992.

Gabriele, Salvatore. "Rendiamo l'isola più accogliente." *Giornale di Sicilia* (Palermo), June 4, 1992.

Filippi, Antonella. "E la donna si veste da uomo, che rivoluzionario, Armani." *Il Giornale di Sicilia* (Palermo), June 20, 1992, p. 24.

Ciuti, Ilaria. "Signore e Signori vi insegno un sogno." *La Repubblica* (Rome), June 24, 1992.

Giacomini, Silvia. "Tra me e Versace nessuna lite." *La Repubblica* (Rome), September 15, 1992.

Desiderio, Eva. "L'America ora mi copia." *La Nazione* (Florence), October 2, 1992.

Pisa, Paola. "Armani, il vestito non fa la dona." *Il Messaggero* (Rome), October 3, 1992, p. 10.

Dubini, Laura. "Armani, facciamo pulizia." *Corriere della Sera* (Milan),

November 17, 1992.

Calabro' Antonio. "Moda, l'Italia s'è mesta." *La Repubblica* (Rome), January 8, 1993, p. 18.

Santini, Galeazzo. "Battere la crisi con la forza della formica." *Class* (Milan) 3 (March 1993), pp. 46–53.

Gatti, Roberto. "Vi voglio vestire da clown." *L'Espresso* (Rome) 10 (March 14, 1993), pp. 132–36.

Altarocca, Claudio. "Brera, voglia di Milano." *La Stampa* (Turin), April 22, 1993, p. 19.

"Una questione di vanità." *Donna* (Milan), May 1993, p. 77.

Frangi, Alessandra. "Non è la mia colpa." *Milano Finanza* (Milan), May 22, 1993, p. 11.

Gorza, Marisa. "Stilsta sovrano." *Lombardia Oggi* (Milan), May 22, 1993, p. 7.

Kalbacker, Warren. "Giorgio Armani." *Playboy* (Chicago), June 1993, pp. 29–33.

Talini, Daniela. "Armani, l'eleganza della A." *Gazzetta Dello Sport* (Milan), June 6, 1993, p. 13.

Veronesi, Daria. "Il successo cucito addosso." *Italia Oggi* (Milan), July 12, 1993, p. 31.

Gabriele, Salvatore. "Così vestirei Pantelleria." *Il Sabato—Il Giornale di Sicilia* (Palermo), September 4, 1993.

Amapane, Antonella. "Io, re della moda per caso." *La Stampa* (Turin), September 18, 1993, p. 13.

Dubini, Laura. "Ma questo è ancora un lavoro serio." *Corriere della Sera* (Milan), October 2, 1993, p. 16.

Amapane, Antonella. "Maestro straight jacket." *La Stampa* (Turin), October 5, 1993.

Beria d'Argentine, Chiara. "La mia donna non è in crisi." *L'Espresso* (Rome) 40 (October 10, 1993), pp. 146–48.

Bevilacqua, Maria Grazia. "Armani l'entusiasta." *Famiglia Cristiana* (Rome) 40 (October 13, 1993), pp. 74–77.

Caccia, Fabrizio. "Allo stadio con stile." *La Repubblica* (Rome), October 17, 1993, p. 8.

Cosi, Marina. "Io, la moda, i divi e la TV." *L'Indipendente* (Rome), October 31, 1993, p. 18.

"Su la testa." *Il Mondo* (Milan) 11 (November 22, 1993), pp. 26–27.

Mancinelli, Antonio. "Giorgio Armani 20 anni dopo." *Mondo Uomo* (Milan), January 1994.

Merenghetti, Paolo. "Vorrei fare lo sceriffo di Milano." *Sette Giorni* (Milan) 1 (January 1, 1994), pp. 62–67.

"Una stella sul petto." *L'Arena* (Verona) 7 (January 8, 1994).

Dondi, Walter. "Armani: io, la moda e il business." *L'Unità* (Rome), February 6, 1994, p. 18.

Aspesi, Natalia. "La mia moda per la seconda Repubblica." *La Repubblica* (Rome), February 21, 1994, p. 21.

D'Agata, Salvatore. "Dieci Armani in uno." *Firma* (Rome) 2 (March 1994), pp. 22–23.

Pende, Stella. "Il mondo di Giorgio." *Panorama* (Milan), March 18, 1994, pp. 76–80.

Casasco, Annamaria. "Vent'anni da raccontare." *Sorrisi e Canzoni TV* (Milan) 12 (March 20, 1994), pp. 38–50.

Fava, Felice. "Armani: il mercato premia solo gli stilisti seri." *Impresa Italia* (Milan) 14 (June 1994), p. 45.

Pisa, Paola. "Io, Giorgio il giovane." *Il Messaggero* (Rome), June 8, 1994, p. 11.

Carloni, Maria Vittoria. "Idoli sì, ma con eleganza." *Panorama* (Milan), June 18, 1994, pp. 123–25.

Casasco, Annamaria. "Armani team." *Sorrisi e Canzoni TV* (Milan), June 26, 1994, pp. 62–66.

Dubini, Laura. "Armani: io autodidatta come Berlusconi." *Corriere della Sera* (Milan), June 27, 1994, p. 30.

Citacov, Marta. "Quell'incontentabile artista." *L'Informazione* (Rome), July 1, 1994, p. 13.

Lo Vetro, Gianluca. "Ho rivoluzionato la moda italiana." *L'Unità* (Rome), July 1,

1994, p. 12.

Brasca, Giovanni. "La mia ambizione? La regia di un film." *Il Mattino* (Naples), July 7, 1994, p. 6.

Vinciguerra, Luca. "Simint—La sfilata più difficile." *Il Sole 24 Ore* (Milan), July 12, 1994.

Camon, Ferdinando. "Lo stile è vita." *Panorama* (Milan), July 15, 1994, pp. 68–75.

Signorini, Alfonso. "Ho 60 anni ma sono un ragazzo." *Noi* (Milan) 29 (July 20, 1994), pp. 66–71.

Pietroni Storace, Elisa. "La libertà di essere belli." *Gazzetta di Parma*, July 27, 1994, p. 5.

Mulassano, Adriana. "Questione di pelle." *L'Informazione* (Rome), August 30, 1994.

Gabriele, Salvatore. "Il piacere di rinnovarsi." *Il Sabato* (Palermo), September 3, 1994, p. 21.

Hill, Andrew. "Fare affari non è più di moda." *Financial Times* (London), September 23, 1994, p. 14.

Ortolani, Renata. "Giorgio Armani taglia e cuce." *Il Corriere Mercantile* (Genoa) 223 (September 28, 1994).

Lo Vetro, Gianluca. "Che moda impossibile." *L'Unità* (Rome), October 8, 1994, p. 10.

Vicedomini, Pascal. "Armani, c'era una volta la moda." *L'Informazione* (Rome), October 21, 1994, pp. 14–15.

Dubini, Laura. "L'America incorona Armani." *Corriere della Sera* (Milan), October 29, 1994.

Fuchs, Catherina and Paul Sahner. "Armani über das Ende der Träume." *Bunte* (Munich) 49 (December 1, 1994), pp. 46–52.

Vicedomini, Pascal. "Armani—uno scandalo trasforma tutto in una passerelle." *L'Informazione* (Rome), December 7, 1994.

Farkas, Alessandra. "Hollywood ai piedi di Armani." *Corriere della Sera* (Milan), December 9, 1994, p. 16.

Satta, Gloria. "Donne, non diventate vittime della moda." *Il Messaggero* (Rome), December 9, 1994, p. 11.

Silipo, Raffaella. "Pfeiffer, la mia preferita." *La Stampa* (Turin), December 9, 1994, p. 13.

Brunetti, Umberto. "Un futuro caldo in mezzo alla gente." *Prima Comunicazione* (Milan) 237 (January 1995), pp. 4–9.

Cardinale, Claudia. "Bilancio fra amici." *Vogue Germany* (Munich), January 1995, pp. 156–94.

Mucchetti, Massimo. "Prima griffe d'America." *L'Espresso* (Rome) 1 (January 5, 1995), pp. 152–53.

Minetti, Maria Giulia. "Ma quale concorrenza . . . la nostra moda è l'unica." *Epoca* (Milan), January 8, 1995.

Lo Vetro, Gianluca. "E ora ognuno si faccia i sessi suoi." *L'Unità* (Rome), January 20, 1995, p. 12.

Windels, Veele. "J'ai decidé d'être moi-même." *De Standaard Magazine* (Mechlin, Belgium), February 3, 1995, pp. 8–11.

Tornabuoni, Lietta. "Armani: tutti i vestiti della libertà." *La Stampa* (Turin), February 6, 1995, p. 15.

Citacov, Marta. "Armani si difende: le reazioni negative ai miei costumi sono superficiali." *L'Informazione*, February 21, 1995, p. 23.

Falck, Jacaranda. "Il fashion discreto della borghesia." *L'Espresso* (Rome) 11 (March 17, 1995), pp. 134–35.

De Chirée, Sylvie. "Giorgio l'enchanteur." *Elle France* (Paris), April 24, 1995, pp. 130–33.

Biagi, Enzo. "Giorgio Armani: la ricerca della perfezione." *Amica* (Milan) 23 (June 10, 1995).

Iantaffi, Stefania and Manuela Scharenberrg. "Claudia Cardinale e Giorgio Armani." *Gala*, July 13, 1995.

Jacaud, Dany. "Giorgio Armani. Le triomphe modeste." *Match* (Paris), July 13, 1995, pp. 32–35.

Amapane, Antonella. "Donne vip sotto le stelle di Roma." *La Stampa* (Turin), July

20, 1995, p. 15.

Desiderio, Eva. "Armani: via le gag della moda." *La Nazione* (Florence), July 26, 1995.

Elkann, Alain. "Io, turista innamorato di un'isola incantata." *La Stampa* (Turin), August 21, 1995.

Mola, Franca. "L'arte di scolpire il tessuto." *Prealpina* (Varese), August 23, 1995, p. 19.

Barzini, Benedetta. "Giorgio Armani: einfach der Grösste." *Bolero* (Zurich) 9 (September 1995), p. 64.

Amapane, Antonella. "Torini ha il mio stile." *La Stampa* (Turin), September 8, 1995, p. 13.

West, C. "The Amazing Armani." *Marie Claire* (Paris), October 1995, pp. 80–83.

Dubini, Cristina. "Questi miei consigli per un guardaroba doc." *Il Giornale* (Milan) 236 (October 7, 1995).

Ouchi, Junko. "Family and Fashion As Seen through the Eyes of Giorgio Armani." *Kateigaho* (Tokyo), November 1995, pp. 171–77.

Serlenga, Lucia. "Revival? No, grazie." *Il Resto del Carlino* (Bologna), November 9, 1995, p. 4.

Falck, Jacaranda. "Mai più donne usa e getta." *L'Espresso* (Rome) 1 (January 7, 1996).

Carloni, Maria Vittoria. "Cerco l'equilibrio per l'uomo del 2000." *Panorama* (Milan), February 1, 1996, pp. 130–33.

Pericoli, Lea. "La pittura aiuta la moda." *Il Giornale* (Milan), February 22, 1996, p. 17.

Gatti, Roberto. "La postina dei miracoli." *L'Espresso* (Rome) 13 (March 29, 1996), pp. 88–90.

Jones, Dylan. "Giorgio Armani the Modernist." *Arena Great Britain* (London), April 1996, pp. 158–59.

Carloni, Maria Vittoria. "Sophia, Fanny e Claudia: le mie vere femme-femme." *Panorama* (Milan), June 6, 1996, 196–99.

Dubini, Laura. "Il lavoro non è tutto, ora l'ho capito." *Corriere della Sera* (Milan), June 27, 1996, p. 15

Birosi, Remo. "Armani a Firenze: scene da uno stile." *Grazia* (Milan) 27 (July 7, 1996).

Baldini, Paolo. "Io orgoglioso di essere piacentino." *Libertá* (Piacenza), July 21, 1996, p. 18, 42–45.

Wayne, George. "Ten Questions You Thought We'd Never Ask. . . ." *Vogue* (New York), August 1996, p. 256.

Gordon, Maryellen. "Armani in New York." *Elle USA* (New York), September 1996, pp. 361–70.

Vaquero, Isabel. "Giorgio Armani descubre su mondo mas secreto." *Woman* (Barcelona) 48 (September 1996), pp. 141–44.

Kemps, Lene. "De vrouwen van Giorgio Armani." *Weekend* (Brussels) 36 (September 4–10, 1996), pp. 186–92.

Hublet, Marianne. "Leçon d'élégance avec Armani." *Weekend La Vie Express* (Paris) 36 (September 6–12, 1996), pp. 36–38.

Carloni, Maria Vittoria. "Io al comando di cento ammiraglie." *Panorama* (Milan), September 26, 1996, pp. 182–85.

Rigalt, Carmen. "Giorgio Armani." *La Revista* 57 (November 17, 1996), pp. 57–62.

Renaux, Pascale. "L'écologie de l'esprit." *Le Soir* (Paris), December 28–29, 1996, p. 8.

Mead, Rebecca. "The interview that shocked the fashion world." *Mode* (New York), December 1996–January 1997, pp. 114–16, 134.

Cesari, Leda. "Leccesi, rubate i colori al vostro Barocco." *Lecce Cronaca* (Italy), January 8, 1997, p. 4.

Dubini, Cristina. "Armani: credo solo in me stesso." *Il Giornale* (Milan), January 14, 1997, p. 16.

Freitag, Michael. "Giorgio Armani." *Frankfurter Allgemeine Magazine* (Frankfurt), January 17 1997, pp. 50–51.

Ahrens, Klaus and Hanno Piucer. "Lo stilista su misura." *Manager* (Milan) 10 (January 27, 1997), pp. 298–306.

Bulbarelli, Paola. "Giorgio Armani." *Mia* (Milan) 1, 2 (February 1997).

Van Versendaal, Dirk. "Der Mythus um meinen Namen Bröckelt." *Amica Germaia* (Hamburg) 5 (February 1997), pp. 226–37.

Dendler, Carolin. "Giorgio Armani." *Bild* (Hamburg) 5 (February 2, 1997), pp. 40–43.

Pavoni, Teodora. "Vesti come ti detta il cuore." *Bella* (Milan) 5 (February 4, 1997), pp. 12–14.

Asnaghi, Laura. "Armani contro tutti nella guerra dello stile." *La Repubblica* (Rome), February 9, 1997, p. 22.

Carloni, Maria Vittoria. "Io, Giorgio, sono fuori dal coro." *Panorama* (Milan), February 27, 1997.

Bottelli, Paola. "Armani: così ridisegno la produzione." *Il Sole 24 Ore* (Milan) 58 (February 28, 1997), p. 8.

Brivio, Serena. "Armani: troppo provincialismo." *La Provincia*, March 5, 1997, p. 5.

Marcolin, Anna. "Niente più diktat." *Messaggero Veneto* (Udine), March 20, 1997, p. 8

Baudot, François. "Armani le feu sous la glace." *Elle France* (Paris), May 19, 1997.

Soli, Pia. "Ieri, oggi e Armani." *Il Tempo* (Rome), June 28, 1997, p. 3.

Righetti, Donata. "Armani: bisogna creare luoghi per i giovani, basta con le dis- oteche lager." *Corriere della Sera* (Milan), July 8, 1997, p. 43.

Bertaso, Gianni. "Rigenerato e soft." *Fashion* (Milan) 1224 (September 26, 1997), p. 22.

Bulbarelli, Paola. "Giorgio Armani: il grande stilista lo fa il mercato." *Il Giornale* (Milan), October 2, 1997, p. 14.

Falck, Jacaranda. "Re Giorgio e i suoi delfini." *L'Espresso* (Rome) 48 (October 4, 1997), pp. 205–07.

Pisu, Renata. "Che fatica essere il ragazzo Armani." *La Repubblica* (Rome), October 5, 1997, p. 29.

McEvoy, Marian. "Armani—He's Swept Away in a Sea of Raves." *Women's Wear Daily* (New York), October 9, 1997.

Novero, Nella. "La razionalità del fashion style." *L'Indipendente* (Rome), October 9, 1997.

Angioni, Martin. "Giorgio Armani: I Owe It to Milan." *The Art Newspaper* (London) 76 (December 1997), p. 22.

Vergoni, Guido. "Lo stile è come il letto di un fiume." *Corriere della Sera* (Milan) 1 (January 1998), pp. 62–66.

Beccari, Tazio. "Gioco con il tempo." *Amica* (Milan), January 9, 1998, pp. 54–56.

Capparucci, Lorella. "Armani: l'uomo? Jeremy Irons." *Il Giorno* (Milan), January 13, 1998, p. 22.

Pisa, Paola. "Armani, ritorno al classico." *Il Messaggero* (Milan), January 18, 1998, p. 12.

Coppet, Anita. "Monsieur Armani." *Marie Claire France* (Paris), February 1998.

Demay, Marie-Noelle and Bertrand Tessier. "Les coulisses du défilé interdit." *Gala* (Paris) 249 (March 19–25, 1998).

Bottelli, Paola. "Armani, 600 miliardi in casa." *Il Sole 24 Ore* (Milan), April 3, 1998, p. 11.

Agosti, Giuseppina. "Qui Giorgio Armani rivive gli anni della sua infanzia." *Libertà* (Piacenza), April 17, 1998, p. 19.

Kujacinski, Dona. "Giorgio Armani." *Gala* (Paris) 25 (June 1998).

Riva, Massimo. "Creo l'Europa della moda tra morbidezza e vigore." *La Repubblica* (Rome), June 1, 1998, pp. 5–15.

Paracchini, Gian Luigi. "Armani: nella storia grazie a quel tailleur." *Corriere della Sera* (Milan), June 7, 1998, p. 14.

Bulbarelli, Paola. "Re Giorgio: in passerella soltanto dei bluff." *Il Giornale* (Milan), July 3, 1998, p. 13.

Di Giovanni, Janine. "Giorgio the King of Good Taste on Life as a Label." *The Times Magazine* (London) August 22, 1998.

Lo Vetro, Gianluca. "Ma al vero stile non serve lo show." *L'Unità* (Rome), November 19, 1998.

Rusconi, Marisa. "Smoking e scarpe da tennis." *L'Espresso* (Rome) 1 (January 7, 1999), pp. 122–24.

Dallai, Margherita. "Ecco la mia isola." *Viaggio* (Milan) 21, 3 (June 1999), p. 53.

————. "Pantelleria amor mio." *Viaggio* (Milan) 22, 3 (July 1999).

Chierici, Maurizio. "Armani. I colori di Pantelleria." *Corriere della Sera* (Milan), July 21, 1999, p. 31.

Pietroni Starace, Elisa. "Giorgio Armani: quell'isola è il mio Puerto Escondido." *Gazzetta di Parma* (Parma), July 25, 1999, p. 16.

Savidan, Dominique. "Je suis trop jeune pour déléguer." *Le Figaro* (Paris), September 28, 1999.

Paracchini, Gian Luigi. "Armani: questa è la mia svolta, la donna del 2000 si ispira a Internet." *Corriere della Sera* (Milan), September 29, 1999, p. 21.

Arosio, Enrico and Jacaranda Falck. "Siate sexy—Educatamente." *L'Espresso* (Rome) 39 (September 30, 1999), pp. 88–92.

Matarrese, Antonella, and Angelo Pergolini. "Armani anno o." *Panorama* (Milan), January 6, 2000, pp. 76–80.

"La mode ne doit pas regarder en arrière." *Le Figaro* (Paris), January 17, 2000.

Gastel, Minnie. "Giorgio Armani 25 anni da protagonista." *Donna* (Milan) 2 (February 2000), pp. 40–51.

Prost, Marie-Laure. "Notre création est faite pour durer." *Cosmétique* (Paris), February 2000, pp. 22–23.

Asnaghi, Laura. "Nata nel 1920 per le divise Usa, la girocollo più trendy è ora un mix di stili. Cotone, tulle, lana dall' impronta hippy." *La Repubblica* (Rome), February 16, 2000, p. 31.

Henno, Martine. "Le roi Giorgio sacré à New York." *Le Figaro* (Paris), February 21, 2000, p. 15.

Hublet Marianne. "Armani et la nouvelle ère." *Weekend le Vif* 8 (February 25, 2000), p. 97.

Munoz, Ana. "Giorgio Armani." *Blanco y Negro* (Madrid), February 27, 2000, pp. 40–49.

Ferrè, Giusi. "La nuova natura del piacere. Piu` seducente la donna, piu` attraente l'uomo. Giorgio Armani percorre l'erotismo. E promette nuovi peccati." *Amica* (Milan), March 2000, pp. 182–89.

Krohmer, Anke. "Colui che dettta la moda." *Playboy* (Rome), March 2000, pp. 137–49.

Molter, Veit. "Klassiker der Moderne: Giorgio Armani 25 Jahre im Dienst der Mode." *Dolce* (Munich) 3 (March 2000), pp. 17–21.

Wilbekin, Emil. "Classic Cuts." *Vibe* (New York) 3 (March 2000), pp. 168–72.

Brunel, Jacques. "La précision du flou Armani." *Vogue* (Paris), April 2000, pp. 184–286.

Webb, Iain R. "Empire Armani." *Elle UK* (London), April 2000, pp. 259–63.

Dean, Syahmedi. "Giorgio Armani. The Silver Years. *Harper's Bazaar* (New York), June 2000.

Selected Writings and Statements by the Artist

Statement in "Un Borsalino in testa." *Il Nuovo Veronese* (Verona), November 19, 1983.

Statement in "Ecco la mia sfida per l'abito del futuro." *L'Unità* (Rome), December 18, 1983.

Statement in "Un po' di mistero non guasta." *Fashion* (Milan), October 6, 1984.

Statement in "Parola di Armani: l'abito fa il monaco." *L'Unità* (Rome), October 6, 1985.

"Tra tricolore e spaghetti." *Incontri*, February 1986.

Statement in Raffaella Carretta, "Il cinquantenne." *Epoca* (Milan) 1888 (December 12, 1986), pp. 26–30.

Statement in "Giorgio Armani Amarcord." *Libertà* (Piacenza), March 17, 1987.

Statement in Fabio Franchini, "E lo stilista Armani le dedica un pensiero." *Gazzetta dello sport* (Milan), March 19, 1987.

"Armani: anche per il tempo va il corto." *Il Messaggero* (Rome), April 10, 1987.

"Armani: autoritratto televisivo." *Libertà* (Piacenza), May 1, 1987.

"Quell'aerea eleganza di Fred Astaire." *Il Giorno* (Milan), July 10, 1987.

"Armani: una maestra nel coraggio di cambiare." *La Stampa* (Turin), September 3, 1987.

"La tradizione vincente." *Il Messaggero* (Rome), September 23, 1988.

Statement in "Jersey—cosa ne pensano gli stilisti." *L'Uomo Vogue* (Milan) 179 (November 1987).

"Modello Cary Grant." *L'Espresso* (Rome), January 8, 1989, pp. 66–67.

"Look and Roll." *Il Messaggero* (Rome), February 24, 1989, p. 14.

Statement in Marina Cosi, "Niente scuola, siamo creativi." *Italia Oggi* (Milan), March 1, 1989, p. 15.

Statement in Adriana Mulassano, "Di Giorgio in Giorgio." *Capital* (Milan), June 1989, pp. 134–41.

"Buttiamoci tra le morbide lane." *Il Messaggero* (Rome), September 10, 1989.

Statement in Marco De Corona, "Molto meglio come eravamo." *Corriere della Sera* (Milan), November 27, 1989.

"Il suo look." *Panorama* (Milan), December 3, 1989, p. 41.

"Un po' largo per i giovani ma sempre inappuntabile." *Il Messaggero* (Rome), December 12, 1989, p. 11.

Statement in Giusi Ferrè, "Armani, i perchè di uno stile." *Amica* (Milan) 8 (February 1990).

"Il piacere di cambiare per lei è un classico." *Il Messaggero* (Rome), March 4, 1990.

"Quell'indispensabile pezzo da novanta." *Il Messaggero* (Rome), April 15, 1990, p. 11.

"Innocenti evasioni." *Il Messaggero* (Rome), November 9, 1990, p. 7.

"Da griffe di abbigliamento a marchio d'impresa." *Mondo Eonomico* (Milan), June 30, 1990.

Statement in Bianca Maria Piccinino, "Giorgio Armani." *Forum Colorum*, July–September 1990, pp. 9–11.

Statement in Glynis Costin, "Signor Glamour." *Fashion Life*, February 1991, pp. 44–46.

Statement in Cristina Tonelli, "Camporese è proprio alla moda." *La Gazzetta Sportiva* (Milan), February 10, 1991, p. 2.

"Moda Carnevale—Risponde Armani." *Oggi* (Milan), February 13, 1991, p. 9.

"Colletti sbarazzini." *Il Messaggero* (Rome), March 2, 1991.

Statement in Roberto Gatti, "Questione di stile." *L'Espresso* (Rome), March 10, 1991, pp. 52–55.

"L'industria dell'abbigliamento secondo Giorgio Armani." *Modena Mondo* (Modena), May 1991, p. 5.

"Niente stravaganza, solo sobrietà." *Il Messaggero* (Rome), October 5, 1991.

Statement in Simona Fassati, "Non per la firma ma per la qualità." *Il Sole 24 Ore* (Milan), October 6, 1991.

"La mia sfida." *Ulisse 2000* (Roma), December 1991, pp. 128–29.

"Un intervento di Giorgio Armani." *Donna* (Milan), December 1991, p. 150.

Statement in "Domenica con Giorgio." *Panorama* (Milan), April 12, 1992, p. 147.

Statement in Emma Franceschini, "E la giacca entra nel museo." *Il Messaggero* (Rome), June 21, 1992.

"L'atelier dei talenti." *Corriere della Sera* (Milan), June 24, 1992, p. 3.

Statement in Giusi Ferrè, "Semplicità al potere, e Armani diventa un simbolo." *Europeo* (Milan) 26 (June 26, 1992).

"Comunicare con stile." *La Repubblica* (Rome), December 17, 1992, p. 21.

"L'opinione: lei vista da liu." *Donna* (Milan), January 1993, p. 76.

"Giusto essere orgogliosi." *La Repubblica* (Rome), February 4, 1993.

"Saint-Tropez." *Marieclaire* (Paris), August 1993, p. 22.

"Un ragazzo dai capelli bianchi." *Sorrisi e Canzoni TV* (Milan), February 1993, pp. 52–53.

Statement in Donatella Polizzi Piazza, "Armani scopre la sua Africa." *Giornale di Sicilia* (Palermo), May 8, 1993, p. 20.

Statement in Sofia Catalano, "E la modella pelle e ossa vinse." *Giornale di Sicilia* (Palermo), May 22, 1993, p. 22.

"Tra lusso e neopovero." *L'Uomo Vogue* (Milan), June 1993, pp. 90–91.

"Piango anch'io le vittime della moda." *La Stampa* (Turin), September 18, 1993, p. 16.

Satement in Luciana Boccardi, "Firmate da Giorgio Armani le divise della nazionale." *Il Gazzettino* (Venice), June 2, 1994.

Statement in Minnie Gastel, "Giorgio Armani—Ricominciare ogni volta." *Donna* (Milan), July 1994, pp. 134–37.

"Bellezza contro scandalo." *La Stampa* (Turin), September 9, 1994.

"Femminilità senza volgarità." *La Voce* (Milan), October 1, 1994.

Statement in "La parola d'ordine è: formazione." *Corriere Lavoro* (Milan), October 28, 1994, p. 3.

Statement in Sara Gay Forden, "Armani: alt alla moda spettacolo." *La Stampa* (Turin), November 25, 1994.

Statement in Giusi Ferrè, "Moda pulita ce la farà." *Europeo* (Milan) 51 (December 28, 1994), pp. 96–100.

"Bella e d'annata." *La Voce* (Milan) 242 (December 31, 1994).

Statement in Isabella Bossi Fedrigotti, "Armani: ho trovato l'America." *L'Espresso* (Rome) 1 (January 5, 1995), pp. 152–53.

"Stilisti dite basta agli anni 60." *La Stampa* (Turin), October 27, 1995, pp. 1–4.

"Armani Disarmed." *Emporio Armani* magazine (Milan) 14 (September 1995–February 1996), pp. i–ix.

"La moda passa, l'arte resta." *Messaggero Veneto* (Udine) September 28, 1996, p. 8.

Statement in Marika De Feo, "Armani bacchetta tutti." *Corriere della Sera* (Milan), February 2, 1997, p. 14.

Statement in R. Cri, "Io, l'amore e i colleghi," *La Stampa* (Turin), February 9, 1997.

"La pagella di Armani: stilisti, razza dannata." *Il Giorno* (Milan), February 9, 1997, p. 10.

"Rompo le regole e ricomincio da me." *Corriere della Sera* (Milan), October 3, 1997, p. 7.

"Come sono cambiati l'uomo e la sua moda da quando è nato Mondo Uomo a oggi?" *Mondo Uomo* (Milan), November–December 1997.

"In equilibrio senza camicia, ma con la giacca. La sfida raffinata che propone un nuovo stile, senza travestiment." *Corriere della Sera* (Milan), January 11, 1998, p. 5.

"La Borsa può attendere." *L'Espresso* (Rome) 32 (August 13, 1998), pp. 126–27.

Statement in Marta Citacov, "La moda punta al recupero dall'identità." *L'uomo Vogue* (Milan) 292 (July–August 1998).

Statement in Paola Bottelli, "Armani: il dubbio di oggi: a chi passare il testimone." *Il Sole 24 Ore* (Milan), October 2, 1998, p. 3.

Statement in "Un gigante che vale 2.400 miliardi l'anno." *Gente Money* (Milan), July 1, 1999, pp. 210–11.

Statement in "Armani lascia? Ancora giovane." *Il Mattino* (Naples), September 29, 1999, p. 10.

Statement in "Armani e Hdp ai ferri corti." *La Repubblica* (Rome), October 6, 1999, p. 42.

"L'inchiesta BBC non ha fatto male alla moda milanese." *Libertà* (Piacenza), December 1, 1999, p. 2.

Statement in Giampietro Baudo, "Giorgio Armani: rigore senza tempo." *Milano Finanza Fashion* (Milan), December 14, 1999, p. 6.

"Non c'è più verità nella moda: opinione di Armani." *Panorama* (Milan), February 24, 2000.

Statement in "Contatti con Gucci, ma non solo." *Il Messaggero* (Rome), February 24, 2000, p. 21.

PHOTO CREDITS

The New York Times described Robert Wilson as "a towering figure in the world of experimental theater." His works integrate a wide variety of artistic media, combining movement, dance, painting, lighting, furniture design, sculpture, music, and text into a unified whole. His numerous awards and honors include an Obie award for direction (1986), the Golden Lion award for sculpture from the Venice Biennale (1993), the Dorothy and Lillian Gish Prize for lifetime achievement (1996), the Premio Europa award from Taormina Arte (1997), and the prestigious Commandeur des Arts et des Lettres from France (2002).

A native of Waco, Texas, Wilson was educated at the University of Texas and Brooklyn's Pratt Institute. By the late 1960s he was acknowledged as one of the leading figures in Manhattan's avant-garde theater. Working with his Byrd Hoffman School of Byrds, he developed highly regarded pieces such as *Deafman Glance* (1970) and *The Life and Times of Joseph Stalin* (1973). His 1976 opera *Einstein on the Beach*, written with composer Philip Glass, achieved worldwide acclaim and altered conventional perceptions of opera as an art form.

Throughout the world, Wilson has staged both original works and productions from the traditional repertoire, including his *the CIVIL warS*—a collaborative, multinational epic performed on three continents (1983–85)—Wagner's *Parsifal* in Hamburg (1991), and Mozart's *The Magic Flute* in Paris (1991–99). In 1999 he presented his acclaimed production of Wagner's *Lohengrin* at the Metropolitan Opera in New York, and in 2002 the Zurich Opera performed Wagner's entire *Ring* cycle under his direction.

Wilson's artworks have been shown in museums and galleries internationally. Extensive retrospectives have been presented at the Centre Georges Pompidou, Paris, and the Museum of Fine Arts, Boston. He has mounted installations in numerous locations, including the Venice Biennale, the Museum Boijmans Van Beuningen in Rotterdam, London's Clink Street Vaults, and the Vitra Design Museum in Weil am Rhein, Germany.

Each summer Wilson develops new work at the Watermill Center in eastern Long Island, a theater laboratory that brings together students and experienced professionals in a multidisciplinary environment dedicated to creative collaboration. Work is currently under way to raise funds for the center as a year-round facility.

PROJECT TEAM

Solomon R. Guggenheim Museum

CURATORIAL

Germano Celant, *Senior Curator of Contemporary Art*

Harold Koda, *Guest Curator*

Susan Cross, *Associate Curator*

Karole Vail, *Assistant Curator*

Lisa Panzera, *Project Assistant Curator*

Ilaria Dupré, *Research Assistant*

Shannon Bell, *Intern*

MANAGEMENT

Lisa Dennison, *Deputy Director and Chief Curator*

Marc Steglitz, *Deputy Director, Finance and Operations*

Karen Meyerhoff, *Director of Exhibition and Collection Management and Design*

Marion Kahan, *Exhibition Program Manager*

Pepi Marchetti Franchi, *Executive Associate to the Director*

Jessica Ludwig, *Project Manager*

EXTERNAL AFFAIRS

Betsy Ennis, *Director of Public Affairs*

Kendall Hubert, *Director of Corporate Development*

Nic Iljine, *European Representative*

Laura Miller, *Director of Marketing*

Helen Warwick, *Director of Individual Giving and Membership*

LEGAL

Gail Scovell, *General Counsel*

Brendan Connell, *Assistant General Counsel*

Stefanie Lieberman, *Acting Assistant General Counsel*

FINANCE

Amy West, *Director of Finance*

Christina Kallergis, *Senior Financial Analyst, Budget and Planning*

CONSERVATION

Carol Stringari, *Senior Conservator*

Denyse Montegut, *Consulting Textile Conservator and Fiber Analyst*

Joanne Dolan, *Consulting Textile Conservator*

REGISTRARS

Meryl Cohen, *Head Registrar*

Marylouise Napier, *Registrar*

Kaia Black, *Project Registrar*

FILM AND VIDEO

Ultan Guilfoyle, *Film Consultant*

Paul Kuranko, *Media Arts Specialist*

Reginal Leigh Harper, *Film Clip Coordinator*

Concetta Pereira, *Production Coordinator, Graphics*

PUBLICATIONS

Anthony Calnek, *Deputy Director for Communications and Publishing*

Elizabeth Levy, *Director of Publications*

Elizabeth Franzen, *Managing Editor*

Jennifer Knox White, *Editor*

Cindy Williamson, *Assistant Production Manager*

Esther Yun, *Assistant Production Manager*

Domenick Ammirati, *Assistant Editor*

Melissa Secondino, *Assistant Production Manager*

Meghan Dailey, *Associate Editor*

Rachel Shuman, *Administrative Assistant*

Victoria Rich, *Photographic Researcher*

Susan McNally

PHOTOGRAPHY

David Heald, *Head Photographer*

Ellen Labenski, *Associate Photographer*

Kim Bush, *Manager of Photography and Permissions*

Catalogue Design

Matsumoto Incorporated

Takaaki Matsumoto, *Art Director, Designer*

Larissa Nowicki, *Designer*

Thanh X. Tran, *Designer*

Delphine Barringer, *Office Manager*

Exhibition Design

Robert Wilson, *Designer*

Michael Galasso, *Music*

A. J. Weissbard, *Lighting Designer*

Serge Von Arx, *Collaborator for Visual Design*

Michael Galasso and Peter Cerone, *Sound Design*

Jakob Friis Nielsen, *Administrative Assistant*

Elisabetta di Mambro, *Change Performing Arts, Producing Director*

Royal Academy of Arts

Professor Phillip King CBE, *President*

Lawton Fitt, *Secretary*

EXHIBITION ORGANISATION

Norman Rosenthal, *Exhibitions Secretary*

Simonetta Fraquelli, *Project Director*

Sunnifa Hope, *Project Administrator*

Susan Thompson, *Armani Registrar*

Mark Clark, *Project Chief Art Handler*

Sascha Machiedo, *Project Manager for Fabrication, Construction and Installation*

Erica Svec, *Head Dresser*

COPYRIGHT

Miranda Bennion, *Photographic and Copyright Manager*

FINANCE

Dominic Anghileri, *Finance Director*

Kay Butler, *Deputy Finance Director*

ARCHITECTS

Peter Schmitt, *Surveyor to the Fabric*

Alex Dobbs, *Architect*

MARKETING

Katharine Jones, *Head of Marketing*

Alice Holman, *Marketing Officer, Print and Production*

Pamela Bhanvra, *Marketing Officer, Tourism*

Livia Ratcliffe, *Marketing Officer, Promotions*

PRESS

Caroline Atkinson, *Head of Press*

Sarah Davies, *Press Officer*

Sophie Martin, *Press Assistant*

CORPORATE FUNDRAISING

Jane Marriott, *Head of Corporate Fundraising*

Gwen Communier, *Corporate Events Manager*

Susannah Gould, *Sponsorship Administrator*

EVENTS

Malcolm Colin-Stokes, *Head of Special Events*

Lucy Daynes, *Events Organiser*

FACILITIES

Dave Vobes, *Facilities Manager*

FRIENDS OF THE ROYAL ACADEMY

Sarah Cook, *Head of Friends*

COMPUTER INSTALLATION

David Aston, *IT Director*

Andrew Gorczycki, *Deputy IT Manager*

RA ENTERPRISES LTD

David Breuer, *Chief Executive*

John Barford, *Head of Commercial Operations*

Nick Tite, *Head of Publishing*

RA PUBLICATIONS

Peter Sawbridge, *Editor*

Fiona McHardy, *Editorial Assistant*

Carola Krueger, *Production Manager*

Harry Burden, *Production Assistant*

RA MAGAZINE

Sarah Greenberg, *Editor*

Sam Phillips, *Assistant Editor*

Kim Jenner, *Business Manager*

Jane Grylls, *Advertisement Manager*

Tom Uglow, *Listings and Production Editor*

MERCHANDISING

Selina Fellows, *Production Development Consultant*

Ella Riley, *Buyer*

Alice Payn, *Buyer*

Matt Thomas, *Merchandiser*

Amanda Dodridge, *Merchandise Assistant*

Ryan Lawyer, *Warehouse Manager*

Noah Crutchfield, *Shop Manager*

Construction

Keith Spriggs, *Devonshire House Associates*

Legal Counsel

Elizabeth Robertson, *Jones Day*

381

Mrs Frederick Bienstock
Mr Mark Birley
Dame Elizabeth Blackadder OBE RSA RA
Sir Victor and Lady Blank
Mr Peter Bowring CBE
Mr and Mrs Michael Bradley
The Britto Foundation
Mr Jeremy Brown
Mrs Ian Buckley-Sharp
Mrs Richard Burton
Mrs Alan Campbell-Johnson
Mrs Lily Cantor
Mr F A A Carnwath CBE
Jean and Eric Cass
The Marquise de Cérenville
Mr and Mrs George Coelho
Carole and Neville Conrad
David J and Jennifer A Cooke
Mr and Mrs Sidney Corob
Tom Corrigan
Julian Darley and Helga Sands
The Countess of Dartmouth
Mr Keith Day and Mr Peter Sheppard
Mr and Mrs Hans de Gier
Peter and Kate De Haan
Anne Dell Provost
Lady de Rothschild
Dr Anne Dornhorst
Sir Philip Dowson PPRA and Lady Dowson
John Drummond FCSD Hon DES RCA
Mr and Mrs D Dymond
Professor Dyson and Dr Naylor
Mr and Mrs Nicholas Earles
Lord and Lady Egremont
Mr and Mrs Peter Ellis
Mr and Mrs John and Fausta Eskenazi
Mary Fedden RA
Mr Bryan Ferry
Mrs Donatella Flick
Flying Colours Gallery
Mr and Mrs George Fokschaner
Mr and Mrs Edwin H Fox
Mrs R M Fox
Mr Monty Freedman
Michael and Clara Freeman
A Fulton Company Limited
The Baron and Baroness of Fulwood
Jacqueline and Jonathan Gestetner
The David Gill Memorial Fund
Mr and Mrs Simon Gillespie
Patricia Glasswell
Michael Godbee
Mrs Alexia Goethe
Sarah and Alastair Ross Goobey
Sir Nicholas and Lady Goodison's Charitable
    Settlement
Piers and Rosie Gough
Ms Angela Graham
Sir Ronald Grierson
Mr Roger Hatchell and Mrs Ira Kettner
David and Lesley Haynes
Sir Denys and Lady Henderson
Mrs Margarita Hernandez
Mrs Alexander F Hehmeyer
Mr and Mrs Alan Hill
Russell and Gundula Hoban
Anne Holmes-Drewry
Sir Joseph Hotung
Mrs Sue Howes and Mr Greg Dyke
Mr and Mrs Allan Hughes
Mrs Pauline Hyde
Simone Hyman
Mrs Manya Igel
Mr Oliver Iny
Mr S Isern-Feliu
Ian and Barbara Jackson
Sir Martin and Lady Jacomb
Mr and Mrs Ian Jay
Mr and Mrs Harold Joels
Mr D H Killick
Mr and Mrs James Kirkman
Joan H Lavender
Mr Peter Leaver
Mr George Lengvari
The Lady Lever of Manchester
Colette and Peter Levy
Mrs Rosemarie Lieberman
Susan Linaker
Mrs Livingstone
Miss R Lomax-Simpson
Mr and Mrs Mark Loveday
Richard and Rose Luce
Mrs Marilyn Maklouf

Mr and Mrs Eskandar Maleki
Mr and Mrs Michael (RA) and Jose Manser
Mr and Mrs M Margulies
The Lord Marks of Broughton
Marsh Christian Trust
Mr and Mrs Stephen Mather
Mr Brian Mayou and Dr Susan Mayou
Mrs M C W McCann
Gillian McIntosh
Mr and Mrs Andrew McKinna
Sir Kit and Lady McMahon
The Mercers' Company
Mrs Kathryn Michael
Mrs Alan Morgan
Thomas F Mosimann III
Mr and Mrs Carl Anton Muller
N Peal Cashmere
Mr and Mrs Nordby
Mr and Mrs Simon Oliver
Mrs Lale Orge
Mr Michael Palin
Mr and Mrs Vincenzo Palladino
Mr Gerald Parkes
Mr Vasily Pasetchnik
John H Pattisson
Mrs Wendy Becker Payton
The Pennycress Trust
Mr Andrew S Perloff
Philip S Perry
John and Scheherazade Pesaute-Mullis
Mr David Pike
Mr Godfrey Pilkington
Mr and Mrs A Pitt-Rivers
Mr and Mrs William A Plapinger
John Porter Charitable Trust
Mr Ian M Poynton
Miss Victoria Provis
The Quercus Trust
John and Anne Raisman
Sir David and Lady Ramsbotham
Martin Randall Travel Ltd
Mr T H Reitman
The Roland Group of Companies Plc
Mr and Mrs Ian Rosenberg
Paul and Jill Ruddock
Mr and Mrs Derald H Ruttenberg
Mrs Mortimer Sackler
Lady (Robert) Sainsbury
Mr and Mrs Victor Sandelson
Mr and Mrs Bryan Sanderson
Mr and Mrs Hugh Sassoon
Mr S Schaefer and Ms O Ma
The Schneer Foundation, Inc
Carol Sellars
Dr and Mrs Agustin Sevilla
Dr Lewis Sevitt
The Countess of Shaftesbury
Lord and Lady Colin Sharman
Mr and Mrs William Sieghart
Alan and Marianna Simpson
Mrs Margaret Simpson
Mr and Mrs Mark Franklin Slaughter
Mrs Jack Steinberg
Mr and Mrs R W Strang
Mrs D Susman
The Swan Trust
Mr and Mrs David Swift
Mr John Tackaberry
Group Captain James B Tait and Irene
    Bridgmont
Mrs Mark Tapley
The Tavolozza Foundation
Mr and Mrs John D Taylor
Mr and Mrs Julian Treger
Miss M L Ulfane
Visa Lloyds Bank Monte Carlo
Mrs Catherine Vlasto
Mr and Mrs Ludovic de Walden
John B Watton
The Hon Mrs Simon Weinstock
Edna and Willard Weiss
Mrs Hazel Westbury
Rachel and Anthony Williams
Mr Jeremy Willoughby
The Right Hon Lord and Lady Young of
    Graffham
and others who wish to remain anonymous

SCHOOLS PATRONS GROUP
Silver Patrons
Arts and Humanities Research Board
The Brown Foundation, Inc., Houston

The D'Oyly Carte Charitable Trust
The Gilbert & Eileen Edgar Foundation
The Eranda Foundation
Mr and Mrs Jack Goldhill
The Headley Trust
Fiona Johnstone
The David Lean Foundation
The Leverhulme Trust
The Henry Moore Foundation
Newby Trust Limited
Edith and Ferdinand Porjes Charitable Trust
Paul Smith and Pauline Denyer Smith
The South Square Trust
The Starr Foundation
Sir Siegmund Warburg's Voluntary Settlement
The Harold Hyam Wingate Foundation

Silver Patrons
The Stanley Picker Trust
The Radcliffe Trust
The Celia Walker Art Foundation

Bronze Patrons
The Lord Aldington
The Candide Charitable Trust
The Charlotte Bonham-Carter Charitable Trust
The Selina Chenevière Foundation
Denise Cohen Charitable Trust
Mr Simon Copsey
May Cristea Award
Keith and Pam Dawson
The Delfont Foundation
Mr Alexander Duma
The Marchioness of Dufferin and Ava
Mr Hani Farsi
Hirsh London
Ken and Dora Howard
The Lark Trust
Mrs Lore Lehmann
Mr John Martin
Claus and Susan Moehlmann
Miranda Page-Wood
N Peal Cashmere
The Worshipful Company of Painter-Stainers
Pickett
Peter Rice Esq
Mr Iain Henderson Russell
Mr and Mrs Anthony Salz
Mr and Mrs Robert Lee Sterling Jr
The Peter Storrs Trust
Mr and Mrs Denis Tinsley
and others who wish to remain anonymous

GENERAL BENEFACTORS
Mr and Mrs John Coombe
Miss Jayne Edwardes
P H Holt Charitable Trust
The Ingram Trust
The Catherine Lewis Foundation
Sally and Donal Main
and others who wish to remain anonymous

AMERICAN ASSOCIATES OF
THE ROYAL ACADEMY TRUST
Major Benefactors
The Annenberg Foundation
Mr and Mrs Sid R Bass
The Brown Foundation Inc, Houston
Citigroup
Mr Edwin L Cox
Mr and Mrs Eugene V Fife
Mr Francis Finlay
Mrs Henry Ford II
The Drue Heinz Trust
The Horace W Goldsmith Foundation
Mr and Mrs Donald P Kahn
Mrs Katherine K Lawrence
The Henry Luce Foundation
Mr and Mrs John L Marion
Mr and Mrs Jack C Massey
Mr Hamish Maxwell
Mr and Mrs George McFadden
The Estate of Paul Mellon KBE
Ms Diane A Nixon
Leon B Polsky and Cynthia Hazen Polsky
Mrs Arthur M Sackler
Mrs Edmond J Safra
Mrs Louisa S Sarofim
Ms Kathleen D Smith
The Starr Foundation
Mr and Mrs Robert Lee Sterling Jr

Alfred Taubman
Mr and Mrs Vernon Taylor Jr
The Eugene and Clare Thaw Charitable Trust
The Honourable John C Whitehead
Mr and Mrs Frederick B Whittemore

Benefactors
Mr and Mrs Herbert S Adler
The Blackstone Group
Mr and Mrs Roderick C Gow
Mrs Melville Wakeman Hall
Ms Frances S Hayward
Mrs Jeanne K Lawrence
Sony Corporation of America

Sponsors
Mrs Deborah Brice
Mrs Jan Cowles
Mr and Mrs Marvin Davidson
Lady Fairfax
Mrs Katherine D W Findlay
Mrs Eva G de Garza Laguera
David Hockney, RA
Mr James M Kemper Jr
Mrs John P McGrath
Mr David McKee
Mr David Murdock
Mrs Milton Petrie
Mr and Mrs William Rayner
Mr and Mrs John R Robinson
Mr Richard Steinwurtzel
Arthur Ochs Sulzberger and Allison Stacey
    Cowles
Virgin Atlantic

Patrons
Ms Helen Harting Abell
Mr and Mrs Steven Ausnit
Elizabeth and Stephen Bechtel Jr Foundation
Mr and Mrs Raphael Bernstein
Mr Donald A Best
Mr and Mrs Henry W Breyer III
Mrs Mildred C Brinn
Jane and Robert Carroll
Mr and Mrs Benjamin Coates
Ms Anne S Davidson
Ms Zita Davisson
Ambassador Enriquillo and Mrs Audrey Z del
    Rosario
Mrs Charles H Dyson
Mrs A Barlow Ferguson
Mr Richard E Ford
Mrs Raymond C Foster
The William Fox Jr Foundation
Mr and Mrs Lawrence S Friedland
Eleanor and Eugene Goldberg
Mrs Betty Gordon
Mrs David Granger
Mrs Rachel K Grody
Mr and Mrs Martin D Gruss
Mrs Richard L Harris
Gurnee and Marjorie Hart
Mr Edward H Harte
Mr and Mrs Gustave M Hauser
Dr Bruce C Horten
Mr Robert J A Irwin
The Honorable and Mrs W Eugene
    Johnston III
Mr William W Karatz
Mr and Mrs Stephen M Kellen
Mr and Mrs Gary A Kraut
Ambassador and Mrs Philip Lader
Mrs Kay Lawrence
Mr and Mrs William D Lese
William M and Sarah T Lese Family Fund
Mr Arthur L Loeb
Mrs Barbara T Missett
Mr Allen Model
Mr and Mrs Paul S Morgan
Mr Paul D Myers
Mr and Mrs Wilson Nolen
Mrs Richard D O'Connor
Mr and Mrs Jeffrey Pettit
Mr Robert S Pirie
Dr and Mrs James S Reibel
Mrs Frances G Scaife
Ms Jan Scholes
Mr and Mrs Stanley DeForest Scott
Ms Georgia Shreve
Mrs Frederick M Stafford
Mr and Mrs Stephen Stamas

Ms Brenda Neubauer Straus
Mrs Matilda Gray Stream
Elizabeth F Stribling
Mrs· Royce Deane Tate
Mrs Britt Tidelius
Mrs Richard Barclay Tullis
Ms Sue Erpf Van de Bovenkamp
Mrs William M Weaver Jr
Ms Deborah White
Mr and Mrs George White
Mrs Sara E White
Dr and Mrs Robert D Wickham
Mr and Mrs Robert G Wilmers
Mr Robert W Wilson
Mr and Mrs Kenneth Woodcock
and others who wish to remain anonymous

CORPORATE MEMBERSHIP OF THE ROYAL ACADEMY OF ARTS

Launched in 1988, the Royal Academy's Corporate Membership Scheme has proved highly successful. Corporate membership offers company benefits to staff and clients and access to the Academy's facilities and resources. Each member pays an annual subscription to be a Member (£7,000) or Patron (£20,000). Participating companies recognise the importance of promoting the visual arts. Their support is vital to the continuing success of the Academy.

CORPORATE MEMBERSHIP SCHEME

Corporate Patrons
Ashurst Morris Crisp
Bloomberg LP
BNP Paribas
B. P.
Debenhams Retail plc
Deutsche Bank AG
Ernst and Young
GlaxoSmithKline plc
Granada plc
John Lewis Partnership
Merrill Lynch
Radisson Edwardian Hotels
Standard Chartered Bank

Corporate Members
Apax Partners Holding Ltd
Atos KPMG Consulting
Bear, Stearns International Ltd
The Boston Consulting Group
Bovis Lend Lease Limited
The British Land Company PLC
Bunzl plc
Cantor Fitzgerald
CB Hillier Parker
Cedar Communications
Christie's
Chubb Insurance Company of Europe
Citigroup
CJA (Management Recruitment Consultants) Limited
Clifford Chance
Credit Agricole Indosuez
De Beers
Diageo plc
Dresdner Kleinwort Wasserstein
F&C Management plc
Fleming Family & Partners
GAM
Goldman Sachs International
Hay Group
Herdez Europa
Hewitt, Bacon and Woodrow
Weil Gotschal & Manges
Zurich Financial Services

Honorary Corporate Patrons
ABN AMRO

Honorary Corporate Members
All Nippon Airways Co. Ltd
A.T. Kearney Limited
Derwent Valley Holdings plc
London First
Yakult UK Limited

SUPPORTERS OF PAST EXHIBITIONS

The President and Council of the Royal Academy would like to thank the following sponsors and benefactors for their generous support of major exhibitions during the last ten years:

ABN AMRO
Masterpieces from Dresden, 2003
Allied Trust Bank
Africa: The Art of a Continent, 1995*
Anglo American Corporation of South Africa
Africa: The Art of a Continent, 1995*
A. T. Kearney
231st Summer Exhibition, 1999
232nd Summer Exhibition, 2000
233rd Summer Exhibition, 2001
234th Summer Exhibition, 2002
The Banque Indosuez Group
Pissarro: The Impressionist and the City, 1993
Barclays
Ingres to Matisse: Masterpieces of French Painting, 2001
BBC Radio 3
Paris: Capital of the Arts 1900–1968. 2001
BMW (GB) Limited
Georges Rouault: The Early Years, 1903–1920. 1993
David Hockney: A Drawing Retrospective, 1995*
British Airways Plc
Africa: The Art of a Continent, 1995
British American Tobacco
Aztecs, 2002
Cantor Fitzgerald
From Manet to Gauguin: Masterpieces from Swiss Private Collections, 1995
1900: Art at the Crossroads, 2000
The Capital Group Companies
Drawings from the J Paul Getty Museum, 1993
Chase Fleming Asset Management
The Scottish Colourists 1900–1930. 2000
Chilstone Garden Ornaments
The Palladian Revival: Lord Burlington and His House and Garden at Chiswick, 1995
Christie's
Frederic Leighton 1830–1896. 1996
Sensation: Young British Artists from The Saatchi Collection, 1997
Classic FM
Goya: Truth and Fantasy, The Small Paintings, 1994
The Glory of Venice: Art in the Eighteenth Century, 1994
Masters of Colour: Derain to Kandinsky. Masterpieces from The Merzbacher Collection, 2002
Masterpieces from Dresden, 2003
Corporation of London
Living Bridges, 1996
Country Life
John Soane, Architect: Master of Space and Light, 1999
Credit Suisse First Boston
The Genius of Rome 1592–1623. 2000
The Daily Telegraph
American Art in the 20th Century, 1993
1900: Art at the Crossroads, 2000
De Beers
Africa: The Art of a Continent, 1995
Debenhams Retail plc
Premiums and RA Schools Show, 1999
Premiums and RA Schools Show, 2000
Premiums and RA Schools Show, 2001
Premiums and RA Schools Show, 2002
Deutsche Morgan Grenfell
Africa: The Art of a Continent, 1995
Diageo plc
230th Summer Exhibition, 1998
The Drue Heinz Trust
The Palladian Revival: Lord Burlington and His House and Garden at Chiswick, 1995
Denys Lasdun, 1997
Tadao Ando: Master of Minimalism, 1998
The Dupont Company
American Art in the 20th Century, 1993
Ernst & Young
Monet in the 20th Century, 1999

Eyestorm
Apocalypse: Beauty and Horror in Contemporary Art, 2000
Fidelity Foundation
The Dawn of the Floating World (1650–1765). Early Ukiyo-e Treasures from the Museum of Fine Arts, Boston, 2001
Friends of the Royal Academy
Victorian Fairy Painting, 1997
Game International Limited
Forty Years in Print: The Curwen Studio and Royal Academicians, 2001
The Jacqueline and Michael Gee Charitable Trust
LIFE? or THEATRE? The Work of Charlotte Salomon, 1999
Générale des Eaux Group
Living Bridges, 1996
Glaxo Wellcome plc
The Unknown Modigliani, 1994
Goldman Sachs International
Alberto Giacometti, 1901–1966. 1996
Picasso: Painter and Sculptor in Clay, 1998
The Guardian
The Unknown Modigliani, 1994
Guinness PLC (see Diageo plc)
225th Summer Exhibition, 1993
226th Summer Exhibition, 1994
227th Summer Exhibition, 1995
228th Summer Exhibition, 1996
229th Summer Exhibition, 1997
Harpers & Queen
Georges Rouault: The Early Years, 1903–1920. 1993
Sandra Blow, 1994
David Hockney: A Drawing Retrospective, 1995*
Roger de Grey, 1996
The Headley Trust
Denys Lasdun, 1997
The Henry Moore Foundation
Africa: The Art of a Continent, 1995
Ibstock Building Products Ltd
John Soane, Architect: Master of Space and Light, 1999
The Independent
Living Bridges, 1996
Apocalypse: Beauty and Horror in Contemporary Art, 2000
International Asset Management
Frank Auerbach, Paintings and Drawings 1954–2001. 2001
Donald and Jeanne Kahn
John Hoyland, 1999
Land Securities PLC
Denys Lasdun, 1997
The Mail on Sunday
Royal Academy Summer Season, 1993
Marks & Spencer
Royal Academy Schools Premiums, 1994
Royal Academy Schools Final Year Show, 1994*
Martini & Rossi Ltd
The Great Age of British Watercolours, 1750–1880. 1993
Paul Mellon KBE
The Great Age of British Watercolours, 1750–1880. 1993
Merrill Lynch
American Art in the 20th Century, 1993*
Paris: Capital of the Arts 1900–1968. 2001
Mexico Tourism Board
Aztecs, 2002
Midland Bank plc
RA Outreach Programme, 1993–1996
Lessons in Life, 1994
Minorco
Africa: The Art of a Continent, 1995
Natwest Group
Nicolas Poussin 1594–1665. 1995
The Nippon Foundation
Hiroshige: Images of Mist, Rain, Moon and Snow, 1997
Peterborough United Football Club
Art Treasures of England: The Regional Collections, 1997
Pemex
Aztecs, 2002
Premiercare (National Westminster Insurance Services)
Roger de Grey, 1996*
RA Exhibition Patrons Group
Chagall: Love and the Stage, 1998

Kandinsky, 1999
Chardin 1699–1779. 2000
Botticelli's Dante: The Drawings for Dante's Divine Comedy, 2001
Return of the Buddha: The Qingzhou Discoveries, 2002
Reed Elsevier plc
Van Dyck 1599–1641. 1999
Rembrandt's Women, 2001
The Royal Bank of Scotland
Braque: The Late Works, 1997*
Premiums, 1997
Premiums, 1998
Premiums, 1999
Royal Academy Schools Final Year Show, 1996
Royal Academy Schools Final Year Show, 1997
Royal Academy Schools Final Year Show, 1998
Virginia and Simon Robertson
Aztecs, 2002
The Sara Lee Foundation
Odilon Redon: Dreams and Visions, 1995
Sea Containers Ltd
The Glory of Venice: Art in the Eighteenth Century, 1994
Silhouette Eyewear
Sandra Blow, 1994
Africa: The Art of a Continent, 1995
Société Générale, UK
Gustave Caillebotte: The Unknown Impressionist, 1996*
Société Générale de Belgique
Impressionism to Symbolism: The Belgian Avant-garde 1880–1900. 1994
Thames Water Plc
Thames Water Habitable Bridge Competition, 1996
The Times
Drawings from the J Paul Getty Museum, 1993
Goya: Truth and Fantasy, The Small Paintings, 1994
Africa: The Art of a Continent, 1995
Time Out
Sensation: Young British Artists from The Saatchi Collection, 1997
Apocalypse: Beauty and Horror in Contemporary Art, 2000
Tractabel
Impressionism to Symbolism: The Belgian Avant-garde 1880–1900, 1994
Union Minière
Impressionism to Symbolism: The Belgian Avant-garde 1880–1900, 1994
Walker Morris
Premiums, 2003
Royal Academy Schools Final Year Show, 2003
Yakult UK Ltd
RA Outreach Programme, 1997–2002
alive: Life Drawings from the Royal Academy of Arts & Yakult Outreach Programme

*Recipients of a Pairing Scheme Award, managed by Arts + Business. Arts + Business is funded by the Arts Council of England and the Department for Culture, Media and Sport.

OTHER SPONSORS

Sponsors of events, publications and other items in the past five years:

Carlisle Group plc
Country Life
Derwent Valley Holdings plc
Dresdner Kleinwort Wasserstein
Fidelity Foundation
Foster and Partners
Goldman Sachs International
Gome International
Gucci Group
Rob van Helden
IBJ International plc
John Doyle Construction
Marks & Spencer
Michael Hopkins & Partners
Morgan Stanley Dean Witter
Prada
Radisson Edwardian Hotels
Richard and Ruth Rogers
Strutt & Parker